CULINARY
COUNTERPOINT
Detroit Symphony Orchestra
COOK BOOK

Dedicated to the musicians
who are the Detroit Symphony Orchestra.

Proceeds from the sale of this book will be used
to benefit the Detroit Symphony Orchestra.

Copyright © 1983 by
The Detroit Symphony League
All rights Reserved
First Edition

ISBN: 0-9611348-0-1
Library of Congress #83-71434

Printed by
Precision Printing
Southfield, Michigan 48076

Second Printing, February, 1989
J&M Reproduction, Troy, Mich. 48083-2833

Many years ago, my thoughts of compiling a cookbook to benefit our great Detroit Symphony Orchestra were somewhat of a dream. The dream has become a reality due, in large measure, to a very supportive committee and a number of extraordinarily dedicated people.

A special thank you to Connie Salloum, past president of the Detroit Symphony League, who initiated this project; to Debbie Tischler, our president, who enabled us to complete the job, and to Carol May, who always had extra time to help or simply to listen.

My deepest gratitude to the W.B. Doner Agency and its staff, specifically Karen Romeyn whose cover and divider designs brought aesthetic excellence to this book; David Smith whose illustrative genius was incorporated in our divider artwork; and to Gerald Farber for his exceptional photograph which graces our cover.

Many, many thanks to John Fischer . . . our printer, primary promoter, problem solver and advisor whose endless hours of constructive, creative assistance did so much, so often, to help Culinary Counterpoint become a reality.

Finally, to my daughter Debbie, who had to fend for herself so frequently while I was working on the project; and to my dear husband Bob, without whose support, encouragement and patience this wonderful book would never have come to be ... A THOUSAND THANKS!

At last, our cookbook is complete. It reflects an incredible measure of hard work and an even greater measure of love. We trust that it therefore also reflects the excellence of our world class Detroit Symphony Orchestra.

Brenda Pangborn
Brenda J. Pangborn,
Chairman
April 1983

PRESIDENT'S MESSAGE

The Detroit Symphony League furthers the interests of the Detroit Symphony Orchestra by increasing public appreciation of its value to the community and by providing substantial financial support through various projects. Such fund raisers are the Music Box Boutique, a Christmas tour of homes, a radio marathon and the Detroit Symphony ASID Showhouse.

The League's membership is innovative and dynamic. The cookbook commitee, with Brenda Pangborn as chairman, has worked tirelessly to produce only the best. They deserve a standing ovation!

Great food — like great music — is art, carefully composed and beautifully executed. The contributors to <u>Culinary Counterpoint</u> join the Detroit Symphony Orchestra in the creation of art.

Deborah A. Tischler
Deborah Tischler
President (1982-83)

CULINARY COUNTERPOINT COMMITTEE

Brenda Pangborn, Chairman and Editor-in-Chief
Sheila Pitcoff, Food Editor
Chris Considine, Layout
Sheila Swanson, Art and Kickoff Co-ordinator
Judy Liberson, Testing
Isabel Smith, Publicity
Nicette Watkinson, Celebrities
Kay Keffer, Volunteers
Winnie Ostrowski, Member at large

ACKNOWLEDGEMENTS

Wine selections by The Merchant of Vino, Southfield, Michigan
Cover violin from Richard Margitza, member of the DSO
Suzanne Boyce and John Merrill, primary testers

Thanks also to the hundreds of individuals, celebrities and restaurants who contributed the recipes which comprise Culinary Counterpoint.

Because of duplication and space limitations, not every recipe submitted could be included in this edition — nevertheless we thank each and every contributor.

The Detroit Symphony League of the Detroit Symphony Orchestra, which celebrated its 43rd anniversary in October 1982, was established in 1939 as the Junior Women's Association. It has grown from the original 10 members to 350 active fund raisers.

The League's primary purpose, "to cultivate by education an appreciation of symphonic music, and to prepare its members for effective support of symphonic music," has not changed much over the years. But its fund raising and community involvement activities have definitely expanded.

In 1981, League president, Mrs. Samuel G. Salloum, recognized the need to reorganize the group in order to broaden its community base, and to encourage a more diverse membership. The name of the organization was changed to the Detroit Symphony League. This move resulted in a large increase in membership, which for the first time included men.

The League's financial contribution to the Orchestra has been close to one million dollars, over half of which was raised in the past 15 years. In recent years the League's full thrust of energy has been devoted to larger and more financially successful projects. The largest project, a joint venture with the Women's Association for the Detroit Symphony Orchestra, is an annual Radio Marathon, now in its eighth year.

With the presentation of this cookbook, the League has entered yet another area of fund raising. We are confident that it will be one of our most successful to date, and that the continued success of this book will be a constant source of funds to benefit the Detroit Symphony Orchestra — the great sound of Detroit.

The Detroit Symphony Orchestra gave its first concert on February 26, 1914, at the Detroit Opera House. During its sixty-nine year history, the Orchestra has become established among the foremost musical organizations of the world and has won the highest critical acclaim wherever it has appeared.

The music directors and principal conductors of the Detroit Symphony Orchestra include Ossip Gabrilowitsch, who led the Orchestra from 1918 until 1936; Victor Kolar, whose career with the Orchestra lasted from 1943 to 1949. Paul Paray conducted the Orchestra for over a decade, from 1951-1963, and from 1963-1973, Sixten Ehrling directed the Orchestra's musical activities. More recently, Aldo Ceccato conducted from 1973 to 1977; Antal Dorati from 1977 to 1981; and finally Gary Bertini from 1981 to present.

Today the Orchestra presents more than 200 concerts, including more than 80 regular subscription concerts at its home, the Henry and Edsel Ford Auditorium. Concerts for students, outstate tour concerts and assorted free public service events suggests the diversity of events in the Orchestra's yearly calendar. The Meadow Brook Music Festival in Rochester, Michigan is the site of the Orchestra's summer home and is recognized as one of the major summer music festivals in the nation.

In recent years the Detroit Symphony Orchestra has increased its stature among the top ranked orchestras by returning to the recording field with a major international label and by first performing in Europe in the fall of 1979. A dramatically successful tour of such major music capitals such as London, Paris and Berlin, produced rave reviews, standing ovations and numerous encores.

LEAGUE OFFICERS

MRS. HOWARD M. TISCHLER
President
MRS. EDWARD S. MAY
President-Elect
MRS. JOHN Y. KEFFER
Vice President-Projects
MRS. ROBERT W. McCAFFREY
Vice President-Membership
MRS. OLIVER A. GREEN, JR.
Vice President-Boutique
MRS. PETER E. PEKKALA
Secretary
MRS. DAVID D. PATTON
Treasurer

MRS. JOSEPH L. DASOVIC
Mailing
MRS. CLARK E. HARRIS
Program-Social
MRS. JAMES L. TOLLEY
Publicity-Historian
MS. LOUIS LEE
Records
MRS. R. LAWRENCE KROOVAND
Special Projects
MRS. S. LAWRENCE POHE
Yearbook

ADMINISTRATIVE STAFF

OLEG LOBANOV
Executive Vice President &
Managing Director
MICHAEL A. SMITH
General Manager
ROBERT J. JONES
Director of Finance
ELEANOR LUEDTKE
Director of Marketing
STEVE HAVIARAS
Director of
Audience Development
SUSAN MARTIN
Director of Development

BETH BERGLUND
Assistant Director of the
Annual Fund
CHUCK DYER
Assistant Director of
Audience Development
RICHARD HANCOCK
Assistant Manager-Operations
PATRICIA KIRCHMAN
Assistant Director of Finance
JOHN ZORN
Assistant Manager-Operations
VERNON C. ALLEN
House Manager

OFFICERS OF THE BOARD

WALTER J. McCARTHY, JR.
Chairman
ROBERT B. SEMPLE
Honorary Chairman
DON C. BECKER
Vice-President and Chairman of
Marketing Committee
WALTER E. DOUGLAS
Vice-President
WILLIAM C. FERGUSON
Vice-President and Chairman,
Orchestral and Staff Relations
WALTER B. FISHER
Vice-President, Chairman of
Financial Management Committee
MRS. FRANK A. GERMACK, JR.
President Women's Association
MORTON E. HARRIS
Vice-President
PIERRE V. HEFTLER
Vice-President
THOMAS H. JEFFS II
Vice-President

ARTHUR L. JOHNSON
Vice-President and Chairman of
Education/Outreach Committee
HARRY A. LOMASON
Vice-President
JOHN W. McNULTY
Vice President
RALPH J. MANDARINO
Vice-President - Treasurer
DONALD R. MANDICH
Vice-President and Chairman of
Development
ALAN E. SCHWARTZ
Vice-President and Chairman of
Nominating Committee
MRS. HOWARD M. TISCHLER
President, Symphony League
PETER P. THURBER
Vice-President and Chairman of
By-laws Committee and Secretary
MRS. R. JAMISON WILLIAMS
Vice-President
MRS. P. ALEXANDER WRIGLEY
Vice-President

7

DORATI
St. Adrian
CH-6318 Walchwil

What music would you want to hear with what dish? It's a legitimate question. Let's not forget , Mozart wrote his greatest Divertimenti as dinner-music.

The opposite question can also be asked: What would you like to taste while listening to this or that musical masterpiece? Indeed, why couldn't a great cook of genius create a dish which would be a "perfect match" to the second act of "Tristan und Isolde", or Tchaikovsky's Violin Concerto?

The genius would, of course, not look to the overly obvious: he surely would not offer the same fish "en blue" to Schubert's "Trout" quintet, nor would we get pheasant or rabbit to the "Hunt" quartet by Mozart. The relationships would be more subtle.

All in all, there seems to be a deeper connection between the musical and culinary arts than one would suspect. Some great musicians are great cooks, many are connoiseur gourmets and all of them are great eaters.

When, on tour with a symphony orchestra — many memories come to the fore — one arrives in a city for the very first time, one only has to follow the members of the orchestra to get to the best restaurant in town: — interestingly, not always a fancy one, but the one with the best food, for certain.

Also, it is probably not just a coincidence that so many Symphony Orchestras publish cookbooks. They must make up quite a sizeable library by now. For years I have contributed recipes to many, illustrated some, and here I am writing my first preface to the newest one.

* * *

To begin with, then, — I cannot cook. I cannot even boil an egg. It will enevitably, get too hard, or comes out too soft, or will even burst, maliciously, no matter how diligently and ambitiously I apply myself to it. The recipes contributed under my name are exquisite, but they are those of my wife's. I only eat the dishes, did not make them, did even less to invent them. My wife creates them galore and they are all light, becoming and delicious.

Also, I never have read a cookbook. That is, I never read any from the first page to the last. But I did read one sentence in one.

It was in Sydney, Australia, where I found myself, for a longish stay, alone in a large apartment, with a superbly appointed kitchen. I decided that I would cook for myself. Not knowing how to go about it, I went to a bookshop to buy a cookbook. There were many to choose from. A tall volume called "Eating All Over the World" caught my fancy. I took it. Indeed, it contained recipes from every country, every region of our globe. The book opened itself on the page of Tibet. That's fine, I thought, I'll begin with a Tibetian dish. Let's see what the Dalai Lama has for lunch. I read: "Take half an ox". That was the end of my short career as would be Escoffier.

* * *

The readers of this book will have better luck, no doubt.
I wish them well, as I do its compilers, publishers and sponsors.
And — by-the-way — I never eat before a concert and very little after. My main meal is breakfast, and I love a good lunch with a glass of fine wine.

Antal Dorati
Conductor Laureate

DETROIT SYMPHONY ORCHESTRA

ANTAL DORATI
Conductor Laureate

KENNETH JEAN
Resident Conductor

MICHAEL KRAJEWSKI
Assistant Conductor

FIRST VIOLINS
Gordon Staples
 Concertmaster
Bogos Mortchikian
 Associate Concertmaster
Joseph Goldman
Gordon Peterson
 Assistant Concertmaster
Misha Rachlevsky
Linda Snedden-Smith
Derek Francis
Alan Gerstel
Nicholas Zonas
LeAnn Toth
Beatriz Budinszky
Malvern Kaufman
Richard Margitza
Margaret Tundo
Elias Friedenzohn
Santo Urso
Ronald Fischer
Lenore Iatzko

SECOND VIOLINS
Edouard Kesner
 Principal
Felix Resnick
 Assistant Principal
Alvin Score
Lillian Fenstermacher
James Waring
Ann Alicia Ourada
Walter Maddox
Roy Bengtsson
Thomas Downs
Robert Murphy
Sofia Novak-Tsoglin
Joseph Striplin
Bruce Smith
Gariel Szitas
Geoffrey Applegate
Marguerite Deslippe

VIOLAS
Nathan Gordon
 Principal
David Ireland
 Assistant Principal
Philip Porbe
Eugenia Staszewski
LeRoy Fenstermacher
Hart Hollman
Walter Evich
Gary Schnerer
Catherine Compton
Glenn Mellow
Darryl Jeffers

VIOLONCELLOS
Italo Babini
 James C. Gordon Chair
 Principal
Marcy Chanteaux
 Assistant Principal
John Thurman
Mario DiFiore
David Levine
Barbara Fickett
Debra Fayroian
David Saltzman
Paul Wingert
Carole Gatwood

BASSES
Robert Gladstone
 Principal
Raymond Benner
 Assistant Principal
Stephen Molina
Maxim Janowsky
Linton Bodwin
Stephen Edwards
Donald Pennington
Craig Rifel

HARP
Elyse Ilku
 Principal

FLUTES
Ervin Monroe
 Principal
Shaul Ben-Meir
Robert Patrick
 Assistant Principal
Clement Barone

PICCOLO
Clement Barone

OBOES
Donald Baker
 Principal
John Snow
Robert Sorton
 Assistant Principal
Treva Womble

ENGLISH HORN
Treva Womble

CLARINETS
Paul Schaller
 Principal
Douglas Cornelsen
Laurence Liberson
 Assistant Principal
Oliver Green

E-FLAT CLARINET
Laurence Liberson

BASS CLARINET
Oliver Green

BASSOONS
Robert Williams
 Principal
Kirkland Ferris
Paul Ganson
 Assistant Principal
Lyell Lindsey

CONTRABASSOONS
Lyell Lindsey

FRENCH HORNS
Eugene Wade
 Principal
Bryan Kennedy
Corbin Wagner
Willard Darling
Mark Abbott
 Assistant Principal
Keith Vernon

TRUMPETS
Ramon Parcells
 Principal
Kevin Good
Alvin Belknap
 Assistant Principal
Gordon Smith

TROMBONES
Raymond Turner
 Principal
Joseph Skrzynski
Nathaniel Gurin
 Assistant Principal
Thomas Klaber

TUBA
Wesley Jacobs
 Principal

TIMPANI
Salvatore Rabbio
 Principal
Robert Pangborn
 Assistant Principal

PERCUSSION
Robert Pangborn
 Principal
Norman Fickett
 Assistant Principal
Raymond Makowski
Sam Tundo

KEYBOARD
Ray Ferguson
Muriel Kilby

LIBRARIAN
Elkhonon Yoffe
Charles Weaver, assistant

PERSONNEL MANAGER
Oliver Green
Steven Molina
 Assistant Personnel Manager

10

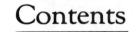

Contents

Contents

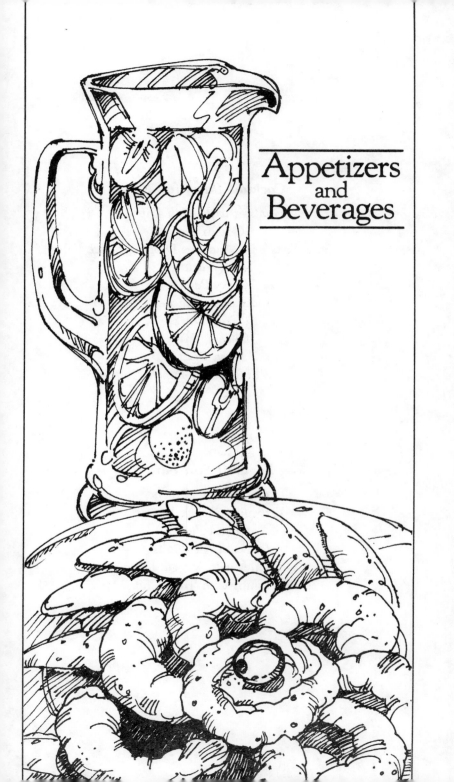

Appetizers
and
Beverages

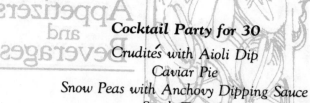

Cocktail Party for 30

Crudités with Aioli Dip
Caviar Pie
Snow Peas with Anchovy Dipping Sauce
Steak Tartare
Hanky Pankys
Individual Quiches
Crab Dip
Cheese Tray
Fresh Fruit
Whiskey Sour Punch

Football Fan Fare

Champagne Punch
Teriyaki Chicken Wings
Gouda Puffs
Cocktail Meatballs
Crudités with Veggie Dip
Tortilla Chips with Taco Chip Dip

CRAB ARTICHOKE APPETIZER

2   cans crabmeat, drained
1   14-ounce can artichokes,
      drained and cut into pieces
1   can mushroom soup

6 to 10 mushrooms, chopped
      and sautéed
¼   cup dry Sherry
3   drops Tabasco

In a saucepan combine ingredients and heat thoroughly. Transfer to a chafing dish. Serve with crackers.
Note: After dip is mixed, it may be refrigerated until ready to heat and serve.

Serves about 20
Preparation time: 15 minutes
Easy

Kathie O'Rourke

CURRY DIP

Best when prepared a day ahead

½   cup sour cream
1   cup mayonnaise
2   tablespoons green onion
      including tops, chopped
1½ tablespoons lemon juice

½   teaspoon salt
½   teaspoon A-1 Sauce
½   teaspoon Worcestershire
      sauce
1½ tablespoons curry powder

Combine all ingredients and blend well. Serve with raw vegetables.

Makes about 2 cups

Mary Tolley

VEGGIE DIP

Serve with crudités as an appetizer or snack

⅔   cup mayonnaise
½   cup sour cream
1   tablespoon onion flakes
1   tablespoon parsley, chopped

1   teaspoon Beau Monde
      seasoning
1   teaspoon dill weed

Combine ingredients, mix well and refrigerate.

Tina Pohe

MEXICAN CHILI DIP

Serve with tostadas

½	cup ground beef	1	8-ounce can refried beans
¼	cup chopped onion	½	cup sharp Cheddar cheese
¼	cup hot taco sauce	¼	cup chopped green olives
1½	teaspoons chili powder	¼	cup chopped onion
½	teaspoon salt		

Brown meat and onion in skillet. Drain off fat. Add hot sauce, chili powder and salt and mix well. Add beans and mash mixture thoroughly. Cook over low heat for 30 minutes.

Transfer to chafing dish and serve garnished with cheese, olives and remaining chopped onion.

Preparation time: 15 minutes
Cooking time: 30 minutes

Jackie Ong

RICH MAN'S DIP

This is excellent with crisp, fresh vegetables

1	can condensed tomato soup	½	cup chopped green pepper
1	8-ounce package cream cheese	½	cup chopped celery
1	package unflavored gelatin	1	cup mayonnaise
½	cup chopped onion	2	6-ounce cans shrimp, drained

In a saucepan heat the soup with the cream cheese. Beat in the gelatin then remove from heat; let cool for ½ hour. Beat in the remaining ingredients. Refrigerate for 2-3 hours before serving.

Serves 8-10
Easy

Richard Hayman
DSO "Pops" Conductor

CRABMEAT DIP I

2 3-ounce packages cream cheese with chives	⅔ cup mayonnaise
1 7¾-ounce can crabmeat, well drained	Dash of Tabasco sauce
	Dash of Worcestershire sauce
	Paprika

Preheat oven to 350 degrees.
Combine all ingredients except paprika and mix well. Sprinkle with paprika and bake until bubbly and hot.
To serve cold: Refrigerate 2-3 hours to let flavors blend.

Preparation time: 15 minutes
Baking time: 30 minutes
Easy

Nina Rabbio
DSO

TACO CHIP DIP

3-4 avocados	¾ pound shredded Monterey Jack cheese
2 teaspoons lemon juice	
3 tablespoons mayonnaise	1 cup diced black olives
3 tablespoons sour cream	1 cup chopped tomatoes
1 package taco seasoning	1 cup chopped green onions
¾ pound shredded sharp Cheddar cheese	

Mash the avocados with the lemon juice and place in the bottom of a glass serving dish. Combine the mayonnaise, sour cream and taco dip and mix well; layer mixture over the mashed avocados. Layer the Cheddar cheese, the Monterey Jack cheese, olives, tomatoes and onions. Refrigerate until ready to serve. Serve with taco chips.

Serves 8-12
Preparation time: 15 minutes
Chill
Easy

Lenore latzko
DSO

CRAB DIP II

1 8-ounce package cream
  cheese, softened
1 7½-ounce can crab meat
¼ cup mayonnaise
1 teaspoon onion juice or
  1 tablespoon finely minced
  onion

1 teaspoon prepared mustard
Dash salt
2 tablespoons white wine
Optional: 1 clove garlic, minced

Combine ingredients in a chafing dish and heat. Serve with crackers
or chips.

Preparation time: 15 minutes
Easy

Carol A. Meyer

SPINACH DIP

1 package frozen chopped
  spinach, thawed and drained
  well
1 small onion, finely chopped
1 can water chestnuts, drained
  and minced

1 package Knorr's vegetable
  soup mix
1 cup mayonnaise
1 cup sour cream

Combine ingredients and mix well. Serve with crackers or party rye.

Preparation time: 15 minutes
Easy

Kathie O'Rourke

ARTICHOKE DIP

Serve with crackers or pita bread

1 cup mayonnaise
1 cup Parmesan cheese, grated
Garlic to taste

1 9-ounce can artichoke
  hearts, mashed

Preheat oven to 350 degrees.
Combine all ingredients and mix well. Place in baking dish and bake
for 30 minutes.

Judy & Larry Liberson
DSO

ANOTHER TERRIFIC CRAB DIP

1   8-ounce package cream
    cheese
2   tablespoons mayonnaise
¼   teaspoon salt
Dash Worcestershire
Dash pepper

2   tablespoons horseradish
1   tablespoon chopped onion
1   7-½ ounce can crabmeat,
    flaked
⅓   cup slivered almonds

Preheat oven to 375 degrees.
Combine all ingredients, except almonds, and blend well. Place in ovenproof baking dish and sprinkle with almonds. Bake for 15 minutes or until hot and bubbly.

Serves 6
Preparation time: 15 minutes
Baking time: 15 minutes
Easy

Eileen Hitz

GUACAMOLE

The flavors become more intense as this chills, so be careful with the pepper

2   very ripe, large avocados
1   medium onion, minced
Juice of 2 lemons

1   small Jalapeno pepper,
    seeded and minced, or,
    to taste
Salt to taste

Peel and pit the avocados. Mash well and combine with remaining ingredients. Use as a dip with corn chips.

Makes 2 cups

Eleanor Luedtke

A cheese tray usually has a combination of Cheddar: Cheshire, New York, or Canadian: Bleu: English Stilton, Gorgonzola or Roquefort; and Swiss: Gruyere or Jarlsberg. Creamy cheese are usually served with dessert.

BEER DIP

½ pound Swiss cheese, shredded

½ pound sharp Cheddar cheese, shredded

12 ounces beer

1 package onion soup mix

Combine ingredients and heat until cheeses are melted. Transfer to a chafing dish. Serve with chunks of bread.

Preparation time: 10 minutes
Easy

Inez Redman

CHILI CON QUESO DIP

1 pound processed American cheese

½ pound Cheddar cheese

½ cup seeded, diced tomatoes

½ cup finely chopped onions

2 tablespoons minced parsley

2 hot, green chili peppers (or more), chopped

2 drops Tabasco sauce

Place cheese in top of double boiler and melt. Add remaining ingredients; heat until onions are soft. Transfer to chafing dish. Serve with tortilla chips.

Serves 10
Preparation time: 20 minutes
Can be made ahead and reheated

Jackie Ong

SPEEDY PATÉ

This tastes as though you had slaved over a hot stove all day

1 8-ounce package Braunschweiger

½ cup finely chopped walnuts

½ cup sweet butter

¼ cup finely minced onion

¼ cup brandy

Place all ingredients in the container of a blender or in a food processor fitted with the steel blade. Blend well. Chill for several hours to allow flavors to blend.

Brenda Pangborn

HUMMUS

1 20-ounce can chick peas, drained
1 clove garlic
3 tablespoons olive oil
3 tablespoons lemon juice
1½ teaspoons coarse (Kosher) salt

Freshly ground pepper to taste
1 tablespoon tahini (sesame seed paste)
Chopped parsley for garnish

Combine all ingredients except parsley in a food processor fitted with the steel blade or in a blender and process until smooth. Garnish with parsley and serve with Syrian flat bread or pita bread cut in wedges.

Makes 2 cups
Preparation time: 10 minutes
Easy

Anne Simons

SALMON MOUSSE WITH RED CAVIAR

2 1-pound cans red salmon
¼ cup cider vinegar
½ cup dairy sour cream
2 tablespoons prepared horseradish
2 envelopes unflavored gelatin
⅓ cup lemon juice

1 teaspoon seasoned salt
1 teaspoon salt
1 teaspoon prepared mustard
1 cup heavy cream, whipped
1 4-ounce jar red caviar, chilled

Drain salmon; remove any bones and skin. Break into small pieces. Put salmon and vinegar in a blender in small batches and puree. Turn into a 1½-quart bowl. Fold in sour cream and horseradish. Sprinkle gelatin over lemon juice and let stand for 5 minutes. Set over pan of boiling water and stir to dissolve. Gradually stir into salmon mixture. Add salts and mustard and blend well. Fold in whipped cream. Turn into a 1½-quart mold (a fish mold is ideal). Refrigerate, covered, for four hours.

To serve: Invert mold over a platter and place a hot damp cloth over mold. Shake lightly to release. Spoon caviar over mousse.
Serve with cocktail rounds or crackers.

Virginia Andreae

HORS D' OEUVRE PIE

A colorful, easy to prepare, appetizer

1 9-inch pie shell
12 ounces cream cheese
2 ounces Bleu cheese

½ cup mayonnaise
½ teaspoon onion salt or garlic
   salt

Garnishes: Cherry tomatoes cut in half, thinly sliced mushrooms, chopped parsley, chopped egg, sliced ripe olives.

Preheat oven to 425 degrees.
On large baking sheet, pat pie shell into an 11-inch circle. Pierce thoroughly with a fork and bake for 8 minutes or until lightly browned. Let cool, then place on a serving platter.
Beat cheeses, mayonnaise and salt until fluffy and spread evenly on the pastry. Cover with plastic wrap and chill at least 4 hours. Before serving, place the tomatoes in a circular pattern on the outside of the pie shell, cut side down. Then place the mushrooms, parsley, eggs, and olives in circles starting from the row of tomatoes going toward the center of the shell. Chill.
When ready to serve slice into wedges.
Note: Eggs and vegetables may be prepared in advance and refrigerated until ready to decorate.

Serves 10
Preparation time: 45 minutes before chilling shell
5 minutes to decorate   Eleanor Pekkala

SHRIMP PATÉ

1½ pounds shrimp, cooked,
   shelled and deveined
½ cup butter
Juice of 1 small onion (about
   10 drops)

1 tablespoon dry Sherry
Dash of mace
½ teaspoon dry mustard
Salt and freshly ground pepper
   to taste

Grind the shrimp briefly in a food processor. Combine the remaining ingredients and spoon mixture into a 2-cup mold. Refrigerate until ready to serve. Serve with crackers or dark bread.

Serves 10-12
Preparation time: 15 minutes   Chuck Dyer

LAYERED CRAB SPREAD

Expensive, but worth it

LEVEL 1

12 ounces cream cheese, softened
2 tablespoons Worcestershire sauce
1 tablespoon lemon juice
2 tablespoons mayonnaise
1 small onion, minced
Dash garlic salt

LEVEL 2 SHRIMP SAUCE

1 cup ketchup or chili sauce
2 tablespoons prepared horseradish
2 tablespoons lemon juice
1 tablespoon brown sugar
1 teaspoon onion juice
1 teaspoon Worcestershire sauce
½ teaspoon salt
¼ teaspoon M.S.G., optional
6 drops Tabasco Sauce or to taste

LEVEL 3

1 8-ounce package crabmeat, thawed and drained
Parsley

In bowl of mixer, combine ingredients for level 1. Mix well and spread in shallow glass pie plate.

Combine ingredients for level 2 and spread desired amount of shrimp sauce to cover cream cheese mixture. Top with crabmeat and sprinkle with parsley.

Cover with plastic wrap and refrigerate overnight. Pour off any excess liquid. Serve with crackers.

Barabara Suhay

CHICKEN SPREAD

Great for the cocktail hour

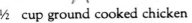

½ cup ground cooked chicken
1 tablespoon chopped onion
2 tablespoons ground almonds
1 teaspoon chopped parsley
Salt and pepper to taste
Mayonnaise

Combine all ingredients except the mayonnaise. Add enough mayonnaise to bind the mixture. Shape into a large ball and chill until serving time. Serve with party rye or crackers.

Serves 4-6
Preparation time: 20 minutes
Chill

Babette Posen

BABA GHANOOJ

This is a traditional and very popular appetizer. Serve with pita bread cut into fourths for easy handling

1 large eggplant	2 tablespoons lemon juice
1 clove garlic, minced	1 teaspoon salt
¼ cup tahini (sesame seed paste)	Optional: Smoke flavoring

Cut eggplant in half and place cut side down on a charcoal grill or place on a cookie sheet and bake in a 350-degree oven until very soft. Peel and mash the eggplant and put it through a strainer. Add tahini, lemon juice, and salt to taste. If eggplant was baked in an oven, add some smoke flavoring for a more authentic taste. Chill. If mixture is too thick, thin with a little water or lemon juice.

Note: All quantities may be altered to suit taste.

The Sheik Restaurant
Detroit, Michigan

STEAK TARTARE

½ cup finely minced onion	1 teaspoon ground pepper
4 anchovy fillets	1 tablespoon Cognac
1-2 large cloves garlic, mashed	Dash Tabasco
2 egg yolks	2 pounds fresh ground top round, sirloin or tenderloin, with no fat, ground five times
1 tablespoon Worcestershire	
2 tablespoons capers	
1 heaping teaspoon Dijon mustard	
1 teaspoon parsley, minced	Additional parsley for garnish

Mix all ingredients, except meat, and make into a paste. Add meat and incorporate thoroughly. Form into loaf or put into a bowl to mold and chill.

When ready to serve place on a bed of lettuce and garnish with fresh parsley. Serve with small party rounds of pumpernickel and rye.

Preparation time: 20 minutes
Chill overnight
Easy

Carol Ann May

LIPTAUER CHEESE

This is an easy, attractive and delicious spread for the hors d'oeuvre table.

1	8-ounce package cream cheese, softened	1	heaping teaspoon caraway seeds
½	cup butter, softened	2	teaspoons capers, drained and chopped
1	teaspoon dry mustard		
1	tablespoon Hungarian paprika	¼	cup sour cream
		2	anchovies or ½ teaspoon salt
1	tablespoon minced onion		

Beat the cream cheese and butter until smooth. Add the mustard, paprika, and onion and blend well. Fold in the remaining ingredients. Chill 24 hours before serving.

Yield: 2 cups
Preparation time: 15 minutes
Chill: 24 hours
Easy

Lee Barlow

EGGPLANT CAVIAR

1	large eggplant	1	tablespoon white vinegar
¼	cup chopped parsley	1½	teaspoons lemon juice
1	small onion, finely chopped	1	teaspoon salt
		2	cloves garlic, minced
½	teaspoon sugar	¼	teaspoon freshly ground pepper
3	tablespoons olive oil		

Preheat oven to 350 degrees.

Oil a baking sheet and sprinkle with salt. Cut eggplant in half lengthwise and place, cut side down, on the sheet. Bake for 45 minutes or until eggplant is tender. Remove from oven and let stand until cool enough to handle. Peel and finely chop the pulp. Let drain in a colander for 15 minutes.

Combine the eggplant with the remaining ingredients. Cover and refrigerate for 24 hours. Check for seasoning and adjust if necessary. Serve with pita bread cut into fourths or with crackers.

Makes about 2 cups

Paula Stevens

CAVIAR PIE

8 eggs, hard-cooked, shelled and chopped	½ cup finely chopped Bermuda onion
2½ cups sour cream, divided	6-8 ounces well drained caviar, black or red
½ cup mayonnaise	

Line the bottom of an 8-inch cake pan with waxed paper.
Mix eggs, ½ cup sour cream, mayonnaise and onion. Press into pan and chill for a few hours. Just before serving, unmold onto a plate and frost with sour cream. Gently spread caviar on top. Serve surrounded by crackers and lemon wedges.
Can make a day ahead and keep in refrigerator.
Do not freeze.

Marcy Chanteaux
DSO

BAR CHEESE

A tavern-style crock of cheese

1 pound sharp Cheddar cheese	2-3 teaspoons Dijon mustard
1 3-ounce package cream cheese or ¼ cup butter, softened	2 jiggers brandy
	2 jiggers kirsch

Place Cheddar cheese and cream cheese or butter in the container of a food processor fitted with the steel blade; blend well. Add the mustard and with machine running, slowly add the brandy and kirsch. If mixture is very dry, it may be necessary to add 1-2 teaspoons good quality olive oil. Place mixture in a crock and refrigerate. Serve at room temperature.
Note: Any leftover bits of cheese and last drops from liqueur bottles can be added to the crock. Just blend in with the original mixture. Keeps indefinitely.

Bobbi Pincus

26

CHRISTMAS CABBAGE

This is delicious and very colorful

1   cup raw red cabbage, finely shredded
½   cup green pepper, finely chopped

¼   cup crumbled Bleu cheese
Mayonnaise or sour cream

Combine the cabbage, green pepper and cheese; blend well. Mix with mayonnaise and/or sour cream to a spreading consistency. Chill well. Serve with crackers.

Marlynn Barnes

VEGETARIAN CHOPPED LIVER

1   pound fresh string beans
3   large onions, chopped
3   tablespoons vegetable oil

4   eggs, hard cooked
½   cup chopped walnuts
Salt and pepper

Cook the beans until done. Drain and chop in a food processor fitted with the steel blade. Sauté the onions in the oil until golden. Combine all ingredients and season to taste with salt and pepper. Process until mixture is finely chopped. Transfer to a serving dish and form into a mound. Chill.
Serve with party rye or pumpernickle.

Marti Miller

HOLIDAY OR ANYTIME SPREAD

1   cup grated sharp cheese
1   8-ounce package cream cheese, softened
2   tablespoons milk
1   2½-ounce jar dried beef, cut up
2   tablespoons minced onion

2   tablespoons minced green pepper
Dash pepper
½   cup sour cream
¼   cup chopped nuts
½   cup chopped ripe olives

Combine ingredients and mix well. Place in a pie plate and bake in a 350-degree oven for 15 minutes.
Serve with crackers

Sandy Kroovand

27

SMOKED SALMON PARTY BALL

Something deliciously different

1   1-pound can salmon
1   8-ounce package cream
    cheese, softened
2   teaspoons grated onion
1   teaspoon horseradish

1   teaspoon lemon juice
1   teaspoon salt
¼   teaspoon liquid smoke
½   cup chopped pecans
2   tablespoons chopped parsely

Drain, bone, remove skin and flake salmon. Combine salmon, cheese, onion, horseradish, lemon juice, salt and liquid smoke. Mix thoroughly and refrigerate for several hours.

Combine pecans and parsley. Shape salmon into a ball or a log and roll into nut mixture. Chill for at least 1 hour or until ready to serve.

Preparation time: 15 minutes
Chill: 3-4 hours
Easy

Inez Redman

SAVORY SHRIMP PATÉ

1   can tiny shrimp
2   green onions, including
    green tops, finely chopped
3   tablespoons butter, melted
1   8-ounce package cream
    cheese, beaten

2-3 shakes Tabasco sauce
Salt to taste
Garnish: Sliced olives, sliced
    pimento or red pepper,
    paprika

Rinse and drain shrimp. Mix the green onions with the melted butter, cream cheese, Tabasco and salt. Combine with the shrimp and refrigerate until ready to serve.

For those with an artistic touch, shape by hand into a fish and use an olive slice for an eye and a slice of pimento or red pepper for a big smile, and sprinkle with paprika. Serve with fish-shaped crackers.

Serves 4-6

Thomas F. Russell

MUSHROOM MOUSSE

¼	cup butter	2	egg yolks
1	pound mushrooms, chopped,	2	teaspoons Sherry
1	onion, chopped	½	cup heavy cream
1	tablespoon lemon juice	1	teaspoon Worcestershire sauce
½	cup beef or chicken broth	½	teaspoon salt
1	package unflavored gelatin	⅛	teaspoon pepper
1	3-ounce package cream cheese		

In a large skillet melt the butter; add the mushrooms, onion and lemon juice and cook over medium heat for 15 minutes. Place broth in a saucepan and sprinkle gelatin over top. Let stand for 5 minutes to soften then cook over low heat until the gelatin is dissolved. Let cool. In a blender combine the mushroom mixture, broth, cream cheese, egg yolks and Sherry; blend until smooth. Stir in cream, Worcestershire sauce, salt and pepper. Pour into a 1-quart ring mold; chill for at least 5 hours.

Serves 15
Preparation time: 40 minutes
Chill

Martha Bowman

BEER CHEESE

1½	pounds shredded sharp Cheddar cheese	¼	teaspoon Tabasco sauce
2	tablespoons Worcestershire sauce	¼	teaspoon salt
		½	teaspoon freshly ground pepper
2	cloves garlic	1	12-ounce can stale beer

Place all ingredients in a blender or a food processor fitted with the steel blade. Blend until pureed. Place in a crock and chill for at least 6 hours — preferably overnight. Serve with crackers.

Keeps for 2-3 weeks
Easy

Janet Hanson

ROQUEFORT CHEESE BALL

¼ pound Roquefort cheese
¼ cup Old English cheese
1   3-ounce package cream cheese
1   tablespoon Worcestershire sauce
1   teaspoon finely chopped onion
½ cup finely chopped parsley, divided
½ cup finely chopped pecans, divided

Combine the cheeses, Worcestershire sauce and onion and beat with a mixer until smooth. Add ¼ cup parsley and ¼ cup pecans and incorporate thoroughly. Form into a ball, wrap in waxed paper, and chill overnight.

After chilling, combine the remaining parsley and pecans and coat cheese ball with the mixture. Let stand 24-28 hours before serving.

Beth Berglund

HOT CRAB COCKTAIL SPREAD

1   8-ounce package cream cheese
1   tablespoon milk
2   teaspoons Worcestershire sauce
1   7½-ounce can crab meat, drained, cartilage removed
2   tablespoons chopped green onion
2   tablespoons toasted slivered almonds

Preheat oven to 350 degrees.

In a bowl combine the cream cheese with the milk and Worcestershire sauce. Add crab meat and green onions; blend well. Transfer to a shallow baking dish. Garnish with almonds. Bake until heated through — about 15 minutes.

Serve warm with crackers.

Makes 2 cups
Preparation time: 10 minutes
Easy

Kitty Talcott

SNOW PEAS WITH LEMON-ANCHOVY DIPPING SAUCE

2 egg yolks
3-4 tablespoons Dijon mustard
1 2-ounce can anchovies, with liquid
Juice of lemon
1 shallot, finely chopped
1 cup vegetable oil

¼ cup sour cream, optional
Salt and freshly ground pepper
1 tablespoon capers, drained and rinsed
Additional capers for garnish
2 pounds fresh snow peas, strings removed

In the container of a blender or food processor fitted with a steel blade, combine the egg yolks, mustard, anchovies, lemon juice and shallot. Mix until foamy and pale. With machine still running, slowly drizzle in oil, stopping occasionally to allow oil to be absorbed. If sauce is very stiff, add sour cream until creamy in consistency. Add salt and pepper to taste; stir in capers. Cover and refrigerate.

Before serving, garnish with additional capers.

Crisp peas in ice water. Drain well and arrange in sunburst pattern on a flat basket. Place a bowl of the dipping sauce in the center.

Serves 10-12
Preparation time: 15 minutes
Make ahead
Easy   Linnoah Grenzke

CHICKEN LIVER PATE

½ cup butter
2 pounds chicken livers
2 medium onions, chopped
1 rib of celery with leaves, finely chopped

2 teaspoons curry powder
1 teaspoon paprika
Salt and freshly ground pepper to taste
2 tablespoons Cognac

Melt the butter. Sauté the chicken livers, onions and celery. Add the curry powder, paprika, salt and pepper. Cover and cook over low heat for 8 minutes; cool for fifteen minutes. Place in blender or food processor fitted with a steel blade, add Cognac and blend until smooth. Put into a mold and chill until firm.

Rose-Marie Mebus

MARINATED SHRIMP

1	cup chopped celery	2½	tablespoons celery seed
3½	tablespoons salt	1	2¼-ounce bottle capers
¼	cup pickling spices		with juice
2½	pounds shrimp	2-3	dashes Tabasco
1¼	cups vegetable oil	4	medium onions, sliced into
¾	cup white vinegar		thin rings
1½	tablespoons salt		

Bring 3 quarts of water to boil. Add celery, salt and pickling spices. When water returns to a boil, add the shrimp and cook just until shrimp are pink. Allow to cool in water and drain. Shell and devein shrimp. In a bowl, combine the oil, vinegar, salt, celery seed, capers with juice and Tabasco sauce. Mix well. Alternate shrimp and onions in layers and cover with marinade. Cover and refrigerate for at least 24 hours.

Serves 20
Preparation time: 1 hour
Refrigerate: 24 hours
Easy

Winnie Ostrowski

HANKY PANKYS

Freeze well for instant hors d'oeuvres

1	pound bulk pork sausage	½	teaspoon oregano
1	pound ground beef	½	teaspoon onion or garlic salt
1	pound Velveeta cheese, cubed	2	packages party rye bread

Brown the sausage and hamburger; drain well. While meat is still hot, mix in the cheese. Add spices and mix well. Cheese will melt into hot meat and mixture will become spreadable.

Spread on rye bread and broil until hot and bubbly, or bake in a 350-degree oven.

To freeze, place on cookie sheets and put in freezer. When frozen transfer to plastic bags and seal well.

Eleanor Pekkala

SWEET GEFILTE FISH

FISH STOCK

Water
1   large onion, sliced
1   large carrot, sliced
¼   cup sugar

½   teaspoon pepper
2   tablespoons salt

Fill a large kettle half way with water and place over medium heat. Add the remaining ingredients and bring to a boil.

FISH

2½   pounds Whitefish
2½   pounds Pickerel
2   onions, finely chopped
2   eggs, uncooked
2   eggs, hard cooked and chopped
¼   cup sugar

¼   teaspoon pepper
1   teaspoon salt
¼   cup water
¼   cup matzo meal
1   large, carrot, finely grated

Chop or grind fish thoroughly. Add the onions and eggs, continuing to chop. Add the sugar, pepper, salt, matzo meal and grated carrot; mix thoroughly. Form fish into ovals and lower into the simmering fish stock. Reduce heat to a simmer, cover pot, and cook for 3 hours.

Serves 10-20   Henia Ciesla

RHODE ISLAND SHRIMP

The stuffing is also excellent for stuffing mushrooms . . . just top with some grated Parmesan cheese

⅔   cup Ritz cracker crumbs
⅓   cup Italian seasoned bread crumbs
½   cup butter, melted
2   tablespoons red wine

12-15 large sized shrimp, shelled, deveined and split down the back
Additional red wine

Place a small amount of wine in the bottom of an ovenproof baking dish large enough to hold the shrimp in one layer. Combine all ingredients except the shrimp; mix well. Stuff shrimp with the cracker mixture and place in a baking dish. Bake for 25 minutes in a 350-degree oven.

Serves 4   Denise Nett

MEATBALLS IN PLUM SAUCE

PLUM SAUCE

2   12-ounce jars plum jam
3   8-ounce jars Dijon mustard
1   1-inch piece of fresh ginger
     peeled or ½ teaspoon ground
     ginger

¾   cup ketchup
½   cup orange juice
¼   cup soy sauce
2   6-ounce cans pineapple juice

In a large saucepan, combine all ingredients and mix well. Simmer for 30 minutes. While sauce is cooking, make the meatballs.

MEATBALLS

2   pounds ground beef or pork
2   cups fine bread crumbs
1   8-ounce can water chestnuts,
     finely chopped
1   large onion, chopped
3   eggs

2   teaspoons salt
2   teaspoons oregano
2   teaspoons sage
3   cloves garlic
½   teaspoon pepper

Place the meat, breadcrumbs and water chestnuts in a large bowl. Place the remaining ingredients in a blender and puree. Add the pureed mixture to the beef. Blend well with your hands. Form into 1-inch balls and add to the simmering sauce. Simmer for 15 minutes then transfer to a chafing dish.

Yield: 100 meatballs
Preparation time: 30 minutes
Cooking time: 1 hour

Kathy Walters

CURRY CANAPES

1   4-ounce can chopped ripe
     olives
¼   cup chopped green onions
¾   cup Cheddar cheese,
     shredded

¼   cup mayonnaise
¼   teaspoon curry powder
Pinch salt
10 slices bread, crust removed
     and quartered

Preheat broiler. Combine ingredients and mix well. Spread on small thin squares of bread. Broil until cheese is melted.

Marlene Thomas

STUFFED GRAPE LEAVES WITH AVGOLEMONO SAUCE

These can be made well in advance and frozen

LAMB BROTH

4	cups water	Juice of 2 lemons	
1	lamb neck bone	½	cup white wine

Combine ingredients and bring to a boil. Skim off the froth that rises to the top and simmer for 15 minutes. Use to poach the stuffed grape leaves.

ROLLS

1½ pounds ground beef
3 pounds ground lamb
2 cloves garlic, minced
2 medium onions, finely chopped
½ cup pine nuts
2 cups cooked rice

3 tablespoons dry mint leaves
½ cup finely chopped fresh parsley
Salt and freshly ground pepper
3 jars grape leaves, carefully washed
4 cups lamb broth

In a large pan, brown the meat. Drain off the fat and add the garlic and onions. Cook for 10 minutes. Add remaining ingredients except the grape leaves and broth.

Spread the leaves out on paper towels. Place a rounded tablespoon of stuffing mixture on the edge of each leaf. Roll up, tucking in the edges. Continue working until all the stuffing is used.

Place the rolls in the lamb broth. Cover with a dish weighted down with a can, and poach for 1½ hours.

AVGOLEMONO SAUCE

4 egg yolks
Juice of 1 lemon
1 cup poaching liquid

Beat the yolks until light. Continue beating while you add the lemon juice and slowly add the broth.

Yield: 200 small rolls

Chris Considine

SPINACH PUFFS

2	10-ounce packages frozen chopped spinach
6	eggs
¾	cup butter, melted
1	large onion, chopped
1	clove garlic, minced
1	teaspoon pepper
2	cups dry Pepperidge Farms stuffing
½	cup grated Parmesan cheese

Cook the spinach; drain well. Beat the eggs then add the butter. Add remaining ingredients; mix well. Scoop by the teaspoonful and form into balls. Freeze on a cookie sheet lined with waxed paper. When they are firm, store in plastic bags until needed.

To serve: Remove from the freezer and bake in a 350-degree oven for 25 minutes. It is not necessary to defrost before baking. Serve with mustard sauce.

Yield: 40 spinach balls
Preparation time: 10 minutes
Baking time: 25 minutes
Freeze
Easy

Babette Posen

MUSTARD SAUCE

Serve as a dip for Spinach Puffs

½	cup dry mustard
½	cup white vinegar
¼	cup sugar
1	egg yolk

Combine the mustard and vinegar in a small bowl. Let stand at room temperature for 4 hours. Transfer to a small saucepan. Combine the sugar and egg yolk and mix well. Add to the saucepan and cook, stirring, until slightly thickened. Chill. Remove from refrigerator 30 minutes before serving.

Harriet Samuelson

Store freshly made horseradish in a dark bottle as it turns gray when exposed to light.

SPANAKOTIROPETES

Spinach-Cheese Puffs

These delicious pastries can be made ahead and baked just before serving

2	eggs	2	tablespoons chopped parsley
1	medium onion, quartered	1	tablespoon chopped fresh dill, or 1 teaspoon dill weed
½	pound Feta cheese, crumbled		
1	8-ounce package cream cheese, softened		Dash pepper
1	10-ounce package frozen chopped spinach, thawed	1	package phyllo or strudel leaves
		1	cup butter, melted

Combine the eggs, onion and cheese in the container of a food processor fitted with the steel blade, or in a blender, and process until smooth. Add the cream cheese and process until thoroughly incorporated. Squeeze as much liquid as possible from the spinach. Add spinach, parsley, dill and pepper to the cheese mixture and process just until combined. Refrigerate for at least 1 hour.

Stack 2 pastry leaves on a smooth, flat surface; cover remainder with plastic wrap to prevent drying. For each puff, cut a strip 2 inches wide and 16 inches long, cutting through both leaves. Brush with melted butter, then place a rounded teaspoon of the filling on one end of the strip. Fold one corner to opposite side, forming a triangle. Continue folding, keeping the triangle shape, to the other end. Arrange the filled pastries on an ungreased jelly-roll pan. Repeat the remaining pastry until filling is used up.

Bake in a 375-degree oven for 20 minutes, or until golden brown. Serve hot.

Note: If desired, pasties may be filled, then wrapped well and frozen in a single layer until ready to bake and serve.

Yield: 48 hors d'oeuvres   Bess Psihas

PIROZHKI
(Pea-rosh-key)

Serve with clear chicken or beef soup, on the "zakuska" appetizer table or presented alone as a first course.

PASTRY

4	cups flour	1	cup chilled lard, cut into
½	teaspoon salt		¼ inch bits
1	cup chilled butter, cut into	8-12	tablespoons ice water
	¼ inch bits		

Combine the flour, salt, butter and lard in a deep bowl. With your fingers, rub the flour and fat together until they resemble coarse meal. Pour in ½ cup ice water and gather dough into a ball. If it crumbles, add up to ¼ cup more ice water, 1 tablespoon at a time, until the particles adhere. Wrap the ball in waxed paper, and chill for 1 hour. On a lightly floured board, shape the pastry in a rectangle 1 inch thick then roll it into a strip about 21 inches by 6 inches. Fold the strip into thirds to make a 3 layered packet, 7 inches by 6 inches. Turn the pastry around and again roll it out lengthwise into a 21x6 inch strip. Fold into thirds and roll out as before. Repeat procedure two more times, ending with the folded packet. Wrap pastry in waxed paper and refrigerate for 1 hour.

FILLING

¼	cup butter	6	tablespoons chopped fresh
3	cups finely chopped onions		dill or 3 tablespoons dried dillweed
1½	pounds lean ground beef	2	teaspoons salt
3	hard cooked eggs, finely chopped	¼	teaspoon freshly ground black pepper

In a large, heavy skillet, melt the butter. Add the onions and cook, stirring occasionally, over moderate heat for 8-10 minutes or until they are soft and transparent but not brown. Add the beef and cook briskly, breaking up lumps with a fork, until no traces of pink remain. Chop the mixture finely, and combine with the eggs, dill, salt and pepper. Blend thoroughly and taste for seasoning.

ASSEMBLY

Preheat oven to 400 degrees.

On a lightly floured board, roll the dough into a circle about ⅛-inch thick. With a 3-3½-inch cookie cutter, cut out as many circles as you can. Gather the scraps into a ball and roll out again, cutting additional circles. Roll each circle into a thin oval. Drop 1 tablespoon of the filling in the center of each circle. Flatten filling slightly, and fold one long side of the dough up over the filling, almost covering it. Fold in the two ends about ½ inch, and then fold over the remaining long side of the dough. Place the pirozhki, seam side down, on a buttered baking sheet. Bake for 30 minutes, or until golden brown. Note: These are not very difficult to make, but do take time. After baking, they can be frozen. To thaw, remove from freezer, place in brown paper bag in a 350-degree oven for 10-15 minutes.

Davida Raber

ZUCCHINI SQUARES

Delicious!

3 cups unpeeled thinly sliced zucchini, with peel	1 tablespoon chopped parsley
1 cup Bisquick	½ teaspoon salt
½ cup finely chopped onion	Dash pepper
½ cup Parmesan cheese	½ teaspoon marjoram or oregano
½ cup vegetable oil	1 clove garlic, minced
4 eggs, beaten	

Preheat oven to 350 degrees.
Grease a 9x13-inch pan. Combine ingredients and mix well. Spread in pan. Bake 30-40 minutes until brown. Cut in squares and serve hot.

Yield: 3 dozen hors d'oeuvres
Preparation time: 10 minutes
Baking time: 25 minutes
Easy

Anne Meda

MY FAVORITE CRABMEAT HORS D'OEUVRE

¼ cup butter, softened
1 8-ounce package cream cheese, softened
1 tablespoon minced onion
1 egg yolk
1 7½-ounce can crabmeat
1 package English muffins

Cream the butter and cream cheese. Add onion, egg yolk and crabmeat and mix well. Spread evenly to edges of the English muffin halves. Cut each half into quarters and place on an ungreased cookie sheet. Broil until hot, bubbly and lightly browned.
To freeze: Place uncooked hors d'oeuvres on cookie sheet in single layer and freeze until solid. Transfer to airtight plastic bags. Remove from freezer 1 hour before broiling.

Yield: 48 hors'oeuvres
Preparation time: 15 minutes

Janice D. Cohen

STUFFED MUSHROOMS

These take a while, but they're worth the effort

2 pounds fresh mushrooms
¼ cup butter
1 cup seasoned bread crumbs
1½ cups Swiss cheese, grated
1½ tablespoons parsley
2 tablespoons chopped fresh dill
2 eggs, lightly beaten
¼ cup lemon juice

Preheat oven to 350 degrees.
Wash mushrooms and drain. Remove stems and set aside. Melt the butter in a large skillet. Toss mushroom caps in the melted butter, remove from pan and place on cookie sheets. Chop stems and brown in butter. Add remaining ingredients and cook until mixture is stringy. Stuff caps and bake for 15 minutes.
May be prepared ahead and baked just before serving.

Karen Schaupeter

TERIYAKI CHICKEN WINGS

3 to 3½ pounds chicken wings (about 20)

½	cup ketchup	1	teaspoon salt
¼	cup dry white wine	1	teaspoon ground ginger
¼	cup soy sauce	1	clove garlic, crushed
2	tablespoons sugar		

Cut ½-inch tip off each chicken wing; separate at joint. Place the chicken in a single layer in an ungreased baking dish. Mix remaining ingredients and pour over the chicken. Cover and refrigerate, turning occasionally, for at least 1 hour.
Heat oven to 375 degrees.
Remove chicken from the baking dish, reserving sauce. Place the chicken on a rack in broiler pan lined with aluminum foil. Bake for 30 minutes, basting occasionally with reserved sauce. Turn chicken and bake, basting occasionally until chicken is nicely glazed, 20-30 minutes.

Serves 8-10
Preparation time: 10 minutes
Cooking time: 1 hour
Easy

Carmella Gusfa

ROQUEFORT CRACKERS

Keep these in your freezer — slice and bake for a quick, delicious hors d'oeuvre.

2¼	cups flour	1	cup (4 ounces) crumbled
½	cup powdered sugar		Roquefort cheese, or
½	teaspoon salt		Bleu cheese
½	teaspoon white pepper	3	tablespoons cream Sherry
1	cup butter	1²⁄₃	cups walnuts, chopped

Sift together the flour, sugar, salt and pepper. Cut in butter and cheese until mixture resembles small peas. Sprinkle with Sherry and blend to a stiff dough. Add 1 cup nuts. Shape into a log and roll in remaining nuts. Wrap in plastic wrap and chill.
Slice ¼-inch thick and bake in a 400-degree oven for 8 minutes. Cool and serve, or store and serve later.

Sheila Mohr

HOT SAUSAGE BALLS

2	pounds bulk sausage meat	1½	cups barbeque sauce
2	cans water chestnuts, chopped		

Preheat oven to 350 degrees.
Combine the sausage meat and water chestnuts; mix well. Form into small balls about the size of large marbles. Place on the rack of a broiler pan and bake for 1 hour.
Heat barbeque sauce in a chafing dish and add sausage balls.

Preparation time: 10 minutes
Easy

Betty Gerisch

ARTICHOKE SQUARES

1	14-ounce can artichoke hearts	¼	teaspoon salt
½	cup Italian Dressing, divided	¼	teaspoon pepper
		½	teaspoon oregano
1	small onion, chopped	2	cups shredded Cheddar cheese
1	clove garlic, quartered		
4	eggs	2	tablespoons minced parsley
¾	cup white bread crumbs (about 1½ slices)		

Preheat oven to 325 degrees.
Cut artichoke hearts into quarters and marinate in ¼ cup dressing for 10-15 minutes. Drain.
Sauté the onion and garlic in ¼ cup dressing for 5 minutes. Drain and remove garlic. Beat eggs. Add bread crumbs and seasonings and stir in cheese, artichokes and onions. Put into greased 8x8-inch pan. Bake for 30 minutes. Cool 10 minutes before cutting into squares.

Serves 10
Preparation time: 20 minutes
Baking time: 30 minutes
Easy

Linnoah Grenzke

PIROSHKES

A favorite old Russian recipe — always served with soup

2   small onions, finely chopped
1   pound ground round
1   pound mushrooms with
    stems, finely chopped
2   eggs, hard cooked and
    chopped

Salt and pepper
6   packages refrigerated biscuit
    dough each containing
    10 biscuits
Vegetable oil

Sauté the onion and meat until meat is browned. Drain off fat. Add the mushrooms, chopped eggs and seasoning to taste.
Separate bisquits into ten pieces and roll out each into a circle on a lightly floured board. Put 1 generous teaspoon of filling in the center of each circle, roll up, being sure to tuck in sides, and seal.
Put vegetable oil in skillet to a depth of ¼ inch and fry rolls on medium heat until nicely browned. Serve hot or at room temperature.

Yield: 60 rolls
Preparation time: 1 hour
Cooking time: 30 minutes
Easy

Sophia Nowak-Tsoglin
DSO

GOUDA PUFFS

Impressive, and very quick to prepare

1   4-ounce package
    refrigerator crescent rolls
Dijon mustard
1   small Gouda cheese round

1   egg white mixed with 2
    teaspoons water
Sesame or caraway seeds

Preheat oven to 350 degrees.
Lay the crescent rolls flat on a lightly floured cutting board. Lightly roll out the dough then spread generously with mustard. Remove the wax from the cheese and place in center of the dough. Wrap dough around the cheese and seal with the egg-water mixture. Sprinkle liberally with sesame or caraway seeds. Bake for 20 minutes. Remove from the oven and let rest for 10 minutes, then cut into small pie shaped pieces and place on a serving dish.

Makes 16-24 puffs
Easy

Holly Barnett

INDIVIDUAL QUICHES

4 ounces cream cheese
¼ cup milk
½ cup mayonnaise
¼ cup minced onion
¼ teaspoon salt

2 eggs, beaten
¼ cup chopped black olives
¼ cup chopped smoky link
   sausages
4 ounces grated Swiss cheese

In the top part of a double boiler, combine the cream cheese, milk, mayonnaise, onion and salt. Cook, stirring constantly, until cheese has melted and ingredients are well mixed and creamy. Remove from heat and allow to cool slightly. Stirring constantly, add some of the hot cream cheese mixture to the beaten eggs, then add egg mixture to the hot cheese mixture. Stir in the olives, sausage and Swiss cheese. Coat 24 tart pans with vegetable cooking spray. Fill each tart cup to the top. Bake in a 350-degree oven for 18-20 minutes or until quiches rise and are golden brown.

Makes 24 hors d'oeuvres   Anne Simons

OLIVE PUFFS

A make ahead hors d'oeuvre. Keep on hand for unexpected guests

2 cups grated sharp Cheddar
   cheese
½ cup butter, softened
1 cup flour
½ teaspoon salt

1 teaspoon paprika
¼ teaspoon Tabasco sauce
3 8-ounce jars small stuffed
   green olives, well drained

Blend together the cheese and butter. Blend in the flour, salt, paprika and Tabasco. Wrap each olive in some of the cheese mixture and form into a ball. Freeze on cookie sheets until firm then store in freezer in plastic bags until needed.
To serve, preheat oven to 400 degrees. Bake frozen puffs for 10-15 minutes.

Yield: about 70 puffs
Easy   Mary Alice Bird

HOT MUSHROOM ROLLS

1 large onion, finely chopped
1 teaspoon butter
¾ pound fresh mushrooms, finely chopped
¼ teaspoon salt
⅛ teaspoon freshly ground pepper
1 8-ounce package cream cheese, softened

½ teaspoon Worcestershire sauce
¼ teaspoon garlic powder
½ teaspoon M.S.G. (optional)
Loaf of thinly sliced white bread
½ pound butter, melted

Saute the onion in the butter until lightly golden. Add the mushrooms and sauté for 2 minutes; remove from heat. Season with salt and pepper. Taste and adjust seasoning. Add the cream cheese and mix thoroughly until smooth. Stir in the Worcestershire sauce, garlic powder and M.S.G. Allow to sit for at least 1 hour for flavors to blend.

Cut the crusts from the bread. Spread each slice with the mushroom mixture and roll as for a jelly roll. Fasten with toothpicks until set. Refrigerate for at least 1 hour for easy slicing.

When ready to serve, cut each roll into ¼ inch slices and brush generously with melted butter on one side only. Broil until lightly browned.

Serves 10-12
Preparation time: 25 minutes

Mrs. Kent D. Johnson

YANKEE CLAM COCKTAIL BROIL

1 8-ounce package cream cheese, softened
1 clove garlic, crushed
1 teaspoon Worcestershire sauce

Dash salt
1 7½-ounce can minced clams, drained well
Toasted rounds or melba toast

Combine all ingredients and blend well. Heap on toast rounds, covering edges well, and broil. Serve at once.

Betty Gerisch

TERIYAKI MEATBALLS

1 pound hamburger	1 teaspoon ginger
½ cup soy sauce	1 clove garlic, chopped
¼ cup water	

Form hamburger into 1-inch balls. Place in a large flat roasting pan. Combine remaining ingredients and pour over the meatballs. Cook for 1 hour, uncovered, in a 275-degree oven. Serve hot.

Preparation time: 10 minutes
Cooking time: 1 hour
Easy   Janet Cox

HOT SUSSEX SMOKIE

1 pound smoked haddock or cod, filleted and skinned	1 cup shredded Cheddar cheese
1 bay leaf	1 cup dry white wine
3 cups water	Freshly ground pepper
¼ cup butter	Grated Parmesan cheese
¼ cup flour	

Place the haddock and the bay leaf in the water. Simmer until fish flakes easily, about 10 minutes. Cool slightly. Melt the butter in a saucepan and add the flour. Mix well and cook the roux, stirring constantly, for 2-3 minutes for the flour to cook. Remove the fish from the stock and strain the liquid. Slowly add 2 cups of the poaching liquid to the roux, stirring constantly until mixture is smooth. Bring to a boil and simmer for 15 minutes, stirring occasionally. Add the Cheddar cheese, the wine and pepper to taste. Continue cooking until the sauce is smooth and thick.

Flake the fish into the sauce and transfer to 6 small ramekins. Sprinkle with Parmesan cheese and run under a broiler until the cheese is golden brown, or, bake in a preheated 450-degree oven for 10 minutes.

Serves 6
Preparation time: 30 minutes   Gillian Von Drehle

ELIZABETH'S ESCARGOTS

Elizabeth's Restaurant in Northville, Michigan features a seasonal five course repast in an intimate Victorian house.

32 escargots	12 cloves garlic, minced
Red wine	¼ cup chopped parsley
6 tablespoons Cognac	¾ cup clarified butter
2 shallots, chopped	1-2 tablespoons Chartreuse
2 bay leaves	liqueur
3 tablespoons hazelnuts, chopped	Salt
	French bread
1 tablespoon butter	Butter

Rinse escargots at least 3 times and pack in container. Pour on enough red wine to cover. Add Cognac, shallots and bay leaves; cover and refrigerate overnight.

Sauté the hazelnuts in butter and set aside. Combine the garlic and parsley; set aside. Drain the escargots and sauté in butter for 2 minutes. Add the Chartreuse, turn off the heat then add the garlic-parsley mixture. Season with salt to taste.

For each serving, hollow out a piece of French bread. Brush liberally with melted butter and toast in oven. Insert the cooked escargots in the hollowed out bread. Pour the garlic-parsley mixture over and sprinkle with sautéed hazelnuts.

Serves 4
Preparation time: 40 minutes   Beth and Doug Campbell

HERBED CHEESE CRESCENTS

2 packages refrigerated crescent rolls	1 5-ounce container herb or garlic cheese, spread, softened

Open dough flat, and spread generously with softened cheese. Cut each perforated section into two triangles, and roll up from wide end to tip. Bake according to package directions.

Makes 40 hors d'oeuvres
Easy   Brenda Pangborn
                                                 DSC

47

COCKTAIL REUBENS

14 slices dry rye bread, toasted
Prepared mustard
1   16-ounce can sauerkraut, drained and cut into small pieces
6   ounces sliced corned beef, finely snipped

2   cups (about 8 ounces) Mozzarella or Swiss cheese, shredded
½   cup mayonnaise or salad dressing

Preheat oven to 375 degrees.
Spread toast lightly with mustard and place on ungreased baking sheet. Mix sauerkraut, corned beef, cheese and mayonnaise. Spread about ⅓ cup of the sauerkraut mixture on each slice of toast. Bake until hot and cheese is melted, about 10 minutes. Cut sandwiches in fourths.

Makes 56 hor d'oeuvres   Carmella Gusfa

SHRIMP AKRON CITY CLUB

1   pound shrimp, cooked
1   cup mayonnaise
½   cup chili sauce
½   teaspoon chutney
½   teaspoon hot sauce

1   teaspoon Worcestershire
½   teaspoon paprika
Pinch of cayenne
Parmesan cheese
2   tablespoons butter, melted

Preheat oven to 350 degrees.
Put shrimp in 1-quart casserole or in individual ramekins. Combine mayonnaise, chili sauce, chutney, hot sauce, Worcestershire, paprika and cayenne. Adjust seasoning to taste. Pour sauce over shrimp. Sprinkle with cheese and drizzle with melted butter. Bake for 20 minutes or until lightly browned.
If prepared in casserole, serve with buttered toast.
If prepared in individual ramekins, serve with buttered toast on the side.

Serves 6
Preparation time: 10 minutes
Baking time: 20 minutes
Easy   Ann Muir

COCKTAIL MEATBALLS

1	pound ground beef	2	tablespoons butter
1	teaspoon M.S.G. (optional)	3	tablespoons unsulfured
¾	teaspoon salt		molasses
¼	cup chopped onion	1	teaspoon prepared mustard
¼	cup milk	3	tablespoons vinegar
1	tablespoon dry bread	¼	cup ketchup
	crumbs	¼	teaspoon thyme
1	tablespoon flour		Optional: Minced green pepper

Combine meat, M.S.G., salt and onion; blend well. Mix together the milk and bread crumbs, add to the meat and mix until all ingredients are thoroughly incorporated. Form into ¾-inch balls and roll in flour. Melt the butter in a skillet; add meatballs and sauté until browned on all sides.

Combine the remaining ingredients and blend until smooth. Pour sauce over meatballs and simmer, stirring occasionally, until sauce thickens and meatballs are nicely glazed, about 8-10 minutes. Transfer to a chafing dish and serve hot.

Serves 8-10
Preparation time: 30 minutes
Easy

Diane Varisto

SHRIMP NIBBLERS

1	8-ounce package shredded	1	teaspoon dill, or to taste
	Cheddar cheese		18-20 slices white bread
1	cup mayonnaise	1	pound cooked shrimp

Combine the cheese, mayonnaise and dill; set aside. Remove crust from the bread then cut each piece into quarters. Spread some of the cheese mixture on each piece of bread and top with a whole shrimp. Dab with additional cheese spread. Refrigerate until ready to serve. To serve, broil for 5 minutes.

Makes about 80 hors d' oeuvres
Easy

Alice Riedl

SHRIMP-SCALLOP MEDLEY

1 pound fresh spinach,
trimmed, cooked and
drained
3 green onions, finely chopped
Pinch of thyme or dill
1 tablespoon butter
1 clove garlic, minced

2 tablespoons vermouth
Pinch of thyme
4 large shrimp, cleaned
and butterflied
½ pound scallops, rinsed
1 tablespoon lemon juice
Salt and freshly ground pepper

Combine the cooked spinach, onions, and thyme or dill. Mix well and divide between 2 individual oven-proof dishes. Cover with foil and keep warm in oven.

Melt the butter in a skillet. Add the garlic, vermouth and thyme, and cook, stirring, until butter begins to sizzle. Add the shrimp and scallops and stir-fry until just done — about 7 minutes. Add the lemon juice and season to taste with salt and freshly ground pepper. Remove baking dishes from oven and, with a slotted spoon, place the shellfish on the spinach. Pour the juices over.

Serve with sliced tomatoes sprinkled with oregano.

Serves 2
Preparation time: 15 minutes

Toula Patsalis
Kitchen Glamor, Inc.

ONION PASTRY

1 package Pepperidge Farms
puff pastry
2 large yellow onions,
chopped
½ pound bacon, chopped

2 tablespoons flour
1 egg
Salt, pepper and nutmeg
Egg wash: 1 egg mixed with
1 tablespoon cold water

Remove pastry from freezer and let thaw. Sauté onions and bacon; simmer for 15 minutes. Stir in the flour and remove from heat; let cool. Roll out half the dough into a rectangle ⅛-inch thick. Beat egg and add to onion mixture. Add salt, pepper and nutmeg to taste; mix well. Place filling on dough to within one inch of the edge. Brush the edge with egg wash. Roll out the other half of dough and place on top of the onion mixture. Press edges together. Brush top with egg wash and make slits for air to escape.

Heat over to 375 degrees and bake pastry for 40-50 minutes or until pastry is golden brown.

John Snow
DSO

EGG NOG

12	eggs, separated	2	cups rum
1½	cups superfine sugar	2	quarts heavy cream, whipped
4	cups whiskey, brandy or bourbon		Freshly grated nutmeg

Beat the egg yolks until pale. Slowly add the sugar, beating constantly, until smooth and lemon colored. Very slowly stir in liquors. Carefully add the whipped cream and let stand for 1 hour.
Beat the egg whites until stiff but not dry. Fold into first mixture. Transfer to a punch bowl and sprinkle top with freshly grated nutmeg.

Serves 16   Sidney Bramson

HOT BUTTERED RUM

1	cup butter	1	teaspoon cinnamon
½	cup firmly packed brown sugar	1	pint vanilla ice cream, softened
½	cup sifted powdered sugar		Rum or Brandy
1	teaspoon nutmeg		Boiling water

Cream together the butter, brown sugar, powdered sugar, nutmeg and cinnamon. Blend in the softened ice cream and place in freezer.
To serve: Place 2-4 tablespoons of the frozen mixture in a large mug. Add 1-2 shots of rum or brandy, fill with boiling water and stir. Sprinkle with nutmeg . . . enjoy!

Serves 16-20   Hart Hollman
                                                                               DSO

GRANNY'S ICED TEA

3	cups water	2	cups orange juice
2	cups sugar	2	cups lemon juice
8	cups tea, brewed	1	cup fresh mint leaves

Bring water and sugar to a boil in a 6-quart saucepan; boil for 5 minutes. Add the tea, orange juice, lemon juice and mint. Let steep, uncovered, for 1 hour. Strain off the mint leaves and serve over ice. Store in refrigerator in covered jars.

Makes 18 cups   Marianne Endicott

BACCIO PUNCH

1	block of ice or ice ring	1	cup Anisette
2	cups grapefruit juice		Sugar to taste
2	cups gin		Fresh fruit
2	cups soda water	2	cups Champagne

Place ice block or ice ring in a large punch bowl. Add the juice, gin, soda water and Anisette; mix well. Garnish generously with fresh fruit slices. Just before serving, stir in the Champagne. Serve in wine glasses.

Makes 9 cups   Marilyn Van Giesen

52

RICH HOT CHOCOLATE

1 teaspoon mocha flavored instant coffee mix
2 teaspoons instant hot cocoa mix

Water
2-3 drops almond or vanilla extract
Half and Half

Place coffee mix and cocoa mix in cup. Fill with water to ¾ full. Add extract and fill to top with Half and Half.

Serves 1

Ann Alicia Ourada
DSO

HART'S DELIGHT

1 lemon slice
Granulated sugar
1 ounce Old Bushmill's Irish Whiskey

1 ounce Kahlua
5 ounces coffee
Whipped cream

Rub rim of a stemmed Irish Coffee glass with lemon juice. While still wet with the juice, dip the rim in sugar to coat well. Place the rim over an open flame using Sterno or a gas stove, and turning glass slowly, heat until the sugar starts to bubble. Remove from heat and add the Irish Whiskey.
Return glass to the flame. Tip and rotate the glass, coating sides evenly and heating the whiskey. Tip the glass to ignite the warmed whiskey, hold upright, and continue swirling glass until the flame dies down. Add Kahlua and coffee, top with a dollop of whipped cream, and sprinkle with additional Kahlua. Serve with a small napkin wrapped around the stem — the glass will be hot.

Serves 1

Hart Hollman
DSO

ANNIVERSARY PUNCH

1   bottle liquor (bourbon, rye)
1   cup cranberry juice
¼   cup lemon or lime juice
Dash Angostura bitters

1   1 liter (33.8 ounces) bottle
    soda water
2   bottles Champagne
Fruit for garnish

Mix the whiskey, juices and bitters and refrigerate. When ready to serve, pour into a punch bowl over an ice mold. Add the soda water and Champagne. Garnish with fruit.

Serves 20   Inez Redman

WHISKEY SOUR MIX

1   6-ounce can frozen orange
    juice concentrate
1   6-ounce can frozen lemonade
    concentrate

36 ounces water
4   ounces Rose's lime juice
1   cup sugar, or to taste
1   egg white

Combine all ingredients and refrigerate. Mix with whiskey in equal portions.

Enough for about 30 sours   Bob Allison
                                            "Ask Your Neighbor"

PERFECT IRISH COFFEE

The hot whiskey-laced coffee is sipped through the velvety cream

1½ teaspoons sugar
1   cup hot strong black coffee

1   jigger Irish whiskey
1   tablespoon whipped cream

Heat a stemmed goblet. Add the sugar and just enough of the hot coffee to dissolve the sugar; stir well. Add the whiskey and fill the glass to within 1-inch of the rim with additional hot coffee. Float the cream on top, but do not mix it into the drink.

Serves 1   Peggy McCourt

SLUSH

A refreshing summer drink

7	cups water	12	ounces lemon juice
3	cups sugar	3	cups brandy, gin, or vodka
2	cups hot water		Chilled 7-Up
4	green tea bags		
1	12-ounce can frozen orange juice		

Mix together the water and sugar. Bring to a boil, stirring, until the sugar is completely dissolved. Let cool.

Pour hot water over tea bags and allow to cool completely. Squeeze out tea bags and discard. Add undiluted orange juice, lemon juice, and sugar mixture blending well. Add the liquor, mix and freeze.

To serve: Put two ice cream scoops of Slush in a glass and fill with 7-Up.

Serves 15-25   Carol Herbst

BENNER'S BLENDER BRUNCH

My solution to quickie nutrition. A healthy drink to have throughout the day or in place of breakfast or lunch.

1½	cups orange juice	3	heaping tablespoons Millers bran
1	heaping tablespoon Brewer's yeast	½	green pepper, chopped
1	heaping tablespoon soy protein powder	1	carrot, chopped
1	heaping tablespoon dry cottage cheese	1	rib celery, chopped
			Optional: fruits and vegetables to taste

In the container of a blender place the orange juice, Brewer's yeast, protein powder, cottage cheese and Millers bran; blend until combined. Add vegetables and any optional fruit and process until liquified.

Serves 1-2   Ray Benner
Preparation time: 5 minutes   DSO

FRUIT CORDIAL

1   quart ripe raspberries,   1½   cups superfine sugar
     strawberries or pitted   1   bottle (fifth) vodka
     cherries, washed

Combine ingredients, mix well, and let stand for 1 month.

Rebecca Hubert

MUG DELIGHT

1   ounce brandy*   Boiling water
1   ounce Creme de Cacao*   Whipped topping
1   tablespoon instant coffee
     powder

Combine the brandy, Creme de Cacao and coffee in a mug. Fill with hot water, mix, and add a dollop of whipped topping. Sprinkle with additional Creme de Cacao, serve, and *smile!*
Depending on degree of inner warmth desired!

Serves 1

Hart Hollman
DSO

HAWAIIAN CHAMPAGNE PUNCH

Ice ring   1   quart ginger ale
1   46-ounce can Hawaiian   1   bottle domestic Champagne
     Punch   Orange slices and strawberries
1   6-ounce can frozen   for garnish
     lemonade, thawed

Make an ice ring by filling a medium-sized ring mold with bottled water and freezing. Pour the punch and lemonade in a large punch bowl. When ready to serve, add the ginger ale, Champagne and the ice ring. Float orange slices and strawberries on top.

Makes 12 cups

Vera Heidelberg

CHAMPAGNE PUNCH

2 bottles white champagne, chilled
1 bottle club soda, chilled

1 bottle Sauternes, chilled
⅓ bottle apricot brandy
Fresh strawberries

Mix all liquids in a large punch bowl. Make a decorative ice mold and float on top of punch. Garnish with fresh strawberries.

Serves 12   Marilyn Jakubowski

SANGRIA

1 orange, thinly sliced
1 lemon, thinly sliced
¼ cup superfine sugar
½ cup Cointreau

½ cup brandy
½ gallon red Burgundy, chilled
1 liter club soda, chilled
Ice

Combine the orange, lemon, sugar, Cointreau and brandy. Let macerate at room temperature until ready to serve. Add the Burgundy, soda and ice; stir.

Note: In summer add a cup each of strawberries, raspberries and blueberries. In winter add a small package of frozen mixed fruit with juice. For white sangria, use dry white wine.

Serves 12   Jean Murray

SPICED PERCOLATOR PUNCH

Witches Brew

2   32-ounce bottles cranberry juice
1   46-ounce can unsweetened pineapple juice
1   cup brown sugar

4   teaspoons whole cloves
12 inches stick cinnamon, broken
Peel from ¼ orange, cut in strips
2-3 cups light rum

In a 24 cup percolator, combine the cranberry juice, pineapple juice and brown sugar. Place the cloves, cinnamon stick pieces and orange peel in basket of percolator. Assemble coffee maker, plug in, and percolate until light indicates done.

Just before serving, remove basket and stir in rum to taste. Keep hot.

Makes about 20 cups   Sheila Pitcoff

BLINKING STAR

This authentic Russian cocktail was given to us with a little bit of humor from our own inimitable Misha, who says, "It's all in the way you steer it."

First, you take a large empty glass. Fill it with 3½ ounces Vuodka. Zen you very slowly add another 3½ ounces Vuodka — steer it and drink very carefully.

Misha Rachlevsky
DSO

TEXAS CLOUD

1½ ounces Amaretto
1   ounce white creme de cacao

3   scoops French vanilla ice cream
1   fresh strawberry

Combine all ingredients, except the strawberry, in the container of a blender and process until well blended. Serve in a chilled, stemmed glass. Garnish with the strawberry.

Serves 1   "Bobi" at Beau Jack's

STRIP AND GO NAKED

Two of these and you'll . . .

1 can frozen lemonade
   concentrate
Using lemonade can to
   measure add:

1 can bourbon
1 can beer
5 to 6 ice cubes

Mix well in a blender! WOW!

Marcy Chanteaux
DSO

KAHLUA

2 cups sugar
2 cups boiling water
2 tablespoons vanilla

2 cups instant coffee powder
1 quart (not fifth) Vodka

Mix the sugar, water and vanilla and let cool. Add the coffee and vodka; mix well and put in bottles. Let sit for 30 days.

Makes about 1½ quarts
Preparation time: 10 minutes
Sitting time: 30 days
Easy

Joe Ann Goodman

WHISKEY SOUR PUNCH

1 12-ounce container frozen
   orange juice concentrate
1 6-ounce container frozen
   lemonade concentrate
1 16-ounce jar maraschino
   cherries, drained
1 tablespoon Angostura
   bitters

1 tablespoon sugar
1 liter (33.8 ounces) bottle
   club soda
½ cup whiskey sour mix
1 pint whiskey

Combine 3 ounces of orange juice concentrate and ½ jar of cherries. Mix well. Place in a mold and freeze overnight.
To serve: Combine the remaining orange juice and lemonade and mix well. Pour into a punch bowl. Add club soda, whiskey sour mix and whiskey and blend well. Float the cherry ice mold on top.

Susan Murphy

HEALTHY NOGS

PINEAPPLE-BANANA NOG

1   6-ounce can pineapple juice
1   tablespoon milk

1   tablespoon honey
1   medium banana

ORANGE NOG

1   glass orange juice
2   tablespoons milk

1   tablespoon honey

APRICOT NOG

2   6-ounce cans apricot juice
¼   cup milk

2   tablespoons honey

STRAWBERRY-BANANA NOG

1   cup fresh strawberries
1   cup milk

½   small banana, cut up
1   tablespoon honey

Mix all ingredients in a blender and process until smooth. Serve cold.

Lloyd Buck

HOT MULLED CIDER

A non-alcoholic drink for apres ski

1   gallon apple cider
3   cinnamon sticks
1   tablespoon whole cloves
2   cups orange juice

1   orange, sliced
1   lemon, sliced
Cinnamon sticks for stirring

In a large kettle, boil cider with spices for 5 minutes. Add the orange and lemon slices. Serve in mugs with cinnamon sticks.

Serves 16
Preparation time: 10 minutes
Easy

Jeanine Collins

Soups

Cuisine on a Shoestring

Mixed Green Salad
French Canadian Ragout
Buttered Noodles
Russian Dark Pumpernickle Bread
Snow Pudding

Wine Suggestion

Spanna-Dessilani (1978)
A hearty but soft red wine

Après Ski Buffet

Spiced Percolator Punch
Cheese Fondue
Smoked Salmon Party Ball
Piroshkes
Misha's Borscht
Beer Bread
Lemon Garlic Chicken
Crusty Topped Kugel
Steamed Fresh Green Beans
Chocolate Cheesecake
Baked Fruit

Wine Suggestions

Macon-Lugny Latour (1981)
A rich white
or
St. Joseph-Jaboulet Aine (1980)
A rich and warming red

FROSTED FRESH TOMATO SOUP
WITH PESTO GARNISH

Light and delicious

SOUP

7 large, ripe tomatoes, peeled, or one 35-ounce can tomatoes with juice
1 small onion
1 clove garlic, minced
1½ teaspoons salt
¼ teaspoon freshly ground pepper
1 teaspoon sugar
5 tablespoons creme fraiche or sour cream
1 teaspoon minced parsley
1 teaspoon curry powder
Creme fraiche or lightly salted sour cream for garnish

Place tomatoes, onion, garlic, salt, pepper and sugar in a blender and process until smooth. Push through a sieve into a large bowl and beat in the remaining ingredients with a wire whisk until the mixture is smooth and creamy. Serve very cold in chilled soup mugs. Garnish with a dollop of creme fraiche or lightly salted sour cream, and sprinkle with pesto.

PESTO

1 cup chopped fresh basil leaves
⅓ cup minced parsley
3 tablespoons minced fresh tarragon
3 tablespoons minced fresh chervil
3 tablespoons minced fresh chives
1 clove garlic
Juice of 1 lime
⅔ cup olive oil
Salt and pepper to taste

Place all ingredients except the oil in a food processor fitted with the steel blade. Blend for 1-2 seconds. With the machine running, slowly add the oil in a thin stream and blend until smooth. Add salt and pepper to taste.

Serves 6
Makes 1½ cups
Keeps in refrigerator 2-3 weeks

Charity de Vicq Suczek

MISHA'S BORSCHT

Misha's Borscht has been served often at his Nightcap with Mozart series and has appeared in the Detroit Free Press in the "Best Cook on the Block" series.

2½ to 3 pounds round bone beef, bone included
3-4 large beets, peeled and quartered
2 medium bay leaves
3½ to 4 quarts water
Salt and freshly ground black pepper to taste
1 small head green cabbage, coarsely chopped

3 large carrots, grated
1 medium Spanish onion, finely chopped
4 medium potatoes, peeled
Juice of ½ large lemon
6-8 ounces tomato paste, to taste
Sour cream

In a large soup pot or kettle, combine the whole piece of meat, beets, bay leaves and water. Season lightly with salt and pepper. Bring to a boil skimming froth off the top several times as needed. Reduce heat, partially cover, and simmer for 1 hour.

Remove the beets with a slotted spoon and set aside to cool. To the pot, add the cabbage, carrots, onion and two of the whole peeled potatoes. Pour in the lemon juice and stir. Grate the cooled beets and add to the pot. Bring the mixture to a boil, reduce heat and simmer another hour, partially covered.

Remove the potatoes from the pot and mash and return to the pot. Dice the two remaining raw potatoes and add to the soup. Simmer for 30 minutes, or until the potatoes are cooked. Add tomato paste and simmer an additional 30 minutes. Cool and refrigerate overnight; the soup should be served the day after preparation for maximum blending of flavors.

Serve very hot with a dollop of sour cream on top of each serving.

Makes about two gallons

Misha Rachlevsky
DSO

BAKED MINESTRONE

1½ pounds lean beef stew meat, cut into 1¼-inch cubes
1 cup coarsely chopped onion
1 teaspoon minced garlic
1 teaspoon salt
¼ teaspoon pepper
2 tablespoons olive oil
3 10½-ounce cans condensed beef broth
2 soup cans water
¾ teaspoon basil
¾ teaspoon oregano
1 16-ounce can tomatoes, with liquid
1 15½-ounce can kidney beans, with liquid
1½ cups thinly sliced carrots
1 cup small shell macaroni
2 cups sliced zucchini
Parmesan cheese

Preheat oven to 400 degrees.
Combine the beef, onion, garlic, salt, pepper and oil in a Dutch oven. Brown, uncovered, in the oven for about 40 minutes, stirring 1 or 2 times. Reduce heat to 350 degrees. Add the broth, water, and seasonings. Cover and cook for 1 hour or until the meat is almost tender. Stir in the tomatoes, beans, carrots and macaroni. Sprinkle zucchini on top, cover and return to the oven for 40 minutes, or until macaroni is cooked. Serve with Parmesan cheese.

Makes 3½ quarts   Dorothy Williams

AVOCADO AND OLIVE SOUP

This unusual soup is delicious hot or cold

3 cups milk
1 large avocado, peeled
1 can condensed cream of celery soup
1 can condensed cream of chicken soup
½ cup chopped celery
½ cup chopped olives
¼ cup minced onion
Salt and freshly ground pepper to taste
Sour cream and additional sliced olives for garnish

Combine all ingredients, except the sour cream and sliced olives, in a large saucepan and cook for 8-10 minutes. Cool, then puree in a blender. Pour into bowls and serve with a dollop of sour cream and a sprinkling of chopped olives.

Serves 6-8
Preparation time: 25 minutes
Easy   Chuck Dyer

HUNGRY MUSICIANS' POTATO-CELERY SOUP

This makes a great snack for two after a late evening concert or a delicious soup course before an elegant dinner.

4   medium Michigan potatoes, scrubbed and diced
2   chicken bouillon cubes

4   ribs celery, chopped
Salt and pepper to taste
Chopped parsley

Place 4 cups of water in a medium saucepan; bring to a boil. Add the potatoes, bouillon cubes, celery and seasoning. Simmer until potatoes are tender. Sprinkle with chopped parsley. "Musicians and friends are now ready for a hearty serving of delicious soup!"

Serves 4

Ervin Monroe
DSO

CREAMY ZUCCHINI SOUP

2   tablespoons butter
½   cup sliced scallions
6   medium zucchini, thinly sliced
2   13¾-ounce cans chicken broth
2   tablespoons dry Sherry

⅛   teaspoon pepper
⅛   teaspoon salt
Dash nutmeg
1   cup light cream
3   tablespoons grated fresh Parmesan cheese

In a large saucepan, melt the butter. Sauté scallions until softened. Add the zucchini and chicken broth and bring to a boil. Lower heat and simmer 8-10 minutes or until zucchini is tender. Allow mixture to cool 10-15 minutes. In blender or food processor, process cooled zucchini mixture in small batches until smooth. Return mixture to saucepan. Stir in the Sherry, pepper, salt and nutmeg. Bring to a boil, remove from heat, then stir in the cream and cheese. Serve hot, or cover and chill in refrigerator for 3-4 hours.

Serves 8
Preparation time: 40 minutes

Davida Raber

SPRING SOUP

6 cups strong chicken broth
½ cup carrots, cut in fine julienne
½ cup green peas
¾ cup raw spinach, finely chopped

¼ cup green onions, sliced
2 tablespoons chopped fresh parsley
Salt and white pepper to taste

Heat the broth. Add the carrots and peas and simmer for 5 minutes. Add the remaining ingredients and simmer for 3 minutes longer. Serve immediately.

Serves 6-8
Preparation time: 20 minutes
Easy   Paula Stevens

CREAMY CAULIFLOWER SOUP

1 medium cauliflower, cut into tiny florets
¼ cup butter
⅔ cup chopped onion
2 tablespoons flour
2 cups chicken broth

2 cups light cream
½ teaspoon Worcestershire sauce
¾ teaspoon salt
1 cup grated Cheddar cheese
Chopped chives or parsley

Cook cauliflower in salted water. Drain, reserving 1 cup liquid. Melt the butter; add the onion and cook until soft. Blend in the flour. Add the broth and cook, stirring, until mixture comes to a boil. Stir in the reserved cooking liquid, cream, Worcestershire sauce and salt. Add the cauliflower and heat to boiling. Stir in the cheese and cook until cheese is melted. Sprinkle with chives or parsley.

Serves 8
Preparation time: 30 minutes
Easy   Kathie Ninneman

RUSSIAN BORSCHT

Great in the summer, served cold

1	tablespoon salt	2	tablespoons vinegar
1½	quarts water	1	teaspoon sugar
1	pound lean beef, cubed	2	tablespoons butter
1½	cups shredded raw beets	½	small head cabbage,
¾	cup shredded carrots		shredded
¾	cup shredded white turnips	Freshly ground black pepper	
	or rutabagas	2	bay leaves
1	medium onion, chopped	Sour cream	
2	tablespoons tomato puree		

Add salt to the water and heat. Add the meat and simmer until tender, about 1½ hours. Meanwhile, in a large saucepan, combine the beets, carrots, turnips, onions, tomato puree, vinegar, sugar and butter. Cover and simmer for 15 minutes, stirring frequently. Add the cabbage and cook 10 minutes longer. Add the cooked vegetables, pepper and bay leaves to the meat and broth. Adjust seasonings and cook until the vegetables are tender.

Serve warm or cold, topping with a dollop of sour cream just before serving.

Serves 6-8
Prepare ahead

Nancy Burrows

LENTIL SOUP

1	cup dried lentils	2	bay leaves
1	cup chopped onion	½	teaspoon cumin
2	cloves garlic, minced	Pinch of thyme	
2	cup shredded carrots	Pinch of turmeric or curry	
4	ribs celery, chopped		powder
2	tablespoons chopped fresh	Salt and pepper to taste	
	parsley	2	tablespoons lemon juice
3	cups chicken broth	Optional: 1 cup cubed cooked	
3	cups water		chicken

Combine all ingredients except the lemon juice and chicken. Cover and simmer for 50-60 minutes or until lentils are tender. Stir in the lemon juice and chicken and heat thoroughly.

Sue Fishman

CREAM OF PEANUT SOUP

This recipe goes back to the 20's

2	tablespoons butter	¼	cup finely grated onion
2	tablespoons flour	⅔	cup creamy or chunky
4	cups milk		peanut butter
2	tablespoons grated onion	3	tablespoons grated sharp
½	teaspoon pepper		Cheddar cheese
1	teaspoon salt		

Melt the butter in a large saucepan over medium heat. Add the flour and blend in well. Gradually stir in the milk and mix until well blended. Add remaining ingredients and bring to a boil. Simmer over low heat for 15 minutes. Serve hot or cold.

Serves 6-8
Preparation time: 15 minutes
Cooking time: 30 minutes
Easy

Ida Allen

HOT BEER SOUP

3	12-ounce bottles light beer	½	teaspoon cinnamon
½	cup sugar	¼	teaspoon salt
4	egg yolks		Freshly ground pepper to taste
⅓	cup sour cream		

In a heavy 5-quart saucepan, bring the beer and sugar to a boil over high heat, stirring constantly, until sugar is dissolved. Remove from heat. In a small bowl, beat the egg yolks. Beat in the sour cream, a little at a time, then add ¼ cup of the beer mixture. Stir in seasonings, and add to the beer mixture a little at a time. Cook over low heat, stirring constantly, until slightly thickened. **Do not boil.**

Serves 4
Preparation time: 20 minutes
Easy

Bob Allison
"Ask Your Neighbor"

MUSHROOM-BARLEY SOUP

All this needs is a crisp green salad and crusty French bread

1	pound fresh mushrooms, rinsed and drained	1	bay leaf
6	tablespoons butter, divided	½	cup barley
1	cup chopped onions	¼	cup chopped parsley
1	clove garlic, minced	1½	cups chopped celery with leaves
3	cups strong beef broth	1½	cups chopped carrots
1½	quarts water	¼	cup dry Sherry or Port wine
3	tablespoons tomato paste	1	pint sour cream
1	teaspoon salt		

Freshly ground black pepper to taste

Chop half the mushrooms and slice remaining half pound. In a large saucepan, melt 4 tablespoons butter. Add the chopped mushrooms, the onion and garlic and sauté until onions are soft and transparent. Stir in the broth, water, tomato paste, salt, pepper and bay leaf. Heat to boiling; stir in the barley. Reduce heat, cover, and simmer over low heat for 1 hour.

Add the parsley, celery and carrots. Cook, covered, for 30 minutes, or until the carrots are tender and the barley is cooked. In a medium skillet heat the remaining butter. Add the reserved mushrooms and sauté for 5 minutes. Add mushrooms and Sherry to the kettle.

When ready to serve, ladle into bowls and top with a dollop of sour cream.

Serves 8
Easy   Diana Wise

CREAM OF CUCUMBER SOUP

2	cups peeled and chopped cucumber, with seeds removed	¼	cup chives
		¼	cup celery leaves
		3	sprigs of parsley
1	cup chicken stock	2	tablespoons butter, softened
1	cup light cream	1	tablespoon flour

Put all ingredients into a food processor or blender and mix until smooth. Add salt and white pepper to taste. Serve hot or cold.
To serve hot: Sprinkle with dill.
To serve cold: Top with additional minced cucumber.

Serves 4
Prepare ahead   Barbara June

CARROT SOUP

Great for a picnic

16 thin carrots	4 ounces cream cheese
4 cups clear chicken broth	Chopped parsley for garnish
1 small onion, sliced	Nutmeg

Scrape the carrots and cut into chunks. In a saucepan, heat the chicken broth. Add carrots and onion and simmer until carrots are soft, about ½ hour. Place in a blender or food processor fitted with the steel blade. Add the cream cheese, and process until liquified.
To serve: Ladle into bowls and garnish with parsley and nutmeg.
Variation: Substitute curry powder for nutmeg.

Serves 4
Preparation time: 45 minutes
Served hot or cold
Easy   Phylis Dyer

GAZPACHO

6 green onions	1 teaspoon seasoned salt
1 medium green pepper	¼ teaspoon freshly ground black pepper
2 cups cucumber, peeled only if waxed	¾ teaspoon Worcestershire sauce
1 cup celery	¼ cup wine vinegar
3 large tomatoes	¼ cup tarragon vinegar
1 quart tomatoes or V-8 juice	2 drops Tabasco sauce
1 clove garlic, minced	
1 tablespoon vegetable oil	

Coarsely chop all vegetables; refrigerate in a covered bowl. Combine remaining ingredients, blend well and refrigerate.
One hour before serving, combine vegetables and liquid and return to refrigerator.

Serves 8
Preparation time: ½ hour in food processor
Chill
Easy   Arleen McCaffrey

PERSIAN COLD CUCUMBER SOUP

½ cup dried currants or raisins

⅓ cup coarsely chopped walnuts

⅔ cup plain yogurt

¾ cup light cream

1 hard boiled egg, finely chopped

¼ cup green onions, finely chopped

1 cucumber, peeled and finely chopped

Salt and freshly ground pepper to taste

Chopped dill for garnish

Soak the currants in hot water to cover for 5 minutes or until plump. Drain and place in a large bowl with the walnuts. Stir in the remaining ingredients except the dill. Refrigerate for 3-4 hours. Garnish with dill.

Serves 4
Preparation time: 20 minutes
Chill
Easy
Holly Barnett

COLD STRAWBERRY SOUP

This is a wonderfully refreshing and lovely summer soup

2 pints strawberries

1 cup orange juice

¼ cup sugar

½ cup red wine

1 tablespoon cornstarch

1 cup heavy cream

Sour cream

Wash berries well. Set aside 6-8 nice ripe berries. Puree the remaining strawberries in a blender or food processor fitted with the steel blade. Transfer to a large saucepan; add the orange juice and sugar. Heat to boiling and cook until sugar dissolves. Combine the wine and cornstarch and add to the strawberry mixtures; cook until soup is clear. Remove from heat. Let cool for 15 minutes; add the heavy cream and blend well. Chill until ready to serve — at least 3 hours.
To serve: Ladle into bowls or mugs, top with a dollop of sour cream and garnish with a whole strawberry.

Serves 6-8
Preparation time: 20 minutes
Easy
Jean Smith

HUNGARIAN GOULASH SOUP

A hearty soup for a cold winter night

2	onions	½	teaspoon marjoram
2	tablespoons vegetable oil	1	teaspoon caraway seeds
¼	teaspoon paprika		Water
1	teaspoon vinegar	2	tablespoons flour
1	pound diced beef (soup meat)	2	medium potatoes, peeled and diced
1	tablespoon tomato puree		

Slice the onions into thin rings. Sauté in oil until transparent. Add the paprika and vinegar and mix well. Add the meat, tomato puree, spices and 2 cups of water; simmer for 1 hour or until meat is tender. Make a paste of flour and a little water and add to the meat. Add the potatoes and 4 more cups of water and cook 15 minutes longer or until potatoes are done.

Note: For more intest coloring, when soup is done, sauté ½ teaspoon paprika in a little oil; add 2 tablespoons water and 1 tablespoon tomato puree. Bring to a boil and add to the soup.

Serves 4-5
Preparation time: 45 minutes
Cooking time: 1½ hours

Joan Garrett

CREAM OF BOURBONNAISE

2	tablespoons butter	1	quart chicken broth
3	tablespoons water		Salt and pepper
3	leeks, diced	1	cup light cream
2	potatoes, sliced	2	tablespoons snipped chives

Simmer the butter, water and leeks for 5 minutes. Add the potatoes and broth; simmer 15-20 minutes, or until potatoes are soft. Liquify mixture in blender or food processor fitted with the steel blade. Add salt and pepper to taste.

To serve hot: Add cream, heat, place in bowls and sprinkle with chives.
To serve cold: Refrigerate soup. Before serving, add cream, ladle into bowls, and garnish with chives.

Serves 4
Preparation time: ½ hour

Patricia Ann Molloy

SELJANKA

Fish Soup Made Simple

The proportions in this traditional Scandanavian fish soup are easily altered according to taste. Feel free to experiment with stock and vegetable quantities.

½	cup butter	1	tablespoon capers
5	carrots, sliced	3	tablespoons flour
2	onions, chopped	Fish or vegetable stock	
3-4	potatoes, peeled and diced	2	pounds fresh or frozen salmon or whitefish filets, cut into serving pieces
4	tomatoes, peeled and chopped		
1	pound mushrooms, sliced	Sour cream and parsley for garnish	
2	dill pickles, chopped		
1	teaspoon marjoram		
1½	cups pitted black olives, sliced		

In a large kettle, melt the butter. Add remaining ingredients except for the flour, stock and fish. Cook over low heat for 10-15 minutes until the vegetables are partially cooked but still crisp, stirring frequently to prevent sticking. Add enough water to the flour to make a thick paste and add to the kettle; heat to boiling. Add enough stock to make desired quantity of soup — let your taste be your guide. About 15 minutes before serving, add the fish. Simmer until fish flakes when touched with a fork. Serve with a dollop of sour cream and chopped parsley.

Salme Lohuaru
Horseshoe Valley Resort
Barrie, Ontario

CREAM OF VEGETABLE SOUP

3	tablespoons butter	¼	cup long grain rice
2	leeks, chopped (white part only)	12	asparagus stalks cut into 1-inch pieces
1	medium onion, chopped	½	pound fresh spinach, torn into bite-sized pieces
2	medium potatoes, cubed		
2	large carrots, sliced	2	cups milk, scalded
1½	teaspoons salt	½	cup heavy cream
¼	teaspoon pepper		Dill weed
6	cups water		Paprika

Heat the butter in a large saucepan. Add the leeks and onion and cook over low heat, stirring constantly, for 5 minutes. Add the potatotes, carrots, salt and pepper; cook for 2 minutes, stirring. Add the water and bring to a boil. Stir in the rice, cover and simmer for 10 minutes. Add the lower, tougher parts of the asparagus; cook for 10 minutes. Add the tips; cook for 5 minutes, then add the spinach and cook for 3 minutes longer or until vegetables are just tender. Stir in the hot milk. Season to taste with additional salt and pepper.

Stir in the cream and heat, but *do not boil*. Sprinkle with dill and paprika for color. Serve immediately.

Serves 6-8
Preparation time: 1 hour
Easy

Marilyn Van Giesen

CRAB BISQUE

You won't believe how good and easy this is

1	can condensed tomato soup	1	7½-ounce can crab meat with juice, cartilage removed
1	can condensed beef bouillon soup	3	cups Half & Half
1	can condensed green pea soup — without bacon or ham		Sherry

In a saucepan over low heat, slowly combine the soups, whisking until smooth. Add the crabmeat with juice and Half & Half and mix. Add Sherry to taste.

Serves 8-10
Preparation time: 15 minutes
Make ahead, but do not freeze
Easy

Marcy Chanteaux
DSO

CREAM OF MUSHROOM SOUP

½ pound fresh mushrooms, thinly sliced
2 cups water
3 chicken bouillon cubes
2 thick slices onion

¼ cup butter
3 tablespoons flour
3 cups milk
Salt and pepper
Freshly chopped parsley

Place the mushrooms, water, bouillon cubes and onion in a large kettle. Bring to a boil and simmer, covered, for 20 minutes. Melt the butter in a small saucepan and blend in the flour. Gradually add the milk and cook, stirring constantly, until slightly thickened. Add mixture to the mushroom broth and season with salt and pepper to taste. Sprinkle with chopped parsley and serve hot.

Makes about 1½ quarts   Mado Lie

CHEESE 'N CARROT CHOWDER

An epicurean delight

3 tablespoons butter
1½ cups chopped celery
1 cup shredded carrot
¼ cup sliced green onion
2 cans condensed cream of potato soup
1 14½-ounce can chicken broth
½ cup water
2 tablespoons snipped parsley

2-3 drops hot pepper sauce
2 cups (8 ounces) shredded Cheddar or Colby cheese
1 13-ounce can evaporated milk
3 tablespoons dry Sherry
Additional chopped green onion for garnish

In a large saucepan, melt the butter. Cook the celery, carrot and green onion until tender but not brown. Add the potato soup, chicken broth, water, parsley and pepper sauce. Cook, stirring, until soup boils, then reduce heat. Cover and simmer for 20-25 minutes, stirring occasionally. Stir in the shredded cheese, milk, and Sherry. Heat through, but do not boil. Sprinkle with additional onion if desired.

Serves 6-8
Preparation time: 30 minutes
Easy   Sheila Donenfeld

MAINE FISH CHOWDER

4-5 medium potatoes, peeled and cut in small pieces
1 medium onion, peeled and sliced
1 pound fresh or frozen haddock filets

1 quart milk
1 tablespoon butter
Salt and pepper to taste

Place the potatoes and onions in a pot and add water to just cover. Cook until the potatoes are done. Add the fish and cook until the pieces fall apart. Stir in the milk and return to a boil. Add the butter, salt and pepper; stir, and serve hot.

Serves 4-6
Preparation time: 15 minutes
Easy   Mrs. Robert W. Stewart

GOLDEN AUTUMN CHOWDER

Try this on a cold winter night

2 tablespoons oil
1 pound round steak cut in ½-inch cubes
3 medium potatoes, pared and coarsely chopped
1 medium rutabaga, pared and coarsely chopped
2 cups coarsely chopped cabbage
3 medium carrots, peeled and chopped

2 medium onions, chopped
2 tablespoons chopped parsley
1 tablespoon vinegar
1½ teaspoons salt
1 bay leaf
1 teaspoon sugar
¼ teaspoon pepper
6 cups water

Heat oil in a Dutch oven and brown the meat in small batches. Add remaining ingredients. Simmer, covered, 1 to 1¼ hours or until meat is tender. Remove bay leaf before serving.

Serves 6
Preparation time: 30 minutes
Cooking time: 1¼ hours
Easy   Jeanne and Larry Anderson

BROCCOLI BISQUE

This soup is delicious hot or cold

5¼ cups, or 3 cans, chicken broth
1 medium onion, quartered
2 tablespoons butter
1 teaspoon salt
1-2 teaspoons curry powder
Dash of pepper
1¼ to 1½ pounds fresh broccoli, trimmed and cut into small chunks, or two 10-ounce packages frozen chopped broccoli
2 tablespoons lime juice
8 lemon slices
½ cup sour cream
1 tablespoon snipped chives

Place chicken broth, onion, butter, salt, curry and pepper in a large saucepan. Bring to a boil then add the broccoli. Bring broth to a second boil, reduce heat and simmer, covered, 8-12 minutes or until broccoli is tender. Transfer broccoli and broth to a blender in small batches and process until smooth. Pour soup into a large bowl and stir in lime juice. Cover and refrigerate at least 4 hours.
When ready to serve ladle into small bowls. Top with a lemon slice, a dollop of sour cream and a sprinkling of chives.

Serves 8   Jackie Ong

NANA'S DILL SOUP

We call it Nana's, not because it's her recipe, but because she likes it so much!

1 bunch fresh baby dill, tender part only
6 cups chicken broth
3 medium potatoes, peeled and cut in chunks
3 medium onions, chopped
Salt
Sour cream
Chopped chives

Wash the dill well. Place in a large pot with the chicken broth, the potatoes and onions. Cover and cook until potatoes are soft. Remove from heat, place in blender and process until pureed. Pour the soup into a bowl and season with salt to taste; chill. Serve ice cold with a dollop of sour cream and chopped chives.

Serves 6-8
Preparation time: 45 minutes
Easy   Ruth F. Frank

SEAFOOD BISQUE

Wonderfully rich — great for company

¼	cup finely chopped shallots	½	pound raw shrimp, diced
½	cup finely chopped celery	½	cup butter, melted
½	cup finely chopped fresh, white mushrooms	¼	cup flour
		¼	pound crabmeat, shredded
½	cup finely chopped green onions	3	tablespoons brandy
		4	cups cream
3	tablespoons butter, melted	Salt and pepper	
1½	tomatoes, peeled, seeded and chopped	Tabasco	

Sauté the shallots, celery, mushrooms and green onions in 3 tablespoons butter until limp. Add the tomatoes and cook until they begin to fall apart. Add the shrimp and cook, stirring constantly, until just cooked through.

Blend the ½ cup melted butter and flour together and whisk it into the shrimp mixture. Add the crabmeat and cook, stirring constanly, until the soup is thick and bubbly. Flame with the brandy, stir in the cream and bring to a simmer. Season with salt, pepper and Tabasco to taste.

Serves 8
Can be prepared up to 2 days ahead

Christopher A. Blunt
Chef/Owner Beggar's Banquet
E. Lansing, Michigan

NAVY BEAN SOUP

2	pounds navy beans	Butter
4	quarts water	Salt
1½	pounds smoked ham hocks	Pepper
1	onion, chopped	

Wash the beans in hot water until they are white. Place in a large kettle with the water and ham hocks. Sauté the onions in a little butter and add to pot. Simmer, covered, for 3 hours. Add salt and pepper to taste.

Serves 8-10
Preparation time: 15 minutes
Cooking time: 3 hours
Easy

Dorothy Brennan

CORN CHOWDER

⅓ cup finely cut bacon,
   salt pork or 3 tablespoons
   oil
½ cup minced onion
2½ cups finely diced raw
   potatoes (about 3 potatoes)

1 teaspoon salt
Water
1 17-ounce can creamed corn
   with liquid
1¼ cups milk
Pepper

In a saucepan, fry the bacon or pork until crisp and golden brown. Add the onions and sauté slowly over low heat until tender and transparent. Add the potatoes, salt and just enough water to barely cover the potatoes. Cook until potatoes are tender — about 10 minutes — do not drain. Add the corn and liquid, milk, and pepper to taste. Heat thoroughly.

Serves 5

Mal Sillars
WDIV

CREAM OF BROCCOLI SOUP

2 heads broccoli
½ cup water
6 tablespoons butter
6 tablespoons flour
2 cups milk

2 cups light cream or half and
   half
1 bay leaf
1½ teaspoons herb salt
2 vegetable cubes

Place broccoli and water in pressure cooker and cook for 2 minutes or steam broccoli for 10 minutes on top of stove; drain and discard broth.

In saucepan, mix butter and flour. Add milk, cream and bay leaf. Cook until thick over medium heat. Add herb salt and vegetable cubes. Put ½ to ¾ of broccoli with ⅓ of soup base into a blender. Mix well. Add to remaining soup base. Cut up the remaining broccoli into bit-sized pieces and add to the soup. Cook until heated through.

Serves 4 as a meal, 6 as a first course
Preparation time: 15 minutes
Easy

Ann Alicia Ourada
DSO

CAPE COD CHOWDER

¾ pound haddock
¼ cup chopped celery
¼ cup chopped onion
1 8-ounce can minced clams
    with broth
6 ounces shrimp
1 6-ounce can evaporated milk

2 cups whole milk
Salt and pepper to taste
3 tablespoons butter
¼ cup frozen baby peas
Optional: ¼ cup frozen corn
2 large potatoes,
    cooked and diced

Cut fish into bite-size pieces; place in a kettle with the celery and onion. Add enough water to just cover and simmer until fish begins to turn white. Add the remaining ingredients except the peas and corn, and potatoes. Simmer until fish is cooked and chowder thickens slightly. Add the vegetables and cook only until heated through.

Serves 4
Preparation time: 20 minutes
Easy
                                                    Thelma Shapiro

SPLIT PEA SOUP

1 hambone with at least 1
    pound ham attached
1 pound dried split peas

1 medium onion
1 cup quick barley
Salt to taste

In a large kettle cover hambone with water. Bring to a boil and simmer for 1 hour. Meanwhile, rinse peas and chop the onion. Add the peas and onion to the kettle; simmer on low heat for one hour longer, stirring occasionally to prevent soup from sticking to the bottom of the pot. Remove hambone and ham. Add the barley and cook for 20 minutes, or until barley is tender. Meanwhile, cut the ham into small pieces and return to the pot. Add salt to taste. If soup is too thick, add water until soup is desired consistency.

Serves 8-10
Cooking time: 2½ hours
Easy
                                                    Maimu Looke

HEARTY LENTIL SOUP

2	medium onions, chopped	8	medium carrots, sliced
6	cups water	4	ribs of celery, chopped
1½	cups lentils, washed	½	teaspoon marjoram
1	bay leaf	⅓	cup chopped fresh parsley
4	large tomatoes, peeled and chopped		Salt and pepper to taste

In a large pot, lightly sauté the onions. Add the remaining ingredients; bring to a boil. Lower heat and simmer for 2 hours.

Judy and Stephen Molina
DSO

"Beautiful soup! Who cares for fish, game, or any other dish? Who would not give all else for two pennysworth only of beautiful soup?

Alice in Wonderland
Lewis Carroll

For a really rich flavored soup, brown the bones, meat and vegetables in a hot oven before adding to the cold water.

Salads

Salads

Vegetarian Dinner

Chilled Carrot Soup
Curried Vegetables with Brown Rice
Suji Halwa
Fresh Fruit with Yogurt

Wine Suggestions
Grand Cru (1981)
A dry but fruity California Chenin Blanc;

Summer Dinner

Persian Cold Cucumber Soup
Beef Dijon Salad
Hot Cheese Bread
Summer Pudding

Wine Suggestions
(Soup Course)
Pinot Grigio-Jermann (1981)
A fresh, crips white

(Main Course)
Fleurie-DuBoeuf (1982)
A light, quaffable red

BIBB LETTUCE WITH TARRAGON DRESSING

Easy and elegant

TARRAGON DRESSING

¼ cup lemon juice or vinegar
¼ teaspoon dry mustard
¾ cup olive oil
1 clove garlic, crushed
½ teaspoon salt
½ teaspoon freshly ground
 pepper

½ teaspoon dried tarragon,
 or more to taste
1 tablespoon chopped fresh
 parsley
1½ teaspoons snipped
 chives
1 teaspoon capers, crushed

Whisk together the lemon juice, mustard, olive oil, garlic, salt and pepper. Add tarragon and blend well. When ready to serve add parsley, chives and capers; mix well.
Toss with Bibb lettuce and serve with fresh croutons.

Winnie Ostrowski

YOGURT SALAD

3 cups plain yogurt
2 cucumbers, peeled, seeded
 and grated
3 green onions, chopped
½ teaspoon basil

¼ cup walnuts
½ cup raisins
½ teaspoon salt
Optional: ½ teaspoon mint,
 ½ teaspoon summer savory

Combine ingredients and mix well. Serve chilled.
Variation: Can add milk and make into a cold soup.

Serves 6-8
Preparation time: 15 minutes
Prepare ahead
Chill

Marlene Thomas

Squeeze fresh lemon juice over potatoes and vegetables. This will eliminate the need for salt.

BEET AND PINEAPPLE SALAD

An unusual combination and so good

1	16-ounce can whole beets	1	5-ounce jar horseradish
1	20-ounce can unsweetened crushed pineapple	2	packages lemon flavored gelatin
			Sour cream

Drain beets, pineapple and horseradish but reserve the juices. Combine reserved juice with enough water to make 2½ cups liquid. Heat mixture to boiling, add gelatin and cook until gelatin is dissolved. Shred the beets and combine with the pineapple and horseradish. Use more horseradish if a more "peppy" flavor is desired. Stir in the gelatin mixture and mix well. Pour into 1½-quart mold; chill until firm.
Serve on lettuce with sour cream.

Serves 10-12
Preparation time: ½ hour
Prepare up to a day ahead
Easy

Kay Keffer

HARRAH'S SALAD

1	head lettuce	½	cup mayonnaise mixed with a few drops of vinegar
2	ribs celery, finely sliced		
1	onion, sliced and separated into rings	½	pound bacon, fried until crisp, then crumbled
1	cup sour cream		Grated Parmesan cheese
½	cup sugar		

Tear lettuce into bite-size pieces and place in the bottom of 9x13-inch pan. Add a layer of celery, then a layer of onion. Mix the sour cream and sugar. Crumble bacon.
Sprinkle salad with the sour cream mixture; the mayonnaise mixture, then the crumbled bacon. Top with Parmesan cheese to taste. Cover tightly with foil and refrigerate for at least 3-5 hours before serving.

Serves 4-6
Preparation time: 20 minutes
Chill 3-5 hours

H. Robert Reynolds

86

SPINACH SALAD

DRESSING

1   cup vegetable oil
½   cup vinegar
¾   cup sugar
⅓   cup ketchup

1   teaspoon Worcestershire
    sauce
1   medium onion, grated

Combine ingredients and mix well. Let stand in refrigerator overnight.

SALAD

1   package fresh spinach,
    washed and broken into
    bite-sized pieces
5   strips bacon, fried and
    broken into bits
1   can bean sprouts, drained, or
    1 cup fresh sprouts

3   eggs, hard cooked and
    chopped
Optional: 1 cup water chestnuts,
    sliced

Combine ingredients and toss lightly. Just before serving, pour dressing over salad.

Serves 4
Easy
                                                    Peggy Dasovic

---

SEVEN LAYER SALAD

Place in a large bowl in layers:

½   head lettuce, shredded
½   medium green pepper,
    chopped
3   stalks celery, chopped
3   green onions chopped
1   package frozen peas,
    defrosted and drained

½   cup mayonnaise mixed with
    3 tablespoons sugar
2   cups shredded Mozzarella
    cheese
5   slices bacon, cooked and
    crumbled

Cover and refrigerate overnight.

Serves 6
Preparation time: 30 minutes
Chill overnight
Easy
                                                    Joe Ann Goodman

CRAB AND RICE SALAD

Delicious

1 7½-ounce can crabmeat, drained and cartilage removed
3 cups cooked rice, cooled
1 10-ounce package frozen peas, blanched, cooled, and drained
4 stalks celery, chopped

⅓ cup sliced green onions
½ cup sour cream
1 cup mayonnaise
1 tablespoon seasoned salt
1 tablespoon fresh lemon juice
Salt and pepper to taste
Curry powder

Combine all ingredients except the curry powder. Chill for 24 hours. To serve, mound on lettuce leaves and sprinkle with curry powder to taste.

Makes 4-6 servings
Preparation time: 15 minutes, excluding rice preparation
Chill overnight

Anne Meda

MARINATED CHERRY TOMATOES

1 pint cherry tomatoes
6 tablespoons olive oil
6 tablespoons vinegar
1 tablespoon finely chopped fresh dill or 1½ teaspoons dried dill

2 green onions, minced
2 tablespoons minced parsley
Salt and freshly ground pepper

Place tomatoes in a strainer set in a deep bowl. Pour boiling water over to cover and let stand one minute. Immediately plunge tomatoes into ice water; drain well. Peel off and discard the skins. Let tomatoes drain briefly on paper towels then transfer to a serving bowl. Add the remaining ingredients and toss gently.
Cover and refrigerate. Can be prepared up to 3 days ahead.

Serves 12
Preparation time: 15 minutes
Chill

Carol Ann May

SUPER SPINACH SALAD

2 pounds fresh spinach, washed and dried
Salt and pepper
2 teaspoons sugar, divided
½ pound bacon, fried and crumbled
6 eggs, hard cooked and chopped, divided
1 package frozen peas, thawed
1 medium onion, chopped
1 cup mayonnaise
½ cup sour cream
1 cup shredded Swiss cheese

Tear spinach into bite-size pieces; layer on the bottom of a glass salad bowl. Sprinkle with salt, pepper and 1 teaspoon sugar. Add the bacon in one layer. Sprinkle half the chopped eggs over the bacon. Add salt and pepper to taste and the remaining sugar. Combine the peas and onions and put on top of the bacon. Combine the mayonnaise and sour cream and spread over the salad. Top with the cheese and remaining chopped eggs.

Serves 6   Ann Marie Dahn

SHRIMP MOLD SEGOVIA

This was served at an after-glow for Andre Segovia in 1979

1 can condensed tomato soup
1½ packages unflavored gelatin
1 8-ounce package cream cheese
1 cup mayonnaise
2 4½-ounce cans shrimp or ½ pound fresh shrimp, crumbled
¾ cup finely chopped onions
1 cup finely chopped celery
½ teaspoon Worcestershire sauce

Heat the soup and add the gelatin; stir until dissolved. Melt the cheese in the hot soup and blend well. Beat in mayonnaise. Add shrimp, onions, celery and Worcestshire sauce. Pour into an oiled 5-cup ring mold and refrigerate until firm.
Note: Can be put into individual molds and served as a small salad.

Serves 12
Preparation time: 30 minutes
Make ahead
Easy   Jean Collinson

FROZEN FRUITCAKE SALAD

1 cup sour cream
½ small (4½-ounce) carton Cool Whip, thawed
½ cup sugar
2 tablespoons lemon juice
1 teaspoon vanilla
1 13-ounce can crushed pineapple

2 medium bananas, diced
½ cup chopped walnuts
Any 2 of the following to make mixture equal 4½ cups:
  Raspberries
  Canned peaches
  Canned Bing cherries
  Mandarin oranges

In a mixing bowl blend the sour cream and Cool Whip. Add the sugar, lemon juice and vanilla. Fold in the fruit and nuts, and turn mixture into a 4½-cup ring mold. Freeze for several hours or overnight. To serve, remove from freezer and let stand for 10 minutes, then unmold. Serve cold.

Sue Currier

LEMONADE JELLO MOLD

1 large package lemon Jello
3 cups boiling water
1 6-ounce can frozen lemonade concentrate, thawed

1 8-ounce container Cool Whip
Fresh fruit

Dissolve the Jello in the boiling water. Add the lemonade, mix well and refrigerate until gelatin is thickened but not set. Beat in the Cool Whip and pour into a 6-cup ring mold. Garnish with fresh fruit in the center and around the ring.

Note: For variation, whipped cream or sour cream may be substituted and 1 cup well-drained fruit may be added.

Preparation time: 10 minutes
Chill
Easy

Dorothy Hack

PASTA SALAD COPENHAGEN

The ingredients in this salad can be varied to create almost endless combinations. Try pieces of tongue, Jarlsberg or Cheddar Cheese, blanched green beans or asparagus . . .

1 pound shell pasta or rotini	**Vinaigrette**
1 pound Danish ham	5 tablespoons chives
½ pound Havarti cheese	¼ cup fresh chopped dill or
2 green peppers	2 tablespoons dried dill
2 sweet red peppers	weed
3 cucumbers, peeled	Salt and pepper to taste
2 ripe tomatoes	

Cook pasta in a large kettle of boiling water until just barely tender. There is only one way to know if the pasta is done, and that is to taste it. Pasta will be ready when it is barely tender and still quite firm. Drain pasta and submerge it in cold water to stop the cooking process. When completely cold, drain it well. Slice the ham, cheese, green and red peppers and cucumbers into pieces slightly larger than your little finger. Cut the tomatoes in wedges. Toss vegetables in a bowl with the drained cold pasta. Pour in the vinaigrette and mix with your hands. Add the chives and dill and season with salt and pepper. Let the salad stand at room temperature for 30 minutes before serving to allow flavors to blend. Taste before serving and add more herbs, salt and pepper if desired.

VINAIGRETTE

1 large clove garlic mashed to a paste with ½ teaspoon salt	⅓ cup white wine vinegar
	1 teaspoon fresh thyme or
2 tablespoons Dijon mustard	½ teaspoon dried thyme
1 cup olive oil	Salt and pepper to taste

Add the garlic paste to the mustard and blend well. Pour in the oil and whisk until dressing has become thick. Whisk in the vinegar, herbs, salt and pepper. Taste for seasoning.

Serves 6-10

Sandi Cooper
Complete Cuisine, Ltd.
322 S. Main Street
Ann Arbor, Michigan

DUBLIN POTATO SALAD

Ideal from March 17 through Labor Day

2 tablespoons vinegar
1 teaspoon celery seed
1 teaspoon whole mustard seed
3 large potatoes, pared and cubed
2 teaspoons sugar
½ teaspoon salt
2 cups finely shredded cabbage

1 12-ounce can corned beef, chilled and cubed
¼ cup finely chopped dill pickle
¼ cup sliced green onion
1 cup mayonnaise
¼ cup milk
½ teaspoon salt

Combine the vinegar, celery seed, and mustard seed; set aside. Cook the potatoes in boiling salted water until al dente (or O'Dente). Drain well, and while potatoes are still warm, cover with the vinegar mixture, sugar, and ½ teaspoon of salt.

To serve: Add the cabbage, corned beef, pickle and onion. Combine the mayonnaise, milk and ½ teaspoon salt. Pour over the salad and toss lightly.

Serves 8
The potatoes can be prepared ahead of time   Patty Maguire Young

SHRIMP REMOULADE

2 cloves garlic, minced
⅓ cup horseradish mustard
2 tablespoons ketchup
2½ teaspoons paprika
¼ teaspoon cayenne pepper, or to taste
1 teaspoon salt

⅓ cup tarragon vinegar
½ cup olive oil
½ cup chopped green onions with tops
1 pound shrimp, cooked and cleaned
Lettuce

Combine all ingredients except shrimp and lettuce; shake well. Place shrimp in a bowl. Pour the dressing over and let marinate in the refrigerator for several hours.

Serve on beds of lettuce.

Serves 6
Preparation time: 10 minutes
Refrigerate: several hours
Easy   Sheila Swanson

PEACHY GELATIN SALAD

2 cups water, divided
½ cup syrup from canned peaches
1 small package lemon gelatin
1½ cups canned peach slices, well drained

1 cup sour cream
½ cup cranberry sauce
1 small package raspberry gelatin

Peach layers: Heat ½ cup water with the peach syrup in a small saucepan. Dissolve the lemon gelatin in the hot liquid and cool to room temperature. Arrange a row of the peach slices in the bottom of an 8½-inch ring mold. Spoon in just enough gelatin mixture to cover the peaches and chill until firm. Blend the sour cream into the remaining gelatin and chill until thickened. Fold remaining peaches into the sour cream-gelatin mixture and spoon carefully over the chilled layer. Return to refrigerator until firm.
Cranberry layer: Heat the cranberry sauce with 1½ cups water. Dissolve the raspberry gelatin in the hot liquid, remove from heat and cool until slightly thickened. Carefully pour into the mold over the peach layers. Chill for at least 2 hours or until set.
To serve: Unmold onto a serving plate and fill center of ring with salad greens and additional peach slices.

Serves 8   Mrs. Kent D. Johnson

SWEET AND SOUR ZUCCHINI

This can be served cold as salad or hot as a side dish

4 medium zucchini
¼ cup wine vinegar
2 tablespoons sugar
Olive oil

Freshly ground pepper
Garlic
Nutmeg

Slice the zucchini into rounds, salt them and leave to "sweat" for an hour. Rinse and pat dry. Sauté zucchini quickly in a small amount of olive oil. When still crisp tender, season with pepper, garlic and nutmeg to taste. Add the vinegar and sugar and cook for a few more minutes.

Serves 6
Preparation time: 15 minutes
Easy   Helen Addison

BENGALESE SALAD

SALAD

2 cups diced cooked chicken
1 cup sliced celery
1 orange, peeled and sectioned
1 large banana, cut into chunks
½ medium cucumber, scored and sliced
½ cup peanuts, chopped
Watercress

In a large bowl combine chicken, celery, orange, banana, cucumber and peanuts. Toss together lightly and set aside.

DRESSING

½ cup sour cream
2 tablespoons chopped chutney
1 teaspoon grated orange peel
1 teaspoon lemon juice
¼ teaspoon curry powder
¼ teaspoon seasoned salt
Dash pepper

Combine ingredients and chill for one hour. Just before serving pour dressing over salad and toss gently. Serve on a bed of watercress. Note: Yogurt may be used instead of sour cream for a slightly different flavor.

Serves 4
Preparation time: 20 minutes
Chill: 1 hour
Easy

Carol Meyer

AVOCADO SALAD

¼ cup golden seedless raisins
4 ripe, unblemished avocados
Safflower oil
¼ cup pine nuts
Salt to taste
Juice of one lemon

Pour boiling water over the raisins; cool and drain. Halve the avocados and carefully remove rind. Lightly coat halves with oil and cut into eight even slices. Gently fan slices out onto serving plates. Sprinkle with raisins and pine nuts, salt lightly and sprinkle generously with the lemon juice.

Serves 8

John Merrill

ROSOLJE

This is a traditional smorgasbord dish to be served at parties or holidays in Scandinavia. It is an absolute MUST on Christmas Eve.

SALAD

6-8 potatoes, boiled in jackets and cooled

2   8-ounce cans red beets, diced (save liquid)

3   eggs, hard cooked (two diced, one saved for decoration)

8-12 radishes, diced (save 2-3 whole for decoration)

2   cucumbers, peeled and diced

3-4 dill pickles, chopped

1   small onion, finely chopped

¾   pound veal, stewed and diced or ½ pound ham

1   jar herring fillets in sour cream

Peel the potatoes and cut in chunks. Combine remaining ingredients and toss with potatoes.

DRESSING

1½ cups sour cream

2-3 tablespoons beet liquid

1   teaspoon dry mustard

½   teaspoon horseradish, or to taste

¼   teaspoon freshly ground pepper

Salt to taste, depending on the herring used

Prepare dressing and pour over salad; mix well. Salad will be pink. Decorate with wedges of hard-boiled eggs and radish roses. Refrigerate at least six hours or overnight.

Prepare ahead   Mall Kionka

HOMEMADE RANCH DRESSING

1   cup buttermilk or sour cream

1   cup mayonnaise

2   teaspoons M.S.G. (optional)

½   teaspoon garlic powder

½   tablespoon onion powder

2   tablespoons chopped chives or parsley

Optional: ¼ cup Sherry

Combine and let stand overnight

Makes 2-2½ cups   Natalie Payne

MOLDED ASPARAGUS SALAD

¾ cup sugar
½ cup vinegar
1 tablespoon lemon juice
1 cup water
½ teaspoon salt
1 envelope unflavored gelatin dissolved in ½ cup cold water

1 cup chopped celery
½ cup chopped pecans
2 whole pimentos, chopped
1 10½-ounce can asparagus, drained and cut up
½ cup chopped stuffed olives

Combine the sugar, vinegar, lemon juice, water and salt and boil for 2 minutes. Add softened gelatin to the vinegar mixture and stir until dissolved. Chill until mixture is the consistency of unbeaten egg whites. Fold remaining ingredients into chilled gelatin. Spoon into 1½-quart mold and refrigerate until firm.

Serves 8-10
Preparation time: 1 hour
Make day before

Virginia Hatzenbeler

HOT CHICKEN SALAD

SALAD

1 quart (5 pounds) cooked chicken, cut into bite-size pieces
1 quart chopped celery
1 cup slivered almonds
⅔ cup chopped green pepper

¼ cup minced onion
¼ cup chopped pimento
1 teaspoon salt
¼ cup lemon juice
1¼ cups mayonnaise

TOPPING

3 cups crushed potato chips   ⅔ cup grated cheese

Preheat oven to 350 degrees.
Mix all ingredients, except topping, and place into a casserole. Top with potato chips and grated cheese. Bake 30 minutes.

Serves 12
Preparation time: 15 minutes, excluding preparation of chicken
Baking time: 30 minutes
Easy

Flo Harris

ORIENTAL SALAD

Longer marinating improves flavor

SALAD

1 bunch broccoli, cut into florets	2 cups sliced fresh carrots
	1 cup fresh bean sprouts
1 head cauliflower, cut into florets	2 cups fresh pea pods
	½ cup sesame seeds

Combine vegetables. Toss with Champagne Vinaigrette and chill thoroughly, tossing occasionally. Allow to marinate until flavors are well blended.

CHAMPAGNE VINAIGRETTE

1¼ cups olive oil	3 teaspoons minced shallot
½ cup Champagne vinegar or white wine vinegar	½ teaspoon salt
	Pepper to taste

Combine ingredients and blend well.

Serves 12-14   Bonnie Lockwood

MO-MO'S TOMATO ASPIC

Serve as a salad or an entree

3 cups V-8 juice	2 packages unflavored gelatin softened in 1 cup cold water
6 whole cloves	
2 bay leaves	
Pinch oregano	1 6-ounce can crabmeat, flaked
2 tablespoons brown sugar	
2 tablespoons vinegar	2-3 eggs, hard cooked and chopped
1 tablespoon lemon juice	
Tabasco sauce to taste	2-3 sweet pickles, chopped
¼ teaspoon seasoned salt	1 rib celery, chopped
1 tablespoon horseradish	

In a medium saucepan combine the juice, cloves, bay leaves, oregano, vinegar, lemon juice, Tabasco, salt, sugar and horseradish. Simmer over low heat for 30 minutes. Strain into a bowl through a large sieve. Add remaining ingredients, mix well, and pour into an 8-cup mold. Refrigerate until firm.

Serves 10-12   Mary Cunningham

SALADE OLIVYE

A traditional and delicious Latvian mixed vegetable salad

4   medium carrots, sliced
4   medium potatoes, boiled
2   hard cooked eggs, chopped
1   can peas, reserving half
    the juice
4   small sweet or dill pickles,
    chopped

1   onion sliced or 1 small
    bunch green onions, chopped
2   cloves garlic, minced
Optional: ¾ cup salami, bologna,
    chicken or beef, cubed
Sour cream or thick salad
    dressing

Boil the carrots until crisp tender. Cut potatoes into bite-size pieces and combine with the carrots, chopped eggs, peas with juice, pickles, onions and garlic. Add meat, if desired, and toss gently. Add enough sour cream or salad dressing to taste and blend well. Chill for several hours before serving.
Note: Amounts and types of vegetables can be changed according to seasonal availability.

Serves 8-10
Preparation time: 20 minutes
Easy

Lydia and Elkhonon Yoffe
DSO

FARMER'S CHOP SUEY

Fast, easy and colorful. Great for brunch.

1   pound creamed cottage
    cheese
½   cup sour cream
6   green onions, chopped
½   cup chopped radishes
½   cup chopped green pepper

1   cup chopped cucumber
½   tomato, seeded and chopped
Optional: 1 cup shredded
    cabbage, 2 ribs celery,
    chopped

Combine the cottage cheese and sour cream and blend well. Add the remaining ingredients and mix. Serve immediately or refrigerate until needed.

Serves 4-6
Preparation time: 15 minutes
Easy

Barbara Goldman

BROCCOLI SALAD

Always a hit

SALAD

2 heads broccoli
1 pound mushrooms, thinly sliced
2 green onions, finely chopped

Cherry tomatoes
Optional: Water chestnuts and celery slices

Cut the tops from the broccoli, reserving the stalks for another use. Wash florets well. Place the broccoli, mushrooms and onions in a large bowl.

DRESSING

½ cup sugar
1 teaspoon salt
1 teaspoon paprika
1 teaspoon celery seed

1 tablespoon onion powder
¼ cup cider vinegar
1 cup vegetable oil

Combine the sugar, salt, paprika, celery seed and onion powder in a jar and mix well. Add the vinegar and oil, shake well, and pour over vegetables. Toss gently then refrigerate for 1 hour or longer to allow flavors to blend.
Garnish with cherry tomatoes.

Serves 8-12   Eleanor Pekkala

CRANBERRY SALAD

2 3-ounce packages strawberry gelatin
2 cups boiling water
1 16-ounce can whole cranberry sauce

1 cup applesauce
½ cup port wine
1 cup chopped walnuts or other nutmeats

Dissolve gelatin in boiling water. Add remaining ingredients. Pour into a 9x12-inch glass dish; chill overnight. Cut into squares and serve on a leaf of lettuce.

Serves 12
Preparation time: 15 minutes
Chill overnight   Margaret Bluhm

ROMAINE SALAD

SALAD

2 heads Romaine lettuce
1 pound bacon fried until crisp
2 tomatoes, peeled and cut into eighths

½ cup freshly grated Romano cheese
1 bunch green onions, sliced
1 cup croutons

Wash lettuce, dry and tear into bite-sized pieces. Crumble the bacon and combine with the lettuce and remaining ingredients and toss lightly.

DRESSING

2 cloves garlic, mashed
1 teaspoon freshly ground pepper
½ teaspoon salt

1 cup good quality olive oil
Juice of one lemon
1 egg boiled in shell for 30 seconds

Combine the ingredients and mix well. Chill. When ready to serve, pour over the salad and toss lightly.

Janette Hitchcock

MELLOW POTATO SALAD

Deliciously different

12 large potatoes
2 medium onions
2 Granny Smith apples

¾ cup mayonnaise or to taste
1 tablespoon tarragon or to taste

Boil potatoes until tender. When cool enough to handle, peel and cut into chunks. Cut onions into large dice. Core apples but do not peel; cut into chunks. Combine the potatoes, onions and apples and toss gently. Add mayonnaise and tarragon to taste. Refrigerate at least 3 hours before serving.

Serves 8-12
Chill 3 hours
Easy

Glenn Mellow
DSO

SMOKED FISH SALAD

After having smoked my own lake trout, we made this up one evening for a light summer meal and have enjoyed it many times since.

DRESSING
Juice of one lemon

½ cup spicy Italian dressing

Combine ingredients and set aside.

SALAD
Bibb lettuce, Romaine lettuce, and spinach

1 medium sweet red onion, thinly sliced

½ green pepper, thinly sliced

½ red pepper, thinly sliced

¼ pound sharp Cheddar cheese, shredded

1 pound smoked fish, separated into chunks

2 medium tomatoes, cut into wedges

Coarsely ground pepper to taste

In a large bowl, tear salad greens into bite-size pieces. Add the onion, peppers and cheese and toss with just enough of the dressing to coat salad lightly. Place on the individual salad plates, then add the fish. Decorate with tomato wedges and serve with coarsely ground pepper.

Serves 4
Preparation time: 15 minutes
Ingredients may be prepared ahead of time, individually wrapped and refrigerated until ready to assemble and serve.

Joe and Jane Muer

ITALIAN DRESSING

2 ounces fresh Romano cheese, grated to a powder

1 clove garlic, finely minced

1½ teaspoons Dijon mustard

½ cup fresh lemon juice

2 cups olive oil

Pinch of oregano

Place all ingredients in a blender or food processor and mix well. Store in refrigerator.

Yield: 2¾ cups

Linda Smith
DSO

ARTICHOKE HEART SALAD

SALAD

1 14-ounce can water-packed artichoke hearts

6-8 small canned water chestnuts, thinly sliced

3 tablespoons thinly sliced mushrooms

1 small onion, sliced into thin rings

Combine all ingredients and toss well.

DRESSING

¼ cup vegetable oil

4 teaspoons white wine vinegar

1 tablespoon mayonnaise

⅛ teaspoon dry mustard

1 tablespoon snipped chives

⅛ teaspoon salt

⅛ teaspoon pepper

Combine ingredients and mix well. Pour over salad, toss gently and chill until ready to serve.

Serves 4
Preparation time: 15 minutes
Chill
Easy

Glenn Mellow
DSO

RUSSIAN SALAD DRESSING

For many years I thought this recipe originated from the Detroit Athletic Club. I later learned that my uncle, a manager of the DAC, had given the chef the recipe from my maternal grandmother.

1 12-ounce bottle chili sauce

1 16-ounce jar mayonnaise

6-8 small canned beets, chopped

2-3 hard boiled eggs, chopped

2 green peppers, diced

Combine ingredients and mix well — the mixture will be lumpy. Refrigerate overnight to allow flavors to blend. Serve over Bibb lettuce.

Food processor method: In processor bowl fitted with steel blade, chop the green pepper. Add chili sauce and mayonnaise and give one or two turns to blend. Add the beets and turn once or twice to chop. Add the eggs, turn once or twice, until mixed.

Sue Currier

BEAN SPROUT SALAD PERLMAN

Itzhak Perlman, violinist extraordinaire, and culinary hobbyist, gave this recipe to us during a reception after a DSO opening night concert.

SALAD

1 pound bean sprouts	2-3 green onions, chopped

Boil enough water in a large pot to completely cover sprouts. Drop the bean sprouts in and boil for 3-4 minutes, until barely cooked. Immediately drop sprouts into a bowl of ice water to stop the cooking. Drain and place in a bowl.

DRESSING

3 tablespoons soy sauce	¼ teaspoon ginger
1 tablespoon vinegar	½ teaspoon sesame oil

Combine all ingredients and mix well. Pour over the bean sprouts and toss lightly. Chill for at least 30 minutes.

To serve, sprinkle with chopped green onions.

Serves 6
Preparation time: 15 minutes
Chill
Easy   Itzhak Perlman

TOFU DRESSING

Excellent on salad or cooked cold vegetables

½ pound soft tofu, drained	1½ teaspoons spike (herb spice mixture)
1 tablespoon oil	
2½ tablespoons cider vinegar	½ teaspoon honey
1 tablespoon tamari or soy sauce	¼ teaspoon salt
	⅛ teaspoon garlic powder
1 green onion, finely minced	Freshly ground pepper

Combine all ingredients in the container of a blender and process until well combined and smooth.

Makes ¾ cup   Felix Resnick
                                                           DSO

ANTIPASO SALAD

This excellent salad is from the Roostertail

3 cups olive oil
2 small cans pitted black olives, drained
2 small jars pitted green olives, drained
1 head cauliflower, cut into florets
2 bunches fresh broccoli, cut into florets
8 carrots, cut in 1-inch julienne pieces

2 ribs celery, thinly sliced
6 zucchini, thinly sliced
4 Spanish onions, thinly sliced
4 pounds hard salami
1 1-pound can tomato paste
Oregano
Salt and pepper
Garlic powder

In a large pot heat the olive oil over medium heat. Add the olives and cook for 2 minutes. Add remaining vegetables and salami; cook for 5 minutes. Pour off all oil, return pot to heat. Add the tomato puree and spices to taste; mix well. Cook over low heat for 20 minutes. Taste for seasoning.
Serve chilled on a bed of lettuce.

Serves 15-20   Diane and Tom Schoenith

BEEF DIJON SALAD

SALAD
2 cups cooked, rare beef cut into julienne strips
½ cup sliced celery

⅓ cup chopped green onions
¼ cup capers

Combine ingredients and toss gently.

DIJON DRESSING
½ cup vegetable oil
3 tablespoons red wine vinegar
1 tablespoon Dijon mustard

½ clove garlic, minced
Dash of hot pepper sauce
Salt and pepper to taste

Combine dressing ingredients and mix well. About one hour before serving, pour over salad and toss to allow salad to marinate.
Serve on bed of lettuce.

Tina Pohe

TABOOLEY

The authentic Lebanese way to eat tabooley is to use fresh grape or Romaine lettuce leaves to scoop up the salad.

SALAD

½ cup medium grain cracked wheat
2 bunches fresh parsley, stems removed
1 bunch green onions
1 green pepper
1 thin cucumber
4 medium tomatoes
1 cup fresh mint leaves or
2 tablespoons dried mint

Place the wheat in a bowl, cover with cold water and let soak for 1 hour. Finely chop all vegetables. Drain the wheat and firmly squeeze out all water with your hands. Place all vegetables except the tomatoes in a mixing bowl and add the wheat. Pour on dressing and toss well. Place salad in a bowl and garnish the edge of the bowl with chopped tomatoes.

DRESSING

⅓ cup lemon juice
½ cup vegetable oil
Salt and pepper to taste

Combine ingredients and mix well.

Serves 6-8
Connie Salloum

TACO SALAD

1 medium head of lettuce
1 pound sharp Cheddar cheese, shredded
3 tomatoes, chopped
1 pound chopped cooked beef or chicken
½ large bag taco chips, or to taste
1 bottle sour cream and chive salad dressing
Taco sauce to taste

Tear the lettuce into bite-sized pieces. Toss with the cheese, tomatoes, beef and taco chips. Pour on salad dressing and taco sauce to taste. Toss lightly.

Serves 8
Preparation time: 15 minutes
Easy
Pat Goldner

CURRIED SPINACH SALAD

DRESSING

2 tablespoons white wine vinegar

⅔ cup vegetable oil

1 tablespoon finely chopped chutney

1 teaspoon curry powder

1 teaspoon salt

1 teaspoon dry mustard

¼ teaspoon liquid hot pepper sauce

Combine ingredients and mix well. Let stand at room temperature for at least 2 hours.

SALAD

2 pounds fresh spinach

¾ cup dry roasted Spanish peanuts

½ cup raisins, softened

⅓ cup sliced green onion

2 tablespoons sesame seeds

3 red or Golden Delicious apples, with skin

Clean spinach and remove tough leaves and stems. Tear into bite-sized pieces. Wrap well and chill. Just before serving core and slice the apples. Combine the spinach, peanuts, raisins, green onion, sesame seeds and sliced apples. Pour dressing over and toss.

Serves 12
Preparation time: 20 minutes
Prepare ahead and chill
Easy

Margaret Sellgren

SALAD DRESSINGS - Put several cloves of garlic in a bottle with red or white wine vinegar. In 2-3 weeks you'll have a delicately flavored garlic vinegar for salad dressing.

CUCUMBER SALAD

This is especially delicious with Chicken Paprikas

4   medium cucumbers
1   teaspoon salt, divided
½   cup vinegar

½   cup sour cream
Freshly ground pepper
Paprika

Peel the cucumbers and slice very thinly. Place half the cucumbers in a mixing bowl and sprinkle with ½ teaspoon salt. Add the remaining cucumbers and sprinkle with remaining salt. Toss gently, cover, and refrigerate for at least 1 hour.

To serve: Squeeze out as much liquid as possible, then add the vinegar and sour cream. Mix well. Sprinkle with pepper and paprika to taste. May be made in advance and refrigerated.

Serves 4
Preparation time: 15 minutes
Refrigerate
Easy

Beatriz Staples
DSO

COLD PEA AND MUSHROOM SALAD

SALAD

3   pounds fresh peas or 2
     packages frozen peas
1   tablespoon sugar

½   pound mushrooms, sliced
1   tablespoon fresh basil or
     1 teaspoon dried

At least one hour before serving, cook peas with the sugar until crisp tender; drain. Mix with remaining ingredients and chill. Serve with vinaigrette sauce.

VINAIGRETTE

6   tablespoons olive oil
2   tablespoons wine vinegar

½   teaspoon salt

Combine and mix well. Pour over salad and toss.

Serves 6-8
Preparation time: 15 minutes
Easy

Virginia Hatzenbeler

TARRAGON-MUSTARD DRESSING

1   egg
1   tablespoon mayonnaise
¼   cup Dijon mustard
¼   cup tarragon vinegar
1   teaspoon dried tarragon

1   clove garlic
Salt and pepper to taste
1   cup olive oil
1   cup vegetable oil

Combine all ingredients, except the oils, in a blender or in the bowl of a food processor fitted with the steel blade. Process until well mixed. With the motor still running, slowly add the oil in a steady stream until thoroughly incorporated. Taste for seasoning. Refrigerate.

Makes 3 cups

Lee Barlow

CHICKEN RICE SALAD

Delicious and mildly exotic. A lovely luncheon dish. Serve with fruit and avocado slices.

SALAD

1   package Chicken
    Rice-a-Roni
2   small jars marinated
    artichoke hearts, drained,
    juice reserved

2   green onions, thinly sliced
½   green pepper, thinly sliced
3   cups cooked chicken breast,
    cut in bite-sized pieces

Cook Rice-a-Roni according to package directions. Let cool then add the drained artichoke hearts, onions, greet pepper and chicken. Toss gently.

DRESSING

¼-½ teaspoon curry powder
½   cup mayonnaise

Liquid from artichoke hearts

Combine ingredients and mix well. Pour over salad and toss until well coated. Refrigerate until cold.

Serves 6
Preparation time: 35 minutes
Easy

Eileen Hitz

CRANBERRY-EGGNOG WREATH

WREATH

1　envelope unflavored gelatin
2　cups eggnog
1　3-ounce package raspberry
　　gelatin

1　cup boiling water
1　10-ounce jar cranberry-
　　orange relish
Sugared cranberries for garnish

In a medium saucepan soften the gelatin in 1 cup of the eggnog. Heat and stir until gelatin is dissolved; add remaining eggnog. Turn into a 5-cup ring mold and chill until gelatin is almost firm.

Dissolve raspberry gelatin in 1 cup boiling water. Add the cranberry relish and stir well. Chill until partially set. Pour over the eggnog layer; chill overnight.

Unmold, then fill the center with sugared cranberries.

SUGARED CRANBERRIES
2-3 cups cranberries
Egg white
Sugar

Coat the cranberries with egg white then roll in the sugar. Let sit on a cookie sheet until dry.

Serves 8　　　　　　　　　　　　　　　　　　　　Martha Bowman

HONEY-MUSTARD DRESSING

Great with spinach salad

¾　cup vegetable oil
¼　cup cider vinegar
¼　cup honey

¼　cup Dijon mustard
2　cloves garlic, finely minced
Freshly ground pepper to taste

Combine ingredients in a jar and shake well. Refrigerate until ready to use.

Makes 1½ cups
Easy　　　　　　　　　　　　　　　　　　　　Kay Warner

SHRIMP PARADISE SALAD

DRESSING

2 tablespoons lemon juice	½ teaspoon salt
2 tablespoons dry white wine	½ teaspoon paprika
1 teaspoon honey	½ cup olive oil

Combine all ingredients in a bottle and shake well. Chill.

SALAD

1 large pineapple	1 tablespoon lemon juice
1 large orange	1 pound shrimp, cooked,
1 avocado	cleaned and chilled

Cut pineapple in half lengthwise; remove core and pulp, reserving shell for serving. Slice pulp. Peel and section oranges. Peel and slice avocado and sprinkle with lemon juice. Fill pineapple shell with sliced pineapple, oranges and avocado. Arrange chilled shrimp on top. Serve with Paradise Dressing.

Serves 6
Preparation time: 15 minutes
Easy

Sheila Swanson

CAESAR SALAD

1 large head romaine lettuce	1 tablespoon red wine vinegar
½ can anchovies, finely chopped	1 egg yolk
	Juice of ½ lemon
2 cloves garlic, finely chopped	Salt
3 tablespoons oil, safflower or olive	½ cup grated Parmesan cheese

Wash lettuce, dry well, and tear into bite-size pieces. Set aside.
In a bowl mash together the anchovies and garlic. Add oil and vinegar; blend. Add egg yolk and lemon juice and blend. Add salt to taste. Pour over lettuce and toss until lettuce is well coated; add Parmesan cheese and toss again.
Serve immediately.

Serves 4-6
Preparation time: 15 minutes
Dressing can be made ahead and refrigerated.
Easy

Leslie Carney

RIBBON LAYERED JELLO SALAD

Can also be used as a dessert

2	cups milk	2	cups sour cream
1	cup sugar	2	teaspoons vanilla
2	envelopes unflavored gelatin	4	3-ounce packages Jello, using
½	cup cold water		different flavors

Boil the milk and add sugar. Dissolve unflavored gelatin in ½ cup water; then add to the hot milk. Add the sour cream and vanilla and beat until smooth; set aside.

Mix the first box of Jello using 1½ cups water. Place in a 9x13-inch glass dish. When completely set, spoon on 1½ cups of the filling. Refrigerate until firm.

Mix the second box of Jello as before using only 1½ cups of water. Spoon on top of filling layer and refrigerate until set. Continue method until filling and remaining Jello are used up. Jello should be on top and bottom layers.

To serve, cut into squares.

Serves 12-15   Terry Salciccioli

LEMONADE DRESSING FOR FRUIT SALAD

Serve in a silver bowl — elegant

1	6-ounce can lemonade	½	teaspoon salt
⅓	cup sugar	1	cup heavy cream
2	eggs slightly beaten		

Combine the lemonade, sugar, eggs and salt in the top section of a double boiler. Cook over simmering water, stirring constantly, until mixture is thickened and coats a spoon. Remove from heat and chill quickly by immersing in a bowl with ice cubes.

Whip the cream until stiff but still glossy. Fold into lemonade mixture and chill.

Makes 1 pint   Rose-Marie Mebus

SWEET POTATO SALAD

Great at barbecues

5 cups water
1½ pounds sweet potatoes
2 medium ribs celery, thinly sliced
1 small onion thinly sliced
1 medium orange, peeled and cut into sections
½ teaspoon grated orange peel
½ cup mayonnaise
2 tablespoons orange or pineapple juice
½ teaspoon dry mustard
¼ teaspoon salt
Ground pepper to taste
¼ teaspoon ground ginger
Lettuce leaves for serving

Heat water to boiling. Add the potatoes, cover and cook for 30-35 minutes or until tender. Drain well. When the potatoes are cool enough to handle, remove skin and cut into ½-inch cubes.

Add the celery, onion and orange sections. Combine the remaining ingredients, except lettuce, and pour over potatoes. Mix well. Refrigerate until cold, at least 2 hours. Serve in a bowl lined with lettuce leaves.

Preparation time: 1 hour
Refrigerate: 3 hours

Carmella Gusfa

HEARTS OF PALM SALAD

Deliciously different

SALAD
4 cups hearts of palm, cut into chunks
1 cup cubed pineapple
¼ cup chopped dates
¼ cup candied or preserved ginger, chopped

Combine and toss gently.

DRESSING
¼ cup lime sherbet
2 tablespoons mayonnaise
2 tablespoons crunchy peanut butter
Pineapple juice

Mix sherbet, mayonnaise and peanut butter well. If necessary, thin with a little pineapple juice.

Serves 4
Preparation time: 20 minutes

Sheila Swanson

MANDARIN SALAD

SALAD

Greens for 4-6 people
1   cup chopped celery
2   green onions with tops, thinly sliced

1   11-ounce can mandarin orange segments, drained

Combine ingredients and toss gently.

DRESSING

¼   cup vegetable oil
2   tablespoons red wine vinegar
2   tablespoons sugar
1   tablespoon chopped parsley

¼   teaspoon salt
Dash pepper
Dash Tabasco sauce

Combine ingredients and shake well.

TOPPING

¼   cup sliced almonds

1½   tablespoons sugar

Cook the almonds and sugar over low heat until the sugar is melted and nuts are coated.
Just before serving, toss salad with dressing to taste and sprinkle with topping.

Ellie Tholen

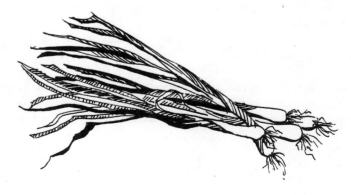

113

FIRE AND ICE TOMATOES

SALAD

12	large tomatoes, peeled and quartered	2	large red onions, sliced in rings
2	large green peppers, sliced in rings	2	large cucumbers, peeled and sliced

Place tomatoes, green peppers and onions alternately in a salad bowl. Just before serving, add cucumbers.

DRESSING

1½	cups wine vinegar	1	tablespoon mustard seed
1	tablespoon celery seed	1	teaspoon salt
¼	teaspoon cayenne pepper	2-3	tablespoons sugar, to taste
¼	teaspoon black pepper	½	cup water

Mix vinegar, seasonings, sugar and water together. Boil for 1 minute or until the sugar is dissolved. While still hot, pour over vegetables. cool and chill.
This relish will keep in refrigerator several days before addition of the cucumbers.

Serves 12 generously   Sheila Mohr

SUPER SLAW

Perfect for the food processor

1	medium head cabbage	½	bag miniature marshmallows
2	medium carrots	½	cup mayonnaise
1	20-ounce can crushed pineapple, well drained	½	cup slaw dressing

Shred the cabbage and carrots in a food processor. Add the drained pineapple and marshmallows and toss. Combine the mayonnaise and slaw dressing and gently fold into the salad. Chill.

Serves 8-10
Preparation time: 15 minutes
Easy   Debbie Tischler

SHOW STOPPER SALAD

MARINADE

1	cup vegetable oil	1	tablespoon dill weed
1	cup cider vinegar	1	teaspoon salt
½	cup prepared Italian dressing	1	teaspoon garlic salt
1	tablespoon sugar	1	teaspoon pepper
1	tablespoon M.S.G. (optional)		

Combine ingredients and mix thoroughly.

SALAD

1	head broccoli, cut in florets	1	bunch carrots, thinly sliced
1	head cauliflower, cut in florets	4	ribs celery, thinly sliced
1	pound mushrooms, thinly sliced		

Combine all vegetables and toss with marinade. Let sit for 24 hours, turning occasionally. Drain well before serving.

Serves 15-20
Refrigerate 24 hours

Deane Taylor

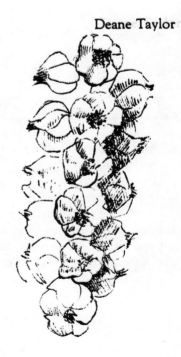

"No cook who has attained mastery over her craft ever apologizes for the presence of garlic in her productions."

Ruth Gottfried
The Questing Cook

115

TROPICAL SALAD WITH LIME DRESSING

SALAD

1 can hearts of palm, cut into chunks
2 bananas, sliced and tossed with ½ teaspoon lemon juice
1 20-ounce can pineapple chunks, drained
1 cup chopped dates
1 11-ounce can mandarin oranges, drained
1 cup chopped Macadamia nuts or walnuts
6 dried apricots, cut into quarters
Romaine lettuce and fresh spinach

Combine ingredients and toss gently.

DRESSING

1 pint lime sherbet
¼ cup mayonnaise
1 cup chunky peanut butter
¼ cup lemon juice

Combine ingredients in a blender and process until thoroughly blended — about 15 seconds. Pour over salad and toss.

Serves 8-10
Preparation time: 30 minutes
Chill
Easy

Ruth Greenbaum

APPLE AVOCADO SALAD

4 tart apples, peeled, cored and sliced
1 ripe avocado
Juice of 2 lemons
¼ cup chopped salted peanuts
Vinaigrette dressing
Bibb lettuce
1 bunch crisp watercress

Toss the apple and avocado slices with lemon juice. When ready to serve, drain off excess juice. Add the nuts and toss with vinaigrette to coat lightly. Serve on a bed of Bibb lettuce; garnish with watercress.

Chris Considine

Breads

Midnight Breakfast Buffet

Shrimp Paté with Pumpernickel Party Slices
Orange Muffins
Eggs Royale
Sautéed Chicken Livers
Strawberry Bread
Sinful Souffle
Hot Fruit Compote

Wine Suggestions

Napa Cellars
Sauvignon Blanc
or
Kabinett Sharzhoffberger
German Riesling

Sunday Brunch

Freshly Squeezed Orange Juice
Fresh Fruit Cup
Scrambled Eggs
Baked Honey Wheat Cakes
The Best Sour Cream Coffee Cake
Coffee   Tea   Milk

Wine Suggestions

Champagne
or
Vouvray

BANANA CARROT BREAD

½ cup butter, softened
¾ cup sugar
2 eggs
1½ cups very ripe bananas, mashed, about 4 bananas
1¾ cups flour
2 teaspoons baking powder
½ teaspoon baking soda
½ teaspoon salt
½ teaspoon cinnamon
¼ teaspoon cloves
1 teaspoon vanilla
1 cup chopped walnuts or pecans
1 cup grated carrots

Preheat oven to 350 degrees.
Cream together the butter and sugar. Add the eggs, one at a time, beating well after each addition. Stir in the mashed bananas. In a separate bowl, combine the flour, baking powder, soda, salt, cinnamon and cloves. Add to the creamed mixture and incorporate thoroughly. Stir in the vanilla, nuts and carrots.
Pour mixture into a buttered loaf pan. Bake for 1 hour or until a toothpick inserted in the center comes out clean. Cool in pan for 20 minutes; then remove and cool on a wire rack.

Preparation time: 30 minutes
Baking time: 1 hour
Easy

Carolyn Conlin

CARROT BREAD

⅔ cup salad oil
1 cup sugar
2 eggs
1½ cups flour
1 teaspoon soda
½ teaspoon ground cinnamon
1 cup grated carrots

Preheat oven to 350 degrees.
Combine all ingredients in a large mixing bowl. Beat for two minutes on medium speed of electric mixer. Spoon into a greased 9x5-inch loaf pan. Bake for 55 minutes or until a toothpick inserted in the center comes out clean.

Yield: 1 loaf
Preparation time: 25 minutes
Baking time: 1 hour
Easy

Barbara June

PEAR BREAD WITH APPLE BUTTER

This tastes even better the next day

BREAD

½   cup butter
1   cup sugar
2   eggs
2   cups flour
½   teaspoon salt
½   teaspoon baking soda

1   teaspoon baking powder
⅛   teaspoon nutmeg
¼   cup yogurt or buttermilk
1   cup chopped pears
1   teaspoon vanilla

Preheat oven to 350 degrees.
Cream the butter then gradually add the sugar. Add the eggs, one at a time, beating well after each addition. Combine the flour, salt, soda, baking powder and nutmeg. Add to the egg mixture alternately with the yogurt. Stir in the pears and vanilla. Pour into a buttered 9x5-inch loaf pan. Bake for 1 hour.

APPLE BUTTER

2   cups unsweetened
    applesauce
¼-½ cup sugar, to taste
1   teaspoon cinnamon

¼   teaspoon allspice
⅛   teaspoon ginger
⅛   teaspoon cloves

In a 1½-quart heavy saucepan combine all ingredients. Bring to a boil and cook for 30 minutes, stirring often. Let cool.

Martha Bowman

KATHY'S SWEET ROLLS

ROLLS

1   cup milk
4   cups flour
⅓   cup sugar
1   teaspoon salt
1   cup shortening

1   package yeast
2   eggs
Melted butter
Sugar
Cinnamon

Scald the milk and let cool to 110-115 degrees. Combine the flour, sugar and salt. Cut in the shortening until it resembles coarse meal. Dissolve the yeast in the lukewarm milk. Beat the eggs and add to the milk mixture. Add to the dough, mix well and refrigerate overnight.

Divide the dough into 4 parts. Roll in a circle ¼ inch thick on a floured surface. Spread with some melted butter and sprinkle with sugar and cinnamon. cut into pie shaped pieces. Roll each piece toward the point and press to seal. Let raise for 1 hour.
Preheat oven to 350 degrees and bake rolls for 20 minutes. Let cool, then frost.

FROSTING

¼	cup butter, softened	1	egg
2	cups powdered sugar	1	teaspoon vanilla

Cream the butter with the sugar. Add the egg and vanilla and incorporate thoroughly. Spread on cooled rolls.

Kathy Snow

POPPY SEED BREAD

¼	cup poppyseeds	2½	cups plus 2 tablespoons flour
1	cup buttermilk		
1	cup butter	1	teaspoon baking powder
1¾	cups sugar	½	teaspoon baking soda
4	eggs, separated	¼	teaspoon salt
½	teaspoon almond extract	½	cup sugar
1	teaspoon vanilla extract	1	teaspoon cinnamon

Preheat oven to 350 degrees.
Soak poppy seeds in the buttermilk for 15 minutes. Cream the butter and 1¾ cups sugar. Add the egg yolks and extracts; mix well. Sift together the flour, baking powder, soda and salt. Add alternately with the buttermilk and seeds.
In a separate bowl, beat egg whites until they form still moist peaks. Thoroughly mix ¼ of the whites into the batter than gently fold in remaining whites.
Pour ½ of the batter into a greased Bundt or tube pan. Mix together the ½ cup sugar and cinnamon. Sprinkle half the mixture over the batter. Add remaining batter and sprinkle with remaining cinnamon and sugar. Bake 45-50 minutes or until a toothpick inserted in center comes out clean.

Preparation time: 25 minutes
Baking time: 50 minutes

Whitney Jill Sale

STRAWBERRY BREAD

Incredibly delicious

3 cups flour
2 cups sugar
1 tablespoon cinnamon
1 teaspoon baking soda
1 teaspoon salt

4 eggs, well beaten
1 cup oil
2 small packages frozen
   strawberries, thawed
Optional: 1 cup chopped nuts

Preheat oven to 350 degrees.
Sift together the flour, sugar, cinnamon, soda, and salt. Beat in the eggs then add the oil, strawberries and nuts. Mix thoroughly. Pour into 3 greased loaf pans. Bake 45 minutes to an hour, or until a toothpick inserted in the center comes out clean. Let stand in pans until nearly cool.

Preparation time: 30 minutes
Baking time: 45 minutes
Freezes well
Easy   Linda Thompson

CHEESE STOLLEN

CAKE
½ cup butter
1 cup sugar
2 eggs
Grated rind of 1 lemon
1 teaspoon almond extract

4 cups flour, sifted
4 teaspoons baking powder
½ pound cottage cheese
¼ pound slivered almonds
½ pound raisins

TOPPING
½ cup butter, melted

Powdered sugar

Preheat oven to 350 degrees.
Cream the butter with the sugar. Add the eggs, lemon rind and almond extract and mix well. Sift the flour with the baking powder and add to creamed mixture alternately with the cottage cheese. At this point the dough will be very stiff so mixing should be completed by hand. Add the nuts and raisins and incorporate thoroughly.

Divide into 2 well-greased loaf pans and bake 40-45 minutes or until tops spring back when touched. Remove from oven and immediately brush tops well with the melted butter. Sprinkle generously with powdered sugar.

Yield: 2 loaves
Preparation time: 20 minutes
Baking time: 35 minutes

Elizabeth Steger
DSO

When baking bread in a glass pan, lower heat 25 degrees.

GEORGIA PEACH BREAD

Peachy . . . a nice change of pace

3	cups sliced fresh, ripe peaches (3-4 peaches)	1	teaspoon cinnamon
6	tablespoons sugar	1½	cups sugar
2	cups flour	½	cup solid vegetable shortening
1	teaspoon baking powder	2	eggs
1	teaspoon baking soda	1	cup pecans, finely chopped
¼	teaspoon salt	1	teaspoon vanilla

Preheat oven to 325 degrees.
Place peaches and 6 tablespoons of sugar in container of blender or in a food processor fitted with the steel blade; process until pureed. There should be about 2¼ cups.
Combine the flour, baking powder, soda, salt and cinnamon; set aside.
Cream remaining sugar and shortening; add the eggs and mix well.
Add peach puree and dry ingredients; mix until well moistened. Stir in the nuts and vanilla.
Pour batter into 2 well-greased and floured 9x5-inch loaf pans. Bake for 55-60 minutes or until a toothpick inserted in the center comes out clean. Cool for 10 minutes in pans, then turn out on a rack and let cool completely.

Yield: 2 loaves
Preparation time: ½ hour
Baking time: 1 hour
Easy

Barbara June

TROPICAL BRUFFINS

½ cup sugar
1 egg
¼ cup milk
⅔ cup Grape-Nuts cereal
1 8-ounce can crushed pineapple, with juice (reserve 2 tablespoons of juice for glaze)

1 cup mashed bananas (2 large)
2 cups biscuit mix
1 teaspoon salt
Glaze:
1 cup powdered sugar
2 tablespoons reserved pineapple juice

Preheat oven to 425 degrees.
Combine the sugar, egg and milk; mix well. Add cereal, pineapple and juice, bananas, biscuit mix and salt. Stir only until moistened. Fill greased muffin tins ⅔ full. Bake for 20 minutes.
Combine powdered sugar and pineapple juice and blend until smooth. While muffins are still hot, dip tops into glaze.

Makes 12
Preparation time: 20 minutes
Baking time: 20 minutes

Mary Powanda

APPLE-PUMPKIN BREAD

An interesting and delicious variation on a popular theme

2 cups flour
1 tablespoon baking powder
½ teaspoon baking soda
½ teaspoon salt
2 teaspoons cinnamon
½ teaspoon freshly grated nutmeg
¼ teaspoon ground cloves
½ teaspoon ground ginger

½ cup plus 2 tablespoons sweet butter, softened
1½ cups sugar
2 eggs
1 cup pumpkin
2 cups shredded tart unpared apples
Powdered sugar

Preheat oven to 350 degrees.
Combine the flour, baking powder, soda, salt, cinnamon, nutmeg, cloves and ginger; set aside. Cream the butter and sugar in a large mixing bowl. Add the eggs and pumpkin and mix until light and fluffy. Add the apples and incorporate thoroughly. Stir in the dry ingredients and mix well. Turn into 2 well-buttered loaf pans and bake

124

for 45-50 minutes or until a toothpick inserted in the center comes out clean. Remove from oven and let cool on a wire rack for 5 minutes. Remove from pans and let cool completely. Sprinkle powdered sugar over the loaves.

Yield: 2 loaves
Preparation time: 25 minutes
Baking time: 50 minutes
Easy   Margaret Worthington

ORANGE MUFFINS

Juice and rind of 2 oranges | 1 cup sugar
(about ⅓ cup juice) | 2 eggs
½ cup golden raisins | 1 teaspoon baking soda
2 tablespoons brandy | 1 cup buttermilk
1 cup butter | 2 cups flour
| 1 cup brown sugar

Preheat oven to 400 degrees.
Grate the orange peel and combine with the raisins. Let soak in the brandy. In a large bowl, cream together the butter and sugar. Add the eggs and beat until well mixed. Dissolve the baking soda in the buttermilk and add alternately with the flour to the egg mixture. Add the orange rind, raisins and brandy. Fill paper lined cupcake tins ¾ full with the batter and bake for 25-30 minutes or until muffins are golden brown and a toothpick inserted in the center comes out clean. Remove from oven.
Mix the brown sugar with the orange juice and drizzle the glaze over the hot muffins. Serve warm.

Yield: 18 muffins
Preparation time: 20 minutes
Baking time: 20 minutes
Freezes well   Reiko Kubo
Easy   Bob Shafer

MUFFINS — Never beat muffin batter, stir only until moistened.

APRICOT BRAN BREAD

Delicious . . . serve anytime

1	cup chopped dried apricots	½	cup brown sugar
Boiling water		1½	cups whole bran cereal
3	tablespoons honey	1	cup milk
1½	cups flour	2	eggs
4	teaspoons baking powder	⅓	cup oil
1	teaspoon salt		

Preheat oven to 350 degrees.

Pour enough boiling water over the apricots to cover. Let stand for 10 minutes then drain well. Combine the apricots with honey. Sift together the flour, baking powder and salt; add the sugar. In another bowl, mix the bran, milk, eggs and oil. Add to the flour mixture then stir in the honey coated apricots. Pour into a 9x5-inch greased loaf pan. Bake for 1 hour or until a toothpick inserted in the center comes out clean. Let cool, remove from pan and wrap well. Serve the next day.

Yield: 1 loaf
Preparation time: 20 minutes
Baking time: 1 hour
Easy   Marilyn Van Giesen

BISHOP'S BREAD

3	cups prepared biscuit mix	¼	cup slivered almonds
¾	cup sugar	¼	cup candied or maraschino cherries, halved
1	egg		
1¼	cups orange juice	¼	cup raisins
1	tablespoon grated orange rind	1	6-ounce package butter-scotch morsels

Preheat oven to 350 degrees.

In a bowl, combine the biscuit mix and sugar. Set aside 2 tablespoons of the mixture and add the egg and orange juice to the remaining dry ingredients; beat until thoroughly blended. Combine the reserved biscuit mixture with the almonds, cherries, raisins and butterscotch pieces and toss well to coat evenly; stir into the batter. Pour into a greased and floured 9x5-inch loaf pan or 2-quart mold. Bake for 60-70 minutes or until a toothpick inserted in the center comes out clean.

Remove from oven and cool on a wire rack.

Yield: 1 loaf
Preparation time: 20 minutes
Baking time: 1 hour
Easy Mado Lie

LEMON POPPY SEED BREAD

½	cup milk	⅔	cup butter
1	tablespoon poppy seeds	¾	cup sugar
2	cups flour	2	eggs
1	tablespoon baking powder	1	tablespoon grated lemon rind
1	teaspoon salt		

Preheat oven to 350 degrees.

Combine the milk and poppy seeds; set aside. Sift together the flour, baking powder and salt. In a large mixing bowl cream together the butter and sugar. Beat in the eggs and lemon rind and add the flour mixture alternately with the milk and poppy seeds beginning and ending with the flour. Turn into a greased 9x5-inch loaf pan. Bake for 70 minutes.

Preparation time: 20 minutes
Baking time: 70 minutes
Easy Martha Bowman

THE BEST CORN BREAD

Serve hot with butter — great with chili

1¼	cups flour	1	egg
¾	cup corn meal	1	cup milk
5	tablespoons sugar	2	tablespoons melted butter
5	teaspoons baking powder		

Preheat oven to 375 degrees.
Sift together the flour, corn meal, sugar and baking powder. Beat the egg and milk together and add to the flour mixture. Add the butter and mix well. Spread batter in a greased 8x8-inch pan and bake for 30-35 minutes, until lightly browned around the edges.

Serves 4-6
Preparation time: 15 minutes
Baking time: 35 minutes
Easy

Victoria King
DSO

HEALTHY MUFFINS

1	cup whole-wheat pastry flour, sifted	1	cup yogurt
2	tablespoons double-acting baking powder	4	eggs
½	cup powdered milk granules	1	cup unsweetened shredded coconut
1	cup raw wheat germ	1	cup raisins
2	cups Miller's bran	1	cup walnuts
1	cup milk	3	tablespoons vegetable oil

Preheat oven to 400 degrees.
Into a mixing bowl sift the flour, baking powder and powdered milk. Add the remaining ingredients and stir *only* until moistened. Fill paper baking cups or well greased muffin tins two-thirds full. Bake for 15-20 minutes or until lightly browned.

Yield: 12 muffins

Linda and Bruce Smith
DSO

CHEESE BREAD

1 loaf Italian bread, unsliced	1 tablespoon poppyseeds
10-14 slices Swiss cheese	2 tablespoons minced onion
¾ cup butter, melted	2 tablespoons lemon juice
1 tablespoon Dijon mustard	

Preheat oven to 350 degrees.
Cut top crust off bread and slice ¾ way through. Stuff the cheese slices between the bread slices. Combine remaining ingredients and drizzle over top and sides of bread. Wrap in heavy aluminum foil and bake for 30 minutes.

Serves 8-10
Preparation time: 5 minutes
Baking time: 30 minutes
Easy   Holly Barnett

CRANBERRY MUFFINS

Great for Thanksgiving or any brunch

2 cups flour	½ cup plus 2 tablespoons chopped walnuts or pecans, divided
½ cup sugar	
1 tablespoon baking powder	
½ teaspoon salt	1 tablespoon grated orange peel, divided
1 cup milk	
¼ cup vegetable oil	2 tablespoons sugar mixed with 1 teaspoon cinnamon
1 egg, beaten	
1 cup chopped cranberries	

Preheat oven to 400 degrees.
Combine the flour, sugar, baking powder and salt. Add the milk, oil and egg and mix well. Fold in the cranberries, ½ cup chopped nuts and 2 teaspoons orange peel. Spoon into 12 greased muffin cups. Combine the sugar-cinnamon mixture and the remaining nuts and orange peel. Sprinkle over the muffins. Bake for 20-25 minutes or until a toothpick inserted in the center comes out clean.
Serve warm.

Yield: 12 muffins
Preparation time: 20 minutes
Baking time: 25 minutes
Easy   Rho Blanchard

BAKED HONEY WHEAT CAKES

Serve with Baked Eggs for lovely brunch meal

1	cup cereal	1	cup flour
½	cup wheat germ	1½	teaspoons baking powder
½	teaspoon baking soda	½	teaspoon salt
½	cup hot water	1	cup buttermilk
¼	cup honey	1	egg

Preheat oven to 425 degrees.
In a large bowl combine the cereal, wheat germ, soda, hot water, honey, and flour. Stir until cereal is softened. Add remaining ingredients and pour into a greased jelly roll pan. Bake for 8-10 minutes. Cut into squares and serve with maple syrup.

Serves 5-10
Preparation time: 10 minutes
Baking time: 10 minutes
Easy   Martha Bowman

DILLY BREAD

1	package dry yeast	1	teaspoon salt
¼	cup lukewarm water	1	tablespoon fresh minced
1	cup creamed cottage cheese,		onion
	at room temperature	1	teaspoon dried dill
1	tablespoon butter, melted	1	egg
2	tablespoons sugar	2¼-2½	cups flour

Soften the yeast in the water and let stand for 10 minutes. In a large bowl, combine the yeast mixture with the cottage cheese, butter, sugar, salt, onion, dill and egg. Gradually add the flour and mix until it forms a ball and leaves the sides of the bowl. Cover and let rise until double in size. Stir mixture down and place in a greased casserole. Let stand 30-40 minutes. Bake in a 350-degree oven for 35-40 minutes or until the crust is golden brown. Brush the top with butter and salt lightly. Let stand for 5 minutes before removing from pan.

Preparation time: 15 minutes
Baking time: 40 minutes   Jeanne Schlitters

HEALTHY BREAD

3 tablespoons butter
1 egg, beaten
1 cup skim milk
1 cup water
2 cups whole wheat flour
¼ cup soy flour

¼ cup oat flour (blend rolled oats in blender until powdered)
2 packages bread yeast
1 tablespoon Torula yeast
3-4 cups unbleached flour

Melt butter, add egg, milk and water and heat to 120 degrees. Add the whole wheat flour, soy flour, oat flour, active bread yeast, and Torula yeast; mix for 3 minutes, or until smooth. Knead in enough unbleached flour to make a dough that is firm but moist and slightly sticky to the touch. Knead for 10 minutes by hand or 3 minutes with electric dough kneader.

Place in a greased bowl, cover with a towel, and put in a warm place to rise for 1 hour, until doubled in size. Punch down and divide into two pieces. Shape each piece into a loaf, and let rise 40 minutes to an hour until double in bulk. Bake in a 350-degree oven for 45 minutes.

Debra & Wesley Jacobs
DSO

MEXICAN SPOON BREAD

An old family recipe from Arizona

1 can white corn	⅓ cup oil
1 cup white corn meal	¾ cup milk
2 eggs	1 small can green chilies, chopped
1 teaspoon baking soda	
½ teaspoon salt	1 cup grated Cheddar cheese

Preheat oven to 350 degrees.

In blender, mix all ingredients except chilies and cheese. Pour half of the batter into a well greased 11x7-inch pan. Layer with cheese and chilies and cover with remaining batter. Bake for 40 minutes or until lightly browned.

Note: Although yellow corn and yellow corn meal can be used, white is preferred.

Serves 4-6
Preparation time: 10 minutes
Easy

Robert Williams
DSO

SOUR CREAM CORNBREAD

This is a sweet cornbread . . . a variation of an old favorite. Great hot out of the oven.

1 cup flour	1 cup yellow corn meal
1 teaspoon salt	½ cup sugar
2 teaspoons baking powder	1 egg, well beaten
1 teaspoon baking soda	1 cup sour cream

Preheat oven to 400 degrees.

Sift together the flour, salt, baking powder and baking soda. Add cornmeal and sugar; mix well. Add the egg and sour cream and incorporate thoroughly. Batter will be very thick. Pour into a greased 9-inch square pan. Bake 18-20 minutes.

Serves 9
Preparation time: 15 minutes
Baking time: 20 minutes
Easy

Karen Quarnstrom

IRISH SODA BREAD

Great for breakfast — spread generously with butter and jam

2	tablespoons butter, melted	1	teaspoon salt
1½	cups buttermilk	1	teaspoon baking soda
2	eggs, beaten	1	tablespoon caraway seeds
3½	cups sifted flour	1	cup raisins
¾	cup sugar		

Preheat oven to 325 degrees.
Combine the melted butter, buttermilk and eggs. Blend together the remaining ingredients in a large bowl. Make a well in the center and add the liquid mixture. Stir with a wooden spoon until completely moistened. Scoop out into a greased and floured 2-quart casserole dish. Mound up slightly in the center and cut a cross with a sharp knife ½ inch deep across the entire top of the bread. Bake for 1-1¼ hours or until a toothpick inserted in the center comes out clean.

Freezes well   Pat O'Donnell

BEER BREAD

Men especially love this. It goes very well with chili.

3	cups *self-rising* flour	Pinch of salt	
⅓	cup sugar	1	can beer

Preheat oven to 350 degrees.
Combine all ingredients and stir well. Pour into a greased and floured loaf pan. Bake for 50 minutes or until well-browned. Cool slightly before cutting.

Serves 6-8
Preparation time: 10 minutes
Baking time: 50 minutes
Easy   Jeanne Johnson-Lakey

WHOLE WHEAT-COTTAGE CHEESE ROLLS

Even a novice yeast-baker can master these nutritious rolls

3¾-4 cups whole wheat flour
2 packages active dry yeast
½ teaspoon baking soda
1½ cups creamed cottage cheese
½ cup water
¼ cup firmly packed brown sugar
2 tablespoons butter
2 teaspoons salt
2 eggs

Thoroughly stir together 1½ cups of the flour, the yeast and baking soda. Heat the cottage cheese, water, sugar, butter and salt until just warm. Add the cheese mixture and the eggs to the flour mixture. Beat at low speed on an electric mixer for ½ minute, scraping the bowl constantly then beat for 3 minutes at high speed.

By hand, stir in enough remaining flour to make a moderately stiff dough. Knead on a lightly floured board for 8-10 minutes; place in a greased bowl, turning once. Cover with a linen towel and place in a preheated 150-degree oven. Turn oven off and let dough rise until nearly doubled, 50-60 minutes. Punch down, then shape into 24 rolls. Place in greased muffin tins. Again, place in a preheated 150-degree oven, turn oven off and let rolls rise until nearly doubled. Bake in a 375-degree oven for 12-15 minutes.

Makes 24 rolls   Chris Considine

IRISH FRUIT AND NUT BREAD

An authentic Irish recipe

1¼ cups raisins
1 cup chopped nuts
2 cups sugar
2 cups water
½ cup butter
1 teaspoon cinnamon
1 teaspoon nutmeg
1 teaspoon allspice
½ teaspoon salt
2 eggs, beaten
3 cups unsifted all-purpose flour
½ teaspoon baking soda

Preheat oven to 300 degrees.

In a large saucepan combine the raisins, nuts, sugar, water, butter, and spices. Bring to a boil over low heat. Cool to room temperature by placing saucepan in a sink full of cold water and stirring for about 5 minutes. Add the eggs to the raisin mixture and stir until combined. Add the flour and baking soda; blend thoroughly. Pour into 2 greased 9x5-inch bread pans. Bake for 2 hours.

Peggy Dasovic

CHOCOLATE ZUCCHINI BREAD

This is a delicious variation on a classic tea bread

¾	cup butter	1½	teaspoons baking soda
2	cups sugar	1	teaspoon cinnamon
3	eggs	½	cup milk
2½	cups sifted flour	2	cups shredded zucchini
½	cup unsweetened cocoa	½	cup chopped walnuts
2½	teaspoons baking powder		

Cream together the butter and sugar. Add the eggs, one at a time, beating after each addition. Combine the flour, cocoa, baking powder, soda and cinnamon and add to the creamed mixture alternately with the milk. Stir in the zucchini and nuts. Pour into two greased 8½x4½-inch loaf pans and bake for 45-55 minutes or until a cake tester inserted in the center comes out clean.

Yield: 2 loaves
Preparation time: 50 minutes
Baking time: 1 hour
Easy

Bob Allison
"Ask Your Neighbor"

BRAN MUFFINS

Make in the evening, enjoy in the morning

1	cup boiling water	½	teaspoon salt
1	cup Bran Buds	2½	teaspoons baking soda
1½	cups sugar	2	cups buttermilk, sour milk
½	cup margarine		or plain yogurt
2	eggs	2	cups bran flakes
2½	cups flour, sifted	1	cup raisins

Combine the water and Bran Buds and let cool. Stir in the sugar and margarine. Add eggs, one at a time, beating well after each addition. Sift together the flour, salt and soda. Combine the buttermilk, bran flakes and raisins and add to the Bran Buds mixture alternately with the dry ingredients. Pour into a container, cover and refrigerate. When ready to bake, spoon into greased muffin tins. Bake in a 375-degree oven for 20 minutes.

Yield: 5 dozen
Preparation time: 15 minutes
Baking time: 20 minutes
Keeps 5 weeks in refrigerator
Easy

Vicki Deshaw

RHUBARB BREAD

BREAD

²/₃ cup vegetable oil	1 cup sour milk
1¼ cups brown sugar	2½ cups flour
1 teaspoon vanilla	1 teaspoon baking soda
1 teaspoon salt	1½ cups finely diced rhubarb
1 egg	½ cup chopped nuts

Preheat oven to 325 degrees.

Combine the oil, brown sugar, vanilla and salt. Add the egg and sour milk and blend well. Sift together the dry ingredients; add to the first mixture. Add the rhubarb and nuts and stir only until dry ingredients are thoroughly moistened.

Pour into 2 well-buttered 8x4-inch bread pans. Bake for 55 minutes or until a toothpick inserted in center comes out clean. Let cool for 20 minutes.

Note: To make sour milk, add 1 tablespoon vinegar to 1 cup minus 1 tablespoon milk. Let sit 10 minutes.

TOPPING

½ cup sugar	1 tablespoon melted butter
½ teaspoon cinnamon	

Combine ingredients and sprinkle over warm bread.

Yield: 2 loaves
Preparation time: 30 minutes
Baking time: 45 minutes
Easy

Jeanne and Larry Anderson

To make herb butters, mix 2 tablespoons dried herbs to ½ cup of softened butter. Blend thoroughly. Freeze for easy availability.

Eggs, Cheese, Pasta and Vegetarian Dishes

Italian Buffet

Antipasto Salad
Baked Minestrone
(served in mugs)
Crusty Italian Bread
Green and White Lasagna Swirls
Stuffed Tomatoes
Neapolitan Ice Cream Pie

Wine Suggestion
Rose' such as
Rivera from Italy (1981)

Mexican Dinner

Sangria
Taco Chip Dip
Tortilla Chips
Mexi-Chili Casserole
Fresh Green Beans
Mexican Spoon Bread
Fake Flan

Wine Suggestions
Ideally a Mexican Beer
such as Carta Blanca
But if you insist on
a wine, a simple
California red such as
Heitz Grignolino (1978)

EGGS ROYALE

Perfect for a party brunch

1	pound Canadian bacon or ham cut into julienne strips	½	cup butter
		3	dozen eggs, well beaten
1½	cups condensed mushroom soup	½	pound shredded sharp Cheddar cheese
1	6-ounce can evaporated milk		

Cook the bacon until lightly browned and place in a 9x13-inch baking dish. Combine the mushroom soup with the milk and blend well. In a large frying pan, melt the butter. Add the eggs and scramble until soft but not runny. Let cool, then pour a layer of eggs over the bacon. Pour some of the sauce mixture over the eggs. Repeat the layers until sauce and eggs are used up. Sprinkle top with the grated cheese. Bake in a 350-degree oven for 30 minutes.

Serves 12-15
Preparation time: 30 minutes
Cooking time: 30 minutes

Helen W. Milliken
Former First Lady of Michigan

BAKED EGGS

Can be made the day before and refrigerated — great for brunch

2½	cups bread cubes	½	cup grated Parmesan cheese
2	cups milk	½	pound Swiss cheese, sliced
12	eggs	½	cup dry bread crumbs
	Seasoned salt	1	pound bacon, fried, drained and crumbled
	Pepper		
1	green pepper, chopped	1	stick butter, melted
2	small onions, chopped		

Preheat oven to 400 degrees.
Soak the bread in milk for 10 minutes. Drain milk off, and reserve. Beat eggs slightly, add the reserved milk, salt and pepper to taste, chopped pepper, onions and Parmesan cheese; mix well. Add the bread cubes, mix and pour into a greased 9x13-inch baking dish. Cover with slices of Swiss cheese.
Toss the bread crumbs and bacon with the melted butter and sprinkle on top of casserole. Bake for 15 minutes.

Serves 8
Preparation time: 30 minutes
Baking time: 15 minutes

Marlynn Barnes

DEVILED EGG BAKE

6   eggs, hard cooked and
    shelled
¼   cup mayonnaise or salad
    dressing
2   tablespoons prepared
    mustard
¼   teaspoon salt

1   6½-ounce can tuna, drained
    and flaked
1   can condensed cream of
    shrimp soup
½   cup milk
4   cups hot cooked rice

Halves eggs lengthwise. Remove the yolks and mash in a small bowl. Add mayonnaise, mustard and salt; mix well. Stuff the egg whites with yolk mixture.

In a medium saucepan combine the tuna, soup and milk. Heat, stirring constantly, just until bubbly.

Line a 6-cup shallow casserole with rice. Arrange the stuffed eggs on the rice and spoon tuna sauce over. Bake in a 350-degree oven for 15 minutes or until hot and bubbling.

Note: To double the recipe, use one can cream of shrimp soup and one can of cream of mushroom soup.

Serves 4

Carol and Fergus McWilliam
DSO

SABTAH'S SPINACH OMELET

A great way to use up a lot of odds and ends in the refrigerator

½   pound spinach or Swiss
    chard, stalks removed
8   eggs, beaten
½   pound Monterey Jack,
    Colby or combination of
    cheeses, grated
3   cloves of garlic, minced

¼   cup butter
Pita bread
Tahini
Sliced tomatoes
Optional: grated Parmesan
    cheese added with other
    cheeses

Wash spinach or chard. Remove large stems and cut into strips about ½ inch wide. Parboil for 1 minute, drain and rinse with cold water. Squeeze out excess water.

Combine the eggs, cheese and garlic in a large mixing bowl. Add the spinach; mix thoroughly. Melt the butter in a large non-stick pan. Add the egg mixture and cook over medium heat until it is firm throughout, about 25 minutes. Top should not be runny. Carefully tilt pan let omelet slide out onto a plate. Return omelet to pan to lightly brown the other side then remove to a serving plate.
Serve immediately with pita cut into fourths, Tahini sauce, and sliced tomatoes.

Serves 4-5
Preparation time: 15 minutes   Liz and Shaul Ben-Meir
Cooking time: 30 minutes   DSO

FINNISH PANCAKES

A delicious and delightful brunch dish

5	jumbo eggs	1	cup flour
1	cup milk	¼	teaspoon salt
¼	cup orange juice	½	cup sweet butter
½	cup sugar		Powdered sugar

Preheat oven to 425 degrees.
Place all ingredients, except the butter and powdered sugar, in the container of a blender or a food processor fitted with the steel blade. Process until well blended. Place the butter in a 9x13-inch baking dish and put in the oven until butter is sizzling but not brown. Remove the baking dish and pour batter into the sizzling butter. Bake in the middle of the oven for 20 minutes or until puffed and browned. Remove from oven and sprinkle with powdered sugar.
Note: Batter can be made in advance and refrigerated.

Serves 6-8
Preparation time: 5 minutes
Baking time: 20 minutes
Easy   Elizabeth Johnson

CHEESE FONDUE CASSEROLE

Great brunch dish!

8	slices stale bread	1	teaspoon brown sugar
¼	cup butter, softened	¼	teaspoon paprika
1½	pounds Cheddar cheese, grated	½	teaspoon dry mustard
6	eggs, beaten	2	green onions, finely minced
2½	cups milk		Salt and pepper to taste

Cut crust from the bread. Butter one side and cut into squares. In a 13x9-inch baking dish, arrange bread and cheese in layers, ending with cheese. Mix remaining ingredients; pour over bread and cheese. Refrigerate for 24 hours.

Two hours before serving, remove dish from the refrigerator. Let stand at room temperature 1 hour. Preheat oven to 300 degrees. Place baking dish in a pan of hot water; bake for 1 hour.

Serves 6-8
Preparation time: 25 minutes
Refrigerate overnight
Baking time: 1 hour
Easy

Whitney Jill Sale

BLINTZ SOUFFLE

Easy to prepare and excellent for brunch

12	blintzes, homemade or commercially prepared	1	teaspoon vanilla
4	eggs	1	stick butter, melted
½	cup sugar	1¼	cups sour cream
		¼	cup orange juice

Preheat oven to 350 degrees.

Place blintzes in a single layer in a buttered baking dish. Beat the eggs thoroughly. Combine the remaining ingredients and add to the egg mixture; pour over the blintzes. Bake for 45 minutes.

Rita Weinfeld

MEXICAN CHEESE STRATA

Serve hot after a day on the slopes

4 cups nacho cheese tortilla
   chips, coarsely broken
2 cups shredded Monterey
   Jack cheese
6 eggs, beaten
2½ cups milk
1 4-ounce can green chilies,
   drained and chopped

½ cup chopped onion
¼ cup ketchup
½ teaspoon salt
3-4 drops Tabasco sauce
Whole tortilla chips

Sprinkle the broken tortilla chips over the bottom of a greased 11x7-inch baking dish. Sprinkle with the cheese. In a medium bowl, combine the eggs, milk, chilies, onion, ketchup and seasonings. Mix well and pour over the cheese. Cover and refrigerate for 2-3 hours or overnight.

One hour before serving, remove from refrigerator. Bake, uncovered, in a 325-degree oven for 50 minutes or until set. Garnish with remaining chips.

Serves 4
Preparation time: 15 minutes
Chill
Baking time: 50 minutes
Easy   Marilyn Shuler

"To invite a person to your house is to take charge of his happiness as long as he is beneath your roof."

Brillat-Savarin

BAKED CHEESE SOUFFLE

Terrific for a large crowd

8	slices bread, crust removed	½	teaspoon dry mustard
1¼	pounds shredded sharp	½	teaspoon cayenne pepper
	Cheddar cheese	½	teaspoon salt
6	large eggs, well beaten	1½	cups milk
1	teaspoon minced onion	1½	cups Half & Half

Butter a 9x13-inch baking dish. Cut the bread into cubes and scatter over the bottom of the buttered dish. Sprinkle the cheese on top. Combine the remaining ingredients, mix well, and pour over the cheese. Refrigerate overnight.

Thirty minutes before cooking, remove from refrigerator. Bake in a preheated 350-degree oven for 1 hour.

Note: For variety, add shrimp, ham or chicken.

Serves 10-12
Preparation time: 10 minutes
Baking time: 1 hour
Easy   Elizabeth Johnson

CHEESE FONDUE

Use as a dip for ham, salami, bread, or fresh vegetables

1	clove garlic, cut in half	6	ounces beer
8	ounces sharp Cheddar		Dash of Tabasco sauce
	cheese, shredded	2	tablespoons flour
8	ounces Swiss cheese,	½	teaspoon salt
	shredded	¼	teaspoon pepper

Wipe the inside of the top part of a double boiler with the cut side of garlic clove. Add the cheeses and melt over simmering water. Add the beer, Tabasco, flour, salt and pepper. Heat thoroughly.

Serves 10
Preparation time: 15 minutes   Victoria King
Easy   DSO

CRUSTLESS QUICHE

4	eggs	¼	cup milk or Half and Half
½	pound Jarlsberg cheese, grated	½	teaspoon oregano
		½	teaspoon basil

Preheat oven to 325 degrees.

Beat the eggs. Add the cheese, milk and seasonings. Pour into a well-greased baking dish. Bake, covered, until set, 30-40 minutes.

Variation: Add 1 cup crabmeat, shrimp or chopped fresh tomato before baking.

Serves 2-3
Preparation time: 10 minutes
Baking time: 40 minutes
Easy

Ellen Cale

STRAW AND HAY

Green and white pasta with prosciutto in cream sauce

¼	cup butter	½	cup freshly grated Parmesan cheese
2	tablespoons olive oil		
3	tablespoons chopped onion	2	tablespoons salt
4-6	cloves garlic, chopped	1	tablespoon vegetable oil
6	ounces prosciutto, cut in thin strips	½	pound fresh spinach fettuccine
1	cup creme fraiche	½	pound fresh egg fettuccine
1	cup frozen baby peas, defrosted in hot water		Additional freshly grated Parmesan cheese

In a heavy skillet melt the butter with the olive oil. Add the onion and garlic and sauté until onion is softened. Add the prosciutto and cook until heated. Stir in the creme fraiche and cook, stirring, until mixture is hot and reduced slightly. Add the peas and cook until hot. Remove from heat and stir in the cheese; cover.

In a large kettle, heat 6 quarts of water to boiling. Add the salt and vegetable oil. Stir in the pasta and boil for 2-6 minutes or until al dente. Taste often to make sure pasta does not get overcooked. Drain and toss with the hot sauce. Transfer to a heated platter; serve with additional cheese.

Preparation time: 20 minutes
Easy

Juliette Jonna
"The Merchant of Vino"

GREEN AND WHITE LASAGNE SWIRLS

A great, make-ahead, crowd pleaser

TOMATO-MEAT SAUCE

2	large onions, chopped	1	16-ounce can tomato sauce
3	cloves garlic, minced	1	cup red wine
3	tablespoons oil	1	teaspoon each: basil,
1½	pounds ground beef		oregano, Italian herb
1	pound Italian sausage		seasoning, salt and freshly
1	29-ounce can Italian plum		ground pepper
	tomatoes	½	teaspoon sugar

In a large kettle, sauté the onions and garlic in the oil. In a separate skillet, cook the ground beef and sausage until browned. Drain well, chop into small pieces then add to the onion-garlic mixture. Puree the tomatoes, then add, with the liquid, to the onions. Add remaining ingredients and bring to a boil. Reduce heat and simmer for 2 hours, stirring frequently. Taste for seasoning.

PASTA FILLING

1½	15-ounce containers ricotta cheese	3	eggs
1½	cups grated Parmesan cheese	1½	teaspoons fines herbes
			Freshly ground pepper to taste
1	10-ounce package frozen spinach, thawed and well drained		

Combine all ingredients and blend thoroughly.

ASSEMBLY

½	pound green lasagne noodles	1	pound shredded Mozzarella cheese
½	pound egg lasagne noodles		Grated Parmesan cheese

Cook the noodles according to package directions. When done, drain and place in a pot of cool water.

Grease a 10x15-inch deep baking dish. Spoon a layer of meat sauce on the bottom of pan. Pat the noodles dry with paper toweling and lay out lengthwise on counter top. Spoon 1 generous tablespoon of filling down the center of each noodle; spread mixture evenly with a knife. Roll each noodle up lengthwise and place upright in the pan,

146

alternating the green and white noodles. Pour the remaining meat sauce over, filling the spaces between the noodles. Sprinkle a layer of Mozzarella cheese on top, then some grated fresh Parmesan. Bake in a 350-degree oven for 45-60 minutes, or until hot and bubbly.

Note: For smaller portions, make entire recipe, then place portions of 4 lasagna swirls in freezer-lock bags. Add desired amount of *cooled* meat sauce. When ready to serve, microwave for 7-8 minutes or remove from plastic bag and heat in a 350-degree conventional oven for 30-40 minutes.

Serves 12
Preparation time: 2 hours
Freezes well

Gayle H. Burstein

PASGHETTI PIZZA

PASGHETTI

1	16-ounce package spaghetti	1	cup shredded Mozzarella cheese
2	eggs		
½	cup milk	¾	teaspoon garlic powder
		½	teaspoon salt

Break spaghetti into 2-inch pieces. In a large saucepan, cook according to package directions; drain and cool. Preheat oven to 400 degrees. In a large bowl beat the eggs lightly. Stir in the milk, cheese, garlic powder and salt. Add the cooked spaghetti and stir until thoroughly combined.

Grease a 10x15-inch jelly roll pan and spread the spaghetti in the pan. Bake for 15 minutes; remove from oven and reduce temperature to 350 degrees.

TOPPING

2	1-pound jars spaghetti sauce	3	cups shredded Mozzarella cheese
1½	teaspoons oregano	1	3½-ounce package pepperoni, sliced

Spread spaghetti sauce evenly over the spaghetti. Sprinkle with oregano, then the cheese; top with pepperoni. Return to oven and bake for 30 minutes longer. Let stand at room temperature for 5 minutes before cutting.

Serves 6-8
Preparation time: 30 minutes
Easy

Elaine Harris

SPAGHETTI SAUCE WITH MEATBALLS

Serve hot over freshly cooked spaghetti

SAUCE

¼	cup vegetable oil	½	teaspoon salt
½	cup chopped onions	½	teaspoon pepper
1	clove garlic, minced	½	teaspoon oregano
1	28-ounce can tomato sauce	½	teaspoon basil
1	15-ounce can tomato puree	2	small bay leaves
1	18-ounce can tomato paste	½	cup Parmesan cheese
1	28-ounce can water		

Heat oil in large pot; sauté onions and garlic until golden. Add remaining sauce ingredients and simmer, stirring occasionally, while making meatballs.

Makes about 3 quarts

MEATBALLS

1½	cups bread crumbs	½	teaspoon basil
¼	cup chopped onion	½	teaspoon oregano
1	clove garlic, minced	½	teaspoon pepper
¼	cup Parmesan cheese	3	eggs
2	teaspoons salt	2	pounds ground beef
¼	cup chopped parsley		

Combine ingredients and shape into balls. Add to sauce, cover and cook 3-4 hours, or until sauce is thick. If desired, some Italian sausage may be added at this time.

Serves 6
Preparation time: 45 minutes
Cooking time: 3-4 hours
Prepare ahead
Freezes well

Linda Williamson

SAUCES — Puree any leftover soup to use as a base for a gravy or sauce.

LASAGNA

¼	cup olive oil	½	cup water
1	large onion, chopped	1	pound ground round
2	cloves garlic, minced	1	pound lasagna noodles
6	sprigs parsley, minced	1	stick pepperoni, sliced
3½	cups tomato sauce	¾	cup Parmesan cheese, grated
1	6-ounce can tomato paste		
2	bay leaves	1	pound Ricotta cheese
1	teaspoon salt	1	pound Mozzarella cheese, grated
Pepper to taste			

Heat the oil in a large skillet. Sauté the onion, garlic and parsley until the onion is soft. Add the tomato sauce, tomato paste, bay leaves, salt, pepper and water; stir until well blended. In a separate skillet brown the beef, drain and add to sauce. Cover and cook for 1 hour over low heat.

Cook the noodles al dente. In a 9x13-inch baking dish, alternate noodles, sauce, pepperoni and cheeses in layers ending with Mozzarella cheese on top.

Bake in 350-degree oven for 45 minutes or until hot and bubbly.

Serves 8-10
Preparation time: 45 minutes
Baking time: 45 minutes
Freezes well
Easy   Nicette Watkinson

PASTA WITH CARBONARA SAUCE

¼	pound mild Italian sausage	½	cup parsley
¼	pound thinly sliced cooked ham	3	eggs, well beaten
½	pound hot cooked spaghetti	½	cup grated Parmesan cheese
¼	cup butter	Freshly ground black pepper to taste	

Crumble the sausage and chop the ham. Brown over low heat for 10 minutes, then drain well. Add the spaghetti, butter and parsley and toss until heated through. Add the eggs, cheese and pepper and toss lightly. Serve at once.

Serves 2
Preparation time: 15 minutes
Easy   Terry Gladstone

NUTTY MACARONI AND CHEESE

1	8-ounce package rigatoni, cooked and drained	1	pound creamed cottage cheese
4	tablespoons butter, divided	1	cup sour cream
⅓	cup pitted black olives, chopped	½	cup milk
1	4-ounce jar pimento, chopped		Tabasco sauce and salt to taste
		¼	cup chopped walnuts
Pepper to taste		¾	cup bread crumbs
		¼	cup chopped parsley

Preheat oven to 350 degrees.

In a saucepan melt 3 tablespoons butter. Add the olives, pimento, rigatoni and pepper and toss lightly. Place in a baking dish. Mix the cottage cheese, sour cream, milk, Tabasco sauce and salt. Pour over the rigatoni. Sauté the walnuts and bread crumbs in remaining tablespoon butter until lightly browned. Spread on top of casserole and sprinkle with parsley. Bake 30 minutes.

Serves 6
Preparation time: 20 minutes
Baking time: 30 minutes
Freezes well

Mrs. Henry Ford II

FETTUCINE ALFREDO

Max is well known as one of the great chefs in the Orchestra

1	pound fettucine noodles	1¼	cups unsalted butter, softened
¾	cup heavy cream		Freshly grated nutmeg
1	egg yolk		White pepper
2	cups freshly grated Parmesan cheese		Salt

Cook noodles according to package directions. Place the noodles in a hot serving dish over low heat. Combine cream and egg yolk with a whisk. Add the cheese, butter and cream mixture to noodles, tossing gently. Season with nutmeg, pepper and salt to taste. Serve immediately.

Serves 3-5
Preparation time: 30 minutes
Easy

Maxim Janowsky
DSO

PASTA WITH RICOTTA

2 pounds fresh spinach
1 pound fresh Ricotta cheese
3 eggs, lightly beaten
⅔ cup grated Parmesan cheese
⅓ cup parsley
2 teaspoons salt
½ teaspoon pepper

1 recipe Marinara sauce (see page 155)
1 pound tube type pasta, macaroncelli or elbow macaroni
Parmesan cheese

Preheat oven to 375 degrees.

Rinse spinach well and discard tough stems. Place the spinach in a large saucepan, cover tightly, and cook briefly in the water that clings to the leaves. Cook until leaves are just wilted. Drain well and chop. Combine the spinach, Ricotta, eggs, ⅔ cup Parmesan cheese, parsley, salt and pepper and Marinara sauce; blend well.

In a kettle, bring a large amount of water to a boil. Add the pasta and cook, stirring, for 2 minutes; drain. Add pasta to the Ricotta mixture. Pour into a 2-quart casserole or baking dish and bake 25-30 minutes or until pasta is tender but not mushy. Serve with additional grated Parmesan cheese.

Serves 6-8   Margie Barquist

TINY SHELLS WITH CLAM SAUCE

1 egg
1 cup cream or Half & Half
¾ cup Parmesan cheese
¼ cup chopped fresh parsley
1 8-ounce can minced clams, drained, reserving juice

1 pound cooked tiny egg noodle shells
2 tablespoons butter
½ teaspoon oregano
Garlic salt
White pepper

In a bowl, combine the egg, cream, Parmesan cheese, parsley and reserved juice from clams. Cook the noodles according to package directions, drain and toss with the egg mixture. In a small saucepan melt the butter. Add the oregano and garlic salt and pepper to taste. Add the drained clams and cook until hot. Toss with the shells and serve immediately.

Serves 4
Preparation time: 20 minutes
Easy   Rho Blanchard

MUSHROOM-SPINACH PASTA

Vegetarian's delight

2 cups cream-style cottage cheese
6 ounces cream cheese, softened
2 tablespoons butter
½ cup finely chopped onion
½ pound fresh mushrooms, sliced
⅓ cup dry white wine
½ teaspoon dried thyme, crushed

¼ teaspoon salt
Dash pepper
1 6½-ounce can evaporated milk
1 10-ounce package frozen chopped spinach, cooked and well drained
10 ounces spaghetti, cooked and drained
Grated Parmesan cheese

With an electric mixer, beat the cottage cheese and cream cheese until nearly smooth. Melt the butter in a saucepan and cook the onion and mushrooms until tender. Add the wine, thyme, salt and pepper. Stir in the cheese mixture, milk and spinach; heat thoroughly. Place the hot spaghetti on a large platter; top with the sauce and toss gently. Serve with the grated cheese.

Serves 6
Preparation time: 20 minutes
Easy   Chris Considine

PASTA CON PESTO

This sauce is also excellent with zucchini and other summer squashes

PASTA
2-3 cups flour (all-purpose or semolina pasta flour)
Salt

1 tablespoon olive oil
3 eggs
1 egg yolk

Put 2 cups flour in the bowl of a food processor fitted with the steel blade. Combine remaining ingredients with a fork and add to bowl. Process until dough forms a sticky mass. Add more flour until dough is firm and refuses to "take" any more flour. Knead briefly on a lightly floured board. Let rest, covered with an overturned bowl, for 10-20 minutes before rolling through a pasta machine.

After rolling, let sheets rest on a floured counter or hung over the back of a chair for an additional 20 minutes before cutting.

PESTO

2 cups fresh basil leaves, firmly packed	1 cup grated Parmesan cheese
6 tablespoons pine nuts	1 cup olive oil, divided
4 cloves garlic, minced	Salt and freshly ground pepper

Place basil, pine nuts, garlic and cheese in blender for a food processor fitted with the steel blade. Add ½ cup olive oil and blend to a smooth paste. Slowly drizzle in the remaining oil. Season to taste with salt and pepper. Serve over hot, freshly cooked pasta.

Makes 4½ cups   Marian Impastato

PASTA PRIMAVERA

---

1 pound fettucine or linguine	2 medium carrots, thinly shaved
2 tablespoons olive oil	1 medium sweet red pepper, thinly sliced
1 pound broccoli cut into bite-size pieces	4-6 cloves garlic, minced
3 medium zucchini, unpeeled, thinly sliced	¼ cup chopped parsley
½ pound fresh pea pods, cut into bite-size pieces	2 tablespoons dried basil
	⅓ cup olive oil
	Freshly grated Parmesan cheese

Bring a large pot of water to a boil. Cook pasta according to package directions. In a large skillet, heat the 2 tablespoons of olive oil over medium heat. Add the broccoli, zucchini and pea pods. Stir to coat lightly with the oil, then cover and steam for 5 minutes. Uncover and add the carrots, pepper, garlic, parsley and basil. Replace the cover and continue to cook until the vegetables are crisp-cooked. Drain the pasta and toss with the olive oil. Add to the vegetables and toss gently. Serve immediately with Parmesan cheese.

Serves 4   Benedicta Gray-Sorton
Preparation time: 30 minutes   DSO

HARVEST SPAGHETTI

1   28-ounce can whole
    tomatoes
1   15-ounce can tomato sauce
4   ounces mushrooms, sliced
3   medium zucchini cut into
    cubes
2   medium stalks celery,
    chopped
3   tablespoons minced onion

2   teaspoons dried marjoram
1   teaspoon sugar
¾   teaspoon salt
¼   teaspoon garlic salt
½   cup grated Parmesan cheese,
    divided
8   ounces spaghetti
    Additional grated Parmesan
    cheese

In a Dutch oven, combine all ingredients except cheese and spaghetti. Heat to boiling, reduce heat and simmer 45 minutes, stirring occasionally. Add ¼ cup of the cheese.

Cook spaghetti according to package directions and drain. Remove to a platter and cover with the tomato-zucchini sauce. Sprinkle with the remaining cheese and garnish with parsley, if desired. Serve with additional cheese.

Serves 4
Preparation time: 20 minutes
Cooking time: 1 hour
Easy   Carmella Gusfa

TUNA SAUCE FOR PASTA

Easy to prepare

4   cloves garlic, minced
2   tablespoons olive oil
1   28-ounce can crushed
    tomatoes
1   8-ounce can tomato sauce
4   6½-ounce cans tuna, drained

Dash oregano
Chopped fresh parsley
Chopped fresh basil
3   drops Tabasco sauce, or
    to taste
¼   teaspoon crushed red pepper

In a large saucepan sauté the garlic in the oil. Add remaining ingredients and simmer for 1 hour. Serve with linguine.

Makes about 8 cups sauce   Judy and Stephen Molina
                                                              DSO

MARINARA SAUCE

¼ cup olive oil
2 cups chopped onion
1 small carrot, sliced
2 cloves garlic, minced
4 cups canned Italian plum
  tomatoes

Salt and pepper
¼ cup butter
1 teaspoon dried oregano
1 teaspoon dried basil

Heat the oil in a large skillet. Add the onion, carrot and garlic. Cook, stirring, until golden. Strain the tomatoes and discard the seeds. Add the tomatoes and salt and pepper to taste. Partially cover; simmer for 15 minutes. Put sauce through a sieve, pushing solids through with a spoon. Return to skillet and add remaining ingredients. Partially cover; simmer for 30 minutes.

Makes 3-4 cups   Margie Barquist

For smaller amounts of tomato paste; drop by the tablespoon onto a cookie sheet and place in freezer. When frozen, transfer to a plastic bag, seal well and return to freezer.

155

T.J.'S TEX-MEX LENTIL BURGER

2 cups dried lentils
⅓ cup chopped onion
⅓ cup olive oil
½ teaspoon salt
½ teaspoon pepper
½ cup breadcrumbs
½ cup wheatgerm
3 cups breadcrumbs, for coating

Vegetable oil
12 hamburger buns
T.J.'s Guacamole (see recipe below)
Grated hot pepper cheese
Alfalfa sprouts
2 tomatoes, thinly sliced

Wash the lentils, cover with water and cook until soft. Drain off excess water. Add the onion, olive oil, salt, pepper, ½ cup breadcrumbs and the wheatgerm. Mix thoroughly and form into 12 patties. Coat patties with the remaining breadcrumbs and chill for 1 hour. Fry the burgers in a small amount of vegetable oil until browned on both sides. Toast the hamburger buns, then assemble sandwich. Place the burger on the toasted bun, spread with guacomole, sprinkle with cheese and sprouts then top with a slice of tomato.

Serves 12

Traffic Jam and Snug
Second and Canfield
Detroit, Michigan

T.J.'S GUACAMOLE

6 ripe avocados, peeled and chopped
1 1-pound can tomatoes, drained and chopped
1 onion, chopped
¼ cup mayonnaise
¼ cup sour cream

Juice of 1 lime
2 teaspoons cumin
1 tablespoon chili powder
½ teaspoon salt
¼ teaspoon pepper
⅛ teaspoon hot sauce

Mash the avocados with a fork or in a food processor (do not puree). Combine with remaining ingredients and chill.

Makes 5 cups

Traffic Jam and Snug
Second and Canfield
Detroit, Michigan

MEATLESS MOUSSAKA

2 medium eggplants	1 cup water
2 large onions, chopped	Salt and pepper to taste
1 clove garlic, minced	2 zucchini, thinly sliced
¼ cup oil	2 cups thinly sliced boiled
Additional oil for frying	potatoes
1 cup tomato sauce	¼ cup chopped parsley

Slice the eggplants and let stand in a bowl of salted water for 30 minutes. Combine the onion and garlic and cook in ¼ cup oil until tender. Add the tomato sauce and water and cook for 15 minutes. Season with salt and pepper.

Remove eggplant slices from the water and gently squeeze out excess liquid. Fry in oil as needed until lightly browned; drain on paper towels. Sauté the zucchini until lightly browned and drain.

In a large baking dish, alternate layers of potato, vegetables and tomato sauce. Sprinkle with parsley. Bake in a 400-degree oven for 20 minutes.

Serves 8

Traffic Jam and Snug
Second and Canfield
Detroit, Michigan

TOMATO-CHEESE QUICHE

3-4 ripe tomatoes	Additional freshly ground
Salt and freshly ground pepper	pepper
Olive oil	1 teaspoon dried basil
¾ pound shredded Gruyere or	¼ cup grated Parmesan cheese
Jarlsberg cheese	3 tablespoons butter, melted
1 9-inch quiche crust, baked	
for 10 minutes	

Slice the tomatoes and sprinkle generously with salt, pepper and olive oil. Let stand for ½ hour, turning often, then drain.

Preheat oven to 375 degrees. Sprinkle cheese in bottom of the crust. Place tomato slices on top, sprinkle with pepper, basil and the Parmesan cheese. Drizzle the melted butter over. Bake in upper third of oven for 25 minutes or until lightly browned.

Serves 4-6
Preparation time: 20 minutes
Baking time: 25 minutes
Easy

Brenda Pangborn
DSO

NOODLES ZUIDER ZEE

2 pounds mild or hot bulk sausage	½ cup water
1 small head cabbage, shredded	1 teaspoon salt
	Dash pepper
2 red apples, diced	8 ounces medium egg noodles

In a large skillet, brown the sausage, breaking into small pieces. Pour off excess fat. Add the cabbage, apples, water, and salt and pepper to taste. Cover and simmer until cabbage is just crisp-tender, 5-8 minutes. Meanwhile, cook the noodles according to package directions, then drain and add to the skillet. Mix well, cover, and heat for 1 minute.

Serves 4-6
Preparation time: 30 minutes
Easy

Mary Powanda

EASY RATATOUILLE PIE

1 cup zucchini	½ tablespoon basil
1 cup eggplant	½ tablespoon thyme
Salt	⅛ teaspoon pepper
¼ cup butter	1 cup shredded Monterey Jack cheese
½ cup chopped tomato	
½ cup chopped green pepper	¾ cup Bisquick mix
¼ cup chopped onion	1½ cups milk
1 medium clove garlic, crushed	¼ cup sour cream
¾ teaspoon salt	3 eggs

Cut the zucchini and eggplant into large dice, sprinkle with salt and let stand for 15 minutes. Lightly grease 10-inch pie plate. Heat oven to 400 degrees.

Drain the zucchini and eggplant and pat dry. Melt the butter in a large skillet. Sauté the vegetables and garlic over medium heat, stirring occasionally, until vegetables are crisp tender, 5-10 minutes. Stir in the seasonings and herbs. Spread mixture in a pie plate and sprinkle with cheese. Beat the Bisquick, milk, sour cream and eggs until smooth, about 15 seconds in blender or 1 minute with hand beater; pour over vegetables. Bake for 30 minutes or until a knife inserted between center and edge comes out clean.

Serves 6
Preparation time: 30 minutes
Baking time: 30 minutes
Can be made ahead and freezes well

Cathy Waring
DSO

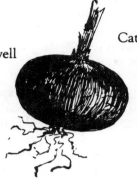

SPINACH PIE

Serve with a Greek salad and hot crusty bread

2	pounds fresh spinach, washed and trimmed	6	eggs, well beaten
1¼	pounds Feta cheese, crumbled	1½	cups butter
		½	cup vegetable oil
1	bunch green onions, chopped	1	pound phyllo dough

Steam the spinach for 5 minutes or until slightly wilted. Place in a large bowl. Add the Feta cheese and chopped onions and mix well. Mix in beaten eggs and set aside.

In a small pot heat the butter and oil until butter is melted. Unwrap phyllo, smooth out and keep covered with damp towels.

Generously grease the bottom and sides of a 9x13-inch baking pan. Brush one layer of dough with melted butter mixture and lay in pan, tucking overlap into sides. Continue this procedure using 8-10 pastry sheets. Place 2 unbuttered sheets on top, then spread spinach mixture over phyllo. Continue buttering and layering the remaining phyllo over the filling. Butter the top layer well and bake in a 350-degree oven for 50-60 minutes.

Freezes well

Sheila Pitcoff

EGGPLANT AND VEGETABLES ITALIAN

This goes especially well with rice or cous-cous

VEGETABLES

2 medium eggplants
1 recipe Italian tomato sauce (see recipe below)
2 large zucchini, unpeeled
½ cup olive oil

1 cup shredded Mozzarella cheese
1 1-pound bag frozen cut green beans, thawed
Grated Parmesan cheese

Peel the eggplant and slice into ¼-inch rounds. Sprinkle with salt and stack the slices on a plate weighted down on top. Let stand for ½ hour or longer to drain. Meanwhile, make the sauce. While sauce is simmering, wash and slice the zucchini ¼ inch thick; set aside. Coat the eggplant slices with olive oil and place ½ of the eggplant slices in the bottom of a 9x13-inch baking dish. Cover with one fourth of the sauce, then add a layer of zucchini and another fourth of the sauce. Sprinkle on the Mozzarella cheese, and place the beans on top. Add half of the remaining sauce, the remaining eggplant slices, then pour on the rest of the sauce. Sprinkle generously with grated Parmesan cheese and bake in a 350-degree oven for 1½ hours or until vegetables are cooked. Let stand for 10 minutes before serving.

TOMATO SAUCE

¼ cup olive oil
1 small onion, chopped
2 cloves garlic, crushed
1 28-ounce can tomatoes
1 12-ounce can tomato paste

2¼ cups water
1 tablespoon oregano
1 tablespoon basil
1 tablespoon thyme
1 tablespoon salt
¼ cup red wine

In a 2-quart saucepan, heat the oil. Sauté the onion until light brown. Add the garlic and cook for 30 seconds. Stir in the tomatoes, tomato paste and water. Add the herbs, salt and wine. Cook over very low heat, stirring occasionally, until thick.

Serves 6-8

Fay Ann Resnick
DSO

VEGETARIAN CHILI

1½   cups sliced carrots
1½   cups green pepper strips
1½   cups sliced celery
½   cup vegetable oil
1   15-ounce can stewed tomatoes
1   15-ounce can tomato puree
1   cup tomato juice
2   1-pound cans kidney beans, drained
1   1-pound can garbanzo beans
2   large cloves garlic, minced
3   tablespoons chili powder
1   teaspoon sugar
½   teaspoon hot sauce
1   teaspoon pepper
Optional: Sour cream, grated cheese, chopped onions for garnish

Sauté the vegetables in the oil until barely tender. In a separate pot combine the remaining ingredients and bring to a boil. Simmer for 10 minutes, then add the vegetables and simmer until vegetables are heated through. Garnish if desired, and serve immediately.

Yield: 3 quarts
Preparation time: 45 minutes
Easy   Janet Monroe

COTTAGE CHEESE LOAF

An unusual recipe that will delight vegetarians

1   large onion, chopped
½   cup butter
3   packages brown seasoning and broth mix
5   eggs, beaten
4   cups small-curd cottage cheese
1   cup chopped walnuts or pecans
4   cups Special K cereal

In a skillet, sauté the onion in the butter. Add the seasoning mix and set aside. In a large bowl, combine remaining ingredients and mix well. Blend in the onion mixture and combine thoroughly. Transfer into a large greased loaf pan and bake in a 350-degree oven for 1 hour. Remove from oven, let cool, then chill. Serve cold.

Preparation time: 20 minutes
Baking time: 1 hour
Easy   Jay Ann Ghent

MILLET, MEDITERRANEAN STYLE

3 cups water
1 cup millet
1 tablespoon olive oil
½ teaspoon salt
1 6-ounce can tomato paste

2 ounces black olives
1 teaspoon basil
Grated Parmesan or Romano cheese

Place the water and millet in a large saucepan and bring to a boil. Add the olive oil and salt and reduce heat to low. Cover and cook for 10-12 minutes until the millet is cooked but the water is not completely absorbed. Stir in the tomato paste, olives and basil and simmer uncovered for 1-2 minutes. Sprinkle with grated cheese.

Serves 4   Barry Shapiro
Preparation time: 20 minutes   DSO

VINE LEAVES WITH CRACKED WHEAT STUFFING

These can also be served as an appetizer

1 cup olive oil, divided
½ pound onions, chopped
½ cup cracked wheat (Bulgur)
1 6-ounce can tomato paste
3 tablespoons pine nuts
3 tablespoons seedless raisins
Salt and allspice to taste
Juice of 2 lemons

3 tablespoons chopped parsley
3 tablespoons chopped celery
½ pound preserved vine leaves or 24 fresh leaves
1 cup fresh lemon juice
1½ cups water

Heat ¼ cup oil in a skillet. Add the onions and sauté until softened and golden. Wash and drain the cracked wheat and add to the pan. Add the tomato paste, pine nuts, raisins, salt, allspice, lemon juice, parsley and celery and mix well.

Soak the leaves in cold water for 1 minute. Gently separate and lay on a wire rack to drain. If using fresh leaves, blanch them for 3 minutes in boiling water, then drain.

Place a heaping teaspoon of the wheat mixture in the center of each leaf, then roll up *loosely* into a cigar shape — be sure to leave enough room for the wheat to swell. Put the unused leaves in the bottom of a pan and lay the filled leaves on top. Combine the remaining olive oil, the cup of lemon juice and the water. Mix well and pour over the stuffed leaves. Press a plate on top to flatten rolls down lightly. Cover pan, bring to a boil, and simmer gently for 45 minutes. Leave in the pan to cool.

Juliette Jonna
The Merchant of Vino

CURRIED VEGETABLES WITH BROWN RICE

This is delicious hot or cold

2 tablespoons vegetable oil
1 onion, coarsely chopped
1 teaspoon salt, or to taste
1 tablespoon curry powder, or to taste
Freshly ground pepper
½ teaspoon cumin
½ bay leaf
¼ cup water
2 medium carrots, thickly sliced on the diagonal
⅔ small butternut squash, skin removed, cut into 1-inch pieces

½ small cauliflower, separated into florets
½ pound broccoli florets, separated
½ pound green beans, cut in 1-inch pieces
1 red pepper, cut in large chunks
6 cups brown rice, made with seasoned liquid and minced onion
1 cup cashew nuts
1 cup raisins

Heat the oil in a Dutch oven. Add the onion and cook, stirring occasionally, until soft. Stir in the salt, curry, pepper, cumin, bay leaf, water, carrots, squash, cauliflower and broccoli. Cover and cook for 10 minutes or until vegetables are crisp tender. Uncover and remove the bay leaf. Add the green beans and red pepper and cook over medium heat until juices are reduced slightly.

Place the rice on bottom of a large, shallow serving dish. Scatter the vegetables over and sprinkle with cashews and raisins.

Serves 8-10

Brenda Pangborn
DSO

WHOLE WHEAT CREPES

3 eggs	½ cup unbleached white flour
1 cup milk	¼ cup whole wheat flour
2 tablespoons butter, melted	Melted butter for frying

Place all ingredients, except the butter for frying, in the container of a blender and mix until well blended. Refrigerate for 1 hour.

Place a crepe pan over medium heat. When hot, remove from heat and brush bottom with melted butter. Pour about ¼ cup batter in pan, tilting to spread batter, and pour off the excess. Return pan to heat and cook until sides are browned and curl slightly. Carefully turn out onto a towel, browned side up, to cool.

Repeat process to make remaining crepes. When cooled, stack with waxed paper between the crepes.

FILLING

½ cup minced onion	1 egg yolk, beaten
¼ cup butter	1 teaspoon salt
2 cups mashed potatoes	

Lightly brown the onions in the butter. Mix in the potatoes, egg yolk and salt. Spread 1 tablespoon of the filling on the browned side of a crepe. Roll up like a jelly roll, tuking in the sides. Repeat process with all crepes.

Heat a large skillet over medium heat. Coat with butter and fry blintzes until both sides are golden brown. Serve with sour cream, yogurt or applesauce.

Note: These can be made ahead and frozen cooked or uncooked.

Makes about 18   Florence Shulman

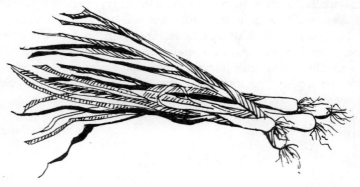

164

Fish
and
Shellfish

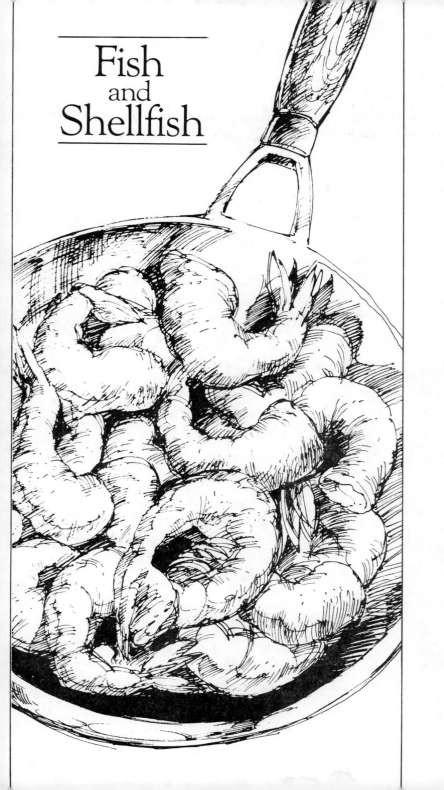

Intimate Dinner For Two

Bibb Lettuce with Tarragon Dressing
Stuffed Brook Trout
Wild Rice Pilaf
Fresh Steamed Brussel Sprouts
Papayas Tucker
Hart's Delight

Wine Suggestions
*A crisp, elegant dry white; such as
the Robert Mondavi Fume Blanc (1980)*

Cape Cod Dinner

Cape Cod Chowder
Steamed Whole Lobsters
Scalloped Corn and Tomatoes
Boiled New Potatoes
Indian Pudding

Wine Suggestions
*A rich, buttery dry white; such as
the Fisher Vineyards Chardonnay (1980)*

SAUMON DE MEAUX

Colorful

THE SALMON

4	¼-pound salmon fillets or steaks, skin removed	2	tablespoons French whole grain mustard
2	tablespoons sweet butter	1	recipe Tomato Beurre Blanc
Salt			
½	cup creme fraiche		

Butter a heavy baking sheet. Space out the four fillets and sprinkle lightly with salt. In a small bowl mix the creme fraiche (see method on page 31) with the mustard, blending well. Coat each portion of salmon with the mustard mixture and refrigerate until ready to broil. Preheat broiler. Set fish under the broiler for 5 minutes, or until the creme fraiche is glazed and dotted with brown. Top with Tomato Beurre Blanc.

TOMATO BEURRE BLANC

1	pound ripe tomatoes, blanched, peeled and seeded	2	tablespoons dry white wine
2	tablespoons olive oil	2	tablespoons white wine vinegar
⅛	teaspoon thyme	1½	tablespoons creme fraiche
Salt and pepper		½	cup cold sweet butter, cut in pieces
1	tablespoon finely chopped shallots		

Cut tomatoes in small cubes. Heat the oil in a skillet and add the tomatoes. Sauté over moderately high heat, stirring constantly, until thick and well-reduced, about 7-8 minutes. Add the thyme and season to taste with salt and pepper.

Place the shallots, wine and wine vinegar in a medium non-aluminum saucepan. Bring to a boil and cook until mixture is reduced to a glaze. Over medium-high heat, whisk in the creme fraiche and quickly reduce liquid to half. Add pieces of butter, one at a time, whisking constantly, moving the pan off and on the heat. When all the butter has been added and the mixture has become thick and fluffy, remove the pan from the heat. Pour the sauce into the tomato puree, adjust seasonings to taste and set sauce in a warm place until ready to serve.

Serves 4

Complete Cuisine, Ltd.
322 S. Main Street
Ann Arbor, Michigan

ORIENTAL TUNA

2   6½-ounce cans white meat tuna packed in oil
1   tablespoon butter
½   cup chopped onion
½   cup sliced water chestnuts
2   teaspoons minced gingerroot
2   cups sour cream
Salt and freshly ground pepper to taste
Cooked rice

Drain the oil from the tuna into a skillet. Add the butter and heat until butter is melted. Add the onion and sauté until soft. Break the tuna into large flakes and add to skillet. Stir in remaining ingredients and cook until just heated through. Serve over hot rice.

Serves 6
Preparation time: 15 minutes
Easy

Chuck Dyer

STUFFED BROOK TROUT A LA CHEF GENE

1   tablespoon chopped shallot
¼   cup King Crabmeat
3   raw shrimp, shelled and butterflied
½   cup Sherry
½   cup sliced raw mushrooms
2   tablespoons clarified butter
Salt and pepper to taste
1   10-ounce boneless whole Brook Trout
¼   cup heavy cream
Chopped parsley and lemon wedges for garnish

Preheat oven to 500 degrees.
In a bowl, combine the shallot, crabmeat, shrimp, Sherry, mushrooms, butter, salt and pepper. Mix well and stuff into the body of the trout. Mixture will be slightly mushy. Place fish into a well-buttered ovenproof sauté pan. Bake for 20 minutes.
Remove fish from the oven and place it on a platter. Add the cream to the pan in which the fish was cooked, stir and pour over the trout. Sprinkle with chopped parsley and serve with lemon wedges.

Serves 2
Preparation time: 15 minutes
Baking time: 20 minutes

Gene Ameriguian, Chef
Little Harry's Restaurant
Detroit, Michigan

SKUMBRIA

This is a MUST on the Scandinavian smorgasbord table

2 pounds fish filets — salmon, haddock, sole or 2 pounds canned salmon, drained	3 whole bay leaves
2 eggs, lightly beaten	3 whole cloves
Flour	10 peppercorns
¼ cup vegetable oil	¼ cup white vinegar
2 medium onions, coarsely chopped	¼ cup water
½ cup grated carrot	¾ cup ketchup
	2 teaspoons sugar
	½ teaspoon salt
	⅓ cup vegetable oil

Dip the fish filets into beaten eggs, then in flour. Sauté in oil until crisp then remove and let cool. If canned salmon is used, omit this step. Arrange the fish in serving dish in a single layer. In a saucepan combine the onions, carrots, bay leaves, cloves, peppercorns, vinegar and water and simmer for 10 minutes. Remove the peppercorns and add the ketchup, sugar, salt and oil. Heat to boiling then pour over the fish. Let cool then refrigerate for at least 12 hours.

Serves 4-6   Mall Kionka

IT'S BATTER, NO MATTER

This is a great batter for fish, chicken, oysters, onion rings, zucchini, mushrooms, etc.

¾ cup cornstarch	¼ teaspoon pepper
¼ cup flour	½ cup fresh ginger ale
1 teaspoon baking powder	1 egg, lightly beaten
½ teaspoon salt	

Combine the cornstarch, flour, baking powder, salt and pepper. Add the ginger ale and egg and stir until smooth.
Use as a coating for any deep-fried foods.
Note: Water or cold beer can be used instead of ginger ale.

Ken Pangborn

BAKED SALMON

Excellent served cold with home-made mayonnaise

1   whole salmon, head and tail   Salt
    removed and prepared for   Crushed red pepper
    baking   Thyme
Butter   Dry white wine

Rinse the fish and dry well. Line a pan with heavy duty foil, butter well and place fish on the buttered foil. Season the cavity of the fish with salt, red pepper and thyme to taste and stuff with 6-8 pats of butter. Pour in wine to depth of ⅛-inch. Fold foil loosely, but completely around the fish. Bake in a preheated 400-degree oven for 15 minutes per pound. After 40 minutes, reduce heat to 350 degrees, remove foil, and continue baking until done.

Preparation time: 15 minutes   Nicette Watkinson

SOLE ROLLS FLORENTINE

¼   cup butter   ½   cup grated Swiss cheese
2   tablespoons chopped onion   1   teaspoon salt
1   package frozen chopped   ¼   teaspoon Tabasco sauce
    spinach, cooked and   6   8-ounce pieces sole filet
    drained   1   can condensed cream of
2   tablespoons flour   mushroom soup
¼   cup wheat germ

Melt the butter. Add the onion and sauté until soft. Add the spinach, flour, wheat germ, cheese, salt and Tabasco and mix well. Divide filling between each fish filet and roll filet up. Place seam side down in one layer in a shallow casserole. Cover with soup. Bake in a 375-degree oven for 25 minutes or until hot and bubbly.

Serves 6
Preparation time: 20 minutes
Cooking time: 25 minutes
Easy   Martha Bowman

SALMON IN PASTRY EXCALIBUR

Worth the time

PASTRY

3	cups flour	⅛	teaspoon salt
¾	cup butter	2	teaspoons ice water

Combine the flour, butter and salt. Add ice water, mix and set aside.

FISH

½	cup butter	1	2½-pound tail-piece of
1	tablespoon raisins		salmon, skinned, filleted
1	tablespoon chopped		and cut in half lengthwise
	almonds	1	egg, beaten

Preheat oven to 425 degrees. Combine the butter, raisins and nuts. Spread half the mixture on one piece of fish; top with the other piece of fish and spread the remaining raisin-nut mixture on top. Roll out pastry large enough to enclose the fish completely and seal around fish. Make a few slashes on top for decoration and brush with the beaten egg. Bake for 35 minutes. While fish is baking, make sauce.

SAUCE

¼	cup butter	1	teaspoon flour
2	shallots, chopped	1¼	cups cream
1	teaspoon chopped	¼	cup dry white wine
	parsley		Salt and pepper
1	teaspoon fresh chervil or	1	teaspoon lemon juice
	½ teaspoon dried	1	teaspoon Dijon mustard
1	teaspoon fresh tarragon or	2	egg yolks
	½ teaspoon dried		

Melt butter in a medium saucepan. Add shallots, parsley, chervil and tarragon and cook until soft. Stir in the flour, cream and wine. Season with salt and pepper to taste; add lemon juice and mustard, and mix well. Beat in the egg yolks. Cook, stirring constantly, until hot. Do not boil or sauce will curdle. Serve over salmon.

Serves 6-8

Martin Wilk, Executive Chef
Excalibur Restaurant
Southfield, Michigan

COLD POACHED SALMON STEAKS
WITH MUSTARD SAUCE

SALMON

Water
1 tablespoon butter
2 tablespoons celery leaves, chopped
2 tablespoons fresh parsley, chopped

1 tablespoon chopped onion
¼ teaspoon thyme
¼ teaspoon marjoram
¼ teaspoon paprika
4-6 salmon steaks cut 1-1¼ inches thick

Fill a skillet ¾ full of water. Add the butter and remaining ingredients except the fish and bring to a gentle boil. using a spatula, carefully add the salmon steaks. Poach on one side approximately 4-5 minutes or until some red appears around center bone. Gently turn steaks over with the spatula and continue to poach for another 4-5 minutes. Remove steaks with slotted spoon, drain over pan and place on a platter. Chill in the refrigerator for 3 to 4 hours.
When cold, remove skin and bones. Serve with mustard sauce.

MUSTARD SAUCE

½ cup mayonnaise
½ teaspoon wine vinegar with garlic
1 teaspoon Dijon mustard
1 rounded teaspoon fresh parsley, chopped

1 rounded teaspoon finely chopped green onions
½ teaspoon mustard seed, crushed

Blend all the ingredients and chill 1-2 hours.

Serves 4-6
Preparation time: 20 minutes
Chill 3-4 hours   Dr. Reginald Zielinski

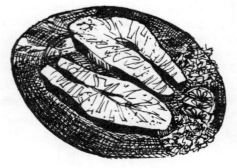

172

TUNA-SWISS QUICHE

A delightful way to serve tuna

2 7-ounce cans tuna, drained
   and flaked
1 cup shredded Swiss cheese
½ cup sliced green onions
1 9-inch pastry shell, baked and
   slightly cooled or 1 10-inch
   Potato Crust (recipe below)

3 eggs
1 cup mayonnaise
½ cup milk
Optional: ⅓ cup slivered
   almonds
Paprika

Preheat oven to 375 degrees.

In a large bowl, combine the tuna, cheese and onion; mix well. Spoon into pie shell. Combine remaining ingredients and slowly pour over tuna mixture. If desired, top with the slivered almonds. Bake for 50 minutes or until a knife inserted in the center comes out clean. Sprinkle with paprika.

Variation: Use Cheddar cheese and salmon

Serves 8
Preparation time: 15 minutes
Baking time: 50 minutes
Easy   Brigitte Krawiec

POTATO CRUST

Perfect for a food processor

1 medium potato
1 small onion
1 egg, lightly beaten
1 teaspoon salt
3 tablespoons whole wheat
   flour

2 tablespoons unhulled
   sesame seeds
1 slice lightly toasted whole
   grain bread, broken into
   small pieces

Preheat oven to 375 degrees.

In a food processor fitted with the steel blade, chop the potato and onion. Change to the plastic blade and add the remaining ingredients. Blend just until thoroughly incorporated.

Lightly butter the bottom and sides of a deep, 10-inch round baking dish. Dust bottom and sides with whole wheat flour. Spread the potato mixture over the bottom and up the sides of the pan. Bake, uncovered, for 40 minutes or until crust is lightly browned. Let cool.

Makes one 10-inch pie crust   Florence Shulman

SALMON LOAF

Perfect for brunch, lunch or a light supper

¾ cup bread crumbs, moistened
    with ¼ cup melted butter
2   eggs, lightly beaten
½   cup milk
1   15½-ounce can salmon,
    drained, skin and bones
    removed
1   teaspoon lemon juice

½   teaspoon salt
Dash of pepper
2   teaspoons, or more to taste,
    finely chopped onion
1   tablespoon melted butter
Garnish: sliced hard cooked
    eggs

Preheat oven to 350 degrees.
Combine the ingredients in order given. Pack firmly into a well-buttered loaf pan and bake for 30-40 minutes. Turn onto a serving platter. Garnish with sliced hard cooked eggs, or slice and serve with mixed vegetables in cream sauce.

Serves 4-6
Preparation time: 10 minutes
Baking time: 40 minutes
Easy   Yetta Dubin

POACHED FLOUNDER

4   filets of flounder
Olive oil
½   teaspoon each: thyme,
    marjoram, basil and tarragon
2   tablespoons vegetable oil

2   tablespoons butter
1   medium onion, chopped
1   cup dry white wine
1   cup heavy cream
Parsley

Cover the bottom of a large shallow baking dish with aluminum foil. Butter the foil well. Coat each filet with olive oil. Mix the herbs together and rub into the fish. In a skillet heat the vegetable oil with the butter; sauté the onions until softened. Place the fish, skin side down in the prepared pan. Place the onions on top of the fish. Pour the wine and the cream over. Bake in a 325-degree oven for 30 minutes or until the fish flakes easily. Garnish with parsley.

Serves 4
Preparation time: 15 minutes
Cooking time: 30 minutes   Hart Hollman
Easy   DSO

COLD SMOKED SALMON WITH CUCUMBER-DILL SAUCE

This takes a while to prepare but it is well worth the time and effort

SALMON

1   whole salmon cleaned
2   cups hickory chips

Fresh dill stalks

Soak hickory chips in water to cover for 1 hour. Place coals in two sections on the outside of a gas or charcoal grill bin. When coals are hot, drain chips and place on top of coals. Lower heat and place whole salmon on grill between the two piles of coals. Cook for about 2 hours, turning once, until flesh is firm and fully cooked. Cool.
Place the salmon on a platter and peel off top layer of skin. Surround with fresh dill stalks. Serve with Cucumber Dill Sauce. When first side has been eaten, turn salmon over and remove skin from fish.

CUCUMBER DILL SAUCE

2   large cucumbers, thinly sliced
1   tablespoon salt
2   cups sour cream
2   cups mayonnaise
2   tablespoons cream-style horseradish

2   tablespoons fresh dill
1   tablespoon tarragon vinegar
1   teaspoon grated onion
¼   teaspoon salt
Pepper to taste

Place the cucumbers in a 2-quart bowl and cover with water. Add salt, mix well, and let sit for 30 minutes. Drain and pat dry. Combine remaining ingredients and mix well. Add the cucumbers and stir lightly. Refrigerate several hours or overnight.

Serves 12-15 as an entree or 10-25 as an appetizer
Preparation time: 2-3 hours
May be prepared up to 2 days in advance

Ann Marie Brown

Put a piece of fresh ginger in the oil when you sauté fresh fish. This will give it a tangy flavor.

TUNA BROCCOLI CASSEROLE

4 eggs	½ cup chopped onion
1 cup sour cream or buttermilk	½ teaspoon salt
2 7-ounce cans tuna, drained	½ cup shredded Swiss or Cheddar cheese
1 pound small-curd cottage cheese	1 large tomato, sliced
2 10-ounce packages frozen chopped broccoli, thawed and drained	½ cup shredded Mozzarella cheese
	¼ cup bread crumbs

Beat the eggs with the sour cream in a large bowl. Stir in the tuna, cottage cheese, broccoli, onion, salt and the cheese. Pour into a greased 9x12-inch baking dish. Bake in a 350-degree oven for 30 minutes. Top with tomato slices, Mozzarella and bread crumbs. Bake 10 minutes longer, until set.

Serves 8-10
Preparation time: 20 minutes
Baking time: 40 minutes
Easy
Joyce Pippel

SOLE WITH FRESH VEGETABLES IN PARCHMENT PAPER

1 tablespoon butter	2 tablespoons dry white wine
½ carrot, shredded	1 6-ounce fresh filet of lemon sole
½ medium celery rib, shredded	
1 large mushroom, sliced	1 cup fresh spinach, washed
½ scallion cut into 3 thin pieces	3 ounces whole shrimp
Salt and freshly ground pepper	1 piece parchment paper, 16x24 inches
2 tablespoons heavy cream	

Preheat oven to 350 degrees.

Melt the butter in a skillet. When hot, add the carrots, celery, mushroom, and scallion and sauté over high heat for 2-3 minutes or until vegetables are crisp-cooked. Season with salt and pepper. Add the cream and wine and cook until most of the liquid has evaporated. Set aside.

Place the parchment on a flat surface. Lay the fish filet in the center.

Place the spinach and shrimp on the sole. Roll the fish around the spinach and shrimp. Season with salt and pepper. Add the vegetable mixture and roll the paper around the fish and vegetables. Seal well; place on a baking sheet and cook for 12 minutes.

To serve, place on a warm plate and permit each guest to open a pouch.

Serves 1

Jim's Garage
Saloon/Restaurant
300 West Larned
Detroit, Michigan

STUFFED FLOUNDER

¼ cup chopped onion	½ teaspoon salt, or to taste
¼ cup butter	Dash of fresh pepper
1 small can chopped broiled mushrooms, drained, liquid reserved	8 6-ounce flounder fillets
	3 tablespoons butter
	3 tablespoons flour
1 7½-ounce can crabmeat, drained, cartilage removed	¼ teaspoon salt
½ cup saltine cracker crumbs	Milk
	⅓ cup dry white wine
2 tablespoons fresh parsley, minced	1 cup grated Swiss cheese
	½ teaspoon paprika

Preheat oven to 400 degrees.

Sauté onion in the ¼ cup butter until tender. Stir in the mushrooms, crabmeat, cracker crumbs, parsley, ½ teaspoon salt and pepper to taste. Spread mixture on each fillet and fold in half. Secure with a toothpick. Place fillets in single layer in baking dish; set aside.

In saucepan, melt 3 tablespoons butter. Blend in the flour and ¼ teaspoon salt. Add enough milk to reserved mushroom liquid to make 1½ cups. Slowly add the flour mixture, blending well. Stir in the wine and cook, stirring constantly, until mixture thickens. Add the cheese and paprika, continuing to stir until cheese is melted. Spoon over stuffed fillets. Bake for 25 minutes, or until fish is flakey.

Serves 8
Preparation time: 30 minutes
Bake: 25 minutes

Carmella Gusfa

COD A LA PROVENCALE

Serve with a salad and steamed green vegetable for a very-low calorie meal

1½ pounds cod fillets
Juice of 1 lemon
Salt and pepper
2 cups finely diced fresh tomato
½ tablespoon minced fresh parsley
3 tablespoons red or white wine

1 teaspoon salt
¼ teaspoon pepper
½ teaspoon thyme
⅛ teaspoon crushed rosemary
1½ tablespoons olive oil
1 small onion, minced
1 clove garlic, minced

Rinse fish fillets, pat dry, and place in a shallow greased baking dish. Sprinkle with lemon juice and salt and pepper to taste. Place the remaining ingredients in a saucepan. Bring to a boil, cover, and cook over medium heat until reduced and thick. Pour mixture over the fish, cover with foil, and bake in a preheated 350-degree oven for 25-30 minutes or until the fish flakes easily. Check after 20 minutes, if there is too much liquid, remove foil for the last 5-10 minutes.

Serves 4
Preparation time: 20 minutes
Baking time: 30 minutes
Easy

Melanie Resnick Wells

SOLE AU GRATIN WITH SHRIMP SAUCE

2 pounds sole fillets, cut in half
¼ cup dry Sherry
2 tablespoons lemon juice
½ teaspoon salt
2 tablespoons butter
2 tablespoons flour
¼ teaspoon pepper
½ teaspoon prepared mustard

1 teaspoon instant chicken bouillon
½ cup heavy cream
½ cup shredded Swiss cheese
1 pound cooked, cleaned, whole shrimp
1 tablespoon minced parsley
3 lemons, sliced

Arrange the fish fillets in a large shallow baking dish. Combine the Sherry and lemon juice and pour over the fish; sprinkle with salt. Bake, uncovered, in a 350-degree oven for 15 minutes. Drain the cooking liquid and add enough water to equal 1 cup; set aside. Melt the butter in a medium saucepan over low heat. Stir in the flour, pepper, mustard and chicken bouillon. Cook over low heat, stirring, until mixture is smooth and bubbly. Remove from heat; add the reserved broth and heavy cream. Bring to a boil and cook, stirring, for 1 minute. Add the cheese and shrimp and cook just until cheese is melted. Transfer to a chafing dish alternating layers of fish and sauce, beginning and ending with the sauce. Garnish with chopped parsley and lemon slices. Keep warm over low flame.

Serves 6-8
Preparation time: 30 minutes   Peggy Dasovic

SCROD IN YOGURT SAUCE

1½	pounds Scrod fillets	1 large clove garlic, minced
Juice of 1 lemon		1 onion, thinly sliced
Salt and pepper		½ cup dry homemade bread
¾	cup plain low-fat yogurt	crumbs
2	teaspoons fresh chopped	Grated Parmesan cheese
	dill, or 1 teaspoon	1 tablespoon butter
	dried dill	

Place fish in one layer in a greased baking dish. Sprinkle with lemon juice and salt and pepper to taste. Combine the yogurt, dill, garlic and salt and pepper to taste and blend well. Spread sauce evenly over the fish. Scatter the sliced onion over all and sprinkle with the bread crumbs and Parmesan cheese. Dot with butter and bake, uncovered, in a preheated 350-degree oven for ½ hour or until fish flakes easily. Note: If fish seems to be drying, cover after 20 minutes with foil until done.

Serves 4-6
Preparation time: 10 minutes
Baking time: 20-40 minutes   Fay Ann Resnick
Easy   DSO

FISH PAPRIKAS STARKER

. . . a delicious traditional Hungarian dish given to us by virtuoso cellist Starker. He noted that it is really his wife's recipe and one of his favorite dishes.

5   pounds fish (carp, whitefish and perch), filleted
2   tablespoons salt
4   large onions, finely chopped

Fish stock (see recipe below)
2   green peppers, coarsely chopped
3   tablespoons paprika

Cut the fish into 2-inch strips and sprinkle with the salt. Let stand for 1 hour. Sprinkle ⅓ of the onions in the bottom of a large kettle. Add a layer of one kind of fish. Continue layering fish and onions, ending with onion. Pour on enough fish stock to cover ⅔ of the fish and onions. Add the green peppers and sprinkle on the paprika. Bring to a boil and cook over low heat until the fish flakes. Season to taste. Let stand for 10 minutes before serving.

To serve cold: Arrange cooked fish in a serving dish. Pour on the fish stock and chill until jelled.

Serves 6

FISH STOCK

1   pound fish heads and bones reserved from Paprikas recipe
1   large onion, chopped
1   tablespoon salt

3   ribs celery, chopped
2   carrots, chopped
Bouquet garni of thyme, parsley and bay leaf

Combine all ingredients. Add water to cover and simmer for 1 hour. Strain.

Janos Starker

*"I don't like to say that my kitchen is a **religious** place, but I would say that if I were a voodoo princess, I would conduct my rituals there."*
Pearl Bailey

DOUBLE SHRIMP CASSEROLE

2	10-ounce cans cream of shrimp soup	½	teaspoon salt
1½	cups milk	⅔	cup shredded Cheddar cheese
1	cup mayonnaise or salad dressing	2-3	cups cooked shrimp
½	cup diced celery	1	8-ounce package medium noodles, cooked and drained
2	tablespoons minced green onion	½	cup chow mein noodles

Preheat oven to 350 degrees.
Combine the shrimp soup, milk, mayonnaise, celery, onion and salt; mix well. Stir in the cheese, shrimp and cooked noodles. Turn into a greased 3-quart casserole. Bake, uncovered, for 30-35 minutes. Top with chow mein noodles and bake for 10 minutes longer.

Serves 8-12
Preparation time: 20 minutes
Baking time: 35 minutes
Can be frozen up to addition of chow mein noodles
Easy   Carmella Gusfa

NEW ENGLAND CLAM SCALLOP

This is served at old-fashioned church suppers in New England. I acquired the recipe from an old friend of my Mother's

3	cans clams with liquor	½	teaspoon salt
2½	cups finely crushed crackers		Pepper to taste
⅓	cup melted butter	1	egg, beaten
¼	teaspoon dry mustard	½	cup milk
1	scant tablespoon Worcestershire sauce		Topping: ½ cup crumbs, butter

Preheat oven to 375 degrees.
Combine all ingredients and blend well. Transfer to a casserole, top with additional crumbs and dot well with butter. Bake for 45 minutes to 1 hour until hot and bubbly, and top is crusty.

Serves 4-6
Preparation time: 15 minutes
Baking time: 1 hour
Easy   Mrs. Robert W. Stewart

RICE AND SHRIMP JAMBALAYA

A delightful way to use leftover ham

4 slices bacon, diced
1 medium onion, minced
½ medium green pepper, diced
2 cups chicken broth
½ cup ketchup
2 tablespoons brown sugar
12 ounces shelled shrimp, cut up

1 cup finely chopped cooked ham
2 tablespoons cornstarch mixed with 2 tablespoons cold water
Salt and pepper to taste
1½ cups hot cooked rice

Fry the bacon until crisp. Remove bacon from skillet, drain well, then crumble. To the skillet, add the onion and green pepper, and cook for 5 minutes. Add the broth, ketchup and brown sugar; cover, and simmer for 15 minutes. Add the shrimp and ham and heat thoroughly. Add the cornstarch mixture and cook, stirring, until mixture thickens. Season to taste. Serve on a bed of hot rice, topped with the crumbled bacon.

Serves 4-6
Preparation time: 30 minutes
Easy

Marcia Wiltshire

SHRIMP CREOLE

1 cup chopped onion
1 cup chopped green pepper
⅓ cup butter
2 tablespoons flour
3½ cups coarsely chopped tomatoes, drained

⅛ teaspoon cayenne pepper
Salt and freshly ground pepper to taste
1½ pounds shrimp, cooked and cleaned
Cooked rice

Sauté the onion and green pepper in butter until softened. Blend in the flour. Add tomatoes, cayenne pepper, salt and pepper, stirring constantly until thickened. Add the shrimp and heat thoroughly. Serve with hot fluffy rice.

Serves 4-6
Preparation time: 15 minutes
Easy

Edward S. May

PESTO FETTUCINE WITH MUSSELS

PESTO SAUCE

3   cloves garlic, finely chopped
1   ounce Pignoli nuts, finely chopped
4   ounces fresh basil, finely chopped
¼   cup olive oil

Combine the garlic and nuts in blender or a food processor fitted with the steel blade. Process to a fine paste. Add the basil and olive oil and process until smooth. Set aside.

MUSSEL COURT BOUILLON

1   cup dry white wine
1   cup clam juice
2   hot peppers
1   onion, coarsely chopped
4   sprigs parsley
4   dozen mussels

Combine ingredients except mussels, in an enamel or stainless steel saucepan and bring to a simmer. Add mussels, cover, and let steam until they open. Discard any that do not open. Remove mussels from their shells and remove the "beards"; set aside.

ASSEMBLY

¼   cup butter
1   red onion, finely chopped
1   cup mushrooms, thinly sliced
1   pound spinach fettucine, cooked and drained
1   pint cherry tomatoes, halved
4   ounces Parmesan cheese, grated
Salt and pepper

Melt the butter in a large sauce pan. When bubbling, add the pesto and mix well. Stir in the onions and mushrooms. Add the drained pasta, the mussels and cherry tomatoes and toss. Add the Parmesan cheese, mix well and season with salt and pepper to taste. Serve with a sprinkling of Parmesan cheese on top.

Serves 4

Jimmy Schmidt
London Chop House
Detroit, Michigan

CRABMEAT CASSEROLE

President Reagan's original White House favorite

1	14-ounce can artichoke hearts, drained	2½	tablespoons flour
1	pound fresh or frozen crabmeat, flaked	1	cup heavy cream
½	pound fresh mushrooms, sautéed in butter	1	teaspoon Worcestershire sauce
2½	tablespoons butter	¼	cup dry Sherry
		¼	cup grated Parmesan cheese

Place the artichoke hearts in a single layer in a casserole dish. Cover with the crab, then the mushrooms. Melt the butter in a small saucepan; stir in the flour. Slowly add the cream, stirring constantly, until the sauce thickens slightly. Stir in the Worcestershire and Sherry. Cook over moderate heat until thick. Pour over the crabmeat and sprinkle with cheese. Bake in a 350-degree oven for 20 minutes.

Serves 4
Preparation time: 20 minutes
Cooking time: 20 minutes
Easy   Bobbi Pincus

SCAMPI DELECTABLE

2	pounds (weight with shells) fresh jumbo prawns	¼	cup olive oil
3	cloves garlic, finely minced	¼	cup melted butter
¼	teaspoon salt	½	cup California white wine
2	tablespoons chopped parsley	2	tablespoons lemon juice
		⅛	teaspoon freshly ground pepper

Shell and devein the prawns, leaving tail intact. Butterfly by splitting lengthwise to 1 inch from head. Combine the remaining ingredients and mix well. Add the prawns and let marinate for several hours. Preheat oven to broil.
Arrange the prawns in a single layer in a shallow oven-proof baking pan. Pour remaining sauce over. Broil for 6-8 minutes, 3 inches from heat. Remove prawns to a serving platter and pour sauce over.

Serves 4   Joe Glover

SHRIMP AND SCALLOPS GRUYERE

Serve with rice or over patty shells

¾	cup plus 3 tablespoons butter, divided	2	teaspoons tomato paste
¾	cup flour	3	teaspoons lemon juice, divided
3	cups milk	1	pound raw scallops
12	ounces grated Swiss Gruyere cheese	½	pound mushrooms
¼	teaspoon garlic powder	1	pound shrimp cleaned and cooked
3½	teaspoons salt, divided	2	tablespoons diced green pepper
¼	teaspoon white pepper		
½	teaspoon dry mustard		

In the top section of a double boiler, melt ¾ cup butter. Add the flour and milk and stir until well combined. Add the cheese and cook, stirring, until cheese is melted. Add the garlic powder, 3 teaspoons salt, pepper, mustard, tomato paste, and 2 teaspoons of the lemon juice; stir well.

Poach the scallops in water to cover with remaining lemon juice and salt for 10 minutes. Drain, reserving ½ cup of the broth. Add broth to the cream sauce.

Sauté the mushrooms in 2 tablespoons butter and add to the sauce. Add scallops and shrimp. Heat for 10 minutes then transfer to a serving dish. Sauté the green pepper in remaining tablespoon butter and sprinkle over the casserole.

Serves 8-10

Marion Smith
DSO

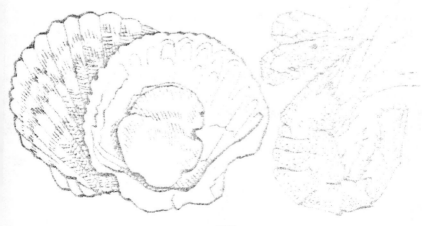

SHRIMP CURRY

½ cup minced onion
5 tablespoons butter
6 tablespoons flour
2½ teaspoons curry powder
1¼ teaspoons salt
¼ teaspoon ginger
1½ teaspoons sugar
1 cup canned beef consommé, undiluted
2 cups milk
1½ pounds shrimp, cooked, shelled and deveined

1 teaspoon lemon juice
2-3 cups cooked rice
Condiments:
1 cup shredded coconut
3 hard-cooked eggs, sieved
1 cup peanuts
1 cup ripe olives
1 cup chutney, chopped
1 cup chopped green pepper
1 cup currants or raisins
1 cup crumbled crisp bacon

Sauté onions in the butter until soft. Add the flour, curry, salt, ginger and sugar; stir and cook slowly 5-8 minutes. Add consommé and milk and cook, stirring constantly, until sauce has thickened and is smooth. Add the shrimp and lemon juice.
Can be made ahead of time and reheated just before serving. Serve with rice, chutney, and at least 3 other condiments.

Serves 4
Preparation time: 20 minutes   Winnie Ostrowski

SHRIMP AMANDINE

1 cup slivered almonds
½ cup butter
1 pound raw shrimp, cleaned and deveined
½ teaspoon salt

Freshly ground pepper
2 tablespoons chopped parsley
Toast points

Sauté almonds in the butter until lightly browned. Remove almonds with a slotted spoon. Add the shrimp and sauté until lightly browned. Combine shrimp with the salt, pepper, parsley and almonds. Serve on toast points.

Serves 4
Preparation time: 15 minutes
Easy
                                          Sheila Swanson

MARYLAND CRAB CAKES

2 tablespoons flour
2 pounds Maryland lump
  crabmeat
2 eggs

½ cup heavy cream
2-3 drops Tabasco sauce
2-4 tablespoons butter

Sprinkle flour over the crabmeat and stir gently to coat. Beat the eggs, cream, and seasonings together and pour over the crabmeat. Mix gently. Melt the butter in a heavy skillet. Drop crabmeat mixture by the tablespoonful into the hot butter and brown, turning once.

Makes about 15 cakes
Preparation time: 20 minutes
Easy

Mrs. Philip Caldwell

SHRIMP STROGANOFF

Easy . . . tastes terrific . . . novel idea

3 pounds uncooked medium
  shrimp, shelled and
  deveined
½ cup butter, divided
½ pound fresh mushrooms,
  sliced
½ cup chopped onion
1 clove garlic, mashed
2 tablespoons flour
1 cup chicken or beef broth

1 tablespoon tomato paste
¾ teaspoon Worcestershire
  sauce
1 tablespoon chopped fresh
  dill or 1 teaspoon dried
  dill weed
1½ teaspoons salt, or to taste
1 cup sour cream
Cooked rice or noodles

Sauté the shrimp in 6 tablespoons butter for 5 minutes. Remove shrimp and add remaining butter, mushrooms, onion, and garlic; cook for 5 minutes. Add the flour and mix well. Stir in the broth, tomato paste, Worcestershire sauce, dill and salt. Simmer for 2 minutes. Stir in the sour cream, mix well, then add the shrimp. Heat but do not boil. Serve with rice or noodles.

Serves 6
Preparation time: 20 minutes
Easy

Pat Young

GRANDMOTHER IVES SCALLOPED OYSTERS

12-16 slices white bread,
    crusts removed, and cubed
1   egg
½ cup heavy cream

Butter
Salt and pepper
1   quart fresh oysters

Preheat oven to 350 degrees.

Butter a 2½-quart casserole then place a layer of bread cubes on the bottom. Mix the egg with the cream and drizzle lightly over the bread. Dot with butter and add salt and pepper to taste. Add a layer of oysters. Continue layering the bread, egg/cream mixture, salt and pepper, butter and oysters until bread and oysters are used up. Bake for 40 minutes. Serve immediately.

Serves 4
Preparation time: 15 minutes
Cooking time: 40 minutes
Easy

Margaret Reynolds

CHEESE SHRIMP CASSEROLE

Great for Sunday brunch or after the concert

6   slices firm white bread,
    crusts removed
4   tablespoons butter, melted
1   cup grated Swiss cheese
2   green onions, chopped
2   tablespoons chopped
    parsley
½ pound small shrimp,
    cooked

3   eggs
½ teaspoon salt
½ teaspoon Dijon mustard
1½ cups milk
½ cup sour cream
Garnish: Cherry tomatoes and
    parsley sprigs

Cut each slice of bread in half on the diagonal. Dip in melted butter. Arrange half of the slices in an unbuttered 8-inch square baking dish; sprinkle with half each of the cheese, onions, parsley and shrimp. Add remaining bread and repeat process.

Beat eggs with salt, mustard, milk and sour cream. Pour over casserole, cover and refrigerate overnight. One hour before serving remove from refrigerator. Let sit at room temperature for 30 minutes. Bake in a preheated 350-degree oven for 30 minutes or until puffed and golden. Cut into squares and serve with cherry tomatoes and parsley sprigs.

Serves 6
Preparation time: 15 minutes
Baking time: 40 minutes
Refrigerate overnight   Louise Lee

SYMPHONY OF SEAFOOD

4	8-ounce lobster tails	⅔	cup flour
2	pounds shrimp, shelled and deveined	2	teaspoons salt
		1	teaspoon paprika
2	7½-ounce cans King crabmeat, drained	¼	teaspoon white pepper
		3	cups light cream
¼	cup butter	1¼	cups dry white wine

Drop lobster tails into a large kettle of boiling water. Cover and simmer for 8 minutes. Remove lobster tails and set aside until cool enough to handle. Add the shrimp to the boiling water; boil for 1 minute then drain. Remove cartilage from crabmeat, leaving pieces as large as possible. Remove meat from lobster shells, and cut into bite-size pieces.

Melt the butter in a Dutch oven. Add the flour, salt, paprika and pepper and stir until smooth. Add the cream and bring to a boil, stirring constantly, until smooth. Reduce heat and simmer for five minutes. Add the wine, lobster, shrimp and crabmeat and blend gently until heated through. DO NOT BOIL.

Serve with parsley and buttered hot wild rice.

Serves 6
Preparation time: 25 minutes   Helene Eagan

COQUILLE ST. JACQUES

1   pound scallops
1   cup dry white wine
1   small onion, chopped
1   tablespoon chopped parsley
2   teaspoons lemon juice
½   teaspoon salt
¼   cup butter
6   tablespoons flour
1   cup light cream
2   ounces Gruyere cheese, grated

Dash of pepper
7-8 ounces canned or frozen crabmeat, drained and flaked
1   cup cooked shrimp
½   cup sliced mushrooms
1½ cups soft bread crumbs mixed with 1 tablespoon melted butter

Combine scallops, wine, onion, parsley, lemon juice and salt. Bring to a boil and simmer for 5 minutes. Drain, reserving 1 cup of liquid. Melt the butter in a saucepan and stir in the flour. Add cream and the reserved scallop liquid. Cook, stirring, until the mixture thickens and bubbles; remove from the heat. Add the cheese and pepper and stir until cheese is melted. Mix in the scallop mixture, crabmeat, shrimp and mushrooms. Spoon into individual casseroles; sprinkle with buttered bread crumbs. Bake in a 350-degree oven for 25 minutes.

Serves 6
Preparation time: 20 minutes
Baking time: 25 minutes

Whitney Jill Sale

SHRIMP AND PARMESAN SUPREME

7   tablespoons butter, divided
1   pound fresh, raw shrimp
    shelled and cleaned
½   pound fresh mushrooms,
    sliced
¼   cup flour
¼   teaspoon dry mustard

Dash cayenne
2   cups heavy cream
5   tablespoons Sherry
½   teaspoon salt
⅓   cup freshly grated Parmesan
    cheese

Melt 3 tablespoons butter in a medium skillet. Add the shrimp and mushrooms. Cook over medium heat, stirring frequently, for 5 minutes or until mushrooms are tender and shrimp turn pink. Remove from skillet and set aside.

Add remaining butter to skillet. When melted, blend in the flour, mustard and cayenne. Stir in the cream all at once and cook, stirring constantly, until mixture thickens and comes to a boil. Add the shrimp and mushrooms and heat thoroughly. Stir in the Sherry, salt and cheese. Serve over rice or pasta.

Serves 6
Preparation time: 15 minutes
Easy

John Fischer

SHRIMP MIJAS

1   tablespoon peanut oil
1   clove garlic, minced
24 large shrimp, peeled,
    cleaned and butterflied
1   cup butter

Juice of ½ lemon
1   tablespoon dry vermouth
Hot cooked rice
1   small jar pimentos cut
    into strips

Heat the peanut oil in a wok or deep fry pan. Add the garlic and shrimp and stir-fry until the shrimp turn pink and begin to curl. In a separate saucepan, melt the butter. Stir in the lemon juice and vermouth. Transfer the shrimp to a shallow ovenproof dish and pour the butter sauce over. Bake in a 350-degree oven for 5-10 minutes or until hot and bubbly. Serve over rice and garnish with pimento strips.

Serves 4
Preparation time: 25 minutes

Jennifer Moore
WDIV-TV

SEAFOOD SURPRISE

Saffron rice is an excellent accompaniment to this delicious dish

¼ cup sweet butter
1 tablespoon olive oil
1 medium sweet onion, thinly sliced
½ sweet red pepper, seeded and cut into thin strips
1 hot banana pepper, seeded and cut into rounds
1 clove garlic, minced
½ chicken breast, skinned, boned, and cut into bite-sized pieces

¼ cup flour
½ pound freshly cooked medium shrimp
½ pound fresh bay scallops
⅛ teaspoon basil
⅛ teaspoon dill
Freshly ground black pepper to taste
½ cup dry white wine or dry vermouth
Juice of ½ lemon

Melt the butter and oil in a large skillet over medium heat. Add the onion, peppers and garlic and sauté until the onion is transparent — 5-10 minutes. Dredge the chicken in the flour and add to the skillet. Cook, stirring occasionally, until the chicken turns white, about 4 minutes. Add the shrimp, scallops, basil, dill and pepper and cook, stirring, until the scallops are firm and cooked, about 5 minutes. Add the wine and lemon juice, stir and cook 5 minutes longer or until the liquid is reduced to a thin sauce.

Serves 4-6
Preparation time: 40 minutes

Dan Harris

SEAFOOD PASTA

½ pound vermicelli
3 tablespoons butter
6 green onions, tops included, thinly sliced
⅓ cup celery, including some of the tops, finely chopped
½ green pepper, chopped
3 tablespoons flour
1½ cups light cream

1 teaspoon lemon juice
½ teaspoon grated lemon rind
½ teaspoon salt
White pepper to taste
1 pimento, chopped
3 tablespoons light Sherry
12 ounces frozen crabmeat, thawed and cut into chunks
Grated Parmesan cheese

Cook the vermicelli according to package directions and drain well. Melt the butter in a skillet over low heat. Add the onions, celery, and green pepper and sauté until onion is transparent. Sprinkle flour over and blend until thick. Slowly blend in the cream, stirring constantly, until mixture thickens — sauce should be fairly thick. Add lemon juice slowly so sauce does not curdle; add rind, salt, pepper, and pimento. Heat thoroughly, then stir in the wine and crab. Cook, stirring, for 10 minutes. Serve over the vermicelli. Sprinkle with Parmesan cheese and serve immediately.

Serves 6
Preparation time: 20 minutes   Marica Wiltshire

SCALLOP AND SIRLOIN KEBOBS

½   teaspoon garlic powder
½   cup oil
3   tablespoons lemon juice
1   teaspoon salt
¼   teaspoon freshly ground
     pepper
2   dashes Tabasco sauce
¼   teaspoon dry mustard

¼   teaspoon sugar
¼   teaspoon thyme
2   pounds sirloin, cut into
     1-inch cubes
2   pounds large scallops
2   limes
½-1 cup butter, melted

Combine the garlic powder, oil, lemon juice, salt, pepper, Tabasco, mustard, sugar and thyme. Mix well and divide between 2 large glass bowls. Place the sirloin cubes in one bowl and the scallops in the other bowl and let marinate for at least 2 hours. When ready to serve, cut each lime into 12 slices. Thread on skewers alternating with the meat and scallops, allowing 3-4 lime slices per skewer. Broil in oven or over hot charcoals for 10-15 minutes, turning to brown evenly. Pour butter over kebobs before serving. Serve with rice pilaf.
Note: Substitute green pepper, pineapple or onion for the limes.

Serves 6-8
Preparation time: 20 minutes
Cooking time: 10 minutes   Joyce Pippel

JEAN-PIERRE RAMPAL
BAKED STUFFED MUSSELS

Moules Farcies au Four

4½	pounds large mussels	½	cup bread crumbs
1	cup white wine	1	egg, beaten
1	cup sweet butter		Salt and pepper to taste
2	cloves garlic, minced		
1	cup parsley, finely chopped		

Soak and scrub the mussels well. Put them in a heavy saucepan with the wine. Cover and cook over high flame for five to eight minutes until they open. Discard those that have not opened. Remove from heat.

Preheat oven to 350 degrees. Mix together the butter, garlic, parsley, and bread crumbs. When combined well, add the egg. Take the mussels out of their shells, wash shells well, split into two halves, and place half of the split shells on a baking sheet. Put the mussels back into the shells and place some stuffing on top. Add salt and pepper to taste. Bake for 10 minutes or until tops are brown and crusty. Serve with lemon wedges.

Serves eight as an appetizer, four as a main course.
Preparation time: 40 minutes
Baking time: 10 minutes

Jean-Pierre Rampal

"Give me books, fruit, French wine and fine weather, and a little music played out of doors, played by someone I do not know."

John Keats

Poultry

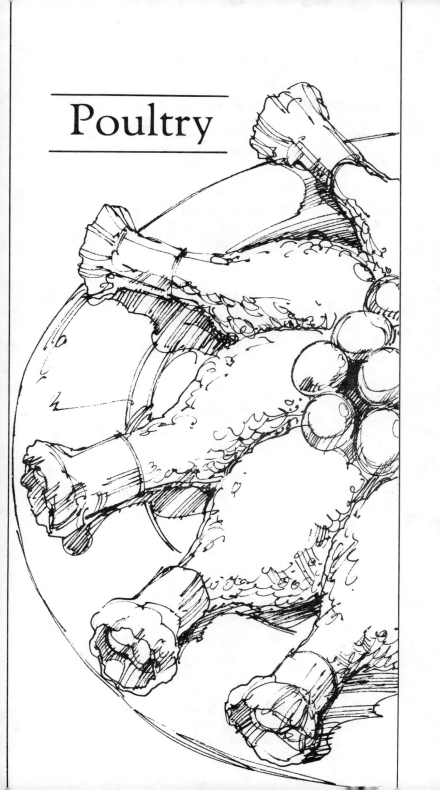

Dinner Before The Concert

Frosted Fresh Tomato Soup
garnished with creme fraiche and pesto
Crusty French Bread
Coq au Vin Blanc
Rice Pilaf
Ratatouille Nicoise
Green Salad with Vinaigrette
Pots de Creme au Chocolate
Cafe   Cognac   Cordials

Charity de Vicq Suczek

Wine Suggestions
A soft, rich white; such as
the Macon-Lugny
from Louis Latour (1981)

Thanksgiving Dinner

Hot Mulled Cider
Peanut Soup served in a Pumpkin Shell
Marinated Cherry Tomatoes
Sour Cream Corn Bread
Roast Turkey with Dressing
Pan Gravy
Cranberry Conserve
Carrot Ring
Yummy Yams
Fresh Broccoli
Creamed Onions
Pumpkin Pie with Praline Topping
Rice Pudding

Wine Suggestions

A soft, rich red wine; such as
the St. Joseph from
Paul Jaboulet Aine (1980)

CHICKEN ALA STELLA

1½ teaspoons salt
1½ teaspoons freshly ground pepper
1½ teaspoons basil
1 tablespoon Italian seasoning
1 teaspoon rosemary
1 teaspoon sage
1 tablespoon parsley
1 whole, young chicken cut in pieces
Olive oil
3 cloves fresh garlic, minced
1½ cups white Reisling wine
1 teaspoon wine vinegar

Mix the salt, pepper, basil, Italian seasoning, rosemary, sage and parsley and rub into the chicken pieces well. Place enough olive oil in a baking pan to cover the bottom with a light film. Add the garlic, wine and vinegar, and place pan in oven until oil is hot. Add seasoned chicken in one layer and turn several times to coat the chicken well. Cover with aluminum foil and bake in a 350-degree oven for 1½-hours. Remove foil and cook for 15 minutes longer until lightly browned.

Serve with rice or homemade pasta, using the natural juices over it.

Serves 4-6
Preparation time: 15 minutes
Cooking time: 1 hour 45 minutes
Easy   Frank D. Stella

RASPBERRY CHICKEN

A simple yet elegant entree

2 tablespoons vegetable oil
¼ cup butter
½ cup chopped onion
6 whole chicken breasts, cut in half
½ cup raspberry vinegar
½ cup heavy cream
¾ cup fresh or frozen raspberries

In a heavy skillet, heat the oil and butter. Add the chopped onion and sauté until soft and transparent. Add the chicken breasts and sauté until partially cooked — about 15 minutes. Stir in the raspberry vinegar, cover and cook until done, about 10 minutes longer. Add the cream and raspberries and heat through.

Serves 3-6
Preparation time: 40 minutes
Easy   Michael Schwartz

LEMON CHICKEN

3 large whole breasts	2 tablespoons vegetable oil
½ cup flour	1 cup chicken broth
Salt and pepper	2 lemons
¼ cup butter	

Bone, split and skin chicken breasts. Flatten between sheets of waxed paper. Combine the flour with salt and pepper to taste and lightly dredge the chicken. Heat butter and oil in a skillet. Brown the breasts then remove from pan; stir in the flour remaining from coating and mix well. Add the broth and juice of 1 lemon. Return chicken to the pan. Thinly slice the remaining lemon and place on top of chicken. Cover and simmer for 5 minutes or until chicken is tender.

Serves 3-6
Preparation time: 25 minutes
Easy   Priscilla Shaw

CHICKEN VERONIQUE

Serve with fluffy rice

4 chicken breasts	Paprika
½ small lemon	2 teaspoons cornstarch mixed
1 tablespoon butter	with 1 tablespoon cold water
⅓ cup dry white wine	¾ cup seedless grapes
2 tablespoons water	
¼ teaspoon instant chicken bouillon	

Rub chicken with the cut lemon. Brown chicken in the butter for 10 minutes. Drain off the fat; add wine, water and bouillon. Cover and and simmer for 25-35 minutes, basting occasionally with the liquid. When done, sprinkle with paprika and remove chicken from pan. Skim off the fat then pour sauce into a measuring cup. Add water to equal ¾ cup and pour liquid back into the pan. Add the cornstarch mixture and cook, stirring, until liquid is thickened. Add the grapes and heat well. Pour over chicken.

Serves 4
Preparation time: 20 minutes
Cooking time: 35 minutes   Sue Droste

LEMON GARLIC CHICKEN

8	breasts of chicken, skinned, boned and halved	2	cups butter, divided
4	eggs, beaten	3	tablespoons lemon juice
½	cup grated Parmesan cheese	6	cloves garlic, minced
1¼	cups flour seasoned to taste with salt and pepper	3	tablespoons parsley
		2	cups fresh mushrooms, sliced

Dry chicken well. Mix the eggs with the cheese. Dip chicken pieces into the flour, then into the egg mixture. Melt ½ cup butter in a large skillet. Brown the chicken in two batches in the hot butter for 5 minutes on each side, taking care to use fresh butter if it gets too browned. Place the chicken in a baking pan in one layer.

In a saucepan, melt the remaining 1½ cups of butter. Add the lemon juice, garlic, parsley and mushrooms. Pour sauce over the chicken and bake in a 350-degree oven, uncovered, for 30 minutes.

Serve the chicken on a bed of hot rice or cooked noodles and drizzle the excess butter over all.

Serves 8
Preparation time: 30 minutes
Cooking time: 30 minutes   Sheila Donenfeld

CORNISH HENS, DETROIT STYLE

Serve with German potato salad

2	Cornish hens	1	cup shredded Swiss cheese, divided
1	teaspoon seasoned salt		
1	cup sauerkraut, divided	2	medium apples, sliced

Rub hens with seasoned salt. Stuff the cavity of each hen with ½ cup sauerkraut and ½ cup cheese. Fasten with skewers.

Place the sliced apples on the bottom of a buttered baking dish. Place the hens on top and bake in a 400-degree oven for 1 hour.

Serves 2-4
Preparation time: 10 minutes
Baking time: 1 hour
Easy   Helen Eagan

CORNISH HENS A LA HANDEL

4   Cornish hens
3   onions, divided
3   large carrots, coarsely
    chopped
3   large celery ribs, chopped
1   cup Kasha (Buckwheat
    groats)
1   cup butter, divided
1   tablespoon vegetable oil
½   pound sliced, fresh
    mushrooms

1   teaspoon sage
1   teaspoon thyme
Salt and pepper
1   cup dry white wine,
    divided
1   cup raisins
1   cup chopped walnuts
1   cup ginger ale
Baby beets
Parsley for garnish

Line a roasting pan with heavy duty aluminum foil leaving at least a 4-inch overlap outside the pan.

Clean and dry the hens well, reserving the giblets. Coarsely chop two of the onions and combine with the chopped carrots and celery. Spread mixture in the bottom of lined roasting pan.

Prepare kasha according to package directions. Chop the remaining onion and sauté it in 2 tablespoons of butter and the oil over medium heat. Add the mushrooms, reserved giblets, sage, thyme and salt and pepper to taste. Add 3 tablespoons of wine and cook for 5 minutes. When kasha is done, add the sautéed onion mixture, the raisins, walnuts and ½ cup of wine. Cover and cook over low heat for 5 minutes. Stuff the hens with the kasha mixture and place on top of the vegetables in the pan. Pour the remaining wine into the cavity of each hen.

Preheat oven to 425 degrees. In a separate saucepan, melt the remaining butter. Brush hens with melted butter and place in the oven for 10 minutes basting several times with butter. When skin is golden brown, pour ginger ale over the hens and cover with a large piece of heavy duty foil sealing well with the overlapped foil. Reduce heat to 325 degrees and roast for 1 hour, basting every 20 minutes. When skin starts to separate at the legs, turn oven to 450 degrees and remove the aluminum cover. Brush with remaining butter and roast, uncovered, for 5 minutes longer.

To serve: Remove the stuffing. Place one hen in the middle of each plate and surround with a "nest" of kasha stuffing. Add several baby beets (eggs in a nest) and garnish with parsley in the cavities of the hens.

Serves 4

Hart Hollman
DSO

CHICKEN BROCCOLI CASSEROLE

2	pounds broccoli, cooked	Salt and pepper
1	2½-3 pound chicken, cooked and boned	2 teaspoons curry powder
		Juice of 1 lemon
2	cans condensed cream of chicken soup	Parmesan cheese
		Paprika
1	cup mayonnaise	Slivered almonds

Place the broccoli and chicken in layers in a 7x11-inch casserole. Combine the soup, mayonnaise, salt and pepper to taste, curry powder and lemon juice. Mix well and pour over the chicken and broccoli. Top with Parmesan cheese, paprika and almonds to taste. Bake in a 325-degree oven for 25-30 minutes or until hot and bubbly.

Serves 4-6
Preparation time: 10 minutes
Cooking time: 30 minutes
Easy   Christine Kiehl

CHICKEN WITH ARTICHOKE HEARTS

Excellent with pea pods tossed in butter

3	tablespoons butter	1 teaspoon white pepper
2	large onions, sliced	Salt to taste
1	large potato, cut into ½-inch dice	8 whole chicken breasts, boned and cut in half
1	clove garlic, minced	Flour
1	cup tomato sauce	¼ cup vegetable oil
1	tablespoon ketchup	
1	14-ounce can artichoke hearts, cut in half, liquid reserved	

Melt the butter in a skillet over medium heat. Sauté onions and potato until onions turn deep brown and begin to carmelize. Add garlic, tomato sauce, ketchup, artichoke hearts, pepper, salt, and ½ of the reserved artichoke liquid. Simmer for 1 hour. Lightly flour the chicken and sauté in hot oil until golden brown and tender. To serve, pour sauce over the chicken.

Serves 8   Laura Britton

ORANGE CHICKEN

1 cup brown rice
2 cups water
1 teaspoon salt
4 whole chicken breasts, skinned, boned and cut in half

1 6-ounce can frozen orange juice, thawed
1 package dry onion soup mix
2 green onions, chopped

Combine the rice, water and salt. Bring to a boil, reduce heat to low, cover and simmer for 1 hour. *Do not remove cover during this time.* Place chicken breasts in a lightly oiled, shallow baking dish. Pour orange juice concentrate over and sprinkle with the onion soup mix and the chopped onions. Cover pan with foil and bake in a 375-degree oven for 30 minutes. Uncover, baste with sauce, and bake for 20 minutes longer or until done. Serve over the rice with the sauce.

Serves 4-8
Preparation time: 15 minutes
Cooking time: 1 hour
Easy   Melanie Resnick Wells

CHICKEN IN SHERRY

6 chicken breasts, boned and halved (12 pieces)
1 pound Canadian bacon, sliced
2 cans condensed cream of celery soup

1 cup Sherry
1 package frozen artichoke hearts, thawed

Wrap each piece of chicken around a slice of bacon. Whisk the soup with the Sherry until smooth. Place chicken bundles in a shallow baking dish. Scatter the artichoke hearts around the chicken and pour soup mixture over. Cover and bake in a 350-degree oven for 1 hour. If desired, uncover the last 15 minutes to brown. Serve with hot rice.

Serves 6
Preparation time: 10 minutes
Baking time: 1 hour
Easy   Sheila Pitcoff

BREAST OF CHICKEN ORIENTAL

½ cup vegetable oil
1 onion, thinly sliced
2 stalks celery, thinly sliced
1 carrot, finely diced
¼ cup water chestnuts, thinly sliced
¼ cup bamboo shoots, sliced
1 cup salad shrimp
2 cups bean sprouts
2 tablespoons brown sugar

¼ cup chopped fresh ginger
3 tablespoons cornstarch, dissolved in ¼ cup soy sauce
6 large whole boneless chicken breasts, skin removed but reserved
Flour
3 eggs, beaten
Fresh bread crumbs, finely ground

Heat oil in large skillet. Add onion, celery, carrot, water chestnuts, bamboo shoots and shrimp; stir until soft. Add the sprouts and cook until softened. Stir in the brown sugar and ginger; and incorporate thoroughly. Add cornstarch-soy sauce mixture and cook, stirring, until thickened. Remove from heat.

Lay chicken breasts flat on table. Divide filling equally in the center of each breast. Fold sides over to cover filling and form an oval. Wrap skin around the breast and chill.

When cold, roll each breast in flour, then in beaten eggs, and then roll in bread crumbs. Heat oil in skillet and cook breasts, turning until evenly browned. Remove from skillet and place on baking sheet in a 400-degree oven for 30 minutes.

Serve with rice and Apricot Ginger Sauce.

APRICOT GINGER SAUCE

3 tablespoons butter
3 tablespoons chopped fresh ginger
¼ cup brown sugar
1 can apricots, sliced

½ cup dry white wine
¼ cup apricot brandy
½ cup water
1 teaspoon cinnamon
½ teaspoon allspice

In saucepan, melt the butter and sauté ginger until soft. Add the sugar and cook, stirring, until smooth. Add remaining ingredients and bring to a boil. Simmer for 20 minutes. Spoon over chicken breasts.

Fred Graczyk, Proprietor
Terence J. Shuster, Chef
Freddie's in West Bloomfield

TOM THE TURKEY SHORTCAKE

A delicious way to use up your Thanksgiving turkey

¾	cup yellow cornmeal	1½	teaspoons baking powder
1	cup boiling water	½	cup butter, melted
1	teaspoon salt	2	cups cooked turkey, cut
3	eggs		in cubes
1	cup milk		

Preheat oven to 350 degrees.
Place cornmeal in a medium mixing bowl. Stir in the boiling water.
Add salt, stir to blend, then set aside. In a small bowl, beat the eggs
with the milk until blended; stir into cornmeal mixture. Add the
baking powder, butter and turkey. Spoon mixture into a buttered
1½-quart casserole. Bake for 45 minutes then cut into squares. Serve
with gravy and a tossed salad.

Serves 6
Preparation time: 15 minutes
Baking time: 45 minutes   Clyde Cleveland
Easy   Detroit City Council

CHICKEN MARENGO

Two chickens cut into eighths		2	tablespoons tomato paste
¼	cup butter	½	cup white wine
1	large onion, diced		Pinch each of thyme and oregano
Minced garlic to taste		½	cup chicken broth
1	cup mushrooms, sliced		Salt and red pepper
2	tablespoons flour		

Brown chicken under broiler. In a large pan, melt the butter and sauté
onions and garlic until glossy. Add the mushrooms and cook 2-3
minutes. Add remaining ingredients and season to taste.
Pour sauce over chicken, cover with foil and bake in a 350-degree
oven for one hour.

Serves 6-8
Preparation time: 30 minutes
Can be made ahead and reheated
Easy   Nicette Watkinson

ROCK CORNISH HENS VICTOR BORGE

Easy and impressive . . . from the "Great Dane"

6	Rock Cornish hens	1-3	tablespoons water
½	cup butter	½	cup light cream
1¼	cups water		Liquid gravy base
	Salt and pepper to taste	½	teaspoon sugar
1	tablespoon flour		Salt and pepper

Rub the insides of the hens with salt and pepper. Tie wings and legs together and sear in butter in a kettle until golden brown — ten to twelve minutes. ("If a clock is not available, play the Minute Waltz ten to twelve times" V.B.) Add the water and let simmer, covered, 30-45 minutes or until tender. Remove birds. Prepare sauce: mix the flour with 1 or more tablespoons of water, just enough to make a thick paste. Stir well into the drippings. Add cream, gravy base and sugar and mix well; add salt and pepper to taste. Pour over hens and serve immediately.

Serves 6
Preparation time: 20 minutes
Cooking time: 45 minutes   Victor Borge

GARLIC CHICKEN SEVERINSEN

This recipe was given to us by Doc Severinsen when he appeared with the Detroit Symphony Orchestra at the Meadowbrook Music Festival in 1982.

3	tablespoons olive oil	1	whole head of garlic (cluster of cloves)
8	boneless whole chicken breasts	1	cup Sauterne

Heat oil in a large skillet. Brown chicken breasts in hot oil. Separate garlic cloves from head, trim ends but leave skin intact. Add garlic and Sauterne to chicken. Cover and simmer over low heat for 45 minutes or until tender.
Serve with couscous or rice.

Serves 8
Preparation time: 15 minutes
Cooking time: 45 minutes
Easy   Doc Severinsen

CHICKEN DIVINE

5 tablespoons butter, divided
8 whole chicken breasts, skinned, boned and cut in half
3 tablespoons brandy
¼ pound mushrooms, sliced

3 tablespoons flour
2 tablespoons tomato paste
1 cup chicken bouillon
1 cup sour cream
Salt and pepper
½ cup grated Parmesan cheese

In a large skillet, melt 3 tablespoons butter; slowly brown the chicken. Heat brandy in a small pan, ignite and pour over the breasts. Remove chicken from skillet. Into the same skillet, put 1 tablespoon butter and sauté mushrooms for five minutes or until lightly browned. Blend in flour and tomato paste. Add the bouillon and stir until sauce comes to a boil. Add the sour cream a little at a time, mixing well; season to taste with salt and pepper. Return chicken to skillet, cover with waxed paper, place lid on pan and cook over low heat for 25 minutes or until tender.
To serve: Arrange chicken on ovenproof platter. Cover with sauce, sprinkle with Parmesan cheese and dot with butter. Run under broiler until brown and bubbly.

Serves 8-16
Preparation time: 30 minutes
Cooking time: 25 minutes   Joan Long

CHICKEN WITH MUENSTER

2 whole chicken breasts, split in half, skinned and boned
Flour seasoned with salt and pepper
½ cup butter, divided

2 tablespoons vegetable oil
½ cup dry red wine
Salt and pepper
12 large mushroom caps, sliced
4 slices Muenster cheese

Slightly flatten the chicken breasts between sheets of waxed paper. Lightly dredge in seasoned flour shaking off the excess. In a medium skillet, heat ¼ cup butter with the oil. Sauté the chicken until lightly browned and cooked through — about 4 minutes on each side. Transfer the chicken to a flame-proof serving dish.
To the pan, add the wine and bring to a boil, stirring in the brown bits

that cling to the pan. Simmer mixture for 3 minutes. Add salt and pepper to taste and pour over the chicken. Heat remaining butter and sauté the mushrooms for 5 minutes; season with salt and pepper. Preheat broiler. Top each chicken breast with a slice of cheese. Divide mushrooms over chicken and spoon some of the liquid on top. Place dish under the broiler for 3 minutes or until cheese is melted.

Serves 2
Preparation time: 30 minutes
Easy

Holly Barnett

CHICKEN DRESSING CASSEROLE

4 large chicken breasts, or 1 3-pound fryer
Broth from poached chicken
1 can condensed cream of chicken soup
1 can condensed cream of mushroom soup

½ cup butter, melted
1 8-ounce package herb seasoned stuffing mix
1 package frozen green beans, cooked and drained
Slivered almonds
Parmesan cheese

Poach chicken until tender. Strain cooking broth and reserve 2½ cups. Bone and cut chicken into bite-sized pieces. Combine broth and condensed soups, mix well and set aside. Melt the butter in a skillet, add stuffing mix and toss well. Put ¾ of the stuffing in 9x13-inch pan and pat it down.

Put the chicken and green beans in layers over the dressing. Pour the soup mixture over and cover with remaining stuffing. Top with almonds and Parmesan cheese. Bake for 1 hour in a 350-degree oven or until bubbly hot.

Serves 8-10
Make ahead
Freezes well
Easy

Judy Harris

ESTHER'S CHICKEN

2	cups uncooked rice	1	cup orange juice
2	cans condensed golden mushroom soup	5	whole chicken breasts, skinned
2	cups Sherry	1	package dry onion soup mix

Wash the rice and spread it in a 9x13-inch baking dish. Combine the mushroom soup, Sherry and orange juice. Pour 1 cup of the orange juice mixture over the rice, and place the chicken on top. Pour the remaining orange juice mixture over the chicken then sprinkle on the onion soup mix. Bake in a 350-degree oven for 1½ hours.
Note: If less salt is preferred, use less onion soup.

Serves 6-8
Preparation time: 15 minutes
Baking time: 1 hour
Easy   Mary Alice Bird

GRANDMA REUTER'S CHICKEN AND NOODLES

1	2½-3 pound chicken	2	chicken bouillon cubes
1	quart poaching broth from the chicken	8	ounces egg noodles, preferably homemade

Poach the chicken and remove the meat — set aside. Skim the fat from the broth and measure out 4 cups. Add the bouillon cubes, chicken and noodles. Cook until noodles are done.

Serves 6-8
Preparation time: 1 hour   Iva Reuter

CHICKEN BREASTS HAVARTI

CHICKEN

6	whole chicken breasts, skinned and boned	1	tablespoon dried tarragon
			Flour
6	slices Havarti cheese, about ⅛ inch thick	2	eggs beaten with 2 tablespoons cream
6	thin slices prosciutto ham		Fresh bread crumbs
6	chunks frozen butter, about ¼ inch thick	2	tablespoons butter
		2	tablespoons oil

Preheat oven to 350 degrees.

Open chicken breasts and pound lightly between sheets of waxed paper until flattened slightly. Place a slice of cheese folded in half on opened boned side of each breast. Place prosciutto on top of cheese. Top with 1 slice of butter and ½ teaspoon tarragon. Fold breast together and press edges shut.

Dredge breasts in flour, dip in egg mixture, then coat with bread crumbs. Place in refrigerator for 30 minutes to set crumbs.

In a large skillet, heat butter and oil. Sauté breasts until lightly browned on both sides and transfer to shallow baking dish. Bake for 20 minutes. Serve with Diable Bearnaise Sauce.

SAUCE

2	tablespoons minced shallot	1	tablespoon Escoffier Sauce Diable
2	tablespoons dried tarragon		
½	cup dry vermouth		Salt
¼	cup wine vinegar (red or white)		White pepper
1	cup sweet butter	2	tablespoons minced fresh parsley
4	egg yolks		
1	teaspoon Escoffier Sauce Robert		

Combine shallots, tarragon, vermouth, and wine vinegar in sauce pan; bring to a boil and reduce to 2 tablespoons. Melt butter until it bubbles. Do not let it brown.

In a blender or food processor, blend egg yolks. Add butter in a thin stream. Blend in tarragon mixture, Sauce Robert and Sauce Diable. Remove from container and season with salt, pepper and parsley.

Maxim Janowsky
DSO

CHICKEN ALLA CARCIOFI

Chicken with Artichoke Hearts

2 tablespoons olive oil
2 whole chicken breasts, skinned, boned and cut into pieces
Flour for dredging
1 egg lightly beaten with 1 tablespoon water

½ cup vermouth or dry white wine
1 cup sliced mushrooms
1 cup artichoke hearts, cut in half
Salt and pepper
Freshly chopped parsley

In a medium skillet, heat the oil. Lightly dredge the chicken pieces in the flour and then dip in the beaten egg. Sauté chicken until white and translucent. Add the wine and cook until chicken is tender. Stir in the mushrooms, cook 3 minutes longer, then season to taste. Add the artichoke hearts and cook until heated through. Sprinkle with parsley and serve immediately.

Serves 2
Preparation time: 20 minutes
Easy

Rho Blanchard

STIR-FRY CHICKEN WITH WALNUTS

5 tablespoons tamari or soy sauce
1 tablespoon cornstarch
2 tablespoons dry Sherry
1 teaspoon freshly grated gingerroot
1 teaspoon sugar
⅛ teaspoon cayenne pepper, or to taste
Vegetable oil

2 green peppers cut in ¾-inch pieces
¼ pound mushrooms, sliced
6 green onions cut in ½-inch lengths
1 cup walnuts
1½ pounds chicken breasts, skinned, boned and cut in 1-inch pieces
2 slices gingerroot

In small bowl blend the tamari, cornstarch, Sherry grated gingerroot, sugar and cayenne pepper. Set aside.
Preheat wok or large skillet over high heat. Add a small amount of oil. When oil is hot, add green pepper, mushrooms, and onions, stir-frying quickly until crisp tender. Remove from wok. Add more oil if

necessary and stir fry walnuts until just golden; remove from wok. Add more oil if necessary and stir-fry chicken with sliced ginger-root 4-5 minutes or until done. Remove gingerroot slices and add tamari mixture. Cook, stirring, until thick and bubbly. Return vegetables and walnuts, cover and cook 1 minute longer until heated. Serve at once over rice.

Serves 4　　　　　　　　　　　　　　　　　　Kevin Good
Preparation time: 15 minutes　　　　　　　　　　　DSO

HUNGARIAN CHICKEN PAPRIKAS

Serve with galuska, egg noodles or rice, and cucumber salad

2　2½-pound fryers, cut up
Salt and pepper
2　medium onions, finely
　　chopped, divided
3　tablespoons bacon fat or
　　other shortening, divided

3　tablespoons sweet
　　Hungarian imported
　　paprika, divided
1　green pepper, chopped
2　cups chicken stock
1½ cups sour cream

Wash and dry chicken pieces and sprinkle generously with salt and pepper. Sauté half the onions in 2 tablespoons shortening until golden. Mix in 1 tablespoon paprika. Add half of the chicken pieces and brown on both sides; transfer to a large pot. Scrape bottom of frying pan and add this to the pot. Sauté remaining onions in re-maining shortening, add 1 tablespoon paprika and brown the remaining chicken. Add to pot along with green pepper and remaining paprika. Add chicken stock, cover and simmer gently for 1½ hours or until chicken is tender.

Before serving, remove chicken and blend sour cream with a small amount of warm broth until smooth. Add sour cream mixture to pot and mix well. Add chicken to sauce and heat just until hot — do not boil or sour cream will curdle.

Note: Entire dish can be made in a crock pot. After browning, put all ingredients, except sour cream, in pot and cook on low for 5-7 hours or until tender.

Serves 6-8　　　　　　　　　　　　　　　　Beatriz Staples
Preparation time: 2½ hours　　　　　　　　　　　　DSO

CLUB CHICKEN CASSEROLE

¼ cup butter
¼ cup flour
1   14½-ounce can evaporated milk
1   cup chicken broth
½ cup dry white wine
3   cups cooked long grain rice
½ cup sliced mushrooms

2½ cups diced white meat chicken
⅓ cup chopped green pepper
¼ cup chopped pimento
1½ teaspoons salt
¼ cup almonds, sliced and toasted

Melt the butter in saucepan and blend in flour. Add evaporated milk, broth, and wine. Cook over medium heat, stirring constantly, until thickened and bubbly. Add the rice, mushrooms, chicken, green peppers, pimento and salt. Pour into a greased 2-quart casserole. Bake uncovered in a 350-degree oven for 40 minutes. Top with almonds and bake 3 minutes longer.

Serves 8-10
Preparation time: 10 minutes
Cooking time: 45 minutes
Easy
Freezes well   Carmella Gusfa

FRENCH CHICKEN LOUISIANA

2   tablespoons butter
1   tablespoon olive oil
2½-3 pounds chicken, cut up, or chicken breasts cut in half
2   teaspoons Italian spices, divided

3   green onions, with tops, cut up
Salt and pepper to taste
1   tablespoon white wine

Heat the butter and oil in pan. Add chicken, cover and simmer for 5 minutes. Sprinkle with 1 teaspoon Italian spices, cover and cook 10-15 minutes longer. Turn chicken over. Add the green onions, salt and pepper to taste, remaining teaspoon of Italian spices, and white wine. Cover and cook for 15 minutes longer or until chicken is tender.

Serves 4-6
Preparation time: 40 minutes to table
Easy   Lee Peters

MITCH'S SPECIAL LEMON CHICKEN

In addition to his "Sing Along" fame, Mitch Miller is well known for his culinary expertise. He says this dish is simple — anybody can prepare it.

¼ cup flour	2 whole chicken breasts, halved, skinned and boned
1 tablespoon salt	
1 tablespoon freshly ground black pepper	2 tablespoons butter
	2 tablespoons chopped fresh parsley
1 tablespoon imported Hungarian paprika	Juice and peel of 2 lemons

In a large bowl, mix together the flour, salt, pepper and paprika. Cut each chicken breast into six pieces and dredge in the flour mixture. Place chicken on a rack and refrigerate for at least 1 hour to allow flavors to permeate the chicken.

Preheat oven to 400 degrees. Place the butter in an oven-proof pan and brown the chicken in the oven — about 4 minutes on each side. Add chopped parsley, lemon juice and peel. Cook 5-10 minutes longer, or until the chicken is tender but still juicy. Serve immediately.

Serves 2
Preparation time: 20 minutes
Easy   Mitch Miller

CHICKEN CASSEROLE

1 cup uncooked rice	Pinch each of thyme, parsley and marjoram
3 cups cooked chicken, cut up	
1 can condensed celery soup	½ cup chicken broth
¾ cup mayonnaise	1 cup sliced almonds

Combine all ingredients except the almonds and place in a 2½-quart buttered casserole. Top with almonds and bake in a 350-degree oven for 45 minutes.

Serves 4-6
Preparation time: 15 minutes
Cooking time: 45 minutes
Easy   Dorothy Brennan

CHICKEN IN CHABLIS

2 whole chicken breasts, skinned, boned, and cut in half
Salt
Nutmeg
2 tablespoons butter

2 tablespoons minced onion
¼ pound mushrooms, quartered
⅔ cup Chablis
1 teaspoon cornstarch mixed with 2 teaspoons Chablis

Sprinkle chicken pieces on both sides with salt and nutmeg. Melt the butter in a skillet and cook chicken until lightly browned. Add the minced onion, mushrooms, and Chablis. Bring to a boil, cover, reduce heat and simmer for 20-30 minutes, or until chicken is tender. Remove chicken to a warm serving platter.

Bring pan juices to a boil and cook, stirring, until liquid is slightly reduced. Stir in the cornstarch mixture and cook, stirring constantly, until thickened. Spoon sauce over chicken or return chicken to skillet and heat through. Serve with pilaf and green beans or asparagus.

Serves 2-4
Preparation time: 40 minutes
Easy   Davida Raber

 ## NATALIE'S CHICKEN

The sauce may be prepared a day ahead. Then simply bake the chicken and reheat the sauce.

CHICKEN
½ cup flour
½ teaspoon salt
¼ teaspoon paprika
⅛ teaspoon pepper
½ teaspoon oregano
3½ pounds chicken, cut up, or 4 whole chicken breasts

¼ cup butter
4 tomatoes, sliced
1 cup sliced mushrooms
½ cup thinly sliced green onions with tops

In a paper bag, combine the flour, salt, paprika, pepper and oregano. Place the chicken in the bag and shake until all pieces are well coated. Melt the butter in a shallow 2-quart casserole and lay the chicken in one layer, skin side down. Bake in a 400-degree oven for 30 minutes or until browned and tender.

Remove the chicken from the oven, turn pieces over, and top with the tomatoes, mushrooms and onions. Pour sauce over and return to oven for 20 minutes or until bubbly hot.

SAUCE

¼ cup butter
Remaining seasoned flour from the coating, plus enough additional flour to make ¼ cup

1½ cups chicken broth
1 cup white wine

Melt the butter in a saucepan. Stir in the flour and cook until bubbly. Remove from the heat and stir in the broth and wine. Return to the heat and cook, stirring, until thick and smooth.

Serves 4
Preparation time: 15 minutes
Baking time: 1 hour
Easy   Natalie Payne

SUPREMES DE VOLAILLE POUR "GAROTA DE IPANEMA"

2 cups black beans
4 cups cold water
½ cup finely chopped raw bacon
¾ cup finely chopped onion
4 cloves garlic, minced
1 cup dry Sherry
½ cup finely chopped carrot
4 cups chicken stock

1 large bay leaf
1 teaspoon leaf thyme
4 whole chicken breasts, boned and split
Salt and pepper to taste
1½ cups heavy cream
5 ounces Boursin fines herbes cheese

Soak beans in the water overnight at room temperature.
Drain and rinse beans. Sauté bacon over low heat for 5 minutes. Add the onion and garlic and cook until onions are soft. Add the beans, Sherry, carrot, stock, bay leaf and thyme. Simmer on low heat for about 1½ hours or until beans are tender.
Season chicken breasts with salt and pepper. Sauté over moderate heat for 4 minutes each side or until done. Remove from pan and keep warm. Deglaze pan with heavy cream and reduce to 1 cup over high heat. Whip in the Boursin cheese.
Divide the beans among 4 plates. Top with sliced chicken breast and a ribbon of Boursin sauce. Serve with brown rice and fresh green vegetables.

Serves   Edward G. Janos, Executive Chef
Money Tree Restaurant
Detroit, Michigan

CHICKEN ENCHILADAS

Crushed corn chips
1 chicken, poached, skinned and boned
½ cup chopped onion
1 4-ounce can green chilies, drained and chopped
2 cups shredded Cheddar or Monterey Jack cheese
1 can condensed cream of chicken soup
1 soup can evaporated milk

Butter the bottom and sides of 9x13-inch baking dish. Sprinkle corn chips liberally to cover the bottom of the pan. Cut chicken into bite size pieces and layer over the chips. Sprinkle with chopped onion, chilies, and cheese. Mix the soup with the milk and pour over the casserole. Bake in a 350-degree oven for 30 minutes until hot and bubbly.

Serves 6
Preparation time: 45 minutes
Baking time: 30 minutes
Easy

Marilyn Shuler

COMPANY CURRIED CHICKEN

Serve with rice or noodles

1 broiler/fryer chicken cut into serving pieces
1 cup orange marmalade
1 tablespoon curry powder
1 teaspoon salt
½ cup water

Butter a 9x13-inch baking dish. Place chicken pieces, skin side down, in dish. In a small bowl combine the marmalade, curry powder, salt and water. Pour over the chicken and bake uncovered, 45-60 minutes, or until chicken is tender. Baste occasionally with the sauce. Remove chicken to platter, skim fat off sauce, and pour over chicken.

Serves 4
Preparation time: 10 minutes
Cooking time: 1 hour
Easy

Mary Powanda

HERBED LEMON CHICKEN

¼ cup olive oil
1 3½-pound chicken, cut into serving pieces
¼ teaspoon each: tarragon, basil, thyme, garlic salt, freshly ground pepper and seasoned salt

1 lemon, thinly sliced
Juice of 1 lemon
Paprika
Additional seasoned salt

Preheat oven to 350 degrees. Pour the olive oil into the bottom of a baking dish large enough to hold the chicken in a single layer. Place the chicken, skin side down, in the dish and sprinkle with the herbs, garlic salt, pepper and ¼ teaspoon seasoned salt. Cover with the lemon slices and sprinkle the juice over the chicken. Bake for 30 minutes. Turn the chicken skin side up and sprinkle with paprika and seasoned salt to taste. Return to oven and bake for 35 minutes longer or until browned and done.

Serves 4
Preparation time: 15 minutes
Baking time: 1 hour
Easy

Janet Hanson

STICKY CHICKEN

2 2½-3 pound chickens, cut up
1 8-ounce bottle Wishbone Russian dressing

1 12-ounce jar apricot preserves
1 package dry onion soup mix

Preheat oven to 350 degrees.
In a saucepan, combine dressing, jam and soup mix. Heat and mix well. Place chicken in a rosting pan large enough to hold in one layer and cover with sauce. Bake 1 hour, uncovered, basting occasionally.

Rosalind Kesner
DSO

NAPA VALLEY CHICKEN

Outstanding and easy

CHICKEN

2½ to 3 pounds chicken parts
Flour seasoned with salt and
   pepper to taste

2 tablespoons butter
2 tablespoons vegetable oil

SAUCE

⅓ cup wine vinegar
1 cup chicken broth
2 teaspoons oregano
2 teaspoons rosemary
1 clove garlic, crushed
2 tablespoons finely chopped
   onion
½ cup ketchup
2 tablespoons brown sugar
   or honey

1 teaspoon salt
½ teaspoon paprika
1 teaspoon soy sauce
1 teaspoon Worcestershire
   sauce
1 cup white wine mixed with
   1 tablespoon flour

Dredge the chicken in the flour. Heat the butter and oil in a skillet; add the chicken and cook until nicely browned. Transfer chicken to a large baking pan.

Combine the ingredients for the sauce and pour over chicken. Cover and bake in a 325-degree oven for 45 minutes. Remove cover and cook 15 minutes longer or until chicken is tender.

Serves 6
Preparation time: 20 minutes
Cooking time: 1 hour
Can make ahead and reheat
Easy

Karen Quarnstrom

CHICKEN QUENELLES WITH PASTA

An epicurean delight

CHICKEN QUENELLES

1	pound boneless chicken breasts, chilled and cut into 1-inch cubes	1	tablespoon grated Parmesan cheese
Salt, pepper and freshly grated nutmeg to taste		1	egg
		¾	cup heavy cream

Process the chicken in a food processor fitted with the steel blade. Add salt and pepper, nutmeg, cheese, egg and cream. Blend thoroughly.

In a large kettle, bring 3 quarts of water to a boil. Using a pastry bag fitted with a round #7 pastry tube, fill the bag with the chicken mixture. Holding the tube over the simmering water, squeeze out about 1 inch of the mixture at a time, letting the quenelles fall into the water. Simmer gently for 2 minutes, then using a slotted spoon, remove quenelles from the water. Continue this process until all the chicken mixture is used. Set aside.

PASTA

2	pounds asparagus, trimmed, scraped and cut into ½-inch lengths	¼	teaspoon freshly grated nutmeg
1	pound green fettucine	1	teaspoon finely minced garlic
1	pound white fettucine	1	cup butter, softened
3	cups heavy cream	1	cup freshly grated Parmesan cheese
Salt and freshly ground pepper to taste		1½	cups toasted pine nuts

Cook the asparagus in salted water for 2 minutes, drain well and transfer to a serving dish. Cook the pasta to the desired degree of tenderness. In a small saucepan, heat the cream, salt, pepper, nutmeg and garlic; bring to a simmer. Drain the pasta and add it to the asparagus. Add the softened butter and pour on the cream sauce. Sprinkle with the grated cheese and pine nuts. Toss well with the reserved quenelles and freshly ground pepper. Serve with additional cheese.

Serves 10-12   Chris Considine

POULET ROQUEFORT

ROQUEFORT BUTTER

¾ cup sweet butter
½ cup Roquefort cheese

½ cup pecans, toasted and
   chopped
4 grinds fresh white pepper

Beat butter until soft and blend in the Roquefort, pecans and pepper. Chill for 30 minutes then form into a thin log and cut into 12 equal pieces.

CHICKEN

6 whole chicken breasts
Salt and pepper
Seasoned flour
2 eggs mixed with
   2 tablespoons of water

Fresh white bread crumbs
¼ cup butter

Remove skin and bones from breasts, leaving the whole breast in one piece. Make a small pocket in the thickest part of the breast on the underside. Season the chicken lightly with salt and pepper. Insert a piece of the Roquefort butter in each pocket and reform the breast to the original shape. Chill for 30 minutes.

Coat chicken carefully with seasoned flour, then dip in the egg wash, then in the bread crumbs. Heat butter in a sauté pan and brown the breasts on all sides. Place in an ovenproof dish and bake in a 350-degree oven for 20 minutes.

Serves 6   Yvonne Gill

TARRAGON CHICKEN

2 pounds chicken breasts,
   skinned and boned
1 cup flour
1½ teaspoons salt
½ teaspoon pepper
¼ cup butter
⅓ cup brandy

1 8-ounce can tiny whole
   onions, drained
½ cup sliced mushrooms
½ cup dry white wine
1 teaspoon tarragon
4 1-inch balls of butter,
   chilled

Cut chicken into serving pieces. Combine the flour, salt and pepper in a paper bag. Add the chicken, close the bag and shake well to coat with the seasoned flour. Melt the ¼ cup butter in a large skillet and brown chicken well. Remove skillet from the heat. In a small pan heat, but do not boil, the brandy. Pour the hot brandy over the chicken and ignite it. Stir until flame dies then add the onions, mushrooms, wine and tarragon. Cover tightly and place over low heat. Simmer for 45 minutes or until tender — do not lift lid for 35 minutes, then check to see if chicken is done, or bake in a 350-degree oven for 45 minutes. Transfer to a hot platter and top with butter balls, allow butter to melt on the hot chicken at the table.

Serves 4
Preparation time: 30 minutes
Cooking time: 45 minutes

Helen Peterson

COQ AU VIN BLANC

6 chicken breasts, or 1 chicken cut into serving pieces	1 tablespoon butter
Lemon juice	1 shallot clove, finely minced
¼ cup butter, melted	1 generous teaspoon flour
Salt and pepper	2 large ripe tomatoes, peeled, seeded and chopped
2 tablespoons oil	½ cup dry white wine or dry vermouth
1 tablespoon butter	
12 mushrooms caps	½ cup mushroom liquor
¾ cup water	1 tablespoon tomato paste
Juice of 1 lemon	Salt and pepper

Rub the chicken with lemon juice and pour the hot butter over them. Let stand at room temperature until ready to use. Then salt and pepper the chicken pieces.

In a large skillet, heat the oil and 1 tablespoon of butter and sauté the chicken until pieces are brown on all sides and almost done — 10-15 minutes on each side. Remove the chicken and keep warm. In a small saucepan, simmer the mushroom caps in the water with the juice of the lemon and 1 tablespoon of butter for 5 minutes. Drain and reserve the liquid. To the juices left in the skillet, add the shallot and flour. Blend well and cook slowly for 3 minutes. Add the tomatoes, and simmer for 3 minutes. Add the wine and mushroom liquor. Simmer the sauce, uncovered, for 15 minutes. Add the tomato paste and season to taste. Return the chicken to the skillet, add the mushrooms and simmer for 5 minutes.

Serves 6
Preparation time: 1 hour
Easy

Charity de Vicq Suczek

BAKED CHICKEN SOUFFLE

A delicious, make ahead entree

9 slices bread, crust removed	4 eggs, well beaten
4 cups chicken, cooked and diced	2 cups milk
4 ounces mushrooms, sliced	1 teaspoon salt
1 can water chestnuts, drained and sliced	1 can cream of mushroom soup
Mayonnaise	1 can celery soup
1 package sliced sharp American cheese	1 2-ounce jar pimento, chopped
	2 cups buttered bread crumbs

Line a buttered 9x13-inch baking pan with the sliced bread. Top with the chicken. Combine the mushrooms and water chestnuts and sprinkle over the chicken. Cover with a thin layer of mayonnaise and top with sliced cheese.

Blend the eggs, milk and salt and pour over cheese. Mix the soups and pimento and spoon over all. Cover with foil and refrigerate overnight. When ready to bake, bring to room temperature. Bake in a 350-degree oven for 1¼ hours. Sprinkle with crumbs on top and bake 15 minutes longer.

Serves 9-12   Whitney Jill Sale

CHICKEN FRANCAISE

1 tablespoon olive oil	Juice of 1 lemon
2 whole chicken breasts, skinned, boned and cut in half	1 teaspoon salt
	Freshly ground pepper to taste
1 small onion, finely chopped	½ cup plus 2 tablespoons white wine, divided
2 tablespoons chopped parsley	1 tablespoon butter
	Grated Parmesan cheese
2 cloves garlic, minced	1 lemon, thinly sliced

Heat the oil in a skillet, and brown the chicken over medium-high heat until golden on each side, adding more oil if needed. Drain chicken on paper towels to remove excess oil and place in a buttered 8x8-inch baking pan; set aside.

To the skillet, add the onion and sauté for 2 minutes. Add the parsley, garlic, lemon juice, salt and pepper, ½ cup wine and butter. Cook, stirring, for 3-4 minutes or until reduced slightly. Add remaining wine and return to a boil, scraping all bits from the bottom of the pan. Pour sauce over the chicken and sprinkle with cheese. Place lemon slices over, cover pan with foil, and bake in a 350-degree oven for 20 minutes. Uncover and bake for 15 minutes longer, or until browned and tender.

Serves 4
Preparation time: 20 minutes
Cooking time: 30 minutes
Easy   Melanie Resnick Wells

MUSTARD CHICKEN

A simple but elegant entree

½ cup Dijon mustard	4 teaspoons crumbled, dried rosemary
3-4 cloves garlic, minced	
2 2½-3 pound chickens, cut up	Pepper to taste
	¾ cup grated Parmesan cheese

Preheat oven to 350 degrees.

Mix the mustard and garlic. Place chicken in a baking dish in one layer. Brush generously with the mustard mixture. Sprinkle with rosemary and pepper and top with Parmesan cheese. Bake, uncovered, until chicken is done — about 1 hour.

Serves 6-8
Preparation time: 10 minutes
Baking time: 1 hour
Easy   Michael Schwartz

HUNAN CHICKEN

1 tablespoon safflower oil
12 Szechwan peppers, crumbled
10 whole Szechwan peppercorns
2 cloves garlic, minced
1 teaspoon minced fresh ginger
2 green onions, chopped
1 whole chicken breast, skinned, boned and shredded
6 fresh mushrooms, sliced
16 snow peas, strings removed
3 napa leaves, shredded
1 tablespoon rice wine
2 tablespoons oyster sauce
1 tablespoon tamari sauce
1 tablespoon hoisin sauce
1 teaspoon sesame oil

Heat the oil in a wok or skillet. Add the peppers, peppercorns, garlic, ginger and onions; cook for 2 minutes. Add the chicken breast and cook until the pieces turn opaque. Make a well in the center and add the mushrooms, snow peas and napa leaves. Stir in the remaining ingredients except the sesame oil and cook for 2 minutes. Remove from the heat and toss with the sesame oil. Serve with steamed brown rice.

Serves 2

Maria Ang
Farrell Shopping Center
29267 Southfield Road
Southfield, Michigan

CHICKEN STRUDEL

This make-ahead dinner can be doubled or tripled

3 tablespoons butter
½ cup mushrooms, chopped
1 onion, chopped
1 clove garlic, minced
3 tablespoons flour
½ teaspoon salt
½ teaspoon pepper
1 cup chicken broth
1 cup light cream
2 egg yolks, beaten
2 cups diced, cooked chicken
3 sheets phyllo dough
Melted butter

Melt the butter in a skillet. Add the mushrooms, onion and garlic and sauté until just dry. Add the flour, salt, pepper and broth. Cook for 5 minutes. Stir in the cream and egg yolks. Add chicken and heat well, but do not allow to boil.
Lay the phyllo dough out flat and keep covered with a damp cloth. Brush one layer with melted butter, add the second layer on top and

brush with melted butter. Repeat procedure with the third layer. Spread the chicken mixture on one end of the dough, and roll up as for strudel. (This is easier to do if the chicken mixture has been made ahead and refrigerated overnight.)

Bake in a 350-degree oven for 30 minutes or until golden.

Note: Spinach or cooked meat can be used instead of the chicken.

Serves 6   Mrs. G. del Gaudio

GOLD COAST STEW

Excellent buffet dish

2	green peppers, cut into rings	½	teaspoon nutmeg
1	medium onion, cut into rings	4	cups cooked chicken, cubed, or leftover turkey or veal
2	tablespoons butter	Rice	
1	6-ounce can tomato paste	Accompaniments:	
¾	cup peanut butter		Grated coconut
3	cups chicken broth, or dissolved bouillon cubes		Chopped peanuts
			Pineapple chunks
1½	teaspoons salt		Sautéed banana slices
1	teaspoon chili powder		Sautéed tomato slices
1	teaspoon sugar		Sautéed eggplant slices

Cook peppers and onion in butter until softened; drain off fat. In a bowl, blend the tomato paste and peanut butter, stir in broth and seasonings and add to onion in pan. Add the chicken and mix well. Cook, stirring, over low heat until heated through.

Serve over hot rice with accompaniments.

Serves 8
Preparation time: 30 minutes
Cooking time: 15 minutes
Freezes well — even with the rice   Rosalind Kesner
Easy   DSO

FIGHTING ISLAND CHARCOAL BROILED DUCK BREASTS

4 freshly killed wild ducks
8 slices bacon
Salt and pepper
2 beef bouillon cubes
1 cup water
1 tablespoon currant jelly
½ teaspoon dry mustard

1 tablespoon Sherry
1 tablespoon red wine *or* brandy
Pinch of marjoram *or* oregano
Salt and pepper
Rind of 1 orange

With a sharp knife, remove the breasts from the ducks, then remove the skin. Cut breasts in half and crimp like a filet mignon and wrap a strip of bacon around securing with 3-4 toothpicks in each breast. Season with salt and pepper.

Very slowly charcoal broil the breasts over a low flame. The breasts should take 4-5 minutes on each side for rare and the bacon will be medium done.

Meanwhile, in a small saucepan dissolve the bouillon cubes in the water. Add the remaining ingredients and mix well. Cook over a low heat until well combined. When duck breasts are done, place them in the sauce for a few minutes. Pass sauce separately.

Serves 4-8   Robert B. Semple

SAUTÉED DUCK BREASTS

4 duck breasts
¼ cup lemon juice
¼ cup butter
1 large onion, chopped
Seasoned salt

8 fresh mushrooms, sliced
1 cup Burgundy wine
2 tablespoons currant jelly
Wild Rice

Bone the duck breasts obtaining 8 pieces. Marinate breasts in lemon juice for 30 minutes, the drain. In a large skillet, melt the butter. Sauté the onion until soft. Add breasts and cook over low heat for 5 minutes; season to taste with salt. Add the mushrooms and wine, cover, and cook until tender. When done, stir in the currant jelly. Serve with wild rice.

Serves 4
Preparation time: 30 minutes   Alice Reisig

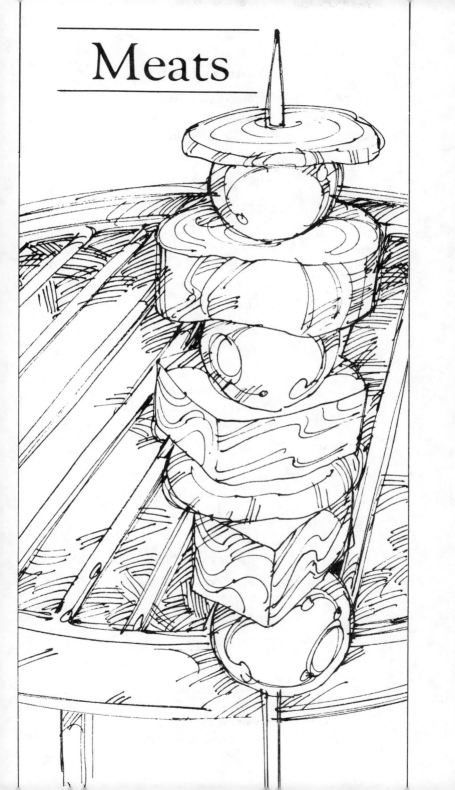

Meats

Christmas Dinner

Hot Buttered Rum
Elizabeth's Escargots
Cream of Bourbonnaise
Irish Fruit and Nut Bread
Cranberry Eggnog Wreath
Standing Rib Roast
Natural Juices
Yorkshire Pudding
Mustard Glazed Carrots
Texas Potatoes
Sugared Walnuts
Plum Pudding
Russian Creme

Wine Suggestions
An elegant, well aged
Bordeaux; such as
a Chateau Leoville-Las-Cases (1970)

Friends 40th Birthday

Shrimp Mold Segovia
Party Rye Slices
Hearts of Palm Salad
Individual Beef Wellingtons
Fresh Asparagus
Broiled Tomatoes
Poached Pears

Wine Suggestions
A rich, hearty red; such as
a Charmes-Chambertin
from A Rousseau (1976)

1982 CHAMPION CHILI

This recipe was entered in the 1982 World Chili Cook-off as the winning Michigan entry, and in the 1981 Cook-off as the Ohio entry. It's great!

6	pounds beef brisket	2	teaspoons salt
1½	pounds pork shoulder	3	onions, chopped
1	cup (6-ounce can) Gebhart's chili powder, or to taste	3	bell peppers, chopped
		1	15-ounce can tomato sauce
2	tablespoons oregano	2	cups tomato juice
¼	cup cumin	1	12-ounce can tomato paste
¼	cup ancho chilies	1	quart bouillon or beef stock
2	Jalapeño peppers, chopped	2	cups beer
2	teaspoons sugar		Water

Chop ¾ of the beef and pork and coarsely grind the remaining meat. In a large kettle, brown the meat and toss with the chili powder, oregano, cumin, chilies, Jalepeño peppers, sugar and salt. Steam the onions and peppers and add to the chili pot. Add the tomato sauce, juice, paste, and stock. Add beer as needed to keep chili slightly moist but not overly wet. Add water as needed.

Adjust chili powder and peppers to individual taste.

Jeanne Johnson-Lackey

JACK KELLEY'S CORNED BEEF 'N CABBAGE

This is an annual St. Patrick's Day dinner

4	pounds corned beef brisket	1	large carrot, sliced
	Cold water	2	pounds small round potatoes, peeled
2	onions, sliced		
1	bunch fresh parsley	2	pounds white cabbage, cut in wedges
1	bay leaf		
	Pepper to taste		

Place beef in a large pot; cover with cold water. Bring to a boil, then discard water; add fresh water to cover. Add remaining ingredients except potatoes and cabbage. Slowly bring to a boil, skimming foam off as it rises to the top. Cover and simmer gently for 4 hours. Remove parsley and add potatoes. Cook for 10 minutes then add the cabbage. Cover and simmer for 20 minutes or until potatoes and cabbage are cooked.

Serves 6-8

Jack Kelley
Detroit Councilman

TOURNEDOS CHASSEUR

¼ cup butter, divided
½ pound mushrooms, cleaned and sliced
2 tablespoons minced shallots
2 1½-inch thick pieces filet mignon

Salt and pepper to taste
½ cup beef broth
¼ cup Madeira wine
2 teaspoons cornstarch

In a skillet, melt 2 tablespoons of the butter and sauté the mushrooms until tender. Add the shallots and sauté 2-3 minutes longer. Remove mushrooms and shallots from pan.

Over moderately high heat, melt remaining butter. When foam subsides, add the filets and sauté 6-7 minutes on each side for rare, longer if desired. Remove meat from pan and season with salt and pepper to taste; keep warm. Pour off fat from skillet and stir in beef broth. Cook rapidly until liquid is reduced to ¼ cup. Dissolve cornstarch in the Madeira and add to the sauce. Cook, stirring constantly, for 1 minute or until sauce is thickened. Add mushrooms, shallots, and meat to sauce and heat thoroughly.

Serves 2
Preparation time: 30 minutes
Easy

Bonnie Lockwood

ROZ'S ROAST

1 2½ pound chuck roast or brisket
Onion powder
Garlic powder
2 tablespoons soy sauce
2 tablespoons red Russian dressing

2 teaspoons dry onion soup mix
2 teaspoons grape jelly
½ cup ketchup
Chopped onion to taste
2 tablespoons red wine

Season meat with the onion and garlic powders to taste. Combine the soy sauce and Russian dressing; mix well and spread on the meat. Sprinkle onion soup mix over and refrigerate for at least 1 hour. Combine the grape jelly and ketchup. Blend well and spread over the roast. Sprinkle with onion and add the red wine. Bake, covered, in a 350-degree oven for 2 hours or until tender.

Serves 4
Easy

Roselyn Liberson

KOREAN BEEF STRIPS

Serve with a crisp, green salad and crusty French bread

½   cup soy sauce
½   cup vegetable oil
½   cup chopped onion
3   cloves garlic, minced
1   tablespoon sesame seeds
2   tablespoons brown sugar
¼   cup Sherry
1   teaspoon finely minced
    fresh ginger
3   pounds boneless beef chuck
    thinly sliced

In a large bowl, combine all ingredients except the meat and mix well. Add the beef and toss to coat thoroughly. Cover and refrigerate overnight.
Barbecue over hot coals for 1 minute on each side.

Serves 6-8
Easy   Roberta Bloom

RINDERROULADEN

1½ to 2 pounds round steak cut
    ½ inch thick
Salt
Freshly ground pepper
Dusseldorf mustard
6   slices bacon, cooked
    and chopped
1   medium onion, chopped
1   large dill pickle, thinly
    sliced
¼   cup butter, divided
Flour
¾   cup condensed beef bouillon
½   cup red wine
Minced parsley for garnish

Pound steak to ¼-inch thickness; cut into 8 serving pieces. Season to taste with salt and pepper and brush lightly with mustard. Top each piece with some of the chopped bacon, onion and pickle. Roll firmly and fasten with thin white cord or toothpicks.
Melt 3 tablespoons butter in a heavy skillet. Dredge rolls with flour and brown on all sides over moderate heat. Add bouillon and wine. Cover and simmer gently until tender, about 1½ hours. Transfer to a warm serving dish.
Combine remaining tablespoon butter with 1 tablespoon flour and blend well. Add to pan drippings and cook, stirring constantly, until thickened. Pour over rolls and sprinkle with minced parsley.
Variation: Use carrot slices instead of pickle.

Serves 6-8
Preparation time: 45 minutes
Cooking time: 1½ hours
Make ahead and reheat   Barb Borseth

MEXI-CHILI CASSEROLE

1½ pounds ground chuck
1 10½-ounce can enchilada sauce
1 8-ounce can tomato sauce
1 tablespoon instant minced onion
1 1-pound can kidney beans, drained
2 cups shredded Cheddar cheese, divided
1 16-ounce package corn chips, divided
¾ cup sour cream

Brown meat and drain. Combine the enchilada sauce, tomato sauce, onion and beans. Mix in the meat, 1½ cups of cheese and all but 1 cup of corn chips. Gently transfer to a 2-quart casserole and bake in a 375-degree oven for 40 minutes.

Mix in the sour cream then sprinkle with the remaining cheese and corn chips. Return to oven for 5-10 minutes longer or until cheese is melted.

Serves 6
Easy
Yolanda McDonald

NEW WORLD MEAT PIE

An English friend of mine once remarked that this was truly the best meat pie he has ever had outside of England.

Top and bottom crust for a 9-inch pie
1 pound ground beef
1 cup grated carrots
1 cup chopped onion
1 teaspoon salt
¼ teaspoon pepper
1 tablespoon chili sauce
½ teaspoon Worcestershire sauce
½ cup grated American cheese
2 tablespoons butter

Preheat oven to 400 degrees.

Line a pie tin with the bottom crust. Combine the beef, carrots, onion, salt, pepper, chili sauce, and Worcestershire sauce and pat into the pie crust. Sprinkle with the cheese and dot with butter. Cover with the top crust, seal and flute. Make a few slits in the crust for steam to escape. Bake for 40 minutes. Serve with cheese sauce.

Serves 4-6
Preparation time: 15 minutes
Baking time: 40 minutes
Easy
Natalie Payne

COMPANY BEEF FILET

A great do-ahead elegant entree

ROAST

1 tablespoon olive oil
3 pounds beef filet or eye
   of rib

2 cups canned
   Madiera sauce

Preheat oven to 450 degrees. Heat the oil in a roasting pan. Add the meat and brown quickly on all sides. place in the oven and roast for 10-12 minutes; it will still be very rare. Let cool. Slice the roast into ½ inch slices, but *do not slice through*, so the meat is attached in one piece at the bottom. Stuff the filling between the slices, then wrap the meat well in foil. May be refrigerated at this point for later preparation, or cooked immediately. If refrigerated, bring to room temperature. Preheat oven to 425 degrees. Roast the beef in the foil for 15 minutes. Heat the sauce, unwrap meat, and pour sauce over and serve.

STUFFING

2 shallots
¼ pound bacon
1 pound mushrooms, coarsely
   chopped
Salt and pepper

2 pounds tomatoes, peeled,
   seeded and chopped
2 tablespoons chopped fresh
   parsley

Place the shallots and bacon in a food processor fitted with the steel blade. Turn machine on and off 5-6 times. Transfer mixture to a skillet and sauté for 1-2 minutes. Add remaining ingredients; cook over high heat, stirring constantly, for 10-15 minutes or until the moisture has evaporated. Cool.

Serves 8-10

Bobbi Pincus
Food Stylist
Cleveland, Ohio

PIN WHEELS

FILLING

¼ cup chopped onion
1 tablespoon vegetable oil
1 pound hamburger

Salt and pepper to taste
2 tablespoons flour
½ cup water

Sauté the onion in the oil until softened. Add hamburger, salt and pepper. Cook until meat is partially done. Sprinkle with flour, mix well, then add the water. Cook, stirring occasionally, until thick. Set aside. Meanwhile, make the dough.

DOUGH

2 cups flour
1 tablespoon baking powder
½ teaspoon salt

¼ cup shortening
¾ cup milk

Sift the flour, baking powder and salt. Cut in the shortening until mixture resembles coarse corn meal. Add milk just until the mixture leaves the sides of the bowl. Turn out onto a lightly floured board and, with a floured rolling pin, roll out to ½ inch thick. When hamburger mixture has cooled, spread on the dough and roll up like a jelly roll. Cut into ¼-inch slices and place on a lightly greased baking sheet. Bake in a 425-degree oven for 15-20 minutes.

Serves 4-6
Preparation time: 45 minutes
Cooking time: 20 minutes

Frances Schlottman

MARINATED BEEF TENDERLOIN

1 cup soy sauce
½ cup olive oil
1 cup Port wine
1 teaspoon thyme
1 bay leaf
1 4-pound beef tenderloin

1 teaspoon pepper
1 teaspoon salt
1 teaspoon Tabasco sauce
1 or more cloves garlic, thinly sliced
½ pound bacon

Combine the soy sauce, oil, wine, thyme and bay leaf in a deep narrow dish. Place the beef in the marinade and let sit at room temperature for 6-8 hours, turning meat frequently.

Just before cooking, preheat oven to 425 degrees. Drain meat from marinade. Combine the pepper, salt and Tabasco and rub into meat. Make small slits in the roast and insert the garlic strips. Wrap the roast in the bacon strips and place in a shallow pan. Roast for 30-35 minutes or until done. Remove and let stand for 5 minutes. Slice and serve.

Linda Williamson

STEAK VICTOR

1   3-pound round steak cut
    1½ inches thick

MARINADE

2   tablespoons Cognac
2   tablespoons lime juice
1   tablespoon salt
¾   teaspoon pepper

2   cloves garlic, minced
¾   teaspoon oregano
¾   teaspoon thyme
¾   teaspoon basil

Combine marinade ingredients and pour over the steak. Let marinate in refrigerator for at least 12 hours, then broil or grill. Slice against the grain as for London Broil.

Serves 6-8
Preparation time: 10 minutes
Marinate
Easy

Babette Posen

STUFFED CABBAGE

1   head cabbage
1   pound ground beef
½   cup raw rice
1   egg, beaten
1   small onion, grated

Salt and pepper to taste
¼   cup lemon juice
¼-½ cup brown sugar
1   cup tomato sauce
Tomato juice or water

Pour boiling water over the cabbage and let simmer for 10 minutes; drain well. Carefully separate leaves reserving the largest ones for stuffing. Combine the beef, rice, egg, onion and seasonings; mix well. Place 2-3 tablespoons of the meat mixture in each cabbage leaf. Roll up securely, tucking in the sides, and fasten with a toothpick. Place in a Dutch oven. Combine lemon juice, brown sugar to taste, and tomato sauce and add to the pot. Add tomato juice or water to cover. Cover and simmer for at least one hour, 2-3 hours would be best for flavors to develop. Adjust lemon juice and sugar to taste.

Serves 6
Preparation time: 30 minutes
Cooking time: 1-3 hours
Easy

Carl Levin
U.S. Senator from Michigan

PAKISTANI KIMA

3 tablespoons butter
1 large onion, chopped
1 pound ground beef
4 tomatoes, diced
1 8-ounce can peas
1 tablespoon curry powder, or to taste
½ teaspoon salt
1 teaspoon paprika
½ teaspoon chili powder
1 clove garlic, minced, or to taste
Rice
Curry condiments: Chutney, coconut, chopped egg, chopped peanuts

Melt the butter in a large skillet. Sauté onion for 5 minutes. Add the beef and tomatoes; cook over low heat for 15 minutes. Stir in the peas with the liquid, and seasonings. Cover and simmer for 30 minutes. Refrigerate overnight to allow flavors to blend. Reheat and serve with rice and curry condiments.

Serves 4
Preparation time: 25 minutes
Cooking time: 30 minutes
Easy
Suzanne Zielenski

LIVER VIENNOISE

¼ cup butter
2 tablespoons olive oil
2 onions, thinly sliced
¼ teaspoon sage
1 pound calves liver, cut into strips
½ cup flour seasoned with salt and pepper to taste
Juice of 1 lemon
1 cup dry white wine
2 tablespoons chopped parsley

Heat the butter and oil in a large skillet. Add the onions and sauté until golden. Sprinkle on the sage, stir, and remove to a bowl. Dredge the liver in seasoned flour. Add to pan and cook quickly over medium-high heat, stirring constantly. Add the onions, lemon juice and wine. Cover and simmer 2-3 minutes. Sprinkle with parsley and serve immediately.

Serves 3-4
Preparation time: 20 minutes
Easy
Brenda Pangborn
DSO

BEEF WITH HORSERADISH SAUCE

6 tablespoons butter, divided
4 pounds top round steak, cut into 1½-inch cubes
2 large onions, thinly sliced
2 teaspoons curry powder
1 1-inch piece ginger root, finely chopped or
  1 teaspoon ground ginger
2 tablespoons Worcestershire sauce

1 teaspoon salt
½ teaspoon freshly ground pepper
1 cup Sauternes or other sweet white wine
1 cup sour cream
2 tablespoons prepared horseradish
2 tablespoons finely chopped parsley

In a large skillet, melt 4 tablespoons butter. Brown the meat, then transfer to a casserole. Add the remaining 2 tablespoons of butter to the skillet and sauté the onions until lightly browned. Transfer onions to the casserole. Add the curry powder, ginger, Worcestershire sauce, salt, pepper and wine. Cover and cook in a 300-degree oven for 3 hours or until the meat is tender.

When ready to serve, combine the sour cream, horseradish and parsley and stir into the meat. Serve with rice.

Serves 10-12
Preparation time: 30 minutes
Cooking time: 3 hours
Easy
                                                        Pat Young

EPICUREAN BEEF CASSEROLE

Serve over noodles with a salad . . . an easy one-dish meal

½ cup fine dry bread crumbs
½ cup flour
2 pounds beef chuck or stewing beef cut in 2-inch pieces

2 cans condensed consommé
1½ teaspoons salt
¼ teaspoon pepper
2 medium onions, sliced
Optional: diced carrots

Preheat oven to 300 degrees.
In a 3-quart casserole mix crumbs with flour; add the meat and toss until meat is well coated. Add remaining ingredients and stir. Cover and bake for 2-3 hours or until meat is tender.

Serves 6
Preparation time: 20 minutes
Cooking time: 2-3 hours

                                        Peggy Tundo
                                        DSO

SHERRIED BEEF

Very easy and ever so good

3	pounds stewing beef	¾	cup Sherry
2	cans condensed cream of mushroom soup	1	package dry onion soup mix

Combine ingredients mixing well. Place in a covered casserole and bake in a 325-degree oven for 3 hours or until beef is tender. Serve with noodles or rice.

Serves 8
Preparation time: 5 minutes
Cooking time: 3 hours
Easy   Kathie O'Rourke

BEEF AND PEA PODS

1	pound flank or round steak, cut into strips	1	large sweet red pepper, thinly sliced
1	tablespoon oil	½	cup water
3	green onions, shredded	2	beef bouillon cubes
½	pound fresh mushrooms, sliced	1	tablespoon cornstarch blended with ¼ cup water
½	pound fresh pea pods		Hot cooked rice or fried noodles

Combine marinade ingredients (see below) in a glass bowl and marinate beef for at least 1 hour.
Heat the oil in a wok or large frying pan; add the onion and sauté for 1 minute. Add the beef; stir-fry until color turns, about 4 minutes. Remove beef with slotted spoon and set aside. Add the mushrooms, pea pods, red pepper, water and bouillon cubes to the wok and bring to a boil. When vegetables are crisp-tender, add the cornstarch mixture and cook until sauce is thickened. Add the cooked beef and stir until hot. Serve hot with rice or fried noodles.
Note: Any combination of fresh vegetables may be used.

MARINADE

1	clove garlic, minced	⅓	cup Sherry or red wine
1	teaspoon white pepper	2	tablespoons soy sauce
1	tablespoon brown sugar	3	tablespoons vegetable oil

Serves 3-4
Preparation time: 15 minutes
Cooking time: 10 minutes   Thomas F. Russell

BRAISED SIRLOIN TIPS

Serve over noodles or rice.

½ cup flour
1 teaspoon salt
¼ teaspoon pepper
2 pounds sirloin tips, cubed
¼ cup butter

½ pound mushrooms, sliced
1 medium onion, diced
1 can condensed consommé
½ cup red wine
1 teaspoon basil

Mix the flour, salt and pepper. Lightly dredge the meat in seasoned flour. Melt butter in a skillet; brown the meat in small batches, removing from pan when well browned. When all meat is browned, return to the pan. Add the mushrooms and onion; cook for 5 minutes. Stir in remaining seasoned flour mixture. Add the consommé, wine and basil, cover, and cook over low heat for 1 hour.

Serves 6-8
Preparation time: 30 minutes
Cooking time: 1 hour
Freezes well
Easy

Marie Draper

PEACH-GLAZED CORNED BEEF SUPPER

3 pounds corned beef brisket
2 cups water
2 medium acorn squash,
   quartered and seeded
4 small apples, cored and
   quartered

½ cup hot water
½ cup peach preserves or
   orange preserves
½ teaspoon ground ginger

Preheat oven to 350 degrees.
Rinse meat in cold water to remove pickling juices. Place meat, fat side up on a rack in a shallow roasting pan. Add water and cover with foil. Bake for 2¼ hours. Remove rack and drain liquid from the pan. Place the squash and apples, skin side down, around meat. Sprinkle squash with salt to taste. Add ½ cup hot water, cover, and bake 45 minutes. Mix the preserves and ginger. Spoon over the meat, apples and squash. Bake, uncovered, 10 minutes longer.

Serves 4-6
Preparation time: 20 minutes
Roasting time: 3 hours

Brigette Krawiec

HIGH-TEMPERATURE RIB ROAST

Remove roast from the refrigerator at least 3 hours before cooking. *Meat must be at room temperature.* Preheat oven to 500 degrees.
Place the roast in a shallow roasting pan, fat side up. Sprinkle with flour and salt and pepper to taste and rub into the meat. Place meat in the oven and roast at 500 degrees according to chart:

2 ribs	4½-5 pounds	25-30 minutes
3 ribs	8-9 pounds	40-45 minutes
4 ribs	11-12 pounds	55-60 minutes

When cooking time is finished, turn oven off. *Do not open oven door at any time.* Leave the roast in the oven for 2 hours, or until oven is lukewarm. Roast will be crunchy on the outside and inside will be able to hold for up to 4 hours.
Note: Oven must be well insulated to do this.

Daniel Shapiro

ALTERNATE METHOD
HIGH-TEMPERATURE ROASTING

Have a 6-pound roast trimmed with the ends of the ribs removed. Preheat oven to 500 degrees. Place the roast in a shallow roasting pan fat side up. Sprinkle with salt and pepper and rub in well. Pour ¼ cup cold water in the bottom of the pan. Place roast in the oven and cook for 15 minutes.
Reduce oven temperature to 400 degrees and roast for 25 minutes longer. Reduce heat to 350 degrees and finish cooking by leaving meat in for 15 minutes for rare, 30 minutes for medium-rare, and longer for well done.

Martha Hood

ON EATING: *"Can you inform me of any other pleasure which can be enjoyed three times a day, and equally in old age as in youth?"*
Charles Maurice Talleyrand Perigord

FOOL-PROOF PRIME RIB

Serve with horseradish sauce

<u>Meat must be cooked *at least* 3 hours before serving</u>. Season to taste and place roast in a shallow baking pan at least 3 hours before roasting to allow to come to room temperature. Meat *must be at room temperature*. Place roast in preheated 350-degree oven and cook for 1 hour. Turn oven off. *Do not open door at any time — leave roast in oven until time to serve*. Forty minutes before serving time, turn oven to 375 degrees. After this final cooking, the meat will be cooked to medium-rare for a roast of 3 or more ribs. For a 2 rib roast, final cooking should be only 35 minutes.

Allow 2 servings per rib   Marie Draper

VIENNESE STUFFED PEPPERS

1 cup rice	1 egg, beaten
2 cups water	Salt and pepper to taste
1 tablespoon butter	2 tablespoons chopped parsley
Pinch of salt	
6 large green peppers	2 teaspoons paprika
1 pound chopped meat	Pinch each of nutmeg, thyme and basil
1 large onion, chopped	
2 cloves garlic, minced	1 16-ounce can tomato sauce

Place the rice in a medium saucepan with the water, butter and salt. Bring to a boil, reduce heat, cover and cook on low for 20 minutes. Wash peppers well and remove seeds. In a large bowl, combine the meat, onion and garlic. Blend in the egg, seasonings and one fourth of the cooked rice; mix thoroughly. Stuff the peppers firmly with the beef-rice mixture. Pour the tomato sauce in a glass baking dish. Place the peppers in the sauce and bake in a 400-degree oven for 1½ hours, basting frequently. Serve with remaining rice.

Serves 6   Eric Knight
                                                Conductor-Arranger

FLANK STEAK FLORENTINE

2 10-ounce packages frozen chopped spinach
2 1½-pound flank steaks
2 eggs
1 cup shredded sharp Cheddar cheese
1 teaspoon sage or poultry seasoning
Dash pepper
1½ cups soft bread crumbs
2-4 tablespoons vegetable oil
1 cup chopped onion
2 cups tomato sauce
1 cup dry red wine
1 teaspoon oregano
2 cloves garlic, minced

Cook and drain spinach well; squeeze out all of the liquid. Pound the flank steaks as thin as possible. Combine the spinach, eggs, cheese, seasoning, pepper and bread crumbs; blend thoroughly. Divide mixture between the steaks and spread evenly. Roll up the meat, starting from the short side and tie with string at 1½ inch intervals.

In a large skillet, brown the meat on all sides in oil. Place meat in a 9x13-inch baking pan. In the same skillet, brown the onions. Add the tomato sauce, wine, oregano and garlic. Simmer for 5 minutes. Pour over the meat and cover pan with foil. Bake in a 350-degree oven for 1 hour 15 minutes. Remove foil and bake for 15 minutes longer. Transfer the meat to a cutting board, remove strings and cut meat into 1-inch thick slices. Serve the sauce separately.

Note: This dish can be prepared ahead of time, except for the baking.

Serves 8   Joan VanVlerah

BEEF STROGANOFF

Serve over hot fluffy rice

3 pounds lean beef
Salt and pepper to taste
¾ cup butter, divided
2 large onions, finely chopped
2 cups sliced mushrooms
¼ cup flour
2 cans condensed beef consomme
¼ cup tomato paste
2 teaspoons dry mustard
6 tablespoons Sherry
2 tablespoons soy sauce
2 cloves garlic, minced
2 tablespoons Worcestershire sauce
1⅓ cups sour cream

Cut meat into narrow strips and season with salt and pepper; set aside for 2 hours. In a large skillet, melt 6 tablespoons butter. Sauté the onions. When softened, add the mushrooms and sauté until browned.

Remove the onions and mushrooms with a slotted spoon; set aside. In the same skillet, sear the meat in batches, then set aside. Add the remaining butter to the skillet and blend in the flour. Add the remaining ingredients and cook just until heated through.

Note: This may be prepared in advance and refrigerated before the sour cream is added.

To serve: Heat in the top section of a double boiler, add the sour cream and stir until heated through.

Serves 8
Preparation time: 30 minutes
Easy

Sheila Swanson

WORLD COOKOFF CHILI

2	tablespoons lard	½	tablespoon ground dried ancho chilis
2	large Spanish onions, diced		
10	cloves garlic, minced	1	tablespoon molasses
2	10-ounce cans beef consommé	3	tablespoons brown stock base
1	14-ounce can tomato puree		Minced pickled jalapeños to taste
1	tablespoon M.S.G. (optional)		
		2	cans beer
4½	ounces Gebhart's chili powder	7	pounds beef chuck or round steak without fat, ⅓ coarsely ground and ⅔ cut into half-inch cubes
2	tablespoons ground cumin		
1	tablespoon ground coriander		
1	teaspoon allspice		Salt to taste

Heat the lard in a large kettle. Add the onions and garlic and cook over medium heat, stirring until soft. Add remaining ingredients except 1 can of beer, the beef and the salt.

In a large teflon lined skillet, sauté the beef 1 pound at a time without any oil, and add to the large pot. Simmer, covered, for 2½ hours, stirring frequently. Do not allow to scorch. Add the remaining can of beer as needed. Consistency should be that of a stew, not a soup. After simmering for 2 hours, adjust seasonings. When done, add salt if needed.

Jim Lark
The Lark Restaurant
6430 Farmington Road
West Bloomfield, Michigan

SOUP STEW

2 tablespoons oil
1 pound stewing beef
2 20-ounce cans white kidney beans
1 28-ounce can tomatoes, crushed
1 cup chopped onions
1 cup diced turnips

1 cup sliced celery
2 cups water
2 teaspoons salt
1 teaspoon sugar
3 tablespoons Worcestershire sauce
¼ teaspoon Tabasco sauce

In a kettle, heat the oil. Add the beef and brown well on all sides. Add remaining ingredients and bake in a 325-degree oven for 4 hours or until meat is tender.

Note: May be made in a slow-cooker for 4-5 hours on low.

Serves 10-12
Preparation time: 15 minutes
Cooking time: 4 hours
Easy
                                              Deane Taylor

POLISH CHOLENT

For the most delicious results, prepare this the night before

10 pounds red or Idaho potatoes
2 medium onions, diced
2 eggs
¼ cup flour or matzo meal

2 tablespoons salt
1 teaspoon pepper
2 teaspoons garlic powder
3 pounds beef flanken, cut in small pieces

Grease a large Dutch oven or stainless steel kettle. Grate the potatoes into the pot and combine with the onions and eggs. Add the flour and seasonings and mix well. Add the flanken, pushing it down into the vegetables. Cover pot, and place in a 300-degree oven. Roast "until you can smell the delicious aroma" then turn temperature to 200 and leave in oven overnight. Do not open the oven door until morning.

Serve for a large noon meal, or refrigerate until 1 hour before serving, then reheat in a 325-degree oven.

Serves 20
Preparation time: 15 minutes
Cooking time: Overnight
Easy
                                              Henia Ciesla

BAKED MEATBALL CASSEROLE

1½	pounds small white onions	1½	pounds small mushrooms, cleaned
1	bunch small carrots	1	10-ounce package frozen peas, thawed
2	pounds ground chuck		
1	egg	1	can condensed cream of mushroom soup
1	cup day-old breadcrumbs		
½	teaspoon marjoram	¾	teaspoon nutmeg
2	teaspoons salt	¾	teaspoon A-1 sauce
¾	teaspoon Worcestershire sauce	¾	teaspoon onion salt
		6	cups mashed potatoes
⅔	cup milk		
⅓	cup vegetable oil	Milk	

Clean onions and cut a small X in the stem end of each onion. Clean carrots and halve lengthwise. Place carrots and onions in a saucepan with 1 inch of salted water and cook, covered, for 20 minutes. Combine meat, egg, crumbs, marjoram, salt, Worcestershire sauce and milk and blend thoroughly with a fork. Form into 1½-inch balls. Heat oil in a large skillet and brown the meatballs quickly. Remove from pan and drain on paper towels. Sauté the mushrooms until tender. Drain on paper towels. Arrange the onions, carrots, meatballs, mushrooms and peas in a 3-quart casserole.

Place the soup, nutmeg, A-1 sauce and onion salt in the skillet. Blend thoroughly, heat, and pour over the meatballs and vegetables. Arrange the mashed potatoes around the casserole and brush with milk. Bake in a 400-degree oven for 35 minutes.

Serves 8
Preparation time: 30 minutes
Baking time: 35 minutes

Marianne Endicott

INDIVIDUAL BEEF WELLINGTONS

This is an elegant main course that can be prepared early in the day

Butter
6 beef filets 1-1½ inches thick,
    4-5 inches around
Salt
Pepper

1 package Pepperidge Farms
    frozen puff pastry shells,
    defrosted in refrigerator
    overnight
1 4-ounce tin liver paste or
    paté de foie gras

Melt enough butter in the bottom of a large skillet to lightly cover. Cook the filets over high heat for 5 minutes on each side. Season lightly with salt and pepper. Remove to a large platter and refrigerate until cold.

Preheat oven to 425 degrees. Remove patty shells from refrigerator and roll out until each is large enough to completely encase a filet. Spread each circle of dough with a thin layer of the liver paté then place a filet in the center and fold the pastry, tucking the seams. Place seam side down on a cookie sheet. Tops may be decorated with any leftover scraps of puff pastry. Bake for 25-30 minutes, until pastry is golden.

Serves 6
Prepare ahead   Carol Ann May

ARGENTINE CASSEROLE

1 pound thin spaghetti
2 pounds ground chuck
2 tablespoons butter
3 cups tomato sauce
1 6-ounce can tomato paste
1 cup mushrooms
2 medium onions, coarsely
    chopped
¼ cup chopped parsley
1 teaspoon oregano

1 teaspoon garlic powder,
    or to taste
Salt and pepper
1 8-ounce package cream
    cheese, softened
2 cups cottage cheese
½ cup sour cream
½ cup chopped chives
2 tablespoons chopped green
    pepper

Cook the spaghetti according to package directions; drain. Brown the meat in the butter then stir in the tomato sauce, tomato paste, mushrooms, onions, parsley, oregano and garlic. Season to taste with salt and pepper. Simmer mixture for 15 minutes. Combine the remaining ingredients in a bowl and mix well.

In a 4-quart buttered casserole, place half the spaghetti; cover with the cheese mixture. Add remaining spaghetti and top with the meat sauce. Bake in a 375-degree oven for 45 minutes or until hot and bubbly.

Note: Can be refrigerated before final baking, and reheated before serving.

Serves 12
Freezes well
Easy   Elly Bundesen

ENCHILADAS SUISSE

This will help stretch your budget

SAUCE

5	tablespoons flour	1½	teaspoons chili powder
¼	cup paprika	2	teaspoons salt
½	teaspoon oregano	¼	cup oil
½	teaspoon cumin	3	cups hot water

Combine the flour and seasonings. Stir in the oil and mix well. Gradually add the hot water and cook until thickened.

ENCHILADAS

1	pound ground beef	½	cup vegetable oil
1	4-ounce can chopped green olives	12	corn tortillas
1	small onion, chopped		Sour cream
½	pound grated Cheddar cheese		Sliced black olives

In a medium skillet, sauté the ground beef until browned. Mix with the chopped olives, onion, cheese and ⅓ cup of the sauce.

Preheat oven to 350 degrees. In another skillet, heat the oil until quite hot. Dip the tortillas quickly in the hot oil to soften them, then dip them in the sauce. Fill each enchilada with some of the meat mixture, roll up and place seam side down in a buttered baking dish. Pour the remaining sauce over them. Bake for 20 minutes.

Remove from oven, top with sour cream and garnish with black olives. Serve immediately.

Serves 6-8
Preparation time: 30 minutes
Cooking time: 20 minutes
Easy   Jeanne Schlitters

BULGUR-GROUND BEEF CASSEROLE

1	pound lean ground beef	1	cup bulgur
2	stalks celery, chopped	1	cup water
1	large green pepper, chopped	½	cup raisins
1	onion, chopped	⅓	cup shelled sunflower seeds
1	clove garlic, minced	1	teaspoon ground cumin
1½	teaspoons salt		
⅛	teaspoon pepper		
1	16-ounce can tomatoes, cut up		

Optional topping: Monterey Jack or Cheddar cheese, shredded or sliced

In large oven-proof skillet cook the meat until well browned; drain off excess fat. Add celery, green pepper, onion, garlic, and salt and pepper and cook until vegetables are crisp-tender. Stir in the tomatoes with liquid, bulgur, water, raisins, sunflower seeds, and cumin. Bake in a 2-quart covered casserole for 35 minutes or until bulgur is tender and mixture is heated through. If cheese topping is desired, remove cover and sprinkle or layer cheese on top 5 minutes before removing from oven.

Serves 6
Preparation time: 15 minutes
Cooking time: 35 minutes
Prepare ahead
Easy

Peggy Tundo
DSO

HAMBURGER QUICHE

½	pound ground beef	½	cup shredded Cheddar cheese
½	cup mayonnaise	⅓	cup chopped green onion
½	cup milk	1	8 or 9-inch unbaked pie shell
2	eggs		
1	tablespoon cornstarch		
½	cup shredded Mozzarella cheese		

Brown the meat; drain off fat. Combine the mayonnaise, milk, eggs and cornstarch and blend until smooth; add to the meat. Add cheeses and onion. Pour into pie shell. Bake in a 350-degree oven for 40 minutes.

Serves 4 to 6
Preparation time: 20 minutes
Cooking time: 40 minutes
Easy

Mary Lou Milliken

FLANK STEAK BOURBON

1　4-pound flank steak, fat
　　removed
½　cup soy sauce
¼　cup bourbon
¼　teaspoon ginger

1　clove garlic, minced
½　cup hot water
¼　teaspoon pepper
4　teaspoons butter
2　teaspoons chopped parsley

Place the meat in a glass dish. Combine the remaining ingredients, mix well and pour over the steak. Let marinate for 2 hours.
Grill the meat over hot coals for 6-8 minutes. Turn meat over and continue cooking until done. Baste frequently with Bleu Cheese Steak Baste.

BLUE CHEESE STEAK BASTE

½　pound Bleu Cheese
¼　cup butter
½　teaspoon dry mustard

1　clove garlic, minced
¼　cup parsley chopped

Combine ingredients and use to baste flank steak.

Preparation time: 10 minutes
Cooking time: 15 minutes
Easy
　　　　　　　　　　　　　　　　　　　　　　Margaret Reynolds

ENCHILADA CASSEROLE

1　pound ground beef
1　teaspoon salt
1　tablespoon chili powder
½　teaspoon oregano
2　tablespoons chopped onion

1　15-ounce can tomato sauce
5　corn tortillas
1　cup grated Monterey Jack
　　cheese

In a skillet, brown the meat. Add the salt, chili powder, oregano, onions and tomato sauce, and simmer for 10 minutes. Layer the tortillas, the sauce and cheese in a shallow 11x7-inch baking dish. Bake in a 350-degree oven for 20 minutes or until cheese is melted.

Serves 4
Preparation time: 20 minutes
Cooking time: 20 minutes
Easy
　　　　　　　　　　　　　　　　　　　　　　Kathie Ninneman

SPRING FLOOD OF 1952 CASSEROLE

In 1952 there was a very bad flood in South Dakota, where I grew up. One of my mother's friends turned on the radio and got this recipe, but missed the name. So we gave it this name for lack of a better one. Also, it was terrific!

1 medium head cabbage
1½ pounds hamburger
1 onion, chopped
1 tablespoon flour
Salt and freshly ground pepper
1½ cups cooked rice

¼ pound mild Cheddar cheese, shredded
1½ cups sour cream mixed with ½ cup milk until smooth
1 cup bread crumbs mixed with ¼ cup melted butter

Chop cabbage coarsely and boil for 5-8 minutes; drain well. In a skillet brown hamburger and onion; drain accumulated fat. Stir in the flour and season with salt and pepper to taste. In a 1½-quart casserole, alternate ½ the hamburger and onion mixture, ½ the cabbage and ½ the rice. Repeat with remaining meat, cabbage and rice. Top with cheese. Pour sour cream mixture slowly over the top; sprinkle with buttered bread crumbs.
Bake uncovered in a 350-degree oven for 30 minutes.

Serves 6-8
Preparation time: 45 minutes
Make ahead and refrigerate
Freezes well

Marcy Chanteaux
DSO

ELEPHANT STEW

This is an interesting and unusual recipe for a large gathering

1 elephant
Salt and pepper to taste

Brown gravy
Optional: 2 rabbits

Cut elephant into bite-size pieces — this should take about two months. Add brown gravy to cover. Cook over kerosene fire at 465 degrees for about 4 weeks or until done. To serve more, the rabbits may be added. Do this only if absolutely necessary as most people do not like to find hare in their stew.

Yield: 3800 servings
Preparation time: 8 weeks
Cooking time: 4 weeks
Easy

TALIVARIA

This recipe was given to me many years ago by my mother

1 pound ground beef	1 1-pound can tomatoes
1 onion, chopped	1 cup sliced mushrooms
1 green pepper, chopped	8 ounces broad noodles,
½ teaspoon chili powder	cooked and drained
Salt and pepper to taste	½-1 cup grated Cheddar cheese
1 can corn, drained	

Brown the beef; drain off excess fat. Add onion and green pepper and cook until tender. Stir in the chili powder, salt and pepper. Add remaining ingredients except noodles and cheese and mix well. Gently toss with noodles, turn into a 1½-quart casserole, and top with grated cheese. Bake in a 350-degree oven for 40 minutes.

Serves 6-8
Preparation time: 30 minutes
Cooking time: 45 minutes
Freezes well   Elizabeth Steger
Easy   DSO

PAN NACHOS

1 pound extra lean ground beef	Shredded lettuce
1 package taco seasoning mix	6 green onions, chopped
1 large package tortilla corn chips	2 tomatoes, chopped
2 cups shredded Mozzarella cheese	8 green olives, cut in half
1 cup shredded Colby cheese	Jalapeño peppers
	Sour cream
	Taco sauce

Brown the beef and prepare the taco mix according to package directions. Preheat oven to 350 degrees. Cover the bottom of a 9x13-inch pan with a generous layer of tortilla chips. Sprinkle beef evenly over the corn chips. Sprinkle on the cheese. Heat in oven until the cheese is melted. Remove from oven and sprinkle on the lettuce, onions, tomatoes and olives.

To serve: Cut with a spatula and place on serving plates. Garnish with Jalapeño peppers, sour cream and taco sauce.

Serves 8-10
Preparation time: 30 minutes
Easy   Paige Pangborn

BEEF AND BEAN SPROUTS

A delicious stay-at-home Chinese entree

2	pounds round steak	¼	teaspoon ginger
3	tablespoons vegetable oil	1	28-ounce can tomatoes
2	cloves garlic, crushed	3	large green peppers, seeded
2	large onions, sliced		and cut in thin strips
1	teaspoon salt	1	pound fresh bean sprouts,
Pinch of pepper			or canned if fresh sprouts are
⅓	cup soy sauce		not available

Cut the meat across the grain into very thin strips. Heat the oil in a skillet. Add the beef, garlic onion, salt and pepper. Cook, stirring, until meat is browned on all sides. Season with soy sauce and ginger. Add the liquid from the tomatoes and cook until meat is tender, about 45 minutes. Add the green pepper and cook for 5 minutes. Add the bean sprouts and tomatoes and cook 3-5 minutes or until heated through.

Serves 6-8
Preparation time: 25 minutes
Cooking time: 1 hour
Easy   Chris Considine

STEAK AU POIVRE

3½	pounds sirloin steak cut	2	tablespoons olive oil
	1½-2 inches thick	1	tablespoon butter
4	teaspoons coarsely ground	½	cup dry white wine
	black pepper	2	tablespoons cream
1	teaspoon salt	¼	cup brandy
3	tablespoons butter		

Cut slashes in the fat on the edges of the steak. Rub the pepper into both sides and sprinkle lightly with salt. In a large, heavy skillet, heat 3 tablespoons butter and the oil over high heat. Add the steak and sear on both sides, lower heat and cook until done to taste.
Remove the meat to a serving platter and add 1 tablespoon butter to the skillet, scraping the browned bits from the bottom of the pan. Add the wine and cream and boil, briskly, until reduced by two-thirds. Add the brandy and heat until warmed. Ignite with a match and pour over the steak.

Serves 6-8   Treva Womble
Preparation time: 30 minutes   DSO

TZIMMES

This is best prepared a day ahead and left to sit in the gravy to let flavors blend.

6-7	pounds boneless beef brisket	¾	cup dried prunes
2	medium onions, sliced	¾	cup dried apricots
Salt and pepper to taste		8	small carrots, cut in chunks
½	teaspoon nutmeg	4	medium potatoes,
2	tablespoons brown sugar		scrubbed and cut in fourths
1¼	cups water	8	small cooked onions

Place meat, fat side down, in large heated Dutch oven or roaster. Add sliced onions and cook over medium heat, turning until meat is well browned on both sides. Add salt, pepper, nutmeg, brown sugar and water. Cover tightly and simmer over low heat or in a 300-degree oven for 1½ hours.

Add the prunes, apricots, carrots and potatoes and cook 45-60 minutes longer, or until vegetables are tender. Remove meat, slice and place on serving platter surrounded by fruit and vegetables.

Yetta Dubin

SUKIYAKI

1½	pounds sirloin steak	½	pound fresh mushrooms, sliced
1	tablespoon vegetable oil		
¾	cup soy sauce	1	10-ounce can bamboo shoots, drained
¼	cup water		
¼	cup sugar	1	small bunch green onions, including tops, cut diagonally
1	medium onion, thinly sliced		
1	green pepper, cut in strips	Hot cooked rice	
3	ribs celery, sliced diagonally		

Cut meat into thin diagonal slices about 2 inches by ½ inch. Heat oil in a large skillet. Brown the meat lightly in the hot oil. In a small bowl, mix the soy sauce, water and sugar. Add half of the mixture to skillet. Push meat to one side of pan. Add the onion, green pepper and celery; cook for two minutes. Stir in the remaining soy sauce mixture, the mushrooms, and bamboo shoots; cook 3 to 5 minutes. Add green onions and cook, stirring, for 1 minute. Serve with rice.

Serves 8
Preparation time: 20 minutes
Easy

Flo Harris

SPINACH MEATBALLS

Easy and economical

2 small onions, finely chopped
2 tablespoons vegetable oil
1 12-ounce package frozen chopped spinach, cooked and drained
1 pound ground veal or beef
1 egg
3 tablespoons grated sharp cheese

½ teaspoon salt
½ teaspoon pepper
½ teaspoon M.S.G. (optional)
Dash of nutmeg or mace
3 tablespoons shortening
3 tablespoon flour
1 can condensed cream of mushroom soup mixed with ½ soup can water

Sauté the onions in the oil lightly browned. Add the onions and the spinach to the ground meat. Add the egg, cheese, salt, pepper, M.S.G., and nutmeg or mace. Mix well and form into balls. Heat the shortening. Roll the meatballs in flour and brown in the hot shortening; transfer to a covered casserole. Pour the soup mixture over the meatballs, cover and bake in a 350-degree oven for 45 minutes. Serve with rice or noodles.

Serves 4
Preparation time: 20 minutes
Cooking time: 45 minutes
Easy   Marilyn Ketchum

CHUCK STEAK

20 inch sheet of foil
½ tablespoon butter
2 pounds chuck steak cut into serving portions, 1 inch thick
1 package onion soup mix
½ pound mushrooms, sliced
½ green pepper, sliced
1 1-pound can tomatoes, drained and chopped, reserving juice

¼ teaspoon salt
Dash pepper
½ cup reserved juice from tomatoes
1 tablespoon A-1 steak sauce
1 tablespoon cornstarch
1 tablespoon chopped parsley

Spread center of foil with butter. Arrange the meat on the foil, slightly overlapping each portion. Sprinkle with the onion soup mix, mushrooms, green pepper and tomatoes. Season with salt and pepper to taste. Mix together the reserved juice, A-1 sauce and cornstarch; pour over meat and vegetables. Bring foil up over the meat and double fold the edges to seal tightly. Bake for 2 hours in a 375-degree oven. When done, roll back foil and sprinkle with parsley.

Serves 4
Preparation time: 20 minutes
Cooking time: 2 hours
Easy

Judy Liberson
DSO

SONNY ELIOT'S BEEF STEW

3   pounds stewing beef, cubed
Flour
⅓   cup vegetable oil
1   clove garlic, minced
1   large onion, sliced
Salt and pepper to taste
1   cup tomato sauce
½   cup beef broth
½   cup Burgundy wine
⅓   cup sugar
1   bay leaf
½   teaspoon thyme

½   teaspoon oregano
½   teaspoon sweet basil
½   teaspoon rosemary
½   pound fresh mushrooms, sliced
1   green pepper, sliced
½   cup fresh peas
2   potatoes, quartered
6   carrots, scraped and cut in 1-inch lengths
3   ribs celery, diced

Lightly dredge meat with flour. In a large heavy Dutch oven, heat the oil on medium-high and sauté the garlic. Add the beef, onion, salt and pepper; cook until meat is nicely browned. Add the tomato sauce, broth, wine and sugar; sprinkle on herbs. Stir to blend; cover and simmer over low heat for 2 hours. Add the vegetables and cook 1 hour longer. If sauce is too thick, thin with a little wine.

Serves 8-10
Preparation time: 45 minutes
Cooking time: 3 hours
Easy

Detroit's own
Sonny Eliot

GROUND BEEF "GRAND STYLE"

This is always popular at church suppers and potluck dinners

1½	pounds ground beef	¼	cup milk
1	cup chopped onion	1	teaspoon salt
1	8-ounce package cream cheese, softened	¼	cup ketchup
1	can condensed cream of mushroom soup	⅓	cup stuffed olives, sliced
		1	can refrigerator biscuits

Brown the ground beef and onion; drain. Combine the cream cheese, soup and milk; blend well. Add the salt, ketchup, olives and browned beef and incorporate thoroughly. Pour into a greased 2-quart casserole. Bake in a 375-degree oven for 10 minutes. Place biscuits around the edge of casserole. Return casserole to oven and continue baking for 15 minutes or until biscuits are golden brown.

Serves 6
Preparation time: 20 minutes
Baking time: 15 minutes
Easy   Debbie Tischler

STEAK DIANE

A classic

3	tablespoons clarified butter	¼	cup dry Sherry
2	rib eye steaks or filet mignons	2	teaspoons steak sauce
2	tablespoons Cognac	1	teaspoon Worcestershire sauce
2	tablespoons minced shallot	1	teaspoon Dijon mustard
2	tablespoons minced parsley	1	tablespoon chives

Heat the butter in a skillet and sauté the steaks until done. In a small saucepan, heat the Cognac until hot but not boiling. Ignite with a match and pour over the steaks. Remove steaks to a platter and keep warm.

Combine the remaining ingredients, except the chives, in the skillet. Bring to a boil and cook, stirring, scraping up the brown bits left from the steaks. Adjust seasonings, then stir in the chives. Pour the sauce over the steaks and serve immediately.

Preparation time: 25 minutes
Easy   Mary Sartell

VEAL WELLINGTON

. . . surprisingly easy

2	tablespoons butter, divided	2	tablespoons vegetable oil
½	pound mushrooms, sliced	1	10-ounce package frozen
2	green onions, thinly sliced		patty shells, thawed
1½	pounds veal rib chops, cut 1-inch thick		

In a small skillet, melt 1 tablespoon butter. Add the mushrooms and green onions and cook, stirring, for 5 minutes or until liquid evaporates. Cover and chill.

Bone the chops and trim off all fat. Melt remaining tablespoon butter and the oil in a wide skillet over high heat. Sear the chops on each side for 1 minute or until nicely browned. Remove from pan; cool then cover and chill.

For each veal medallion, roll out a patty shell on a lightly floured board to an 8-inch circle. Spoon 1 tablespoon of the mushroom mixture in the center of the circle and top with a piece of veal. Close the pastry around the meat with edges overlapping. Place with folded side down on an ungreased, rimmed baking sheet. Cover and chill.

Shortly before serving preheat oven to 425 degrees. Place baking sheet on the lowest rack of oven and bake for 10 minutes. Move pan to highest rack and cook for 10 minutes longer, or until pastry is golden brown. Serve with Mustard Cream Sauce.

Serves 4-6   Sue Eckert

MUSTARD CREAM SAUCE

¼	cup minced shallots or green onions	2	tablespoons Dijon mustard
		1	cup heavy cream
¼	cup dry Sherry		

In a skillet over high heat, combine the shallots and Sherry. Cook until shallots are soft. Stir in the mustard and cream. Cook over high heat, stirring constantly, for 3 minutes or until sauce is thickened and bubbly. Serve hot.

Makes 1 cup   Sue Eckert

Garnish serving trays with fresh fruit or flowers.

VEAL WITH MUSHROOMS

Serve this delicious dish with noodles or rice

1	tablespoon bacon fat	1 cup small fresh mushroom caps
1	clove garlic, minced	
1	onion, chopped	1 tablespoon tomato paste
¾	pound veal, cubed	1 tablespoon water
¼	teaspoon salt	1 cup sour cream
Dash pepper		2 teaspoons paprika

Heat the bacon fat. Add garlic and onions and cook over medium heat until onion is transparent. Add the veal, salt and pepper and cook, stirring, until veal becomes white. Add the mushrooms and cook for 1 minute longer. Add the tomato paste and water, cover and simmer over low heat for 20 minutes or until the veal is tender. Stir in the sour cream and paprika and heat through, but DO NOT BOIL.

Serves 2
Preparation time: 20 minutes
Cooking time: 30 minutes
Easy

Janette Hitchcock

VEAL PICCATA

This is elegant but easy.

2	tablespoons flour	2 tablespoons vegetable oil, divided
½	teaspoon salt	
¼	teaspoon pepper	½ cup dry white wine
1	pound veal, thinly sliced	1 lemon, sliced
2	tablespoons butter, divided	

Combine the flour, salt and pepper. Lightly dredge the veal in the flour mixture. Heat 1 tablespoon butter and 1 tablespoon oil in a medium skillet. Add half the veal slices and cook over high heat until browned on both sides. Remove the veal and brown the remaining slices using the remaining butter and oil. Drain off the excess fat and add the wine and half the lemon slices. Return the veal to the pan, cover, and cook over low heat for 5 minutes. Arrange on a serving platter and garnish with remaining lemon slices.

Serves 2-4
Preparation time: 15 minutes
Easy

Rona Freedland

OSSO BUCCO MILANESE

½ cup flour
Salt and pepper
6 round-bone veal steaks or
   meaty veal shanks
2 tablespoons vegetable oil
2 tablespoons butter
1 carrot, sliced
1 rib celery, sliced
½ cup chopped onion

1 clove garlic, minced
¾ cup tomato puree
¾ cup dry white wine
½ cup water
2 tablespoons chopped
   parsley
Pinch basil
Pinch oregano

Season the flour with salt and pepper to taste. Dredge the veal in the seasoned flour. Heat the oil and butter in a large skillet and brown the meat. Add remaining ingredients, cover, and simmer until veal is tender and liquid is reduced. Serve with Pilaf.

Serves 6
Preparation time: 45 minutes
Easy   Maria Partella

VEAL RAGOUT

3 pounds lean veal, cubed
Salt and pepper
2 tablespoons oil
1 tablespoon butter
¼ cup brandy
1 large onion, coarsely
   chopped
2 cloves garlic, minced

1 28-ounce can tomatoes,
   drained and chopped
1 tablespoon tomato paste
1 bay leaf
1 teaspoon rosemary
1 cup dry white wine
2 cups beef broth
1 cup fresh peas

Sprinkle meat with salt and pepper. Heat oil and butter in a skillet and sauté over medium-high heat, in small batches, until browned on all sides. Heat the brandy, ignite, and pour over the meat, scraping up any browned bits. Transfer meat to a large ovenproof casserole. To the same skillet, add the onion and garlic and cook until softened and lightly browned. Add the tomatoes and tomato paste and cook for 2-3 minutes or until some of the liquid has evaporated. Add remaining ingredients, except the peas, and cook for 5 minutes to reduce slightly. Pour over the veal, cover and cook in a 350-degree oven for 1-1½ hours or until meat is tender. Add peas and return to the oven for 10 minutes. Serve with hot rice.

Serves 6   Ida Allen

VEAL MOREL

Morels give the dish it's unique flavor

8 ounces thinly sliced veal
Salt and pepper
2 tablespoons butter
8 morel mushrooms or regular mushrooms, sliced

2 teaspoons finely chopped shallots or onions
¼ cup light Sherry
¼ cup beef stock
¼ cup heavy cream

Season the veal with salt and pepper to taste. Place sauté pan over high heat. When pan is very hot, add the butter and veal. Brown the meat on both sides. When veal is almost done, add the mushrooms and shallots. Cook for 1 minute then add the Sherry and beef stock. Cook over high heat until liquid reduces in half. Stir in the cream and cook until liquid is reduced to a thick sauce. Serve over noodles or rice.

Serves 2
Preparation time: 15 minutes
Easy   Marilyn Van Giesen

VEAL PARISIENNE

2 pounds veal, very thinly sliced
½ pound fresh mushrooms
2 tablespoons finely chopped onion
¼ teaspoon finely chopped garlic
2 tablespoons flour
1 tablespoon ketchup

2 teaspoons meat extract
½ teaspoon salt
Dash cayenne
1 cup chicken broth
½ cup light cream, divided
2 teaspoons tarragon vinegar
4 tablespoons butter
4 slices ham cut in julienne strips

Brown the veal slowly in butter. Add the mushrooms, onion and garlic. Cook over low heat 3-4 minutes; transfer to platter. To the pan, add flour, ketchup, meat extract, salt and cayenne, stirring until well blended. Gradually add the chicken broth and ⅓ cup cream. Bring to a boil, stirring constantly. Return the veal, onion, mushrooms and garlic to the pan; simmer, covered, 20 minutes, or until veal is tender. Blend in remaining cream and tarragon vinegar; add the ham. If sauce is too thick, thin with some chicken broth.

Serves 4
Preparation time: 45 minutes   Connie Johnston

MUSHROOM STUFFED VEAL TERRINE

1	tablespoon butter	1	egg
1¼	cups sliced fresh mushrooms	¾	cup fresh homemade breadcrumbs
¼	cup finely chopped onion	1	pound ground veal
1	clove garlic, minced	2	tablespoons chopped parsley
¾	teaspoon minced fresh thyme or ¼ teaspoon dried	½	teaspoon Beau Monde seasoning
2	tablespoons sour cream	½	teaspoon finely grated lemon peel

Salt
Freshly ground pepper
3 tablespoons milk

Grease a 7x13-inch loaf pan. Melt the butter in a small skillet over medium-high heat. Add the mushrooms, onion, garlic and thyme and cook for 5 minutes or until most of the mushroom liquid has evaporated and the mushrooms begin to brown. Stir in the the sour cream and cook until syrupy. Season to taste with salt and pepper; set aside. Preheat oven to 350 degrees. Combine the milk and egg in a large bowl and blend well. Add the breadcrumbs and let soak for 5 minutes. Add the veal, parsley, Beau Monde seasoning and lemon peel and mix thoroughly with your hands. Season to taste with salt and pepper. Pat half the veal mixture into the bottom of the prepared pan. Spoon the mushroom mixture over top and spread evenly. Cover with remaining veal mixture, pressing down evenly over the mushrooms. Bake for 1 hour. Drain off accumulated juices and let stand at room temperature for 15 minutes. Cut into thick slices. Serve with mushroom gravy.
Note: To serve cold, top with a second loaf pan, weighted down, and refrigerate overnight until firm in texture.

Serves 6

Carol Ann May

"He who flatters the cook never goes hungry."

Old Proverb

ESCALOPES DE VEAU A LA NORMANDE

8 4-ounce veal scallops
Salt
White pepper
Flour for dredging
6 tablespoons butter, divided

2 tablespoons flour
1 cup heavy cream or creme fraiche
½ cup Calvados

Dry veal with paper towels. Flatten slightly between sheets of waxed paper, season lightly with salt and pepper and dredge lightly with flour. Melt 4 tablespoons butter in skillet and sauté scallops for 2 to 3 minutes on each side, or until slightly browned. Transfer the scallops to a heated serving dish and keep warm.

Add remaining two tablespoons of butter to the skillet and return it to a moderately high heat. When butter has melted and is bubbly, stir in the flour and cook for two minutes. Do not let flour brown. Add the cream and cook the mixture, stirring constantly, until thickened. Add salt and pepper to taste, then add the Calvados. Heat through, but do not boil; pour over veal.

Serves 8
Preparation time: 20 minutes

Winnie Ostrowski

VEAL SCALLOPINE ST. MORITZ

Serve with rice, noodles, or spatzles.

24 slices milk-fed veal scallopine
Salt and pepper
Flour for dredging
2 tablespoons vegetable oil

Mushroom a la Creme Sauce
24 thin slices Prosciutto ham
24 thin slices imported Swiss Gruyere cheese
Parsley for garnish

Pound veal until thin and season with salt and pepper. Dredge in flour and shake off excess. Heat a small amount of vegetable oil until quite hot. Sauté veal quickly until brown on both sides. Arrange veal on a cookie sheet and top each piece with a tablespoon of Mushroom a la Creme Sauce. Place a slice of Prosciutto and Gruyere on each scallop. Put in a 450-degree oven or under broiler for a few minutes until cheese is hot and melted. Garnish with parsley.

MUSHROOM A LA CREME SAUCE

½ onion, chopped
2 tablespoons vegetable oil
1½ cups mushrooms, sliced
¾ cup dry white wine
2 cups heavy cream

1 tablespoon flour mixed
with 1 tablespoon white
wine
Salt and pepper to taste

In a skillet, sauté onion in oil until transparent. Add mushrooms and sauté 1-2 minutes. Add wine and cook until wine has almost completely evaporated. Mix in the cream and cook until reduced slightly. Stir in flour-wine mixture and cook, stirring constantly, until thickened. Season to taste.

Serves 8
Preparation time: 30 minutes

The Bijou
Southfield, Michigan

BENNY GOODMAN
STUFFED BREAST OF VEAL

This delicious traditional recipe was given to us by the "King of Swing".

5 pounds breast of veal
with pocket
2 teaspoons salt or to taste
Pepper to taste

1 teaspoon paprika
½ teaspoon garlic powder
3 tablespoons fat

Sprinkle veal with salt, pepper, paprika and garlic powder. Fill the pocket with the following stuffing and fasten the opening with skewers or thread.

Melt the fat in a roasting pan and place the veal in it. Roast in 350-degree oven for three hours, or until meat is tender. Baste frequently adding a little water if pan becomes dry.

BREAD STUFFING

1 onion, minced
1 green pepper, diced
3 ribs celery, sliced
3 tablespoons fat
6 slices bread

1 teaspoon salt or to taste
Pepper to taste
⅛ teaspoon thyme
1 teaspoon paprika
1 egg

Cook the onion, green pepper and celery in the fat over medium heat for ten minutes, stirring occasionally. Soak the bread in water, squeeze dry and pull into small pieces. Add to the vegetables with salt, pepper, thyme, paprika and egg. Mix well and stuff into veal pocket.

Serves 6-8
Preparation time: ½ hour
Cooking time: 3 hours

Benny Goodman

MOUSSAKA

A delicious Greek classic

MEAT SAUCE

3	medium eggplants	¼	teaspoon cinnamon
1	cup butter		Salt and freshly ground
3	large onions, finely chopped		pepper to taste
2	pounds ground lamb	1½	cups fine bread crumbs
3	tablespoons tomato paste	1	cup freshly grated Parmesan cheese
½	cup red wine		White sauce (see recipe below)
½	cup chopped parsley		

Peel eggplants and slice ¼ inch thick. In a large heavy skillet, melt 4 tablespoons butter and brown the eggplant quickly. Remove from the skillet and set aside.

In the same skillet, melt the remaining butter and cook the onions until lightly browned. Add the ground meat and cook for 10 minutes. Combine the tomato paste, wine, parsley, cinnamon, salt and pepper. Stir into the meat and simmer over low heat, stirring frequently, until all liquid has been absorbed. Remove from the heat.

Preheat oven to 375 degrees. Grease an 11x16x2-inch oven-proof baking dish. Sprinkle bottom with ½ cup bread crumbs. Arrange alternate layers of eggplant and meat in the pan. Sprinkle each layer with Parmesan cheese and bread crumbs. Pour the white sauce over the top. Bake for one hour or until golden. Remove from the oven and cool slightly before serving.

To serve, cut into squares.

Note: the flavor improves if reheated and served the second day.

WHITE SAUCE

½	cup butter	4	eggs, beaten until frothy
½	cup flour		Nutmeg
1	quart milk	2	cups ricotta cheese

In a large saucepan, melt the butter. Stir in the flour and blend thoroughly with a wire whisk. Bring the milk to a boil and gradually add to the butter-flour mixture, stirring constantly. When mixture has thickened and is smooth, remove from heat. Cool slightly, then stir in the beaten eggs, nutmeg and ricotta cheese.

Serves 8-10   Janet Monroe

LAMB SHANKS BRAISED IN BEER

6 large lamb shanks	1 can beer
2 slices bacon	½ teaspoon thyme
6 carrots, chopped	2 bay leaves
12 pearl onions, or green	¼ cup chopped parsley
onions cut into ½-inch pieces	1 clove garlic, minced
2 tablespoons brown sugar	2 tablespoons wine vinegar
2 cups strong beef bouillon	2 tablespoons cornstarch

Remove all fat from the lamb. In a large skillet, fry the bacon until crisp, remove from the pan and drain on paper towels. Brown the lamb shanks in the reserved bacon fat. Remove and drain with the bacon. In the same skillet, brown the carrots and onions; then set aside.

Blot the grease from the pan, leaving the crunchy bits of bacon in the pan. Stir in the remaining ingredients except the vinegar and cornstarch, then return the shanks, bacon and vegetables to the skillet. Simmer, covered, on low heat for 1 hour or until lamb is tender. Remove the bay leaves from the skillet. Combine the vinegar and cornstarch and add to the sauce. Stir until thickened.

Serves 6

Natalie Payne

LEG OF LAMB NEAPOLITAN

5-7 pound leg of lamb	1 medium green pepper,
1 teaspoon salt	coarsely chopped
1 teaspoon crushed oregano	1 clove garlic, minced
4 medium onions, coarsely	1 1-pound 12-ounce can
chopped	tomatoes

Preheat oven to 325 degrees.
Sprinkle lamb with salt and oregano, rubbing it in with your hands. Place meat on rack in shallow roasting pan and roast for 1½ hours. Drain off fat.
Mix together the onions, green pepper, garlic and tomatoes. Pour into pan and use to baste lamb occasionally. Roast lamb one hour longer, or until meat thermometer registers 175 degrees for medium, or desired doneness. Add water to pan during cooking if sauce dries out. Remove meat to a platter and slice. Pass sauce separately.
Goes well with rice.

Serves 6-10 depending on size of roast.
Easy

Kay Keffer

BOBOTIE

South African baked ground lamb curry with custard topping

1	slice homemade-type white bread, 1-inch thick, broken into small bits	½	teaspoon freshly ground pepper
1	cup milk	¼	cup strained fresh lemon juice
2	tablespoons butter	3	eggs
2	pounds coarsely ground lean lamb	1	tart cooking apple, peeled, cored and grated
1½	cups finely chopped onions	½	cup seedless raisins
2	tablespoons curry powder, preferable Madras type	¼	cup coarsely chopped blanched almonds
1	tablespoon light brown sugar	4	small fresh lemon or orange leaves, or 4 small bay leaves
1	teaspoon salt		

Preheat oven to 325 degrees. Combine the bread and milk in a small bowl and let soak for at least 10 minutes. Meanwhile, in a large heavy skillet, melt the butter over moderate heat. When the foam begins to subside, add the lamb and cook, stirring constantly, mashing any lumps, until meat separates and no traces of pink remain. With a slotted spoon, transfer the meat to a deep bowl. Pour off and discard all but 2 tablespoons of fat from the skillet; add the onions. Cook for 5 minutes, stirring often, or until the onions are soft and translucent. Add the curry powder, sugar, salt and pepper, and stir for 2 minutes. Stir in the lemon juice and bring to a boil over high heat. Pour mixture into the bowl with the lamb.

Drain the bread in a sieve set over a bowl and squeeze the bread completely dry; reserve the drained milk. Add the bread, 1 egg, the apple, raisins and almonds to the lamb. Knead vigorously with both hands until the ingredients are well combined. Taste for seasoning and add more salt if desired. Pack the lamb mixture loosely into a 3-quart souffle dish or other deep 3-quart baking dish; smooth top with a spatula. Tuck the bay leaves beneath the surface of the meat.

Beat the remaining eggs with the reserved milk for 1 minute or until frothy. Slowly pour mixture evenly over the meat and bake in the middle of the oven for 30 minutes, or until the custard is a light golden brown.

Serve directly from the baking dish. Bobotie is traditionally accompanied by hot boiled rice.

Serves 6
Preparation time: 25 minutes
Baking time: 30 minutes

Joan Sankowich

PAPOUTZAKIA

Greek stuffed Eggplant

EGGPLANT

4 small eggplants
¾ cup vegetable oil, divided
3 medium onions, thinly sliced
1 pound ground lamb
1 tablespoon tomato paste
2 fresh tomatoes, chopped
Salt and pepper to taste
¼ cup freshly chopped parsley
1 recipe Cream Sauce (see below)

Cut the eggplants lengthwise; remove the pulp and chop finely. Sauté the shells in ¼ cup oil until lighlty browned; set aside. In another pan, sauté the onions in ¼ cup oil until lightly browned. Add the eggplant pulp and lamb and cook for 10 minutes or until browned. Add the tomato paste and chopped tomatoes and cook for 10 minutes. Add salt, pepper and parsley.

Place the eggplant shells in a pan. Add the remaining oil and enough water to come ⅛ inch up the sides of the pan. Stuff the shells with the meat mixture and bake in a 350-degree oven for 30 minutes. Remove from oven and top each shell with Cream Sauce. Place under broiler until lightly browned.

CREAM SAUCE

½ cup butter
6 tablespoons flour
1 quart milk
Salt
White pepper

In a saucepan melt the butter over medium heat. Blend in the flour and stir until smooth. Gradually add the milk, stirring constantly, until the mixture boils. Reduce heat and cook for 5 minutes. Add salt and pepper to taste. Cook, stirring, until the sauce is smooth and thick.

Serves 8   Pat and Yiannis Karimalis

White pepper is black pepper with the husk removed. It is less spicy than black pepper.

HERBED LAMB BALLS WITH COGNAC

These also make delicious hors d'oeuvres

2 pounds ground lamb	1 cup bread crumbs
2 eggs, lightly beaten	¼ cup dry red wine
4 cloves garlic, minced	2 tablespoons vegetable oil
1 teaspoon rosemary	1 onion
¼ cup chopped parsley	¼ cup Cognac
Pinch salt	3 tablespoons tomato sauce
1 tablespoon pepper	1 cup breef broth

Combine the lamb, eggs, garlic, rosemary, parsley, salt and pepper and mix well. In a separate bowl, soften the bread crumbs in the wine; add to meat mixture and mix well. Form into about 30 meatballs. Heat the oil in a large skillet and brown meatballs well. Add the onion and cook, stirring, until wilted. Pour in the Cognac, heat slightly, and ignite; stir until flames subside. Add the tomato sauce and broth. Cover and cook for 30 minutes.

Serves 8-10
Preparation time: 30 minutes
Cooking time: 30 minutes   Mrs. G. del Gaudio

HIGH COUNTRY LEG OF LAMB

If you can read all of this, you have enough energy to make it. It's easy and fun to do.

5 pounds, or larger, leg of lamb	4 large sprigs celery leaves
¼ cup tarragon vinegar	Rounded ¼ teaspoon each: allspice, mace and marjoram
2 quarts buttermilk	2 teaspoons salt
2 large onions, thinly sliced	¼ teaspoon pepper
1 large carrot, sliced	25 whole cloves
2 cloves garlic, crushed	¾ cup dry white wine
10 whole peppercorns	⅓ cup melted bacon fat
5 whole cloves	¼ cup flour
4 large bay leaves	½ cup water
3 juniper berries, optional	½ cup red currant jelly
10 sprigs parsley	1 teaspoon grated lemon rind

Rub lamb thoroughly with the tarragon vinegar. Place in a large pan or crock. Add the buttermilk, onions, carrot, garlic, peppercorns, the 5 cloves, bay leaves, juniper, parsley, celery leaves, allspice, mace, and marjoram. Cover and refrigerate for 4 days, turning twice daily. Keep the meat covered with the buttermilk mixture.

Remove meat from the buttermilk and pat dry. Reserve the buttermilk. Rub the meat with salt and pepper and place in a roasting pan. Stud with remaining cloves. Pour wine and melted fat over the meat. Roast in a 450-degree oven until browned. Reduce heat to 350 degrees and continue to roast for 1½ hours longer. Strain the buttermilk and use to baste the meat frequently.

When meat is done, remove to a platter. Skim off the fat in roasting pan. Blend flour and water to form a paste and stir into the hot liquid. Cook, stirring, until thickened — about 5 minutes. Add the currant jelly and lemon rind and mix until jelly is dissolved. Slice meat and serve with the sauce.

Serves 10 or more   Pat Young

ROAST RACK OF LAMB PROVENCAL

Serve this elegant dish with tomatoes, stewed in olive oil with garlic and parsley.

LAMB

1 7-pound lamb rack prepared with the fat and tissue removed from between the bones.	Kosher salt and freshly ground pepper Dijon mustard

Preheat broiler. Season the meat on all sides with salt and pepper. Wrap bones with foil to protect from burning and place meat under the broiler, turning, until browned on all sides; remove from oven. Spread mustard on the fat side of the lamb and coat well with the Persillade, packing it down firmly. Place lamb on a cookie sheet or sizzling platter in a 450-degree oven and roast until done — about 25 minutes for medium rare.

To carve, slice between the ribs.

PERSILLADE

⅔ cup bread crumbs	2 tablespoons olive oil
6 cloves garlic, minced	⅛ teaspoon savory
½ cup chopped parsley	⅛ teaspoon thyme
Oregano to taste	⅛ teaspoon rosemary

Combine all ingredients and mix well.

Serves 4   The Golden Mushroom
                                                  Southfield, Michigan

ARMENIAN LAMB SHANKS

Serve with Pilaf

4	1-pound lamb shanks	1	28-ounce can tomatoes, drained
¼	cup olive oil		
1	large onion, chopped	1	package frozen green beans
⅓	cup tomato puree	¼	teaspoon oregano
2	green peppers, coarsely chopped	1	teaspoon salt
		¼	teaspoon cayenne pepper
1	cup sliced mushrooms		

Rinse shanks in cold water and pat dry; remove excess fat. Heat the oil in a Dutch oven. Add the lamb and cook over medium heat until browned. Meanwhile, combine remaining ingredients in a saucepan; cook over medium heat for 5 minutes. Pour sauce over the browned lamb shanks, cover, and cook over low heat for 2 hours.

Note: To make in a slow-cooker, place all ingredients in the pot and cook for 5 hours on low. Meat does not have to be browned first.

Serves 4
Preparation time: 20 minutes
Cooking time: 2 hours
Easy   Mrs. Kent K. Johnson

MARINATED SHISH KEBOBS

2	pounds leg of lamb cut into 1½-inch cubes	½	cup cooking oil
2	medium onions, cut into 1½-inch wedges	1	cup red or white wine
		1	tablespoon meat tenderizer
2	green peppers, cut into 1½-inch wedges		Salt and pepper to taste
			Optional: mushroom caps and zucchini chunks
	Cherry tomatoes		

Place the lamb, onions, green pepper and tomatoes in a shallow dish. Combine the oil, wine, tenderizer, salt and pepper and pour over meat and vegetables. Mix gently to coat well. Cover and marinate in refrigerator for at least 2 hours.

When ready to prepare kebobs, remove meat from marinade and thread on skewers alternately with onion, green pepper and tomatoes. Place skewers on a grill 4 to 5 inches from heat. Broil 12 to 15 minutes or until done, turning occasionally, and brushing with marinade.

Note: Since tomatoes do not require as long a cooking time as the meat, it may be preferred to skewer separately and place on grill 4-5 minutes before meat is done.

Serves 8   Connie Salloum

EGGPLANT MOZZARELLA

1 pound Italian sausage
2 medium eggplants
¼ cup vegetable oil
2 cloves garlic, minced
2 tablespoons flour
2 1-pound cans stewed tomatoes, with liquid

2 teaspoons salt
2 teaspoons sugar
1 teaspoon paprika
⅛ teaspoon pepper
⅛ teaspoon dried basil
1 cup grated Mozzarella cheese

Brown the sausage and drain on paper towels. Wash and peel the eggplants; slice 1 inch thick. Heat the oil in a large skillet and cook the eggplant until lightly browned. Remove, drain, and place in a greased 2-quart casserole. Sprinkle sausage over eggplant. Add garlic to the skillet and sauté until lightly golden then remove from skillet. Stir in the flour, tomatoes, salt, sugar, paprika, pepper and basil. Cook, stirring, over medium heat until mixture boils and is slightly thickened. Pour sauce over the eggplant and sausage; top with the cheese. Place in a 375-degree oven and bake for 20 minutes.

Serves 6
Preparation time: 40 minutes
Baking time: 20 minutes
Easy

Karen Pierson

CARAWAY PORK CHOPS

1 cup saltine cracker crumbs
½ teaspoon salt
½ teaspoon pepper
1 teaspoon caraway seeds
4 pork chops

1 egg mixed with 1 tablespoon water
1 tablespoon vegetable oil
1 cup beef broth

Combine the cracker crumbs, salt, pepper and caraway seeds. Dip chops into the egg mixture, then in the seasoned crumbs. Brown chops in the oil, then transfer to a casserole. Add the broth, cover, and bake in a 350-degree oven for 1 hour.

Serves 4
Preparation time: 20 minutes
Cooking time: 1 hour
Easy

Marilyn Ketchum

GLAZED HAM BALLS

These make an excellent entree or, to use as an hors d'oeuvre, make into bite-size balls.

1½	pounds ground ham	2½	cups bread crumbs
1½	pounds ground fresh lean ham or pork	1½	cups brown sugar
		¾	cup vinegar
1¼	cups milk	¾	cup water
3	tablespoons ketchup	1½	teaspoons dry mustard

Combine the ham, pork, milk, ketchup and bread crumbs; blend well. Let stand for 1 hour then form into balls; transfer to a covered casserole.

Melt the brown sugar in a skillet. Add the vinegar, water and mustard. Cook over medium heat for 15 minutes and pour over the ham balls. Bake, covered, in a 350-degree oven for 30 minutes. Remove cover and bake for 30 minutes longer.

Preparation time: 30 minutes
Baking time: 1 hour
Easy

Marilyn Van Giesen

BOILED KIELBASA AND KRAUT

"The Kielbasa & Kraut is a favorite of mine because it's a complete meal and can be stored and reheated indefinitely. Best served with cornbread and buttermilk"

4-5 medium whole potatoes	1½	pounds fresh sauerkraut
3-4 whole onions	1	teaspoon oregano
4-5 cloves garlic, peeled	1	teaspoon crushed red pepper
2 quarts water		
3 pounds kielbasa	2	teaspoons black pepper

Put the potatoes, onions and garlic in 2 quarts of water. Boil for 20 minutes. Add the kielbasa, sauerkraut and seasonings and simmer over low heat for 30 minutes.

Serves 8-10
Preparation time: 10 minutes
Cooking time: 50 minutes

Coleman A. Young
Mayor, City of Detroit

POSCH CHOPS

Always a favorite

2   17-ounce cans sweet
    potatoes
1   21-ounces can apple pie
    filling
1   cup raisins

Ground cinnamon and cloves
    to taste
6   large-end loin pork chops
Salt and pepper

GLAZE

1   jar currant jelly

3   jiggers brandy

Slice the sweet potatoes and place in one layer in ungreased baking dish. Spread the apple pie filling over the potatoes. Sprinkle with raisins and top with cinnamon and cloves.

Brown the pork chops on both sides in a small amount of oil. Sprinkle with salt and pepper to taste. Arrange on top of the potato-apple mixture. Bake, uncovered, in a 350-degree oven for 1 hour.

After 1 hour, melt the currant jelly and add the brandy. Pour over the chops and return to the oven for 15 minutes.

Serves 6
Preparation time: 30 minutes
Cooking time: 1¼ hours
Easy

Sally Posch

SPICY HAM LOAF

An old family recipe

2   pounds lean ham
2   pounds lean fresh pork
1⅓   cups bread crumbs
3   eggs
1⅓   cups milk

1¼   teaspoons cloves
2   teaspoons hot mustard,
       or to taste
½   cup brown sugar, divided

Have the butcher put the ham and pork through a grinder twice. Combine the meat, crumbs, eggs, milk, cloves, mustard and 5 tablespoons of the brown sugar; mix thoroughly. Transfer into two greased loaf pans. Sprinkle with the remaining brown sugar. Bake in a preheated 350-degree oven for 1 hour. Serve with Horseradish Sauce or Mustard Sauce.

Serves 16

Marj. Jewell

TOURTIERE

A traditional French-Canadian Meat and Potato Pie

Pastry for a double crust
  10-inch pie
1 pound ground beef
1 pound ground pork
1 small onion, diced
1 clove garlic
½ teaspoon salt
½ teaspoon savory
¼ teaspoon celery salt or
  pepper
¼ teaspoon ground cloves
½ cup water
3 medium potatoes cut in
  small cubes

Line a 10-inch pie plate with bottom pastry. In a heavy saucepan, combine the remaining ingredients, except the potatoes, and bring to a boil. Reduce heat and cook, uncovered, for 20 minutes or until meat is no longer pink and most of the liquid has cooked off; mixture should not be watery. Remove the garlic clove and let mixture cool. Taste for seasoning.

In another saucepan, boil or steam the cubed potatoes until barely tender. Drain and let cool; add to meat mixture. Spoon into pie shell and cover with top pastry. Seal edges and cut steam vents in top. Bake in a 450-degree oven for 10 minutes. Reduce heat to 350 degrees and bake for 20 minutes or until crust is light brown.

Serves 8   Marie-Paule Hudon-Parcells

ITALIAN CHEESE AND HAM PIE

Delicious

Pastry crust for 3 9-inch pies
1 egg yolk, slightly beaten
1 16-ounce container creamed
  cottage cheese
1 1-pound container Ricotta
  cheese
2 cups diced cooked ham
⅓ cup grated Parmesan cheese
3 eggs
2 teaspoons Italian seasoning
½ teaspoon salt
¼ teaspoon pepper

Roll out ⅔ of the pastry dough and fit into the bottom and sides of a 10-inch springform pan. Brush with egg yolk.

Combine remaining ingredients and mix well. Pour into the prepared crust, folding edges of pastry over the mixture. Roll out the remainder of the pastry and place over the cheese mixture. Brush with some of the egg yolk. Bake in a 375-degree oven for 1 hour. Cool, then refrigerate. Remove from pan and serve cold, or heat in oven for 30 minutes and serve warm.

Preparation time: 30 minutes
Baking time: 1 hour
                                              Colleen Morrison

MARILYN'S QUICHE

1½	cups light or heavy cream	1	pound bulk sausage
4	eggs, lightly beaten	1	onion, grated
1	tablespoon parsley	1	9-inch unbaked pie crust
½	teaspoon salt	½	pound shredded Swiss
¼	teaspoon pepper		cheese, mixed with
¼	teaspoon nutmeg		1 tablespoon flour

Preheat oven to 375 degrees.

Blend the cream, eggs, parsley, salt, pepper and nutmeg together; set aside. In a heavy skillet, crumble the sausage and fry until browned; drain well, reserving 1 tablespoon fat in the skillet. Add the onion and cook until soft.

Put the sausage and onion in the pie shell. Sprinkle the shredded cheese on top, then pour on the egg-cream mixture. Bake for 35-45 minutes or until a knife inserted in the center comes out clean.

Serves 4
Preparation time: 20 minutes
Baking time: 45 minutes
Easy

Marilyn Turner & John Kelly
WXYZ-TV

CRIM DE LA CUSTARD

15	slices bread, crusts removed	½	teaspoon salt
¾	pound sliced sharp cheese	2	tablespoons onion flakes
		½	teaspoon dry mustard
1	10-ounce package frozen chopped broccoli, thawed	¼	teaspoon basil
		¼	teaspoon Worcestershire sauce
2½	cups diced baked ham	¼	teaspoon butter
3½	cups milk		Grated Parmesan cheese
6	eggs		

Layer half the bread slices in a 9x13-inch baking dish. Sprinkle on the cheese, broccoli and baked ham. Cover with the remaining bread slices on top. Combine the milk, eggs, seasoning and butter and pour over the bread. Refrigerate overnight.

Two hours before serving, bring to room temperature. Bake for 50 minutes in a 325-degree oven. Remove from oven and sprinkle generously with Parmesan cheese. Return to oven for 10 minutes longer.

Serves 8-12
Preparation time: 15 minutes
Easy

Mort Crim
WDIV-TV

HAM LOAF

Tastes great cold in sandwiches

1	pound beef	2	eggs
1	pound ham	¼	cup brown sugar
2	cups bread crumbs	1	teaspoon dry mustard
1	cup milk		

Grind the beef and ham together. Combine the remaining ingredients and form into a loaf. Bake in a 350-degree oven for 1½ hours. Serve hot with Mustard Sauce or cold in sandwiches.

Serves 4-6
Preparation time: 15 minutes
Baking time: 1½ hours

Alice Boyce

MUSTARD SAUCE

1	can condensed tomato soup	¼	cup prepared mustard
2	eggs, beaten	2	tablespoons vinegar
2	tablespoons sugar	2	tablespoons butter, melted

Combine ingredients in a small saucepan. Cook, stirring constantly, until mixture begins to boil; remove from heat and serve.

Makes 2 cups

Elizabeth McCartney

SWEET AND SOUR PORK

An extremely simple and tasty way to use left-over pork

3	tablespoons butter	⅓	cup water
1	small green pepper, cut in strips	2	tablespoons vinegar
1	tablespoon cornstarch	1	tablespoon soy sauce
1	cup chunk pineapple, drained	2	cups cooked pork, cubed
⅔	cup pineapple juice, not the juice drained from the chunks	1	fresh tomato, cut into wedges

Melt the butter in a skillet. Sauté the green pepper for 2 minutes. Stir in the cornstarch, pineapple chunks, pineapple juice, water, vinegar, soy sauce and pork. Cook, stirring constantly, until sauce is thick and clear. Add the tomato and heat through for 1 minute.

Serves 4
Preparation time: 20 minutes
Easy

Janette Hitchcock

PORK LOIN STUFFED WITH APRICOTS AND PRUNES

We pride ourselves on our cuisine

12 dried prunes
12 dried apricots
Brandy
1 2-3 pound boneless pork loin
1 teaspoon sage
1 teaspoon thyme
1 teaspoon chopped shallots

½ teaspoon white pepper
1 cup dry white wine
Dijon mustard
Brown sugar
2 cups chicken broth
2 tablespoons butter mixed with 2 tablespoons flour

Combine prunes and apricots in a bowl. Add enough brandy to cover and let soak for ½ hour. Cut a pocket lengthwise in the pork loin. Drain fruit, reserving brandy for marinade. Force the prunes and apricots into pocket and tie roast with string. Combine the reserved brandy with the sage, thyme, shallots, pepper and wine. Pour over meat and let marinate 3-4 hours, turning every 30 minutes. Drain and reserve marinade.

Preheat oven to 350 degrees and roast the pork for 1 hour or until done. Remove roast from oven and increase temeprature to 450 degrees. Cut and discard strings and coat roast well with mustard. Sprinkle with brown sugar and return to oven until nicely browned. Meanwhile, reduce marinade to half then add chicken broth. Pour off juices from roast and add to the sauce. Add butter-flour mixture and cook, stirring, until sauce is thickened. Adjust seasonings to taste.

Serves 8
Preparation time: 30 minutes
Roasting time: 1½ hours

Lee McNew
The Clarkston Cafe
Clarkston, Michigan

POLISH WEDDING MEAT BALLS

A *very old family recipe*

1½ cups bread crumbs
½ cup evaporated milk
½ pound ground pork
½ pound ground veal
½ pound ground beef
2 eggs

1 tablespoon seasoned salt
¼ teaspoon pepper
1 tablespoon chopped parsley
1 tablespoon grated onion
Butter

Combine the bread crumbs and milk; set aside to soak. Combine the pork, veal and beef with the remaining ingredients, except the butter. Add the bread crumbs and blend together, incorporating thoroughly. Form into small balls and brown in butter. Place in a 1½-quart casserole. Bake in a 325-degree oven for 35 minutes. Serve with Sour Cream sauce.

SOUR CREAM SAUCE

1 can condensed cream of
   mushroom soup
1 beef bouillon cube dissolved
   in ½ cup hot water

1 tablespoon soy sauce
1 cup sour cream

Combine the mushroom soup, bouillon, and soy sauce in a heavy skillet. Bring to a boil. Remove from heat, stir in the sour cream and pour over the meat balls just before serving.

Serves 6
Preparation time: 15 minutes
Baking time: 35 minutes
Easy

Marlene Bartkowski

BAKED PORK TENDERLOIN WITH MUSTARD SAUCE

¼ cup soy sauce
¼ cup bourbon

2 tablespoons brown sugar
2 pounds pork tenderloin

Combine the soy sauce, bourbon and brown sugar. Pour over the pork and marinate for several hours, turning meat occasionally. Remove meat from marinade and roast in a preheated 325-degree oven, basting frequently with the marinade, for 1 hour or until done. Carve the tenderloin into thin diagonal slices and serve with Mustard Sauce.

MUSTARD SAUCE

½ cup sour cream
⅓ cup mayonnaise
1 teaspoon dry mustard
1 teaspoon finely minced
    onion

1½ teaspoons vinegar
Salt to taste

At least 1 hour before serving the pork combine the sour cream and mayonnaise and mix until smooth. Stir in the mustard, onion, vinegar and salt and incorporate thoroughly.

Serves 4   Louise Lowell

FRENCH CANADIAN RAGOUT

This recipe has been handed down for many generations

2 pounds ground pork
Flour for dredging
2 large pork hocks, cut in
    2-3 pieces
2 large onions, finely
    chopped

1 3-pound chicken, optional
Salt and pepper
Dash each: cinnamon, sugar,
    allspice, cloves
1 cup flour

Form the ground pork into small balls and lightly dredge in flour; set aside. Rinse pork hocks well and place in a large kettle with the chopped onions and the chicken. Add water to cover and season to taste with salt and pepper. Bring to a boil, lower heat, and simmer for 2 hours or until the water is reduced by half. Remove chicken and pork hocks from the kettle and let cool slightly. Skin and bone the chicken and remove rind from the pork. Return meat to the kettle. Add the pork balls and simmer for ½ hour longer, then add the spices. Meanwhile, place the cup of flour in a heavy skillet. Brown the flour over very low heat, stirring constantly to keep it from burning; this may take up to 30 minutes. Add enough water to make a thin paste and pour slowly into the ragout, stirring constantly, until stew is desired thickness. Served with boiled potatoes and sliced tomatoes.

Serves 12-16   Marie-Paule Hudon-Parcells
                                                                    DSO

A great performance depends on all of the musicians; a great meal depends on all of its supporting parts.

PORK CHOP SUPREME

8 half-pound pork chops   Garnish: Apple rings, parsley

MARINADE

½ cup soy sauce   ½ teaspoon pepper
2 quarts water   ½ teaspoon chopped garlic
½ cup white vinegar   1¼ cups brown sugar
½ cup molasses   1 teaspoon salt

Combine ingredients, bring to a boil, then cool. Place pork chops in a shallow pan and cover with marinade. Cover and place in refrigerator overnight.

Preheat oven to 325 degrees. Drain marinade from the meat and cover the pan containing the pork chops with aluminum foil. Be sure to completely cover and seal the pan well. Bake chops 2½ to 3 hours or until tender. Remove meat from oven. Strain juices into a saucepan.

SAUCE

6 cups apple juice   2 tablespoons cornstarch
½ cup brown sugar   mixed with 1 tablespoon
Salt, pepper garlic to taste   water

To juices in saucepan add the apple juice and brown sugar. Add seasonings to taste and bring to a boil. Mix in cornstarch-water mixture and cook, stirring constantly, until thickened.

When ready to serve, place chops in oven for 10 minutes until heated through. Pour sauce over and garnish with apple rings and parsley.

Serves 8

John Laffrey's Vineyards
Southfield, Michigan

CALIFORNIAN PORK CHOPS

6 pork chops cut ¾ inch thick   1 9-ounce package frozen
1 teaspoon poultry seasoning   artichoke hearts, partially
1 teaspoon salt   thawed
1 can Cheddar cheese soup

Brown the pork chops in a skillet. Sprinkle with the poultry seasoning and salt. Spoon the soup evenly over the meat and top with the artichoke hearts. Cover and simmer 50-60 minutes or until the chops are tender.

Serves 6
Preparation time: 20 minutes
Cooking time: 1 hour
Easy

Ann Rumpsa

Vegetables
and
Side dishes

Middle Eastern Dinner

Baba Ghanooj

Pita Triangles

Tabooley

Papoutzakia

Riz a la Francais

Baklava

Yogurt with Honey

Wine Suggestions
An off-dry, spicey
white wine; such as
the Grand Cru Gewurztraminer (1981)

Picnic Before The Concert

Vegetarian Chopped Liver

Party Rye Slices

Gazpacho

Italian Cheese and Ham Pie

Broccoli Salad

Peach Kuchen

Cheese

Grandma's Iced Tea

Wine Suggestions
A light, dry, crisp white wine;
such as the
Pinot Grigio from S. Jermann (1981)

SPINACH MOLD

Great for dinner parties

3 cups cooked spinach, drained and chopped
⅓ cup fine dry bread crumbs
½ cup minced onion
5 tablespoons butter, divided
½ teaspoon salt
Pepper to taste

½ teaspoon nutmeg
1 cup grated Swiss cheese
5 eggs, lightly beaten
1 cup milk, scalded
1 cup sliced mushrooms
1 can French fried onion rings

Preheat oven to 325 degrees.

Oil a 1-quart ring mold. In a medium bowl, combine spinach and bread crumbs. Cook onion in 2 tablespoons of butter for 10 minutes and add to the spinach. Add the salt, pepper, nutmeg, cheese and eggs. Melt remaining butter with the milk and add to the spinach mixture; mix well. Add mushrooms, mix, and pour into the prepared mold. Sprinkle with onion rings.

Set pan in a larger pan and add water to come half way up the sides. Bake for 35 minutes or until knife inserted in the center comes out clean. Remove from oven and let sit for 5 minutes before unmolding.

Preparation time: 20 minutes
Baking time: 35 minutes   Rose Marie Melbus

TOMATO PUDDING

A sweet vegetable to serve with meat

1 10-ounce can tomato puree
½ cup boiling water
¾ cup brown sugar
¼ teaspoon salt

1½ cups fresh dark bread cubes
¼ cup butter, melted
Optional: 1 scant teaspoon curry powder

Preheat oven to 350 degrees.

Combine the puree, water, sugar and salt; cook over low heat for 5 minutes. Arrange the bread cubes in a well-buttered casserole; pour on the melted butter. Cover with the hot tomato mixture. Bake for 30 minutes.

Serves 4
Preparation time: 15 minutes
Baking time: 30 minutes
Easy   Virginia Andreae

RICE A LA FRANCAIS

This is a traditional Lebanese dish handed down from generation to generation since the time when Lebanon was under French rule.

½ cup butter	1½ teaspoons salt
½ cup pine nuts	1 teaspoon pepper
2 pounds coarsely ground lamb	1 teaspoon allspice
8 cups chicken or turkey broth	4 cups raw long grain rice

Melt the butter in an 8-quart pot. Add the pine nuts and brown lightly. Remove the nuts and 2 tablespoons of the butter and set aside. Sauté lamb in remaining butter until well browned. Add broth and seasonings and bring to a boil over high heat. Stir in the rice, cover tightly, and return to the heat. Bring to a second boil, then reduce the heat to low and cook for 20 minutes. Do not lift the lid. When done, remove from heat and fold in all but 2 tablespoons of the pine nuts. Transfer to a serving casserole. Garnish with reserved nuts.

Variation: Use beef instead of lamb and slivered almonds in place of pine nuts.

Serves 12
Preparation time: 40 minutes

Connie Salloum

FRIED OHIO APPLES

A terrific accompaniment for pork dishes

6 cups apples, about 8 medium	2 tablespoons sugar
5 tablespoons butter	2 tablespoons light brown sugar
1 tablespoon lemon juice	Pinch of salt

Pare and core the apples; cut each into 8 pieces. Heat the butter in a heavy skillet. Add the apples and cook, stirring gently, over medium heat for 15 minutes or until barely tender. Add more butter if necessary. Sprinkle lemon juice and sugars over the apples. Stir once, then cover with a heavy lid and turn off the heat. Let stand, covered, for 15 minutes.

Serves 6-8
Preparation time: 25 minutes
Easy

Louise Lee

SUMMER GARDEN CASSEROLE

1	can tomato sauce or spaghetti sauce	Salt and pepper to taste
1	pound mushrooms, sliced	Pinch of oregano, basil or other herbs to taste
3	small green peppers, diced	Parmesan cheese
3	medium zucchini, sliced	
5	green onions with tops, chopped	

Preheat oven to 350 degrees.
Mix tomato sauce with vegetables; add seasonings. Place in casserole and top with cheese. Bake for 30-35 minutes or until hot and bubbly.

Serves 6
Preparation time: 10 minutes
Cooking time: 30-35 minutes   Marge Barone
Easy   DSO

RATATOUILLE NICOISE

A classic 'do ahead' company dish

1	pound onions, chopped	1	large red pepper, cut into thin strips
6	cloves garlic, minced	1	pound eggplant, peeled and sliced
¼	cup olive oil, divided	1	pound zucchini, trimmed and cut into 1½-inch strips
½	pound tomatoes, peeled, seeded and chopped	1	tablespoon olive oil
1½	tablespoons tomato paste		Salt and pepper to taste
1	teaspoon sugar		
1	teaspoon thyme		
1	bay leaf		

In a large, deep skillet, sauté the onion and garlic in 2 tablespoons of oil over low heat until the onion is golden. Add the tomatoes, tomato paste, sugar, thyme and bay leaf and cook over moderate heat for 10 minutes; set aside. Sauté the pepper, eggplant and zucchini in 2 tablespoons oil over moderately high heat for 5 minutes, adding more oil if needed. Sprinkle with salt and pepper and add them to the onion mixture. Cook, covered, stirring occasionally, for 1 hour and 15 minutes, or until the vegetables are very tender. Correct seasoning, add 1 tablespoon oil and serve warm or at room temperature.

Serves 6   Charity de Vicq Suczek

SCALLOPED CORN AND TOMATOES

20	ounces frozen whole kernel corn	2	teaspoons sugar
½	cup butter, divided	2	teaspoons salt
1	cup thinly sliced onion	1	teaspoon marjoram
4	tomatoes, peeled and chopped	¼	teaspoon pepper
		2	cups soft bread crumbs
		2	teaspoons chopped parsley

Preheat oven to 350 degrees.

Place corn in a buttered 2-quart casserole. Melt the ¼ cup butter in a skillet and sauté the onion until tender and golden, about 5 minutes. Stir in the tomatoes, sugar, salt, marjoram, and pepper. Transfer to the casserole and mix well with the corn.

Using the same skillet, melt the remaining butter. Stir in the bread crumbs and parlsey and sprinkle over the corn mixture. Bake, uncovered, for 30 minutes or until hot and bubbly, and crumbs are browned.

Serves 8
Preparation time: 15 minutes
Baking time: 30 minutes
Easy

Joan Van Vlerah

NORTH SHORE POTATOES

6	tablespoons butter, divided	Dash of freshly ground pepper
2	cups shredded Cheddar cheese	½	medium onion, minced
2	cups sour cream	6	medium potatoes, boiled in skins and refrigerated for 24 hours
½	teaspoon salt		

Melt 4 tablespoons of the butter with the cheese in a double boiler. Add the sour cream, salt, pepper and onion and stir until well blended; remove from heat. Peel the potatoes and grate them into the cheese mixture. Place mixture in a buttered 2-quart casserole and dot with remaining butter. Bake in a 350-degree oven for 45 minutes.

Serves 6-8

Hope Knight

VEGETABLES — *When boiling potatoes to serve whole, cook them in broth with an onion and some freshly ground pepper.*

ZUCCHINI PIE

This unusual combination makes an outstanding side dish.

1   8-ounce can refrigerator
    crescent rolls
⅓   cup salted cashews
2   tablespoons butter
2-3 medium zucchini, with peel,
    thinly sliced
1   onion, finely chopped

1   teaspoon dried dill
Salt and pepper to taste
2   eggs, lightly beaten
1   cup Monterey Jack cheese,
    cubed
Chopped parsley

In a 9-inch pie plate, lay out the rolls to form a pie crust. Place cashews on the bottom of the crust.

In a skillet, melt the butter and sauté the zucchini and onion until translucent. Add the dill and salt and pepper to taste. Pour mixture over the nuts. Cover with the beaten eggs, top with the cheese and sprinkle with parsley. Bake in a 325-degree oven for 40 minutes, or until crust is lightly browned and eggs are set.

Serves 6-8
Preparation time: 20 minutes
Cooking time: 40 minutes
Easy

Susan Murphy

RICE PILAF

¼   cup minced onion
¼   cup butter, divided
2   tablespoons oil
2   cups Carolina rice

Hot chicken stock
2   tablespoons grated
    Parmesan cheese

Preheat oven to 350 degrees.

In a 7-inch ovenproof saucepan, sauté the onion in 2 tablespoons butter and the oil over moderately high heat until the onion is soft but not brown. Add the rice and stir until it is coated with the butter. Pour enough hot chicken stock to cover the rice by ½ inch, bring to a boil, cover tightly, and bake for 30 minutes. Fluff the rice with a fork and add the remaining butter and the cheese.

Serves 6

Charity de Vicq Suczek

ZUCCHINI WITH PESTO SAUCE

6 medium zucchini cut into julienne
Salt
2 cups chopped fresh basil
½ cup olive oil
3 tablespoons pine nuts

2 cloves garlic
1 teaspoon salt
1 cup fresh grated Parmesan cheese
2 tablespoons butter, melted

Place zucchini in colander; sprinkle with salt and let drain while preparing pesto sauce.

Place basil, olive oil, pine nuts, garlic and 1 teaspoon salt in blender or food processor fitted with the steel blade; process until pureed. Transfer to medium bowl. Add cheese and butter; mix well. Rinse zucchini, drain well, and pat dry. Melt butter in a large heavy skillet over medium heat. Add zucchini and sauté until heated through. Add pesto and toss until well coated. Serve immediately.

Serves 6
Sauce can be prepared ahead

Kathy Groustra

POTATOES AND ZUCCHINI EN CASSEROLE

6-8 potatoes, peeled and thinly sliced
2-4 zucchini, thinly sliced
Salt and pepper
Italian seasoned bread crumbs

4-6 ounces shredded Mozzarella or other mild cheese
Butter

Butter a 2-quart casserole and arrange a layer of potatoes in the bottom. Add a layer of zucchini and sprinkle with salt and pepper to taste, bread crumbs and cheese; dot with butter. Repeat process until all the potatoes and zucchini are used up. Cover tightly and bake in a 350-degree oven for 45 minutes or until the potatoes are soft when pierced with a fork. Remove cover and place under a broiler until lightly browned.

Serves 6-8
Preparation time: 20 minutes
Baking time: 45 minutes
Easy

Mario DiFiore
DSO

CARROT RING

Fill the center of the mold with creamed peas for an elegant side dish

2	eggs	½	cup coarsely chopped
1	cup light cream, scalded		blanched almonds
½	teaspoon salt	2½	cups grated raw carrots
½	teaspoon sugar	1½	tablespoons butter
⅛	teaspoon pepper		

Preheat oven to 350 degrees.
Beat the eggs and stir in the scalded cream. Add remaining ingredients except the butter and mix well. Melt the butter in a ring mold and let run around the mold to coat it well; pour the excess into the carrot mixture and blend. Pour into the mold then set mold in a pan of hot water and bake for 30 minutes. Invert mold to serve.

Serves 6-8
Preparation time: 15 minutes
Baking time: 30 minutes
Easy   Ida Mae Massnick

FRIED RICE

2	tablespoons vegetable oil	1	cup cooked peas
4	cups cold, cooked rice	1	cup finely diced carrots,
	Chicken stock		steamed
2	tablespoons soy sauce	½	cup minced green onions,
½	teaspoon sugar		with tops
2	teaspoons Sherry	½	cup sliced mushrooms
2	eggs, beaten		

Heat the oil in a skillet. Gently stir in the rice and separate the grains with a fork. Add the stock a tablespoon at a time until rice is barely moist. Add the soy sauce, sugar and Sherry; mix well. Push rice to one side of the pan and add the eggs. Cook until eggs begin to set, then stir into the rice. Add remaining ingredients and toss.

Serves 6-8
Easy   Kathryn Dahl

CRUSTY-TOPPED BROCCOLI CASSEROLE

This may be made a day ahead and refrigerated

1   package frozen chopped
    broccoli
½   cup condensed cream of
    mushroom soup
1   egg, beaten
½   cup shredded sharp
    Cheddar cheese
½   cup mayonnaise
1   tablespoon minced onion
Salt and pepper to taste
½   cup commercial herb
    stuffing mix
Butter

Cook the broccoli for 5 minutes. Drain well, then mix with the soup, egg, cheese, mayonnaise and onion. Season to taste. Place mixture in a well-buttered casserole and sprinkle on the stuffing mix. Dot with butter and bake for 30 minutes in a 350-degree oven.

Serves 4
Preparation time: 15 minutes
Baking time: 30 minutes
Easy

Peggy McCourt

MAGGIE'S ASPARAGUS CASSEROLE

Great for a busy hostess

2   10-ounce cans cut asparagus
36 saltine crackers, crumbled
½   pound processed American
    cheese, diced
4   hard cooked eggs,
    chopped
1   can cream of mushroom
    soup
¼   cup butter, softened
⅔   cup milk

Drain the asparagus, reserving the liquid. Place ⅓ of the cracker crumbs in the bottom of a well-buttered casserole. Layer half each of the cheese, eggs, asparagus and soup over the crumbs. Place another ⅓ of the crumbs on top and repeat layers, ending with the remaining crumbs. Dot with butter. Add enough of the reserved asparagus liquid mixed with the milk to come ½ inch from the top of the casserole. Bake, uncovered, in a 350-degree oven for 1 hour.

Serves 8
Preparation time: 20 minutes
Baking time: 1 hour
Easy

Maggie Allesee

STUFFED TOMATOES

4 medium tomatoes
¼ cup olive oil
1 tablespoon chopped shallots
½ cup chopped mushrooms
1 teaspoon minced garlic
1 teaspoon fresh thyme or
   ½ teaspoon dried
½ teaspoon dried basil

Pinch of sage
Pinch of rosemary
1 teaspoon salt
½ teaspoon white pepper
1 teaspoon tomato puree
1 egg
½ cup white bread crumbs

Cut tops off tomatoes. Scoop out pulp and place tomatoes in a buttered baking dish. Heat the oil in a saucepan, add the shallots and sauté for 3 minutes. Add remaining ingredients, except the egg and breadcrumbs, and simmer for 3 minutes.

Remove from heat and blend in the egg and breadcrumbs. Check for seasoning; add salt and pepper if needed. When filling has cooled, stuff tomatoes. Place in a 400-degree oven for 15 minutes. Cover with aluminum foil and bake for an additional 20 minutes.

Serves 4
Preparation time: 30 minutes
Cooking time: 35 minutes

Renee Mann

SAUERKRAUT CASSEROLE

½ pound sliced bacon
2 cups chopped onions
2 32-ounce jars sauerkraut,
   drained and rinsed
2 cups cored, pared and
   chopped apples

2 cups chicken broth
1½ cups dry vermouth
⅓ cup packed brown sugar
½ teaspoon pepper
½ teaspoon dried thyme
Apple wedges for garnish

Heat oven to 325 degrees. Fry the bacon in a large skillet until crisp; drain on paper toweling, crumble and set aside. Sauté the onions in the bacon drippings until soft, then stir in the remaining ingredients except bacon and apple wedges. Spoon mixture into a 3-quart baking dish. Bake, covered, until mixture browns and liquid is absorbed — about 4 hours. Top with reserved bacon and apple wedges.

Serves 8
Preparation time: 40 minutes
Baking time: 4 hours
Easy

Holly Barnett

WILD RICE PILAF

1 cup wild rice (6 ounces)	¼ cup sliced green onions
2⅓ cups water	2 tablespoons chopped
1 tablespoon chicken	pimento
bouillon	1 teaspoon grated lemon
1½ cups sliced mushrooms	peel
1½ cups sliced celery	1 tablespoon lemon juice
¼ cup butter	¾ teaspoon salt
1 10-ounce package frozen	½ teaspoon thyme
artichoke hearts, defrosted	⅛ teaspoon pepper

Place rice in a colander and run cold water through for 2 minutes. In a 3-quart saucepan, combine the rice, water and bouillon and bring to a boil. Simmer for 30 minutes; do not drain.
Sauté the mushrooms and celery in the butter. Add the artichokes, onions, pimento, lemon peel, lemon juice, salt, thyme, and pepper. Stir into the rice and transfer to a shallow 2-quart casserole. Cover and bake for 45-60 minutes in a 325-degree oven.

Serves 8-10
Preparation time: 20 minutes
Cooking time: 1½ hours
Easy   Martha Bowman

TEXAS POTATOES

8-10 potatoes	½ cup butter
2 cups Half & Half	½ cup minced onion
1 cup coffee cream	Salt and pepper

Boil the potatoes in skins until fork tender. Let cool, then peel and shred. Pour the Half & Half and cream into a medium saucepan. Add the butter, onion and salt and pepper to taste. Simmer until the butter is melted, then pour over the potatoes. Bake in a 325-degree oven for 1 hour. Potatoes should always be covered with liquid, if not, add more Half & Half.

Serves 8
Preparation time: 10 minutes
Cooking time: 1¾ hours
Easy   Mrs. Dean Richardson

ONION CASSEROLE

Great to prepare ahead and freeze

4 cups sliced onions
6 slices bread, toasted, buttered and cut into 1-inch cubes

2 cups shredded Cheddar cheese
1 cup milk
2 eggs
Salt and pepper to taste

Boil the onions in water to cover until soft. Drain well. In a 3-quart buttered casserole, layer the bread, onions and cheese until used up. Combine the milk, eggs, and seasonings and mix well. Pour over the casserole. Bake in a 350-degree oven for 30-45 minutes until hot and bubbly, and the cheese is melted.

Serves 8-10
Preparation time: 20 minutes
Baking time: 45 minutes
Easy   Holly Barnett

ZUCCHINI-RICE CASSEROLE

1 6-ounce package long grain and wild rice combination
2½ cups water
1 tablespoon butter
3 cups sliced zucchini
2 tablespoons chopped green chilies
1 pound shredded Monterey Jack cheese, divided

1 large tomato, sliced in 6 pieces
1 cup sour cream
½ teaspoon oregano
½ teaspoon garlic salt
2 tablespoons chopped parsley

Cook the rice with the water and butter according to the package directions. Mix the rice with the zucchini, chilies and ¾ of the cheese. Spread in a greased 9x13-inch baking dish. Cover tightly with foil and bake for 40 minutes in a 375-degree oven. Remove from oven and top with the tomato slices. Mix the sour cream, oregano and garlic salt and spread over the tomatoes. Top with the remaining cheese. Broil until the cheese is melted. Sprinkle with parsley.

Serves 12-15
Preparation time: 40 minutes
Cooking time: 1 hour
Easy   Marlene Thomas

SPINACH ARTICHOKE CASSEROLE

This easy, make ahead casseole is excellent for buffets or to take to a party

1 6-ounce jar marinated artichoke hearts
1 teaspoon salt
2 packages frozen chopped spinach, thawed and drained
1 8-ounce package cream cheese, softened

2 tablespoons butter, softened
¼ cup milk
½ cup grated Parmesan cheese
¼ teaspoon pepper

Drain the artichokes and place in the bottom of a greased 1½-quart casserole. Mix the salt with the spinach and place over the artichoke hearts. Beat the cream cheese, add the butter and milk and mix until well blended. Pour over the spinach then sprinkle with the cheese and pepper. If time allows, refrigerate for several hours or freeze if desired.

When ready to serve, remove from refrigerator and let come to room temperature. Bake, covered, in a 350-degree oven for 30 minutes, remove cover and bake 10 minutes longer or until top is lightly browned.

Serves 6
Preparation time: 20 minutes
Cooking time: 40 minutes
Easy

Dody Rothenberg

BEETS IN ORANGE SAUCE

½ cup sugar
1 tablespoon flour
½ teaspoon salt
½ cup orange juice

1 teaspoon grated orange peel
1 1-pound can sliced beets, drained

Blend together the sugar, flour, salt, orange juice and orange peel. Cook over medium heat, stirring, until thickened. Add the beets and heat thoroughly.

Serves 4
Preparation time: 10 minutes
Easy

Mary Powand

ARTICHOKE TORTE

A simple and delightful dish

1 tablespoon butter
2 tablespoons olive oil
2 tablespoons chopped parsley
½ cup chopped green onions
2 10-ounce packages frozen artichoke hearts
½ cup Italian bread crumbs, divided
3 eggs, lightly beaten
1 teaspoon oregano
¾ cup milk
¾ cup grated Parmesan cheese
Salt and pepper

In a medium saucepan, heat the butter and oil. Sauté the parsley and green onions for 3 minutes; cool. Cook the artichoke hearts according to package directions, drain then chop coarsely.

Lightly coat a quiche pan with some oil. Sprinkle with ¼ cup of the bread crumbs. Scatter the chopped artichoke hearts over the bread crumbs. Combine the eggs with the onion mixture and add the oregano, milk, cheese and remaining bread crumbs. Season to taste. Mix well and pour over the artichoke hearts. Bake in a 375-degree oven for 25 minutes.

Preparation time: 20 minutes
Baking time: 25 minutes
Easy

Sue Fishman

CASABLANCA RICE

This unusual side dish compliments steak, lamb, or chicken

2 cups converted rice
1 pound ground lamb or beef
¾ cup sliced blanched almonds
¼ cup blanched, shelled pistachio nuts
¼ cup pine nuts
¼ cup butter
1 teaspoon allspice
Salt and pepper to taste
2 cups chicken or beef broth

Wash rice and soak in water for 10 minutes. Place the lamb in a skillet and cook until browned. Add the almonds and cook until golden. Stir in the pistachios and pine nuts and brown slightly. Strain the rice and stir into the meat mixture. Add the butter and when melted, add the allspice and season to taste with salt and pepper. Stir in the broth; bring to a simmer. Cover skillet and cook over low heat for 1½ hours.

Serves 8-10

Stephanie Germack

QUICK CORN PUDDING

This was given to me by my grandmother

1	1-pound can cream-style corn	1/3	cup commercial bread crumbs
1	1-pound can whole kernel corn, drained	1/2	cup sour cream
1	egg, slightly beaten	1/2	teaspoon salt
		1/8	teaspoon pepper

Combine all ingredients and mix well. Turn into a well-buttered 1½-quart casserole. Place casserole in a pan of boiling water and bake in a 350-degree oven for 40 minutes or until firm.

Serves 8
Preparation time: 10 minutes
Baking time: 40 minutes

Mrs. Monte Clark
Detroit Lions

MUSTARD GLAZED CARROTS

1/4	cup butter	1	pound sliced, cooked carrots
1	tablespoon brown sugar		
1	teaspoon prepared mustard		Chopped parsley for garnish

In a small saucepan, melt the butter. Mix in the brown sugar and mustard. Add the carrots and toss gently. Sprinkle with parsley and serve immediately.

Serves 6

Chris Considine

CHEESE STUFFED ZUCCHINI

6	zucchini, 6-7 inches long	2	tablespoons finely chopped onion
2	eggs, well beaten		
1½	cups shredded Cheddar cheese	1/2	teaspoon salt
		1/2	teaspoon pepper
1/2	cup Ricotta cheese	1/2	cup bread crumbs
2	tablespoons finely chopped parsley	2	tablespoons melted butter

Scrub zucchini well, and cut off the ends. Boil in salted water to cover for 8-10 minutes or until just tender. Allow to cool slightly, then cut in half. Scoop out center pulp, invert, and allow to drain.

Combine the eggs, cheeses, parsley, onion, salt and pepper. Fill shells with mixture. Toss the bread crumbs with the melted butter and sprinkle on top. Bake in a 350-degree oven for 25 minutes. Run under a broiler until brown.

Serves 6

Chuck Dyer

GERMAN POTATO DUMPLINGS

DUMPLINGS

9	medium potatoes	⅔	cup breadcrumbs or farina
3	eggs, well beaten	1	teaspoon salt
1	cup flour	½	teaspoon nutmeg

Boil potatoes in their jackets until soft. Let cool then remove skins and put potatoes through a ricer. Place in a bowl and add the eggs, flour, breadcrumbs, salt and nutmeg. Mix thoroughly and form mixture into dumplings the size of large walnuts. If mixture is too moist, add more breadcrumbs. Drop the dumplings into salted, boiling water. When dumplings rise to the surface, continue boiling, uncovered, for 3 minutes. When done, remove from the liquid. Serve with Dumpling Dressing or gravy.

Note: Uncooked dumpling mixture can be kept refrigerated for several days. Cooked dumplings can be reheated in a double boiler.

DUMPLING DRESSING

1	cup butter	2	tablespoons diced onion
½	cup fresh bread cubes		

Melt the butter in a skillet. Sauté the bread cubes and onions, stirring constantly, until golden brown. Pour over the hot dumplings.

Serves 12

Michael Bric

YORKSHIRE PUDDING

Most often, nowadays, this is served with roast beef. However, in Yorkshire, England, it is made in a 9x13-inch pan and served with gravy before the beef is eaten. This takes the edge off the appetite and helps the economical Yorkshire housewife's budget!

½	cup flour	2 eggs
Pinch of salt		Milk

Place the flour, salt, eggs and ¼ cup milk in the blender. Process until well mixed. Gradually add milk until mixture equals 1¾ cups. Refrigerate for at least 1 hour.

Thirty minutes before the meat is done, heat oven to 425 degrees. Place some beef fat in the bottom of 12 muffin tins. Heat fat until it is "spitting". Re-blend the batter, and fill the muffin tins ¾ full. Place in the oven and bake for 20 minutes or until puffed and browned.

Serves 6-8

Helen Addison

BAKED SPINACH SOUFFLE

2	packages frozen chopped spinach	3	eggs, lightly beaten
1½	cups cottage cheese	¼	cup flour
2	cups shredded Cheddar cheese	2	tablespoons butter, melted

Cook spinach according to package directions; drain well and squeeze out as much water as possible. Combine with remaining ingredients and pour into a well-buttered 1½-quart casserole. Bake in a 350-degree oven for 1 hour.

Serves 6-8   State Senator Jack Faxon

CRUSTY-TOPPED KUGEL

This traditional dish is excellent for buffets. It can stay at room temperature for a long time.

Xmas brunch?

1	pound medium egg noodles	8	eggs, well beaten
½	cup butter, softened	1	quart milk
1	8-ounce package cream cheese, softened	2	teaspoons vanilla
1¼	cups sugar	1	teaspoon lemon juice
		Dash salt	

TOPPING

⅔	cups graham cracker crumbs	1¼	teaspooons cinnamon

Preheat oven to 350 degrees.
Cook noodles according to package directions. Drain and set aside. Cream together the butter and cream cheese. Add sugar and mix well. Blend in the eggs. Add the milk, vanilla, lemon juice and salt. Add noodles and mix thoroughly. Pour into a 9x13-inch baking dish. Mix the graham cracker crumbs and cinnamon and sprinkle on top of noodles. Bake for 1¼ hours or until nicely browned and crusty on top. Let cool at least 30 minutes before serving. Cut into squares.

Serves 8-10
Preparation time: 30 minutes
Baking time: 1¼ hours
Freezes well
Easy

Judy and Larry Liberson
DSO

SPINACH CASSEROLE

Makes spinach haters into spinach lovers

2   10-ounce packages frozen
    chopped spinach, cooked
    and drained
1   8-ounce package cream
    cheese, softened

½   cup milk
1   small onion, chopped
½   cup grated Cheddar
    cheese

Preheat oven to 350 degrees.
Place the spinach in a buttered 1-quart casserole. Combine the cream cheese and milk and beat until smooth; add the onion and mix well. Pour over the spinach and sprinkle with grated cheese. Bake for 20 minutes.

Serves 6-8
Preparation time: 15 minutes
Baking time: 20 minutes
Easy

Kitty Talcott

BROCCOLI AND BLEU CHEESE CASSEROLE

2   tablespoons butter
2   tablespoons flour
1   3-ounce package cream
    cheese, softened
¼   cup crumbled Bleu cheese
    (not Roquefort)

1   cup milk
2   10-ounce packages frozen
    chopped broccoli, cooked
    and drained
⅓   cup crushed Ritz crackers

In a saucepan, melt the butter. Blend in the flour and cheeses — mixture will be lumpy. Add the milk and cook, stirring constantly, until mixture comes to a boil. Remove from heat.
Place broccoli in a 1-quart baking dish. Pour sauce over broccoli and top with the cracker crumbs. Bake in a 350-degree oven for 30 minutes.

Serves 6-8
Preparation time: 25 minutes
Baking time: 30 minutes
Easy

Camille Shy

FRIENDLY SPUDS

Easy to make and always very popular

1	2-pound bag frozen hash brown potatoes	1	cup chopped onions
2	cups sour cream	½	cup butter
1	can cream of chicken soup	8	ounces grated sharp Cheddar cheese
1	can cream of mushroom soup		Salt and pepper to taste

TOPPING

1	cup cornflake crumbs	½	stick melted butter

Preheat oven to 375 degrees.
Thaw potatoes for about 30 minutes. Mix with remaining ingredients, then turn into a 9x13-inch casserole.
Combine the cornflake crumbs with the melted butter and sprinkle on top of casserole. Bake for 1 hour.

Serves 8-10
Preparation time: 5 minutes
Baking time: 1 hour
Easy   Sally Posch

"DIRTY" RICE

1	pound chicken gizzards, finely chopped	½	cup finely chopped green pepper
1	pound chicken livers, finely chopped	2	cloves garlic, minced
¼	cup margarine, melted		Salt and pepper
1½	cups finely chopped onion		Dash cayenne pepper
½	cup finely chopped celery	3	cups hot cooked rice
		½	cup chopped parsley

In a large skillet brown the gizzards and livers in the margarine. Add the onion, celery, green pepper, garlic and seasonings; mix well. Cover and cook over medium heat, stirring occasionally, until vegetables are tender. Add rice and parsley; toss gently. Garnish with additional parsley.

Serves 8
Preparation time: 15 minutes   Rudene Terry

MUSHROOM CASSEROLE

Great for brunch

¾	cup butter	3	tablespoons flour
1½	pounds fresh mushrooms, thinly sliced	1½	cups shredded Swiss cheese
¼	cup chopped onion	4	egg yolks
Salt		3	cups heavy cream
Freshly ground pepper		¾	cup fine, white, buttered bread crumbs

In a skillet, melt the butter. Sauté the mushrooms and onions until tender. Season to taste with salt and pepper. Stir in the flour and cheese. Turn mixture into a 2½-quart casserole. Beat the yolks with the cream; pour over the mushroom mixture. Sprinkle with bread crumbs. Bake in a preheated 375-degree oven for 20 minutes or until set.

Serves 6   Kathryn Dahl

SCALLION RICE

3	cups cooked rice	1	cup sour cream
½	cup finely chopped scallions, including green tops	¼	cup milk
		Tabasco sauce to taste	
		Salt to taste	
1½	cups cottage cheese	Grated Parmesan cheese	

Combine the rice and scallions. Blend remaining ingredients and add to the rice mixture. Place in a buttered 1½-quart casserole; sprinkle with Parmesan cheese. Bake in a 350-degree oven for 25-30 minutes.

Serves 6-8
Preparation time: 15 minutes
Baking time: 30 minutes
Easy   Betty Williams

To make carrot curls, slice the carrots lengthwise into thin strips. Soak strips in ice water until curled. Drain and store in plastic bags until serving time.

VEGETABLE CASSEROLE

2	packages frozen green beans	1	5-ounce can water chestnuts, drained and chopped
1½	cups sour cream		
¾	cup grated sharp Cheddar cheese	4	ounces fresh mushrooms, sliced
2	tablespoons light brown sugar	3	tablespoons chopped pimento
1	tablespoon flour	¾	cup dry coarse bread crumbs
1	tablespoon chopped onion		
1	teaspoon salt	3	tablespoons melted butter
¼	teaspoon pepper		

Cook the beans and drain. Combine the sour cream, cheese, sugar, flour, onion, salt and pepper and add to the green beans. Stir in the water chestnuts, mushrooms, and pimento. Turn into a buttered casserole. Mix bread crumbs with the butter and sprinkle on top. Bake in a 350-degree oven for 25 minutes.

Note: Other vegetables may be substituted for the green beans, and yogurt may be used instead of sour cream.

Serves 6   Myrna Maddox
DSO

CASTILLIAN BEANS

¼	pound pepperoni, thinly sliced	¼	teaspoon pepper
		3	1-pound cans cannellini or white kidney beans, drained
1	cup chopped onion		
1	clove garlic, minced	1	cup chicken broth
1	teaspoon salt	1	4-ounce can green chilies, chopped
1	teaspoon leaf thyme, crumbled		

Sauté the pepperoni in a large skillet for 5 minutes; remove and reserve on paper towels. Sauté the onion and garlic in the pepperoni drippings until soft. Stir in remaining ingredients and the reserved pepperoni. Bring to a boil, stirring once or twice. Transfer to a 2-quart casserole. Bake in a 350-degree oven for 40 minutes.

Serves 8
Preparation time: 20 minutes
Cooking time: 40 minutes
Easy   Natalie Payne

CELERY CASSEROLE AU GRATIN

A nice change from peas, beans, broccoli, etc

3 cups diced celery	1 cup chicken broth
¼ cup slivered almonds	¾ cup Half & Half
½ cup sliced water chestnuts	½ cup grated Parmesan cheese
½ cup sliced mushrooms	½ cup soft bread crumbs
½ cup butter, divided	Parsley for garnish
3 tablespoons flour	

Cook the celery in water to cover for 5 minutes or until tender. Drain off liquid and mix in the almonds, water chestnuts and mushrooms. Pour into a greased 12x8-inch buttered baking dish. Melt 5 tablespoons butter in a saucepan. Add the flour and mix well. Gradually stir in the broth and Half & Half; pour over the celery mixture. Combine the cheese and bread crumbs and sprinkle over casserole. Melt remaining butter and drizzle over top. Bake in a 350-degree oven for 25 minutes. Garnish with parsley.

Serves 8

Alice Reisig

BERKSHIRE BARLEY

A nice change from rice

3 tablespoons butter	1 clove garlic, minced
½ cup chopped onion	½ pound sliced mushrooms,
1 cup barley	sautéed
3 cups canned consommé	Salt and pepper

Melt the butter in a medium skillet. Add the onions and barley and cook, stirring, for 15 minutes, or until lightly browned. Stir in the consommé and garlic and bring to a boil. Cover and simmer for 45 minutes or until barley is tender. Add remaining ingredients and season to taste.

Serves 4-6
Preparation time: 20 minutes
Cooking time: 45 minutes
Easy

Alice Lungershausen

RISOTTO

1	cup raw Risotto	1	teaspoon stem saffron, loosely packed
2	tablespoons olive oil		
¼	cup finely chopped onion	2	tablespoons warm water
¼	cup finely minced prosciutto	Salt to taste	
		2	tablespoons butter
⅔	cup dry white wine	½	cup freshly grated Parmesan cheese
⅛	teaspoon dried, hot red pepper flakes		
1¾	cups simmering rich chicken broth, divided		

Rinse the Risotto and drain it well. Heat the oil in a heavy saucepan. Add the onion and cook, stirring, until it is lightly browned. Add the prosciutto and cook for 1 minute. Add the rice and cook over high heat, stirring constantly, scraping from the bottom, for about 5 minutes or until the rice starts to brown. Add the wine and pepper flakes and mix well. Cook, stirring occasionally, until the wine is almost completely absorbed, about four minutes. Add ½ cup of the broth and cook for 2 minutes. Blend the saffron and water and set aside. Add ½ cup broth to the rice mixture and cook over medium-high heat for 5 minutes, stirring gently and shaking the pan so the liquid is evenly absorbed. Add remaining broth, salt and saffron mixture. Cook over high heat for 6-7 minutes, stirring occasionally, and shaking the skillet. Stir in the butter and remove from heat. Add the cheese and toss gently.

Serves 2-4   Julie Jonna

YUMMY YAMS

Don't wait for Thanksgiving to try this.

4-6	sweet potatoes	1	cup walnuts, coarsely chopped
1½	tablespoons brown sugar		
3	tablespoons honey	1	cup miniature marshmallows

Boil the potatoes until soft. When cool enough to handle, remove the skins and cut into small pieces. Add the brown sugar, honey, walnuts and marshmallows and mix to coat evenly. Place in an oven-proof casserole. Bake in a 325-degree oven for 30 minutes.

Serves 4-6
Easy   Patricia Lemberg

Sauces
and
Condiments

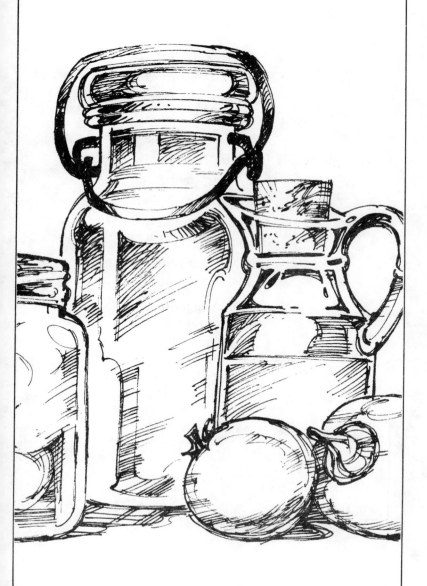

Fourth of July Barbecue
Whiskey Sour Punch
Spinach Puffs with Mustard Sauce
Hors d'Oeuvre Pie
Barbecued Ribs with Barbecue Basting Sauce
Peas and Peanut Salad
Mellow Potato Salad
Fresh Corn on the Cob
Sugarless Apple Pie
Chocolate Trifle

Wine Suggestions
A light, fruity red wine
such as the
Zinfandel from Louis Martini (1978)

BARBECUE BASTING SAUCE

3 cups water
½ cup cider vinegar
½ lemon, unpeeled and left in one piece
1 garlic clove
1 small piece of onion
1 teaspoon soy sauce
½ teaspoon dried sage
Pinch dry mustard
Salt to taste
Cayenne pepper to taste

Combine ingredients in a medium saucepan. Bring to a boil; reduce heat and simmer for one minute. Remove from heat. Use to baste ribs or chicken. Brush meat liberally with sauce before turning over. Cook until done, basting frequently.

Makes 3½ cups

Bobbi Pincus

ALL-PURPOSE BARBECUE SAUCE

2 onions, chopped
2 tablespoons vegetable oil
¾ cup water
¾ cup ketchup
½ cup Worcestershire sauce
½ cup vinegar
3 cloves garlic, minced
¾ cup brown sugar
1 tablespoon salt
1 tablespoon prepared mustard
2 tablespoons chili powder
2 tablespoons paprika

Sauté onion in the oil until soft and translucent. Add remaining ingredients and simmer for 10-15 minutes.

Yield: 5 cups
Preparation time: 30 minutes
Easy

Mary Sartell

TARRAGON BUTTER

½ cup butter, softened
2 teaspoons dried tarragon, finely crumbled
1 shallot, finely minced

Combine ingredients and blend well. Spread on broiled steaks.

Judy Shermar

HORSERADISH MOUSSE

This is great with cold filet of beef or with roast beef

1	envelope unflavored gelatin	½	teaspoon salt
¼	cup chicken broth	1½	cups sour cream
1	small onion, grated	2	egg whites, stiffly beaten
¾	cup freshly grated horseradish		Watercress for garnish

Soak the gelatin in the broth and dissolve over hot water; let cool. Combine the onion, horseradish, salt, sour cream and cooled gelatin; mix thoroughly. Fold in the beaten egg whites. Place in a mold for several hours until set.
To serve: Unmold and garnish with watercress.

Serves 6-8

Lee Muench

EMERGENCY MADIERA SAUCE

For steak or roast beef

¼	cup butter	2	tablespoons tomato paste
1	small onion, finely minced		Salt and pepper
1	clove garlic, minced	2	tablespoons potato starch
2½	cups beef broth	¼	cup Madiera

In a saucepan, over medium heat, melt the butter. Sauté the onion and garlic until the onion is soft. Add the broth, the tomato paste and salt and pepper to taste. Combine the potato starch with the Madiera and add to the mixture. Cook, stirring constantly, until clear and thickened.

Makes 2 cups
Easy

Marla Szymanski

The only way to learn about herbs is to use them — sparingly, until you know each flavor.

BASIC ITALIAN SAUCE

4 cups cooked tomatoes
1 6-ounce can tomato paste
3-4 cloves garlic, minced
2 medium onions, chopped
2 teaspoons oregano

2 teaspoons basil
2 teaspoons sugar
1 teaspoon salt
Pepper to taste
¼-½ cup grated Parmesan cheese

Combine ingredients and simmer for 1-3 hours, or until desired consistency. Use on spaghetti, in lasagne or vegetable stew, or as a pizza sauce.

Preparation time: 15 minutes
Cooking time: 1-3 hours
Easy

Victoria King
DSO

CHILI SAUCE

25-30 fresh, ripe tomatoes
10 medium onions, finely chopped
3 sweet red peppers, finely chopped
1 sweet green pepper, finely chopped

2-3 hot red peppers, minced
2 ribs celery, finely chopped
4 cups brown sugar
3 cups vinegar
4 teaspoons salt

Chop the tomatoes. In a large kettle combine the tomato pulp with the onions, peppers and celery. Add the brown sugar, vinegar and salt. Simmer gently, uncovered, for 2 hours. Seal in hot sterilized jars.

Yield: about 8 pints

Marilyn Ketchum

CHINESE PLUM SAUCE

2 tablespoons plum preserves or orange marmalade
¼ cup vinegar
2 tablespoons sugar

2 tablespoons dry hot mustard
3 tablespoons water
Salt and pepper to taste

Mix the preserves, vinegar and sugar. Combine the dry mustard with the water and stir into a paste. Add to the first mixture, incorporating thoroughly, and season with salt and pepper to taste.

Makes ¾ cup

Bob Allison
"Ask Your Neighbor"

MICKEY'S MUSTARD SAUCE

Use this excellent sauce instead of regular prepared mustard . . . with fish, ham, beef . . .

3 tablespoons Coleman's dry mustard	1 tablespoon flour
	¼ teaspoon salt
¼ teaspoon white pepper	½ cup cider vinegar
2 tablespoons cold water	1 egg, beaten
⅔ cup sugar	1 tablespoon butter

In a saucepan, mix the mustard, pepper and cold water to a paste. Add the sugar, flour, salt and vinegar and mix well. Add the egg and butter, and bring to a boil. Remove from heat, let cool, and stir to blend. Refrigerate.

Makes 1½ cups   Jean Carman

THE BEST AIOLI

This is excellent for vegetables, but, watch out!

6-8 cloves garlic	Juice of 1 lemon
2 egg yolks	1 teaspoon Dijon mustard
Salt and pepper to taste	1 cup good quality olive oil

In a blender or food processor fitted with the steel blade, combine all ingredients except the oil. With the motor still running, slowly add the oil until incorporated.

Yield: 1½ cups
Easy   Paul Landry

VENISON SAUCE

This is delicious as a baste for a roast

2 12-ounce bottles chili sauce	1 cup butter
3 8-ounce jars currant jelly	1 cup Sherry

Combine ingredients, except Sherry, in a medium saucepan. Bring to a boil and cook for 10 minutes. Stir in the Sherry.

Makes 8 cups   Alice Reisig

LEMON BUTTER

This is a fantastic spread on biscuits

1   cup very soft butter
½   cup sugar
Grated rind and juice of
    1 lemon

Pinch of salt
3   eggs

In a medium saucepan whip the butter and sugar. Stir in the lemon rind and salt. In a separate bowl, beat one egg at a time and add to the butter mixture. Mix well. Add the lemon juice and cook over low heat, stirring constantly, for 10 minutes or until mixture has the consistency of custard. Cool before serving.

Makes 1 cup
Preparation time: 15 minutes

Helene Eagan

CREME FRAICHE

1   teaspoon buttermilk

1   cup heavy cream

Mix the buttermilk and cream and heat to lukewarm (not over 85-degrees). Pour into a loosely covered jar and let stand at room temperature, 60-85 degrees, until thickened — about 5 to 8 hours on a hot day or 24-36 hours at low temperature. Stir, cover and refrigerate. Keeps up to 2 weeks in refrigerator.

Makes 1 cup

Winnie Ostrowski

MUSTARD SAUCE FOR FISH

2   teaspoons dry mustard
    mixed with 2 teaspoon water
1   cup mayonnaise
½   cup Dijon mustard

2   teaspoons dry white wine
1   drop Tabasco sauce
Juice of ½ lemon
Dash of Worchestershire sauce

Combine all ingredients; mix thoroughly. Chill at least 2 hours before serving.

Roberta Bloom

TEXAS "DILLY" BEANS

Try these, icy cold, instead of pickles.

2   pounds fresh green beans, trimmed
2   teaspoons cayenne pepper
4   cloves garlic
4   heads fresh dill, or
    4 teaspoons dill seeds

2½ cups water
2½ cups vinegar
¼   cup salt
4   pint canning jars, with lids

Sterilize the jars and lids by boiling for 20 minutes.
Meanwhile, wash beans and trim off both ends. When jars are done, pack the beans lengthwise into the hot jars, leaving ¼ inch head space. To each jar, add ½ teaspoon cayenne, 1 garlic clove, 1 head dill or 1 teaspoon dill seed. In a 2-quart saucepan, combine the water, vinegar and salt and bring to a boil. Immediately pour over the beans, leaving ¼ inch headspace.
Adjust covers and process in a boiling water bath for 10 minutes; remove from water and cool. When cool, tighten lids. Allow to stand for 2 weeks for flavors to blend.

Yield: 4 pints
Lee Muench

SPICED ONION RINGS

These onions are especially good with cold roast beef. Everyone loves them.

1   cup vinegar
1   cup water
1½ cups sugar
1½ teaspoons salt

1   teaspoon whole cloves
½   stick cinnamon
4   cups thinly sliced onion rings

Combine the ingredients, except onions, in a large saucepan and bring to a boil. Add the onions and turn off heat. Let cool then cover and refrigerate for at least 12 hours.

Serves 10-12
Preparation time: 15 minutes
Easy
Janette Hitchcock

GINGER-LEMON PUMPKIN PICKLES

This recipe was brought from Germany by my mother-in-law

1   5-pound pumpkin
20 ounces cider vinegar
Water
2½ cups sugar

1   lemon, thinly sliced
1   3-inch piece of ginger
    root, peeled

Split the pumpkin open, remove seeds and strings. Cut into 1½-inch wide strips and peel off the rind. Cut rind into ¼-inch slices. Reserve pumpkin meat for another use.

Place the pumpkin strips in a crock and pour vinegar over. Add enough water to cover and let soak for 24 hours.

In a large enamel kettle, place pumpkin strips with the vinegar solution and add remaining ingredients. Add water to cover and bring to a boil. Cover and simmer until rinds are transparent and light. After 10 minutes check for taste. Add more vinegar or lemon juice if necessary. Transfer to hot sterilized jars. Cut the gingerroot and place a piece in each jar. Seal immediately.

Lee von Berg

INDIANA BREAD AND BUTTER PICKLES

An old family recipe handed down through at least 3 generations of Indiana residents

1   teaspoon dry mustard
2   teaspoons mustard seed
4   teaspoons salt
1   teaspoon turmeric
2   teaspoons celery seed
4   large onions, sliced

3   red peppers, sliced
3   cups sugar
3   cups cider vinegar
Pinch of alum
4   quarts sliced cucumbers

Combine all ingredients, except alum and cucumbers, and bring to a boil. Add cucumbers; boil 5 minutes. Add the alum. Pack in sterilized canning jars. Can be eaten immediately

Yield: 4-6 quarts
Preparation time: 30 minutes
Keep for months if properly canned
Easy

Trudy Rhoades

CRANBERRY CONSERVE

A delicious alternative to cranberry sauce

1	pound cranberries, washed and picked over	1	lemon, thinly sliced and quartered
1	cup water	¾	cup raisins
2½	cups sugar		Optional:
2	cups pared, diced apples	1	cup walnuts or pecans
½	cup orange marmalade or 1 orange, peeled and diced		

Place the berries, water and sugar in a kettle. Bring to a boil and simmer for 20 minutes or until berries pop. Add the apple, orange or marmalade, lemon and raisins. Cook for 30 minutes or until mixture is thick. Remove from heat and stir in the nuts. Pack in hot sterilized containers and seal.

Yield: About 3 pints

Brenda Pangborn
DSO

PLUM CONSERVE

1	29-ounce can purple plums in syrup	1	orange, peeled, seeded and chopped
½	cup seedless raisins	1	tablespoon lemon juice
1	cup sugar	1	cup walnuts, chopped

Pit the plums and cut in fourths. Combine the plums, raisins, sugar, and orange. Stir until the sugar is dissolved. Bring to a rapid boil then reduce heat to low and simmer mixture for 45 minutes or until very thick; stir often. Add the lemon juice and walnuts and mix well. Seal in hot sterilized glasses.

Yield: (4) 8-ounce jars
Preparation time: 1 hour

Alicia Rosenberg

To make your kitchen smell nice, place 1 teaspoon of whole cloves and ½ orange in 1 cup water. Bring to a boil, then simmer for 15 minutes.

Cookies and Candy

HOLIDAY GIVING

Kahlua in decorative bottles with personalized labels.

Sugared Walnuts offered in a canning jar.
Tie a ribbon around the neck.

Plum Conserve

Beer Cheese in a reusable crock.

An assortment of cookies —
served on a plate that the recipient
will cherish forever.

An assortment of canned goodies —
Carrot Chutney, "Dilly Beans",
and Spiced Onion Rings.

A copy of **Culinary Counterpoint.**

CHOCOLATE TRUFFLE COOKIES

A chocolate lovers delight

1	12-ounce package semi-sweet chocolate chips, divided	1	teaspoon vanilla
¼	cup butter	4	teaspoons instant coffee powder
4	ounces unsweetened chocolate	½	teaspoon baking powder
4	eggs	½	cup flour
1½	cups sugar	4½	cups coarsely chopped walnuts

Preheat oven to 350 degrees.

In the top section of a double boiler over simmering water melt 1 cup chocolate chips with the butter and unsweetened chocolate. DO NOT STIR.

Beat the eggs with the sugar, vanilla and instant coffee powder. When the chocolate has melted, add the egg mixture and blend well. Combine the baking powder and flour and blend into the chocolate mixture. Add remaining chocolate chips and the walnuts and incorporate thoroughly. Drop by the teaspoonful onto a greased cookie sheet. Bake for 5 minutes.

Yield: 4-5 dozen
Easy

Nancy M. Dewar
(Mrs. Robert E. Dewar)

CHOCOLATE PEANUT BUTTER OATMEAL COOKIES

2	cups sugar	½	cup peanut butter
½	cup unsweetened cocoa	1	teaspoon vanilla
½	cup milk	3	cups quick cooking oats
½	cup butter		

Place the sugar, cocoa and milk in a large saucepan. Boil for 1 minute. Add the butter, peanut butter, vanilla and oats; stir well. Drop by the teaspoonful onto waxed paper. Let cool.

Kathy Rich

RUGELACH

They melt in your mouth

1 cup butter, softened	Pinch of salt
1 egg yolk	2 cups flour
¾ cup sour cream	1 tablespoon cinnamon
1 teaspoon vanilla	½ cup sugar
2 cups flour	1 cup chopped nuts
1 teaspoon vanilla	1 cup raisins

Cream the butter. Stir in the egg yolk, sour cream and vanilla and salt. Gradually blend in the flour and mix thoroughly. Wrap the dough in plastic wrap and chill overnight.

Preheat oven to 350 degrees.

Cut dough into 4 pieces; refrigerate remaining dough while working on each section. Take one-fourth of the dough and roll out on a lightly floured board into a circle, ⅛-inch thick. Cut into wedges; sprinkle with cinnamon and sugar and a scattering of nuts and raisins. Roll up the wedges from wide end, pressing tip a bit to make it hold closed. Place on ungreased cookie sheets, tip down, and bake for 20 minutes, or until lightly golden.

Variation: Use apricot jam or peach puree in addition to the nuts and raisins.

These can be frozen in well sealed plastic bags or aluminum foil and used as needed.

Yield: about 48 pastries   Yetta Dubin

KIFLI

CRESCENTS

3 cups flour	6 egg yolks
1 cup butter	½ cup light cream or 3
1 teaspoon salt	tablespoons sour cream

FILLING

1 pound ground walnuts
1 cup sugar
3 egg whites

Combine the flour and butter and mix well; add salt. In a separate bowl, mix the egg yolks and cream and add to flour mixture; mix well.

Pinch off pieces of dough small enough to form balls about the size of walnuts. Place on a cookie sheet and refrigerate overnight.

When ready to prepare, preheat oven to 350 degrees. Remove unbaked dough from refrigerator and let sit at room temperature for 10 minutes. Roll out cookies one at a time into an oval shape about 3 inches long. Place filling in the center, fold over into crescent shapes and press to seal. Place on an ungreased cookie sheet and bake for 15-20 minutes or until golden.

Yield: 60-70 cakes

Eleanor Margitza
DSO

NUT TASSIES

These are delicious any time, but are especially great during the holiday season.

CREAM CHEESE PASTRY

1 3-ounce package cream cheese	½ cup butter, softened
	1 cup flour

Beat the cream cheese and butter. Add the flour and blend well. Form into 24 walnut-sized balls. Press into tiny muffin tins and form into cups. Chill.

FILLING

¾ cup finely chopped nuts	1 teaspoon vanilla
¾ cup firmly packed brown sugar	1 tablespoon butter, melted
1 egg, slightly beaten	Powdered sugar

Preheat oven to 350 degrees.

Combine ingredients, except the powdered sugar, and mix well. Fill prepared cups ¾ full with mixture. Bake for 15-18 minutes. Reduce oven temperature to 250 degrees and bake 10 minutes longer. Let stand for 5 minutes before removing from pans. Cool completely, then sprinkle with powdered sugar.

Yield: 24 cookies
Preparation time: 25 minutes
Baking time: 25 minutes
Easy

Judy Liberson
DSO

CHOCOLATE MERINGUE COOKIES

2 egg whites	¾ cup sugar
⅛ teaspoon salt	1 6-ounce package chocolate
⅛ teaspoon cream of tartar	chips
1 teaspoon vanilla	¼ cup chopped nuts

Preheat oven to 300 degrees.

Beat the egg whites, salt, cream of tartar and vanilla until soft peaks form. Gradually add the sugar and beat until stiff but not dry. Fold in the chocolate chips and nuts.

Cover a cookie sheet with aluminum foil. Drop mixture by the teaspoonful 2 inches apart. Bake for 25 minutes.

Yield: 36 cookies
Preparation time: 20 minutes
Baking time: 25 minutes   Sandy Kroovand

ZUCCHINI COOKIES

These may not sound great, but they sure do taste great!

¾ cup vegetable shortening	1 cup flour
½ cup white sugar	1 teaspoon salt
1 cup firmly packed brown	1 teaspoon cinnamon
sugar	½ teaspoon baking soda
2 eggs	½ cup wheat germ
1 teaspoon vanilla	1 cup raisins, nuts or
1 cup peeled, grated zucchini	combination of both
3 cups uncooked rolled oats	

Preheat oven to 350 degrees.

Cream together the shortening, white and brown sugars, eggs and vanilla. Stir in the zucchini and oats. Combine the flour, salt, cinnamon, baking soda and wheat germ and add to the creamed mixture; mix well. Stir in the raisins or nuts. Drop by the teaspoonful onto 2 greased cookie sheets. Bake for 15-20 minutes, until done.

Preparation time: 20 minutes
Easy   Yolanda McDonald

CREAM CHEESE BROWNIES

CHOCOLATE LAYER

1 package German's Sweet Chocolate	⅛ teaspoon salt
3 tablespoons butter	½ cup flour
2 eggs	1 teaspoon vanilla
¾ cup sugar	¼ teaspoon almond extract
½ teaspoon baking powder	½ cup chopped nuts

Preheat oven to 350 degrees.
Melt the chocolate with the butter over very low heat; let cool. Beat the eggs until lemon colored. Slowly add the sugar and beat until thick. Stir in the baking powder, salt and flour. Blend in the chocolate mixture, vanilla, almond extract and nuts.

CHEESE LAYER

2 tablespoons butter	1 egg
1 3-ounce package cream cheese	1 tablespoon flour
¼ cup sugar	½ teaspoon vanilla

Cream the butter and cream cheese. Gradually add the sugar, beating until fluffy. Blend in the egg, flour and vanilla; set aside.
Spread half the chocolate batter in a greased 9-inch square pan. Top with the cheese mixture, then spoon the remaining chocolate batter over. Bake for 35-40 minutes or until a toothpick inserted in the center comes out clean.

Yield: 16 bars
Preparation time: 30 minutes
Baking time: 40 minutes
Easy

Helen Peterson

QUICK COOKIES

An excellent recipe for beginning cooks

½ cup milk
1 stick butter
2 cups sugar
3 cups rolled oats

5 tablespoons cocoa beverage mix
2 tablespoons peanut butter
1 teaspoon vanilla

In a saucepan bring to a rolling boil, the milk, butter and sugar; cook for 1 minute. Remove from stove and stir in remaining ingredients; blend well. Drop by the teaspoonful onto a piece of waxed paper and let cool.

Yield: 3 dozen cookies
Preparation time: 20 minutes
Make ahead but do not freeze
Easy

Diane Varisto

AUNT MARY'S DATE SQUARES

½ cup butter, softened
1 cup sugar
2 eggs
½ teaspoon vanilla
½ teaspoon salt

1 teaspoon baking powder
¾ cup sifted flour
1 cup finely chopped dates
½ cup chopped walnuts
Powdered sugar

Preheat oven to 350 degrees.
Cream the butter with the sugar. Beat in the eggs, vanilla, salt, and baking powder. Add the flour and mix well. Stir in the dates and nuts and thoroughly incorporate.
Spread in a 7x11-inch greased baking pan and bake for 25 minutes. Remove from the oven and sprinkle with some powdered sugar. Cut into squares while still warm.

Preparation time: 15 minutes
Easy

Marion Smith
DSO

COCONUT MACAROONS

Fast, easy and delicious

1½   cups shredded coconut
⅓   cup sugar
2   tablespoons flour

⅛   teaspoon salt
2   egg whites, lightly beaten
¼   teaspoon almond extract

Preheat oven to 325 degrees.
Combine the coconut, sugar, flour and salt and blend well. Add the egg whites and extract and blend until the mixture is wet. Drop by the teaspoonful onto a greased cookie sheet. Bake for 20 minutes. Remove from pan immediately and let cool.

Yeild: 2 dozen

Linda Williamson

BUTTERHORNS

Excellent for breakfast, brunch or dessert

COOKIES
1   cup butter, softened
12   ounces cream cheese

2   cups flour
Dash salt

Using a hand mixer, cream the butter and cream cheese. Add the flour and salt and blend well. Refrigerate overnight.
Preheat oven to 350 degrees.
Divide the dough into 3 equal parts and form into balls. Dust a pastry board with flour and roll 1 ball at a time into a circle ⅛ inch thick. Cut into 12 equal wedges. Roll each wedge from wide end to narrow edge. Place on an ungreased cookie sheet point side down, 2-3 inches apart. Bake for 30 minutes or until lightly browned. Let cool completely, then frost.

FROSTING
1½   cups powdered sugar
2   tablespoons butter, softened

1   teaspoon vanilla or lemon extract
Milk

Combine the sugar, butter and extract. Add the milk slowly until mixture is a spreading consistency. Spread on each cookie.

Joyce Pippel

CHOCOLATE ALMOND COOKIES

½ cup butter
1 3-ounce package cream cheese
½ cup sugar
1 egg yolk
½ teaspoon almond extract

1 cup flour
¼ teaspoon salt
1 6-ounce package miniature chocolate chips
½ cup slivered toasted almonds

Preheat oven to 350 degrees.
Cream the butter and cream cheese. Add the sugar and blend well. Add the egg yolk and almond extract and mix well. In a separate bowl, combine the flour and salt and gradually add to creamed mixture. Stir in chocolate chips and almonds.
Drop by the heaping teaspoonful onto a greased cookie sheet and flatten slightly. Bake for 12-15 minutes until edges are slightly browned. Cool on a wire rack.

Rita Pitcoff

SALAMI COOKIES

This is an old European recipe. Sounds crazy? Try 'em!

1 cup powdered sugar
1 cup finely ground nuts
½ cup coarsely ground nuts
½ cup raisins
½ cup chopped dates

1 square unsweetened chocolate, melted
1 egg white
Optional: 1 tablespoon rum
Additional powdered sugar

Combine all ingredients and mix thoroughly. Work together to make a *very stiff* dough. Shape dough into 3 logs and roll in powdered sugar. Wrap well in aluminum foil and store for at least 2 weeks to mellow. To serve: Cut into thin slices.
Note: Additional melted chocolate may be used if a more chocolatey flavor is desired; however, add 1 egg white for each additional square of chocolate.

Linda Piljan

"BETTER FOR YOU" CHOCOLATE CHIP COOKIES

Variation on a popular theme

1¼	cups whole wheat flour	1	teaspoon vanilla
1	cup unbleached white flour	½	teaspoon water
1	teaspoon baking soda	2	eggs
1	teaspoon salt	⅓	cup wheat germ
1	cup butter, softened	1-2	cups chocolate chips
¾	cup sugar		Optional: 1 cup chopped nuts
¾	cup brown sugar		

Preheat oven to 375 degrees.

Sift together the flours, baking soda and salt; set aside. Cream the butter and white and brown sugars; add vanilla and water and mix well. Beat in the eggs. Add flour mixture and wheat germ. Stir in chocolate chips and nuts, if desired. Drop by the teaspoonful onto greased cookie sheets. Bake for 10-12 minutes.

Yield: 6 dozen cookies
Preparation time: 25 minutes
Easy

Carol Herbst

CARL GRAPENTINE'S MOTHER'S OATMEAL RAISIN COOKIES

1	cup brown sugar	1	cup sifted flour
½	cup white sugar	½	teaspoon baking soda
¾	cup shortening	¼	teaspoon nutmeg
1	egg	1	teaspoon cinnamon
1	teaspoon vanilla	2¾	cups quick-cooking oats
¼	cup water	1	cup raisins

Preheat oven to 350 degrees.

Cream the brown and white sugars with the shortening until light and fluffy. Add the egg, vanilla and water and mix well. Mix together the sifted flour, baking soda, nutmeg and cinnamon and add to the creamed mixture. Stir in the oats and raisins. Drop by the teaspoonful on lightly greased cookie sheets and bake for 11 minutes.

Carl Grapentine
WQRS-FM 105

CHINESE CHEWS

CRUST

2 cups plus 2 tablespoons flour	1 cup butter
	1 cup dark brown sugar

Preheat oven to 350 degrees.
Combine ingredients and press into a 9x13-inch baking pan. Bake for 10 minutes.

TOPPING

1½ cups dark brown sugar	2 eggs
¼ teaspoon salt	1 teaspoon vanilla
1 cup coarsely chopped pecans	½ teaspoon baking powder

Combine all ingredients and mix well. Spread over the crust, return to oven and bake for 25-30 minutes or until lightly brown. Cool, then cut into squares.

Preparation time: 20 minutes
Baking time: 50 minutes
Easy   Betty Williams

PUMPKIN BROWNIES

An unusual variation on a popular theme

BARS

4 eggs	2 teaspoons baking powder
1½ cups sugar	1 tablespoon cinnamon
1 cup vegetable oil	1 teaspoon salt
1 pound canned pumpkin	1 teaspoon baking soda
2 cups flour	1 cup raisins or chopped nuts

Preheat oven to 350 degrees.
Beat the eggs with the sugar, oil, and pumpkin. Sift together the flour, baking powder, cinnamon, salt and soda. Add to the pumpkin mixture and mix well. Fold in the raisins and spread batter in an ungreased 9x13-inch baking pan. Bake for 30-40 minutes or until the top springs back when lightly touched. Set on a wire rack to cool, then frost.

FROSTING

1 3-ounce package cream cheese, softened	1 teaspoon vanilla
1 tablespoon butter, softened	2 cups powdered sugar, sifted

Combine ingredients and beat well. Frost the cooled brownies and cut into bars.

Yield: 24 bars
Preparation time: 20 minutes
Baking time: 40 minutes
Easy

Paula Stevens

CHEESECAKE COOKIES

CRUST

¼ cup butter	1 cup flour
⅓ cup firmly packed brown sugar	½ cup chopped pecans
	½ cup currant jelly

Preheat oven to 350 degrees.
In a mixing bowl, cream the butter. Add the brown sugar and flour and mix with a pastry blender until mixture resembles coarse corn meal; stir in the pecans. Reserve 1 cup of the mixture for topping, and press remainder on the bottom of an 8-inch square baking pan. Bake for 15 minutes. Let cool then drop jelly by the spoonful and carefully spread over the crust.

FILLING

1 8-ounce package cream cheese	2 tablespoons milk
¼ cup sugar	2 tablespoons lemon juice
1 egg	½ teaspoon vanilla

Beat the cream cheese with the sugar then beat in the egg and milk. Stir in the lemon juice and vanilla and turn into the prepared crust. Sprinkle with reserved crumb mixture and bake for 30 minutes. Cool on a wire rack, then cut into bars or squares.

Yield: 30 cookies

Anne Simons

COOKIES — *Cut leftover pastry into strips. Brush with honey and sprinkle with cinnamon. Bake . . . delicious.*

HOLLY COOKIES

These cookies are colorful on Christmas trays and are so delicious

½ cup butter
24 large marshmallows, cut into small pieces
2 teaspoons green food coloring

2 teaspoons vanilla
4 cups cornflakes
Red cinnamon candies

Melt the butter and marshmallows in the top section of a large double boiler. Add the food coloring and vanilla and mix thoroughly. While still warm, add the cornflakes and stir until well coated.

Lightly butter your hands. Working quickly, make each cookie by dropping some of the mixture into three small sections to resemble three holly leaves. Place two or three cinnamon candies in the center to resemble the holly berries; set aside to cool. Store in tightly covered containers.

Ida Pangborn

GRANDMA'S TEA COOKIES

¼ cup powdered sugar
½ cup plus 6 tablespoons butter, softened
2 teaspoons vanilla
1 teaspoon water

2 cups flour
1 generous cup finely chopped pecans
Additional powdered sugar

Preheat oven to 350 degrees.

Combine the sugar, butter, vanilla and water and mix well. Add the flour and nuts and incorporate thoroughly. Drop by the half-teaspoonful onto 2 greased sheets. Bake for 15 minutes. Remove from oven and sift some powdered sugar over the cookies while they are still warm.

These will keep for a long time if stored in airtight tins. Do not freeze.

Yield: 75 cookies
Preparation time: 15 minutes
Easy

Pat Young

PEANUT COOKIES

½ cup shortening
½ cup sweet butter
2 cups firmly packed light brown sugar
2 eggs
2 cups flour
1 teaspoon baking powder

½ teaspoon baking soda
1 teaspoon vanilla
2 cups quick-cooking (not instant) rolled oats
1 cup corn flakes
1 cup salted peanuts

Preheat oven to 350 degrees.

Cream the shortening, butter and sugar until light and fluffy. Beat in the eggs one at a time, mixing well after each addition. Sift together the flour, baking powder and baking soda. Add to the butter mixture with the vanilla and incorporate thoroughly. Stir in the oats and blend well. Gently fold in the corn flakes and peanuts; mix well. Drop by the teaspoonful on lightly greased cookie cheets 2 inches apart. Bake for 10-12 minutes or until cookies are golden brown. Remove from pan and cool on racks.

Yield: About 80 cookies

Rita Pitcoff

HOT DAYS CHOCO-PEANUT BUTTER SQUARES

2 cups sugar
¾ cup peanut butter
1 6-ounce can evaporated milk
1 4½-ounce package instant chocolate pudding

2 cups quick cooking rolled oats
Optional: ½ cup chopped nuts or 1 cup chocolate chips

In a 10-inch skillet combine the sugar, peanut butter and milk and bring to a slow boil, stirring until peanut butter is melted and sugar dissolves. Remove from heat, add pudding mix and oats and mix thoroughly. If desired, add nuts or chocolate chips and mix well. Turn into an 8x8-inch pan and let cool for 4 hours or overnight. Cut into 1-inch squares.

Yield: 64 bars
Make ahead
Freezes well
Easy

Marge Barone
DSO

COCONUT SHORTBREAD

Excellent and easy

1	pound butter	1	teaspoon vanilla
1	cup sugar	1	7-ounce can flaked coconut
4	cups flour		

Preheat oven to 325 degrees.
Cream the butter and sugar. Add the flour and mix well. Stir in the vanilla and coconut and mix until moistened. Form into 2-inch cylinders and wrap in waxed paper. Chill for one hour.
Slice ¼-inch thick and place on ungreased cookie sheets. Bake for 25-30 minutes.

Yield: 6-7 dozen
Preparation time: 15 minutes
Baking time: 25 minutes   Joe Ann Goodman

CHERRY SLICES

An old English recipe

SHORT CRUST PASTRY

1¼	cups flour	2	tablespoons shortening, chilled
½	teaspoon salt		
½	cup sweet butter, chilled and cut into ½-inch pieces	3-5	tablespoons ice water

In a large bowl, combine the flour and salt. Cut in the chilled butter and shortening using your fingers or a pastry blender. When the mixture resembles coarse corn meal, slowly add the ice water just until the dough holds together. Wrap in plastic and refrigerate for at least 30 minutes.
Preheat oven to 350 degrees. Roll out the pastry into an 11x7-inch jelly roll pan and spread with cherry filling.

CHERRY FILLING

½	cup butter	½	cup chopped glaceed cherries
6	tablespoons sugar		
3	tablespoons flour	½	cup currants
½	teaspoon baking powder	2	eggs, beaten
¼	cup ground almonds		

Cream the butter with the sugar. Mix the flour and baking powder with the almonds, cherries and currants and add to the creamed mixture. Stir in the egg and mix well. Spread evenly over the pastry and bake for 30-40 minutes or until golden brown and firm to the touch. Let cool, then cut into slices.

Gladys Schlesinger

ICED CHOCOLATE BARS

BARS

1	cup butter	2	cups sugar
2	squares unsweetened chocolate	1	cup flour
		2	cups chopped nuts
4	eggs		

Melt the butter and chocolate in a microwave or in the top of a double broiler. Beat the eggs until light and fluffy. Gradually add the sugar, then the chocolate mixture; mix well. Add flour and nuts; incorporate thoroughly. Pour into a greased 9x13-inch pan and bake for 20-25 minutes. Let cool in pan.

ICING

½	cup butter	1½	teaspoons vanilla
3	cups powdered sugar	2-4	teaspoons cream

To make icing, beat the butter with the powdered sugar. Add vanilla and enough cream to make a spreadable consistency. Spread on brownies.

GLAZE

2	squares unsweetened chocolate	2	tablespoons butter

For glazing: Melt the chocolate with the butter and drizzle over the frosting. Let cool, then cut into bars.

Yield: 24 bars
Preparation time: 45 minutes
Freezes well
Easy

Jackie Fitts

"A cook's best friend is her nose."
Mary Aylott

PEANUT BUTTER BARS

This is the answer to more of what you are looking for in a peanut butter cup

½ cup butter, melted
1½ cups powdered sugar
1½ cups graham cracker crumbs
1½ cups crunchy peanut butter

1 12-ounce package chocolate chips melted or 6 ounces each of chocolate chips and butterscotch chips

Melt the butter. Place butter, sugar, graham cracker crumbs and peanut butter in a food processor fitted with the steel blade or in a blender and process until well blended but not wet in consistency. Press into a 9x13-inch glass baking pan. Melt chocolate and/or butterscotch chips in the top section of a double boiler. Spread over peanut butter mixture. Score lightly into squares about 1½ inches each. Refrigerate for 20 minutes, remove and cut through bars.

Yield: 14-16 bars
Preparation time: 15 minutes
No bake

Karen Schaupeter

DELUXE SUGAR COOKIES

1 cup butter, softened
1½ cups powdered sugar
1 egg
1 teaspoon vanilla
½ teaspoon almond extract

2½ cups flour
1 teaspoon baking soda
1 teaspoon cream of tartar
Granulated or colored sugar

Preheat oven to 375 degrees.
Cream the butter and powdered sugar. Add the egg, vanilla and almond extract and mix well. Blend in the flour, soda, and cream of tartar. Cover, then chill for 2-3 hours.
Divide dough in half. Roll out each piece ¼-inch thick on a lightly floured surface. Cut into desired shapes and sprinkle with granulated or colored sugar. Bake for 7-8 minutes.

Yield: 5 dozen

Kathy Snow

SUGAR COOKIES

1	cup butter	1	teaspoon baking soda
1½	cups sugar	5	tablespoons sour milk
2	eggs, lightly beaten	4¼	cups flour
1½	teaspoons vanilla		

Preheat oven to 425 degrees.
Cream the butter with the sugar. Add the eggs and vanilla. Dissolve the soda in the sour milk and add to the butter-sugar mixture. Add flour and mix well.
On a lightly floured board roll out the dough ¼-inch thick. Sprinkle with sugar then cut into desired shapes and press lightly with rolling pin to set sugar. Bake for 5-7 minutes, or until lightly golden.

Preparation time: 20 minutes
Baking time: 6 minutes
Easy

Kathryn Zinn

BUCKEYE BALLS

Kids love to make these!

3	1-pound boxes powdered sugar	1	pound butter, softened
2	pounds smooth or crunchy peanut butter	1	12-ounce package semi-sweet chocolate morsels
		½	stick paraffin

Combine the sugar, peanut butter and butter and beat well. Roll into small balls and refrigerate, covered, overnight.
Melt the chocolate with the paraffin in the top section of a double boiler over hot water. Stick a toothpick in one of the peanut butter balls, then dip into the chocolate; place on waxed paper to harden. Repeat until all candies have been dipped in the chocolate.

Yield: about 60 candies

Sandy Kroovand

"Cookery, the most selfless of all the arts because the least enduring. A bite or two, a little gulp and a beautiful work of thought and love is no more."

Sybil Ryall
A fiddler for Sixpence

RECESS PEANUT CUPS

1	6-ounce package semi-sweet chocolate morsels	2	tablespoons paraffin, melted
4	bars (1.25 ounces) milk chocolate	½	teaspoon vanilla
1¼	cups smooth peanut butter, divided		

In the top section of a double boiler over hot, not boiling, water, combine the chocolate pieces, milk chocolate, ½ cup of the peanut butter and paraffin; stir until smooth. Using half the mixture, divide equally among 24-30 miniature tart or cupcake liners using about 1 heaping tablespoon each. Let set in a cool place for about 5 minutes. Meanwhile, heat the remaining peanut butter and the vanilla in the top of another double boiler over simmering water, and stir until smooth and semi-liquid. Divide mixture equally over the hardened chocolate and let set for 15-20 minutes or until firm.
Top with the remaining chocolate divided equally between the candies. Let set in a cool place for at least 1 hour before serving.

Makes 24-30 cups   Ann Kelly

SUGARED WALNUTS

Put into canning jars and tie with ribbon — makes a great gift

1	teaspoon cinnamon	2	egg whites, lightly beaten
1	cup sugar	1	pound whole walnuts

Preheat oven to 275 degrees.
Mix the cinnamon and sugar; add to beaten egg whites and mix well. Add walnuts and toss until well coated.
Spread on a greased cookie sheet. Bake until top of walnuts turn white. Check every 10 minutes — it will take from 15 to 30 minutes. Turn with a spatula and bake until other side turns white. Remove from oven and let cool. Separate nuts. Place in airtight jars and let stand 24 hours before serving.

Preparation time: 10 minutes
Baking time: 20-40 minutes
Easy   Renee Mann

PEANUT BUTTER AND CHOCOLATE ROLL-UP COOKIES

½	cup shortening	1¼	cups sifted flour
1	cup sugar		Salt
½	cup chunky peanut butter	½	teaspoon soda
1	egg	1	6-ounce package semi-
2	tablespoons milk		sweet chocolate chips

Preheat oven to 375 degrees.
Cream the shortening and sugar. Beat in the peanut butter, egg and milk. Sift together the flour, salt and soda, then stir into the creamed mixture. Place dough on lightly floured waxed paper and roll into a 15-8-inch rectangle. Melt the chocolate chips over hot water. Cool slightly, then spread over dough. Roll as a jelly roll, lifting waxed paper slightly with each turn. Chill for 30 minutes. Slice ¼-inch thick and place on an ungreased baking sheet. Bake for 8-10 minutes.

Grace L. Hath

MAZURKAS

Polish tea cakes

1	cup salted butter	1¾	cups flour
4	eggs, beaten	1	cup sugar
2	cups ground blanched almonds		Jam or preserves

Preheat oven to 350 degrees.
Cream the butter with the eggs until fluffy. Combine the almonds, flour and sugar and gradually add to the butter mixture, beating well after each addition. Pat dough in a greased 10x15-inch jelly-roll pan. Bake for 20 minutes, or until golden brown. Spread top with jam or preserves; let cool for 5 minutes.
To serve: Cut into 2-inch squares.

Yield: 36
Preparation time: 15 minutes
Baking time: 20 minutes
Easy

Anne Bielawski

MOON BALLS

A high-protein, quick energy snack. Kids love them.

½ cup creamy peanut butter   ½ cup granola cereal
½ cup dry powdered milk   ½ cup honey

Combine all ingredients and mix thoroughly. Roll into balls the size of walnuts; refrigerate until firm.

Makes 36
Preparation time: 10 minutes
Easy   Clifford May

DATE DELIGHTS

Colorful and mouthwatering!

¼ cup butter, softened   Red and green food coloring
1   cup powdered sugar   1   box large pitted dates
1   teaspoon vanilla or almond   1   cup walnut halves
    extract   White or colored sugar

Cream the butter with the sugar. Add the vanilla and mix well. Divide the mixture into three parts. Add a few drops of red coloring to one part and a few drops of green coloring to a second part. Leave the third portion white.
Using a knife, fill the opening in each date with some of the creamed mixture. Press a walnut into the mixture, then roll in the sugar.

Ida Pangborn

BAKING — *To test for the freshness of baking soda, add ¼ teaspoon to 1 tablespoon vinegar. If it bubbles, it's usable.*

SUGAR DROP COOKIES

1 cup butter, softened
1 cup sugar
1 egg
1 teaspoon vanilla

½ teaspoon baking soda
½ teaspoon salt
½ teaspoon cream of tartar
2 cups flour

Preheat oven to 350 degrees.
Cream together the butter and sugar. Add the egg and vanilla and incorporate thoroughly. Sift together the soda, salt, cream of tartar and flour and add to the creamed mixture. Drop by teaspoonful onto an ungreased cookie sheet and bake for 10-12 minutes, just until set.

Yield: 6 dozen small cookies

Susan Becker

NUTTY DOUBLE-DECKERS

TOPPING

½ cup chunky peanut butter
½ cup chopped unsalted peanuts

1 cup semi-sweet chocolate morsels

Preheat oven to 350 degrees.
Combine all ingredients and blend thoroughly; set aside.

CRUST

1 cup butter
⅓ cup chunky peanut butter
1¼ cups brown sugar

1 egg yolk
1 teaspoon vanilla
2½ cups flour

Blend the butter and peanut butter until creamy. Add the brown sugar, egg yolk and vanilla and beat until fluffy. Stir in the flour and incorporate thoroughly. Press dough on the bottom of an ungreased 10x15-inch jelly-roll pan. Bake for 15-18 minutes or until dough is firm and lightly browned. Remove from oven.
Using a teaspoon, drop topping evenly over the hot crust. Return to the oven for 2 minutes. Spread melted topping over crust. Cool, then cut into bars. Store in a lightly covered container.

Makes 30 bars
Preparation time: 20 minutes
Baking time: 30 minutes
Easy

Joan VanVlerah

CANDY STRAWBERRIES

2　14-ounce cans shredded coconut
½　cup chopped almonds
Red sugar
1　3-ounce box strawberry gelatin

1　14-ounce can sweetened condensed milk
1　teaspoon strawberry extract
1　teaspoon red food coloring
1　tube green frosting (not the gel)

Spread the coconut on a cookie sheet and allow to dry for 2 days. In a blender, grind the coconut and the almonds together and place in a large bowl. Stir in 2 tablespoons red sugar and the gelatin. Add the milk, strawberry extract, and red coloring and mix well.
Scoop mixture by the teaspoonful and roll into balls in the red sugar. Shape into strawberries making indentations for stems. Allow to set ½ hour or until firm. Add a drop of green frosting to form stems.
Note: These keep well for several weeks in tightly closed tins.

Yield: 50 candies   Shirley Best

OH, FUDGE!

This is an easy to make and delicious fudge

2　3-ounce packages cream cheese, softened
4　teaspoons butter, melted
4　teaspoons corn syrup
Pinch of salt

5　cups sifted powdered sugar
4　ounces unsweetened chocolate, melted
1　teaspoon vanilla
Optional: 1 cup chopped nuts

Line a 9-inch square pan with waxed paper.
Beat the cream cheese. Add the melted butter, corn syrup and salt and mix well. Gradually stir in the sugar, then add the melted chocolate, vanilla, and nuts, if desired; incorporate thoroughly. Press mixture into the prepared pan and chill until firm. Cut into squares and store in refrigerator in a tightly covered container.

Robert Schwartz

CARMEL CORN

1 cup unseasoned popping corn
1 cup minus 1 tablespoon butter

2 cups brown sugar
½ cup corn syrup
1 teaspoon vanilla
½ teaspoon baking soda

Preheat oven to 250 degrees.
Pop the corn. Combine the butter, sugar and syrup and boil for 5 minutes. Add the vanilla and baking soda. Pour over the popped corn and transfer to a buttered cookie sheet. Bake for 1 hour, stirring occasionally.

Preparation time: 15 minutes
Baking time: 1 hour
Easy

Celia Leo

TURTLES

1 6-ounce package peanut butter morsels
½ cup butter, divided
1 14-ounce can sweetened condensed milk, divided

2 teaspoons white vinegar
3 cups pecan halves
1 12-ounce package semi-sweet chocolate morsels
1 teaspoon vanilla extract

In a small saucepan over low heat, melt the peanut butter morsels, 2 tablespoons butter and ⅓ cup of the milk. Remove from heat and stir in the vinegar. Drop by the ½ teaspoonful onto waxed paper-lined cookie sheets. Arrange 3 pecans onto each peanut butter drop to resemble turtle head and legs.
In top of a double boiler, melt the chocolate morsels with the remaining milk, butter and vanilla. Remove from heat, but keep the chocolate mixture over the hot water. Drop chocolate by the heaping teaspoonful over the pecan clusters. Chill for 2 hours or until set. Store, loosely covered, at room temperature.

Yield: about 20 candies

Shirley Best

ENGLISH TOFFEE

1 cup sugar
1 cup butter
3 tablespoons water
1 teaspoon vanilla

3 regular sized (1.45 ounce) Hershey bars
¾ cup finely chopped pecans

In a medium saucepan, cook the sugar, butter, water and vanilla until browned; about 10 minutes. Stir constantly to prevent burning. Pour into a small well-buttered pan. Lay the chocolate bars on top of the hot candy and sprinkle with pecans. Cool, then break into pieces.

Jeanne Schlitters

CHOCOLATE PEANUT CLUSTERS

What a combination!

1 cup smooth peanut butter
1 12-ounce package semi-sweet chocolate morsels

4 cups Spanish peanuts

Melt the peanut butter and chocolate chips in the top section of a double boiler. Stir in the peanuts and coat well. Drop by the teaspoonful on a piece of waxed paper fitted on a cookie sheet; chill. Store in a tightly covered container.

Lloyd Buck

CHOCOLATE PEPPERMINT CLUSTERS

1 12-ounce package semi-sweet chocolate morsels
1 5-ounce can Chinese noodles

1 cup chopped nuts
1 teaspoon peppermint extract

Melt the chocolate in the top section of a double boiler. Do not stir. Remove from heat and mix in the noodles, nuts and extract. Drop by the teaspoonful onto waxed paper and let harden.

Yield: 30 candies
Preparation time: 15 minutes
Easy

Shirley Best

Cakes

Cakes

Children's Birthday Party
Fruit Punch
Pasghetti Pizza
Garlic Bread
Tossed Salad
Birthday Cake
Ice Cream with Hot Fudge Sauce

Refreshments After The Meeting
Almond Paste Coffee Cake
Orange Zucchini Cake
Cheesecake Cookies
Fruit Trifle
Irish Coffee

CHOCOLATE MACAROON CAKE

Really chocolatey!

CAKE

4	egg whites, divided	¾	cup hot coffee
2	teaspoons vanilla, divided	1	teaspoon baking soda
2¼	cups sugar, divided	½	cup sour cream
2	cups coconut, finely grated	½	cup shortening
1	tablespoon flour	3	egg yolks
½	cup unsweetened cocoa	1	teaspoon salt
		2	cups flour, sifted

Preheat oven to 350 degrees.

Beat 1 egg white with 1 teaspoon vanilla until soft mounds form. Gradually add ½ cup sugar, beating until stiff but not dry. Stir in the coconut and 1 tablespoon flour; set aside.

Dissolve the cocoa in the hot coffee, beat the remaining egg whites until soft peaks form. Gradually add ½ cup sugar, and beat until meringue is stiff but not dry; set aside.

Add the baking soda to the sour cream; set aside. Cream the remaining 1½ cups sugar with the shortening. Add the egg yolks, salt, 1 teaspoon vanilla and half of the cocoa mixture. Beat until light and creamy, about 4 minutes. Add the flour, sour cream mixture and the remaining cocoa mixture; blend well, then fold in the meringue mixture.

Turn ⅓ of the batter into a 10-inch tube pan, greased on the bottom. Sprinkle with ½ of the coconut mixture. Continue to layer with ½ the batter, the remaining coconut and then the remaining butter. Bake for 55-60 minutes or until a cake tester inserted in the center comes out clean. Cool completely, remove from the pan, then frost.

CHOCOLATE CREAM FROSTING

1	6-ounce package semi-sweet chocolate morsels, melted	1	egg yolk
		1½	cups sifted powdered sugar
2	tablespoons butter, softened	¼	cup milk

Combine all ingredients and beat until spreading consistency. Frost cooled cake.

Helen Kirchhoff

QUEEN OF SHEBA CAKE

This is a chocolate, chocolate cake.

14	ounces semi-sweet chocolate	1	cup margarine
2	ounces unsweetened chocolate	2¼	cups sugar
1	cup butter	8	eggs, separated
		1½	cups flour, sifted
		½	pound ground almonds

Preheat oven to 350 degrees.
Melt the semi-sweet chocolate, unsweetened chocolate, butter and margarine in the top section of a double boiler over simmering water. Blend in the sugar and set aside. Beat the egg yolks until light; add the chocolate mixture and blend well. Beat in the flour and almonds.
In a separate bowl, beat the egg whites until stiff but not dry. Gently fold beaten whites into the chocolate mixture and transfer to a 10-inch springform pan. Bake for 1¼ hours. When cake is done, the sides will be crisp and the cake will crack, but the center will still be soft. DO NOT OVERBAKE.

Serves 12-20   Nancy Blumenthal

CARROT TORTE

Especially easy with a food processor

CAKE

2	cups sifted flour	2	cups finely grated carrots
2	teaspoons baking powder	1	8½-ounce can crushed pineapple, drained
1½	teaspoons baking soda	½	cup chopped nuts
1½	teaspoons salt	½	cup chopped raisins
1	tablespoon cinnamon	1	3½-ounce can flaked coconut
2	cups sugar		
1½	cups vegetable oil		
4	eggs		

Preheat oven to 350 degrees.
Sift together the flour, baking powder, soda, salt and cinnamon. Add the sugar, oil and eggs; mix well. Add the carrots, pineapple, nuts, raisins and coconut and blend thoroughly. Pour into three 9-inch

round greased and floured pans. Bake for 40 minutes or until a toothpick inserted in the center comes out clean. Cool in pans for 10 minutes then turn out on racks and cool thoroughly. Frost the layers, stack, then frost the top and sides of cake with cream cheese frosting.

FROSTING

½ cup butter, softened
1 8-ounce package cream cheese, softened

1 teaspoon vanilla
1 pound powdered sugar

Cream the butter, cream cheese and vanilla. Sift the powdered sugar and gradually add to the creamed mixture, beating well. If the mixture is too thick to spread, thin with a little cream.

Preparation time: 30 minutes
Baking time: 40 minutes

John Merrill

THE BEST SOUR CREAM COFFEE CAKE

1 cup butter, softened
2 cups sugar
2 eggs, beaten
1 cup sour cream
½ teaspoon vanilla
2 cups flour

1 teaspoon salt
1 teaspoon baking powder
Topping:
   ½ cup chopped nuts
   2 tablespoons brown sugar
   1 tablespoon cinnamon

Preheat oven to 350 degrees.

In a large bowl cream the butter and sugar. Add eggs and mix well. Thoroughly blend in the sour cream and vanilla. Mix in the flour, salt and baking powder.

In a small bowl mix together the topping ingredients. Pour half the batter into a greased and floured 10-inch tube pan. Sprinkle with half the topping. Cover with remaining batter, then the rest of the topping. Bake for 1 hour or until a toothpick inserted in the center comes out clean.

Preparation time: 15 minutes
Baking time: 1 hour
Freezes well
Easy

Thelma Shapiro

BANANA CAKE SUPERB

1 cup sweet butter
2½ cups sugar
6 eggs, well beaten
2 teaspoons baking soda
1 cup sour cream

2½ cups (about 5) mashed bananas
3 cups unsifted flour
Chopped nuts, if desired

Preheat oven to 350 degrees.
Cream together the butter and sugar until light and fluffy. Add the eggs and beat with an electric mixer at medium speed for 2 minutes. Stir the baking soda into the sour cream then add to the creamed mixture. Add the bananas and beat until ingredients are well combined. Add the flour, 1 cup at a time, beating well after each addition. Continue to beat 2 minutes longer. Add chopped nuts to taste, if desired. Turn into a greased and floured 10-inch tube pan. Bake for 1¼ hours or until a tester inserted in the center comes out clean.

Freezes well

Sheila Pitcoff

TOFFEE MERINGUE TORTE

3 egg whites
1 teaspoon vanilla
1 cup sugar
Pinch of salt
¼ teaspoon cream of tartar

2 cups heavy cream, whipped
1 6½ ounce Heath bar, crushed
1 6½ ounce semi-sweet chocolate bar, crushed

Prehet oven to 275 degrees.
Beat the egg whites and slowly add vanilla, sugar, salt and cream of tartar; whip until stiff. Make two 9-inch circles out of brown paper and place on a cookie sheet. Place half of the meringue mixture on each circle and spread evenly to edges. Bake for 1 hour. Turn off heat and leave in oven with door closed at least two hours longer. Cool before finishing torte.

Combine whipped cream and crushed candy bars. Top one meringue layer with ¼ of the whipped cream mixture and set the second layer on top. Frost sides and top with remaining whipped cream mixture. Chill at least eight hours before serving.

Makes one 9-inch torte
Do not freeze

Rhonda and Phil Austin

SNO-BALL CAKE

A wonderful do-ahead dessert

2 packages unflavored gelatin
¼ cup cold water
1 cup sugar
1 cup hot water
1 cup canned, crushed
   pineapple, drained, reserving
   ½ cup juice

3 packages topping mix
1 angel food cake torn into
   bite-size pieces

Dissolve the gelatin in the cold water. Add the sugar and hot water, stirring until the sugar is dissolved. Add the pineapple and juice. Place in refrigerator until slightly set. Prepare 2 packages of whipped topping according to package directions. Fold into the semi-set gelatin. Line a large bowl with plastic wrap and spoon in some of the gelatin mixture. Add a layer of cake, pushing the pieces down into the gelatin. Continue to layer, ending with gelatin mix. Cover with plastic wrap. Refrigerate overnight.

To serve: Invert cake onto a large serving plate and remove plastic wrap. Whip the third package of topping mix and frost the cake.

Serves 10-12
Refrigerate overnight

Julie Stackpoole

WACKY CAKE

1½ cups flour
1 cup sugar
3 tablespoons unsweetened
   cocoa
1 teaspoon baking soda

½ teaspoon salt
1 tablespoon vinegar
¼ cup plus 2 tablespoons oil
1 teaspoon vanilla
1 cup cold water

Preheat oven to 350 degrees.

In an 8-inch square pan combine the flour, sugar, cocoa, soda and salt and mix well. Level mixture off and make three indentations with the back of a spoon. Into one hole add the vinegar, into the second hole add the oil, into the third hole add the vanilla. Pour the water over all and mix well with a fork. Bake for 25 minutes or until a toothpick inserted in the center comes out clean.

Preparation time: 10 minutes
Baking time: 25
Easy

Deborah Elliott

TEXAS SHEET CAKE

Adults and kids alike love this cake . . . especially if one is a chocaholic

CAKE

2 cups flour	1 cup butter
2 cups sugar	¼ cup unsweetened cocoa
½ teaspoon salt	2 eggs, beaten
1 teaspoon baking soda	½ cup sour cream
1 cup water	

Preheat oven to 350 degrees.
Combine the flour, sugar, salt and soda; set aside. Boil the water and add the butter and cocoa; mix well. Add to the dry ingredients and mix well. Add beaten eggs and sour cream and blend. Pour into a 9x13-inch pan. Bake for 20 to 25 minutes or until a toothpice inserted in center comes out clean. Frost immediately

ICING

¼ cup unsweetened cocoa	6 tablespoons milk
½ cup butter	1 pound powdered sugar
	1 teaspoon vanilla

Bring cocoa, butter, and milk to a boil. Remove from heat and beat in the sugar and vanilla. Pour over the hot cake.

Serves 20
Preparation time: 30 minutes
Baking time: 20-30 minutes
Freezes well
Easy

Fran Goldberg

SPICED YOGURT CAKE

The frosting is exceptional!

CAKE

2½ cups flour	¼ teaspoon salt
1½ teaspoons baking soda	¼ teaspoon allspice
1½ teaspoons cinnamon	⅔ cup butter, softened
1 teaspoon baking powder	1⅓ cups brown sugar
½ teaspoon nutmeg	2 eggs
½ teaspoon ground cloves	1½ cups vanilla yogurt

Preheat oven to 350 degrees.

Mix together the flour, baking soda, cinnamon, baking powder, nutmeg, cloves, salt and allspice. Cream the butter with the sugar until light and fluffy. Add the eggs, one at a time, beating well after each addition. Add the dry ingredients alternately with the yogurt, beating on low after each addition. Pour into 2 greased and floured 8x8-inch cake pans. Bake for 30 minutes or until a cake tester inserted in the center comes out clean. Cool in pans for 10 minutes, remove from pans, then place on racks and cool completely before frosting.

COCONUT LEMON FROSTING

1	8-ounce package cream cheese, softened	2	teaspoons grated lemon peel
2	tablespoons butter, softened	2	teaspoons lemon juice
1	pound powdered sugar		Dash nutmeg
		1	cup coconut

Cream together the cream cheese and butter. Add the sugar and blend well. Add the remaining ingredients and incorporate thoroughly. Use to frost between the layers and the top of the cake. Do not frost sides.

Colleen Morrison

VIENNESE TORTE

Delicious

1	6-ounce package chocolate chips	2	tablespoons powdered sugar
½	cup butter	1	teaspoon vanilla
¼	cup water	1	frozen pound cake
4	egg yolks, lightly beaten		Sliced toasted almonds

In a heavy saucepan over medium heat, combine the chocolate, butter and water. Heat, stirring constantly, until blended. Cool slightly, then add the egg yolks, sugar and vanilla, and stir until smooth. Chill until the mixture is a spreading consistency, about 45 minutes.

Slice the frozen cake horizontally into 6 layers. Spread about 2 tablespoons of the chocolate mixture between each layer. Frost the top and sides completely. Sprinkle almonds on top and chill for at least 45 minutes.

Serves 8-10
Preparation time: 25 minutes
Easy

Rona Freedland

CHOCOLATE SAUERKRAUT CAKE

Sounds strange? Tastes great!

½	cup butter	1	teaspoon baking soda
1½	cups sugar	½	cup unsweetened cocoa
3	eggs	1	cup water
1	teaspoon vanilla	1	8-ounce can sauerkraut,
2	cups flour		drained, rinsed and finely
1	teaspoon baking soda		chopped
¼	teaspoon salt		

Preheat oven to 350 degrees.

In a large bowl, cream together the butter and sugar until light and fluffy. Beat in the eggs, one at a time, beating well after each addition. Stir in the vanilla.

Sift together the flour, soda, salt, baking powder and cocoa. Add alternately with the water, to the creamed mixture, beating after each addition. Stir in the sauerkraut. Turn the batter into a 9x13-inch greased baking pan dusted with cocoa instead of flour. Bake for 35-40 minutes or until a toothpick inserted in center comes out clean. Let cool, then frost with Chocolate Sour Cream Frosting.

CHOCOLATE SOUR CREAM FROSTING

1	6-ounce package chocolate morsels	1	teaspoon vanilla
¼	cup butter	¼	teaspoon salt
½	cup sour cream	2½-2¾	cups sifted powdered sugar

In the top of a double boiler, melt the chocolate chips and butter. Remove from heat and add the sour cream, vanilla and salt; mix well. Add 2½ cups of powdered sugar, adding more as needed to make a thick but spreadable consistency.

Pat Lamkins

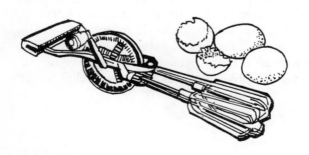

XXX CHOCOLATE TORTE

2	tablespoons unsweetened chocolate	1	cup sugar
6	ounces semi-sweet chocolate	6	eggs
2	ounces unsweetened chocolate	1¾	cups ground almonds
		1½	teaspoons vanilla extract
		¼	teaspoon almond extract
¾	cup butter	½	cup fresh bread crumbs

Preheat oven to 375 degrees.

Line a buttered 9-inch round cake pan with waxed paper. Butter the paper and dust with the cocoa. Melt the chocolates over low heat and let cool slightly. Cream the butter and sugar until light. Beat in the eggs, one at a time, then stir in the remaining ingredients. Pour batter into the prepared pan and bake for 30 minutes or until a tester inserted in center comes out clean. Let cool in pan for 20 minutes, then invert onto a rack and let cool completely; remove waxed paper.

CHOCOLATE BUTTER ICING

4	ounces sweet light chocolate	1	cup sweet butter, softened
4	ounces semi-sweet chocolate	¼	teaspoon almond extract

Melt the chocolates over low heat and let cool slightly. Beat in the butter and extract. Chill until mixture is a spreading consistency.

Cut cake in half to make two layers. Spread one layer with ⅓ of the icing. Place second layer on top and spread top and sides with remaining icing. Chill until set.

Mario DiFiore
DSO

SPRING RHUBARB CAKE

2	cups sugar, divided	1	teaspoon salt
1	egg	1	cup buttermilk
½	cup butter or shortening	1½	cups chopped uncooked rhubarb
2	cups sifted flour		
1	teaspoon baking soda	1	teaspoon vanilla

Preheat oven to 350 degrees.

Cream together 1½ cups sugar, the egg, and butter. Combine the flour, baking soda, and salt; add to the creamed mixture alternating with the buttermilk. Stir in the rhubarb and vanilla. Pour into a greased 9x13-inch baking pan and sprinkle with the remaining sugar. Bake for 40-45 minutes or until a toothpick inserted in the center comes out clean.

Serves 12-16
Preparation time: 15 minutes
Baking time: 45 minutes
Easy

Carol L. May

PISTACHIO BUNDT CAKE

1   package white or yellow
    cake mix
2   4⅛-ounce packages instant
    pistachio pudding mix
4   eggs
½   cup oil

½   cup water
½   cup lemonade or orange
    juice
½ to 1 cup crushed pistachio
    nuts, to taste

Preheat oven to 350 degrees.
Blend all ingredients, including pistachio nuts, in a bowl. Pour into a well-greased and floured 2-quart Bundt pan. Bake for 1 hour or until a toothpick inserted in center comes out clean.
For variety: Use banana pudding mix and 2 mashed ripe bananas and bake in 2 greased and floured loaf pans.

Preparation time: 10 minutes
Baking time: 1 hour
Easy

Ann Alicia Ourada
DSO

CHOCOLATE PISTACHIO BUNDT CAKE

Another interesting variation on the Bundt theme

Prepare the Pistachio Bundt Cake according to directions above. Pour ⅔ of the batter into the prepared pan. Add ¾ cup chocolate syrup to the remaining batter and mix well. Pour over the batter in the pan and spread to edges. Bake according to above directions.
Serve with whipped cream or pistachio ice cream.

Michael Bric

APPLE CAKE

2½ cups sugar, divided
2   teaspoons cinnamon
5   tart apples, peeled and
    thinly sliced
3   cups flour
½   teaspoon salt

4   eggs
1   cup vegetable oil
2   teaspoons vanilla
⅓   cup orange juice
1½ teaspoons baking soda
1½ teaspoons baking powder

Preheat oven to 350 degrees.
Mix 5 tablespoons sugar with the cinnamon and sprinkle on the sliced apples. Toss gently and set aside.

Blend remaining ingredients except the soda and baking powder. Mix on low speed for 1 minute, then increase speed to medium and beat for 3 minutes. Add baking soda and baking powder and mix for 1 minute longer. Pour batter into a greased tube pan, in alternating layers with the apples, beginning and ending with the batter. Bake for 1½ hours or until a toothpick inserted in the center comes out clean.

Serves 16-20
Preparation time: 20 minutes
Baking time: 1½ hours
Easy

Winnie and Doug Frazer
UAW

CRUSHED NUT TORTE

CAKE

1 cup butter	½ pound finely crushed pecans
1 cup sugar	⅓ cup cake flour
3 eggs	Grated rind of 1 lemon

Preheat oven to 350 degrees.
Cream the butter with the sugar and beat for 5 minutes. Beat in the eggs and fold in the pecans until just mixed. Stir in the flour and lemon rind. Pour into 2 greased and floured 9-inch round cake pans and bake for 30-35 minutes or until a cake tester inserted in the center comes out clean. Remove from pans and cool completely.

FILLING

1 8-ounce package cream cheese, softened	½ cup sugar
	1 teaspoon vanilla

Combine all ingredients and cream well. Spread mixture on one layer then stack the other layer on top.

TOPPING
Fresh strawberries
Apricot preserves
Apricot liqueur

Decorate the top with the strawberries, pointed end up. Melt the apricot preserves and add enough liqueur to thin slightly. Paint lightly over the strawberries and torte.

Suzanne Boyce

KEVIN'S DELICIOUS RAISIN CAKE

"I have made and enjoyed this cake since I was 10 years old! It is truly easy to make."

1 cup raisins	1¾ cups flour
⅓ cup butter	1 teaspoon baking powder
1 cup brown sugar	1 teaspoon baking soda
1 cup water	1 teaspoon nutmeg
1 teaspoon vanilla	1 cup chopped walnuts

Combine the raisins, butter, brown sugar and water in a saucepan and bring to a boil. Cook for 3 minutes, stirring, then remove from the heat; add the vanilla, and cool.

Preheat oven to 300 degrees.

Sift the flour and the baking powder. Add the soda, nutmeg, and walnuts and mix. Add to the cooled mixture and beat well. Pour into a greased and floured loaf pan and bake 45-60 minutes or until sides pull away from the pan.

Preparation time: 20 minutes
Baking time: 50 minutes   Kevin Good
Easy   DSO

HAZELNUT CARROT CAKE

This very special carrot cake recipe was given to us by Ilse Dorati, wife of Conductor Laureate Antal Dorati. It has a very unusual texture and health food fadists will love it.

5 eggs, separated	1 teaspoon cinnamon
¾ cup honey	Juice of one lemon
1¼ cups finely grated carrots	Grated zest of one lemon
1 cup toasted hazelnuts (filberts), finely ground	

Preheat oven to 350 degrees.

Grease an 8-inch tube pan. Beat yolks with the honey for 3 minutes. Slowly add the carrots, hazelnuts, cinnamon, lemon juice and peel and incorporate thoroughly.

Beat whites until stiff but not dry. Fold carefully into carrot mixture. Transfer to prepared pan. Bake for 50 minutes or until cake springs back when touched.

Ilse von Alpenheim
(Mrs. Antal Dorati)

HUNGARIAN DOBOS TORTE

CAKE

7	eggs, separated	1	cup sugar
Pinch of salt		1	cup sifted flour

Cut seven 9-inch circles of waxed paper or baking parchment to fit the bottoms of 9-inch cake tins. Grease the bottom of each pan, place waxed paper in, then grease the paper. Preheat oven to 400 degrees. Beat the egg whites with a pinch of salt until soft peaks form; set aside. Beat the yolks with the sugar until lemon colored and thick. Carefully fold in the flour, ¼ cup at a time, until thoroughly incorporated. Gently fold in the beaten egg whites. Fill each of the prepared pans with scant ⅔ cup of the batter, spreading it evenly. Bake for 10-12 minutes until lightly colored. Remove from pan and place on a rack. Invert, remove waxed paper, and cool. Repeat process until all layers are baked. Cool, then frost.

CHOCOLATE CREAM FILLING

1	cup sweet butter, softened	3	tablespoons coffee or liqueur
3½	cups powdered sugar		
1	6-ounce package semi-sweet chocolate morsels, melted	1	egg

Cream the butter, sugar and chocolate until light and fluffy. Beat in the coffee or liqueur and the egg. If mixture is too soft, add more sugar or if too dry, add additional liquid until mixture is a spreading consistency. Spread a thin layer of filling on each cake layer, stack the layers, then frost the sides and top.

Note: For those experienced in handling carmel toppings, you might try the traditional Dobos Torte as follows.

CARAMEL GLAZE

Leave one layer separated from cake and unfrosted. Melt ¾ cup granulated sugar in a non-stick skillet over low heat. Cook until dissolved and light brown — do not touch, it is very hot. Working very quickly, pour carmelized sugar over the unfrosted layer and spread with a spatula. Immediately cut through carmel into wedges. If carmel hardens before done, finish cutting with a knife dipped in boiling water. Place layer on top of cake. If any frosting is left, pipe a decorative border around the torte.

Preparation time: 1 hour   Agi Alpert

ORANGE-ZUCCHINI CAKE

A deliciously different zucchini cake

CAKE

1	cup flour	2	eggs
1	teaspoon baking powder	½	cup All-bran cereal
½	teaspoon baking soda	1½	teaspoons grated
¼	teaspoon salt		orange peel
1	teaspoon cinnamon	1	teaspoon vanilla
½	teaspoon nutmeg	1	cup grated zucchini
¾	cup sugar	½	cup chopped nuts
½	cup oil		

Preheat oven to 325 degrees.
Combine the flour, baking powder, soda, salt, cinnamon and nutmeg; set aside. In a large mixing bowl, beat the sugar, oil and eggs. Stir in the cereal, orange peel and vanilla and blend well. Add the flour mixture, zucchini and nuts and incorporate thoroughly. Spread in a greased 8x8-inch glass pan or a 1½-quart glass baking dish. Bake for 45 minutes or until a toothpick inserted in center comes out clean. Cool, then frost.

ORANGE CREAM CHEESE FROSTING

1	3-ounce package cream cheese, softened	½	teaspoon grated orange peel
1	tablespoon butter, softened	1½	cups powdered sugar
			Milk

In a small mixing bowl, beat the cream cheese, butter and orange peel until light and fluffy. Gradually beat in the sugar. Add milk if necessary, 1 teaspoon at a time, until spreading consistency.

Martha Bowman

OZARK MOUNTAIN MYSTERY CAKE

An old family recipe from Arkansas — everyone loves it

CAKE

2	cups sugar	1	teaspoon salt
2	cups flour	1	17-ounce can fruit cocktail
2	teaspoons baking soda	2	eggs

Preheat oven to 350 degrees.
Mix together the sugar, flour, soda and salt. Drain the fruit cocktail, reserving the liquid. Add enough water to the liquid to make 1 cup.

Mix the liquid into the dry ingredients and stir well. Blend in the eggs. Add fruit cocktail and combine thoroughly. Pour the mixture into a greased 9x13-inch baking pan. Bake for 30-35 minutes or until a toothpick inserted in center comes out clean.

TOPPING

½	cup butter	½	cup evaporated milk
1	cup sugar	½	cup flaked coconut
1	teaspoon vanilla	½	cup chopped nuts

Melt the butter in a saucepan. Add sugar, vanilla and milk and boil for 1 minute. Blend in coconut and nuts and pour over the hot cake. Let the sauce run through cake.

Serves 12
Preparation time: 20 minutes
Baking time: 30-35 minutes
Easy

Phyllis Patton

BANANA WALNUT TORTE

3	cups sugar, divided	¾	cup powdered sugar
3	tablespoons flour	4	teaspoons vanilla
1½	cups chopped walnuts	6	bananas, sliced into rounds
12	egg whites	16	walnut halves
2	quarts heavy cream	¾	cup chopped walnuts

Preheat oven to 350 degrees.

Mix 2 cups sugar; flour and 1½ cups chopped walnuts together. Beat whites until foamy and add remaining cup of sugar slowly, continuing to beat whites until stiff. Fold sugar-nut mixture into whites. Place in pastry bag and pipe mixture onto four 10-inch circles of parchment paper. Bake until crisp and light golden in color. Let cool and trim to 10-inch circles.

Combine the cream, powdered sugar and vanilla in a bowl and beat until stiff. Place meringue layers on a cardboard circle and cover with whipped cream. Place bananas on whipped cream covered meringue layer. Repeat procedure on next two meringue layers, stacking one on the other. Place last layer on top and frost top and sides.

Decorate with whipped cream rosettes and place walnut halves on the rosettes. Make a ½ inch band around the bottom of the frosted torte using chopped walnuts. Chill torte for 2 hours before serving.

Van Dyke Place
Detroit, Michigan

CHRISTMAS FUDGE CAKE

4	ounces unsweetened chocolate	½	cup butter
1	cup light brown sugar	1	cup sugar
1½	cups milk, divided	2½	cups sifted flour
3	eggs	1	tablespoon baking powder
		1	tablespoon warm water

Preheat oven to 350 degrees.

Melt the chocolate in the top part of a double boiler over hot water. Add the brown sugar and ½ cup milk and stir until sugar dissolves and mixture is smooth. Beat one egg lightly and add to the mixture. Set aside to cool.

Cream the butter; gradually add the sugar. Separate remaining eggs. Add the yolks to the butter-sugar mixture and beat well. Alternately add the remaining cup of milk, the flour and baking powder. Beat the egg whites until stiff but not dry. Fold the egg whites into the chocolate mixture, then combine with the water and butter-sugar mixture. Pour into 2 greased 8-inch cake pans. Bake for 25 minutes or until a tester inserted in center comes out clean. Frost with your favorite frosting.

Elizabeth McCartney

RUM CAKE

Rich, buttery and delicious

CAKE

½	cup chopped pecans, dredged in a small amount of flour	½	cup water
		½	cup vegetable oil
1	box Duncan Hines Butter Cake Mix	½	cup rum
		4	eggs
1	package vanilla instant pudding mix		

Preheat oven to 325 degrees.

Grease and flour a Bundt pan. Shake excess flour from pecans then sprinkle nuts in bottom of pan. Combine cake mix, pudding mix, water, oil, and rum and beat well. Add eggs, one at a time, beating after each addition. Spoon over pecans. Bake for 50 minutes.

Remove from oven and let cool for 10 minutes. While cake cools, make sauce.

SAUCE

1 stick butter — DO NOT USE MARGARINE	¼ cup water
1 cup sugar	¼ cup rum

In a sauce pan combine the butter, sugar and water and bring to a boil. Let mixture boil for 2 minutes then remove from heat. Add the rum, stir well, and with cake still in pan, pour the sauce over. Let cool for 1 hour in pan then invert and remove.

Preparation time: 15 minutes

Cecilia Benner
DSO

SUGAR FREE PINEAPPLE CAKE

A superb diet recipe

½ cup butter	1 tablespoon cornstarch
1 teaspoon vanilla	¼ teaspoon nutmeg
2 eggs	½ teaspoon salt
2 tablespoons liquid artificial sweetener	2 cups drained crushed pineapple
1¼ cups flour	1 cup raisins
2 teaspoons baking soda	½ cup chopped walnuts
1 teaspoon cinnamon	

Preheat oven to 375 degrees.

Cream the butter, vanilla, eggs and liquid sweetener until smooth. In a separate bowl, combine the flour, soda, cinnamon, cornstarch, nutmeg and salt; then add to the creamed mixture. Stir in the drained pineapple, raisins and nuts. Bake in a well-greased 8-inch baking pan for 20-25 minutes or until a toothpick inserted in the center comes out clean.

Preparation time: 15 minutes
Baking time: 25 minutes
Easy

Marlene Thomas

ANNE MARIE MAY'S FAMOUS
CHERRY NUT POUND CAKE

"My mother thinks I should have my name in print once in my life and that my good looks aren't going to do it."

1	cup butter, softened	½	teaspoon baking soda
3	cups sugar	1	teaspoon baking powder
1	tablespoon vanilla	½	cup whole maraschino
6	eggs, separated		cherries, drained
1	cup sour cream	½	cup chopped nuts
3	cups sifted flour		

Preheat oven to 350 degrees.
Cream the butter and sugar. Add vanilla and mix well. Add the egg yolks, 3 at a time, beating well after each addition; blend in the sour cream. Add flour, baking soda and baking powder, stirring until ingredients are thoroughly combined. Beat the egg whites until stiff but not dry. Gently fold the egg whites, cherries and nuts into the batter. Turn into a greased 10-inch tube pan. Bake for 1 hour or until a tester inserted in the center comes out clean. Cool for 15 minutes before removing from the pan.

Preparation time: 20 minutes
Baking time: 1 hour

Anne Marie May

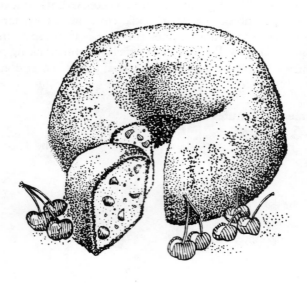

ALMOND PASTE COFFEE CAKE

Stays moist and freezes well

1	cup sugar	1	teaspoon baking soda
½	cup butter	1½	teaspoons baking powder
2	eggs	1	8-ounce can almond paste
1	cup sour cream		or (1) 12-ounce can almond
2	cups flour		filling
Pinch of salt		1	teaspoon vanilla

Preheat oven to 375 degrees.
Cream the sugar and butter; add the eggs and sour cream and incorporate thoroughly. Add flour, salt, soda and baking powder; mix well. Add almond paste or filling and vanilla and blend well. Pour into greased 10-inch tube pan.

TOPPING

½	cup sugar	1½	teaspoons cinnamon
1	cup chopped pecans		

Combine ingredients and blend well. Sprinkle on cake batter and swirl gently into top of batter with a knife. Bake 45 minutes.

Serves 12
Preparation time: 30 minutes
Baking time: 45 minutes

Barb Borseth

CHOCOLATE BANANA POUND CAKE

1	1-pound package Pound Cake mix	2	very ripe large bananas
½	cup sour cream	¼	cup unsweetened cocoa
		1	cup chopped walnuts

Prepare cake according to package directions, substituting the sour cream for the water. Stir in the remaining ingredients and bake according to package directions.

Preparation time: 10 minutes
Baking time: 45 minutes
Easy

Debbie Schwartz

PLUM BUNDT CAKE

Moist and marvelous

CAKE

2 cups self-rising flour
2 cups sugar
1 teaspoon cinnamon
1 teaspoon nutmeg
2 cups chopped pecans

2 small jars babyfood plums with tapioca
1 cup vegetable oil
3 eggs, slightly beaten

Preheat oven to 350 degrees.
In a large mixing bowl, mix the dry ingredients. Combine the liquids and add to dry ingredients. Bake in a greased and floured Bundt pan for 1 hour.

ICING

¼ cup butter
Juice and rind of 1 lemon

1 cup powdered sugar

Melt the butter over low heat; mix in remaining ingredients. Pour half of the icing over cake as soon as it is removed from the oven. Let cake sit for 10 minutes, invert, and pour on the remaining icing.

Preparation time: 15 minutes
Baking time: 1 hour
Easy

Carol Meyer

BANANA CAKE

So moist . . . full of flavor

½ cup butter
1½ cups sugar
2 eggs, lightly beaten
2 cups flour
¼ teaspoon baking powder
¾ teaspoon soda

½ teaspoon salt
3 large very ripe bananas, mashed
¼ cup sour milk or buttermilk
1 teaspoon vanilla

Preheat oven to 350 degrees.
Cream the butter and sugar; add the eggs and mix well. Sift together the flour, baking powder, soda, and salt; add to the creamed mixture and beat for two minutes. Add mashed bananas, milk and vanilla and mix until well blended. Pour into 2 greased and floured 9-inch loaf pans. Bake for 30-35 minutes.

Yield: 2 loaves
Preparation time: 15 minutes
Baking time: 35 minutes
Easy

Kathryn Zinn

Desserts

New Year's Celebration

Mulled Wine
Teriyaki Meatballs
Hot Crab Cocktail Spread
Crisp Crackers
Company Beef Filet
Tomato Pudding
Celery Casserole au Gratin
Romaine Salad
New Year's Gateau
Bonnie's Pear Flan

Wine Suggestions

A full, rich French Champagne;
such as the
Pol Roger Reserve Speciale (1973)

Dessert Buffet

Sac de Bonbon
Banana Walnut Torte
Chocolate Macaroon Cake
Holly Hotel Marble Cheesecake
Nut Tassies
Chocolate Truffle Cookies
Candy Strawberries

Wine Suggestions

A fresh Asti Spumante;
such as the
best selling Gancia

COLONIAL INNKEEPER'S PIE

Serve this lucious pie with whipped cream or softened ice cream.

SAUCE

1½	squares unsweetened chocolate	⅔	cup sugar
½	cup water	¼	cup butter
		1½	teaspoons vanilla

Melt the chocolate with the water; add the sugar and bring to a boil, stirring constantly. Remove from heat and stir in the butter and vanilla. Set aside.

PIE

1	cup flour	½	cup milk
¾	cup sugar	½	teaspoon vanilla
1	teaspoon baking powder	1	egg
1	teaspoon salt	1	9-inch pie crust
¼	cup butter	½	cup finely chopped nuts

Preheat oven to 350 degrees.

Sift together the flour, sugar, baking powder and salt. Add the butter, milk, and vanilla; beat for 2 minutes at medium speed. Add the egg and beat for 2 minutes longer. Pour batter into prepared pie shell. Stir the chocolate sauce and carefully pour over the batter; sprinkle with chopped nuts. Bake 55-60 minutes or until a toothpick inserted in the center comes out clean.

Preparation time: 25 minutes
Baking time: 1 hour

Grace L. Hath

NEVER-FAIL PIE CRUST

1½	cups flour	½	cup vegetable shortening
½	teaspoon baking powder	¼	cup cold water
½	teaspoon salt	2	teaspoons vinegar

Combine the flour, baking powder, and salt. Cut in the shortening with a pastry blender until it resembles coarse cornmeal. Combine the water and vinegar and blend into the pastry mixture.

Divide dough in half. Roll out to fit a 9-inch pie pan. Bake according to pie directions.

Yield: (2) 9-inch pie crusts
Preparation time: 15 minutes
Easy

Diane Varisto

BUTTERSCOTCH PIE

⅓ cup plus 2 tablespoons flour	3 tablespoons butter
1 cup brown sugar	½ teaspoon vanilla
¼ teaspoon salt	1 9-inch pie crust, baked
2 cups milk, scalded	3 egg whites
3 egg yolks, slightly beaten	2 tablespoons sugar

Preheat oven to 350 degrees.

In a medium saucepan combine the flour, sugar and salt. Gradually add the scalded milk and mix well. Cook over medium heat, stirring constantly, until mixture is thick. Add a small amount of the mixture to the beaten egg yolks, then stir yolks into the remaining hot mixture and cook 2 minutes longer. Cool, then add the butter and vanilla. Pour into the baked pie shell.

Beat the egg whites, adding sugar slowly, until stiff but not dry. Spread over the pie and bake 12-15 minutes until browned.

Preparation time: 20 minutes

Tana Beard

SOUTHERN CHESS PIE

This is a traditional and very special Southern recipe. You will love it from the first bite.

1 box yellow *butter* cake mix	1 8-ounce package cream cheese, softened
4 eggs, divided	
½ cup butter, melted	1 box powdered sugar

Preheat oven to 350 degrees.

Combine the cake mix, 1 egg, and the melted butter; mix thoroughly. Press into a 9x13-inch baking pan. Beat the remaining eggs and gradually add the softened cream cheese and powdered sugar. Beat well and spread over the first mixture. Bake for 45 minutes, center will still be runny but will jell as it cools. Let cook, then cut into squares. Note: Chocolate or lemon butter cake mix can be used for variety.

Serves 12-14
Preparation time: 15 minutes
Baking time: 40 minutes
Easy

Jack Fitts

NEAPOLITAN ICE CREAM PIE

Irresistible

3 3½-ounce cans flaked
   coconut
6 tablespoons butter, melted
1 quart vanilla ice cream
1 cup sour cream
½ cup finely chopped toasted
   almonds
¼ cup rum

1 quart chocolate ice cream
1 quart strawberry ice cream
1 square semi-sweet chocolate,
   melted
Garnish: chopped toasted
   almonds and whipped cream
Hot fudge sauce

Preheat oven to 325 degrees.

Combine the coconut and butter and press on the bottom and sides of 2 buttered 9-inch pie plates. Bake for 25 minutes or until the edges are golden. Cool and chill before filling.

In a cold mixing bowl, stir the vanilla ice cream to soften, add the sour cream, nuts and rum. If the mixture becomes too soft, return to freezer until nearly firm. Spread half the mixture in each pie shell. Using a small or medium ice cream scoop, shape the chocolate and strawberry ice cream into balls and arrange some of each on top of the vanilla ice cream. Cover with plastic wrap and freeze. To serve, drizzle with the melted chocolate and top with additional almonds if desired. Cover with whipped cream and serve with hot fudge sauce.

Variations: Graham cracker or chocolate cookie crusts can be used. Any flavors of ice cream may be substituted.

Yield: 2 pies

Sheila Donenfeld

MARY'S KEY LIME PIE

The best . . . and so easy

2 eggs
1 can sweetened condensed
   milk·

½ cup *fresh* lime juice
1 graham cracker crust

Preheat oven to 375 degrees.

In the bowl of a mixer, beat the eggs with the milk until well blended. Stir in the lime juice and beat well. Let rest for 10 minutes then pour into the crust. Bake for 10 minutes, remove from oven and let sit until cooled. Enjoy!

Preparation time: 5 minutes
Baking time: 10 minutes
Easy

The Sea Shanty
Lauderhill, FL

HARBOR PIER PEANUT BUTTER PIE

CULINARY COUNTERPOINT is the first cookbook to receive a copy of this fantastic dessert. They said they would not give it out to anyone else!! MmmMmmGood!

PIE

⅔ cup light corn syrup
¼ cup water
1 quart vanilla ice cream, softened

1 9-inch baked graham cracker crust

Blend together the syrup, water and ice cream. Blend until smooth and pour into pie shell; freeze.

TOPPING

⅔ cup crunchy or creamy peanut butter
¼ cup light corn syrup

Whole Spanish peanuts
Hot fudge

Mix the peanut butter and syrup. Spread evenly over frozen pie filling and top with peanuts; freeze. When ready to serve, slice into wedges and cover with hot fudge.

Serves 6
Preparation time: 15 minutes
Prepare ahead
Easy

The Harbor Pier
Harbor Springs, Michigan

MUD PIE

Rich ... melts in your mouth

1½ cups chocolate wafer crumbs
6 tablespoons butter, melted
1 quart coffee ice cream, softened

Chocolate fudge sauce
Heavy cream, whipped
Sliced almonds, toasted
Shaved chocolate

Combine the cookie crumbs and melted butter. Press firmly into the bottom and sides of a 9-inch pie plate. Put in freezer for ten minutes. Fill with ice cream and top with fudge sauce. Return to the freezer until firm. Garnish with whipped cream, almonds and shaved chocolate.

Serves 6-8
Make ahead
Freezes well
Easy

Judy Harris

MOM'S PUMPKIN PIE

1	30-ounce can pumpkin puree	2	rounded teaspoons ginger
1½	cups sugar	2	cans evaporated milk
1	teaspoon salt	¾	cup whole milk
2½	teaspoons cinnamon	2	9-inch unbaked pie shells

Preheat oven to 425 degrees.
Combine all ingredients and mix well. Pour into the pie shells and bake for 15 minutes. Reduce oven temperature to 350 degrees and bake for 45 minutes longer. Cool before serving.

Yield: Two 9-inch pies
Preparation time: 10 minutes
Baking time: 1 hour
Easy

Ida Pangborn

PRALINE TOPPING

For Pumpkin Pie

2	tablespoons butter	⅓	cup pecans
½	cup firmly packed brown sugar		

Shortly before serving pumpkin pie, melt the butter in a medium saucepan. Add the brown sugar and stir until sugar is dissolved then add the pecans. Sprinkle mixture over the pie shell and broil for 1 minute until bubbly.

Martha Miller

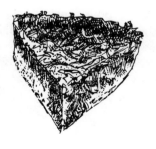

FIVE-PLY PIE

1 3⅝-ounce package lemon pudding
1 egg
¼ cup butter, softened
1 4-ounce package whipped cream cheese
2 tablespoons sugar
1 teaspoon orange rind
1 teaspoon vanilla, divided
1 9-inch baked pie shell
1 3-ounce package orange gelatin
1 cup heavy cream, whipped
1 tablespoon powdered sugar

Prepare pudding mix according to package directions using the egg and ¼ cup butter; let cool. Meanwhile, mix together the cream cheese, 2 tablespoons sugar, orange rind and ½ teaspoon vanilla. Spread into baked pie shell; top with cooled pudding.

Prepare the gelatin according to package directions. When almost set, spread 1 cup of the mixture over the pudding. When almost set, whip the cream with powdered sugar and ½ teaspoon vanilla and spread over the gelatin layer. Refrigerate until ready to serve.

Sue Abrahamsen

CHOCOLATE CHESTNUT PIE

Mouthwatering

1 12-ounce package semi-sweet chocolate morsels
1 15-ounce can chestnut puree
4 tablespoons butter, softened
1 cup chopped walnuts
2 cups coarsely crushed vanilla wafers
1 quart heavy cream, divided
10-15 whole vanilla wafers
Additional chopped nuts for garnish

In the top section of a double boiler, melt the chocolate. Add the chestnut puree, butter, walnuts and crushed vanilla wafers; blend thoroughly. Whip 2 cups of the cream and fold into the chestnut mixture. Spoon into a 9-inch greased pie plate. Place the whole vanilla wafers around the outer edge of the pie. Refrigerate for at least 4 hours. To serve: Whip the remaining cream and cover pie. Sprinkle with chopped nuts.

John Snow
DSO

MAPLE PUMPKIN PIE

3 eggs, lightly beaten	½ teaspoon salt
½ cup sugar	3 cups canned pumpkin
½ cup maple syrup	1 cup light cream
½ teaspoon cinnamon	1 9-inch unbaked pie shell
½ teaspoon ginger	½ cup chopped walnuts

Preheat oven to 400 degrees.
In a large bowl, combine the eggs, sugar, maple syrup, spices, salt, pumpkin and cream. Beat with a rotary beater until smooth. Turn ¾ of the filling into the pie shell. Place on the lowest rack of oven, then pour in the remaining filling. Bake for 55-60 minutes or until the filling is set in the center. Let cool on a wire rack. Decorate with chopped walnuts. Serve warm or cold.

Serves 8
Preparation time: 15 minutes
Baking time: 1 hour
Easy

Jeanne Schlitters

PECAN PIE

3 eggs, lightly beaten	1 teaspoon vanilla
1 cup Maple syrup	3 tablespoons butter, melted
¾ cup sugar	1 cup chopped pecans
⅛ teaspoon salt	1 unbaked 9-inch pie shell

Preheat oven to 350 degrees.
Combine all ingredients except nuts and pie shell and mix well. Fold in the chopped nuts and pour into pastry shell. Bake 35-40 minutes or until a knife inserted in the center comes out clean.

Serves 8
Preparation time: 10 minutes
Baking time: 40 minutes
Easy

Gordon Bowman, Executive Chef
Campus Inn
Ann Arbor, Michigan

CARAMEL ICE CREAM PIE

Delicious

PIE

1	egg white
¼	teaspoon salt
¼	cup sugar
1½	cups chopped walnuts

1	pint coffee ice cream, softened
1	pint vanilla ice cream, softened

Preheat oven to 400 degrees.
Beat the egg white with the salt until stiff but not dry. Gradually beat in the sugar then fold in the walnuts. Turn into a well-buttered 9-inch pie plate. With a spoon, spread the mixture evenly on the bottom and sides, taking care not to cover the rim. Bake for 10-12 minutes, until lightly browned; cool, then chill. Fill with layers of coffee and vanilla ice cream and store in the freezer until serving time. Top with caramel sauce.

CARAMEL SAUCE

3	tablespoons butter
1	cup firmly packed brown sugar

½	cup light cream
1	cup chopped walnuts
1	teaspoon vanilla

In a small saucepan, melt the butter. Add the brown sugar and stir until sugar dissolves. Remove from heat and very slowly stir in the cream. Heat for 1 minute longer, remove from heat and stir in the nuts and vanilla. Serve warm or cold.

Win Schuler Restaurants

FRENCH CANADIAN SUGAR PIE

1½	cups well-packed brown sugar
2	tablespoons flour
1	cup evaporated milk

1	egg, well beaten
½	cup grated coconut, divided
1	8-inch pie crust, unbaked

Preheat oven to 400 degrees.
Mix the brown sugar and flour together in a saucepan. Gradually stir in the evaporated milk and slowly bring to a boil. Simmer on very low heat, stirring constantly, for 5 minutes or until the brown sugar is dissolved. Remove from the heat and slowly pour mixture over

the beaten egg, stirring constantly. Add ⅓ cup coconut and pour mixture into the pie crust. Bake for 10 minutes then reduce heat to 300 degrees for 40 minutes or until the filling is set. Sprinkle on the remaining coconut 10 minutes before pie is done.

Preparation time: 15 minutes
Baking time: 50 minutes
Freezes well
Easy

Marie-Paule Hudon-Parcells
DSO

SUGARLESS APPLE PIE

This is a delicious sugar-free pie for all those calorie counters.

1   6-ounce can frozen apple
    juice concentrate, thawed
1   teaspoon cinnamon
2   tablespoons cornstarch
6   cups tart apples,
    peeled, cored and sliced

½   cup chopped walnuts
½   cup raisins
1   tablespoon butter
Pastry for 2 crust 9-inch pie

Preheat oven to 350 degrees.
Place the undiluted apple juice in a saucepan. Add the cinnamon and cornstarch, and cook, stirring constantly, until thickened. Stir in the apples, walnuts and raisins. Spoon the mixture into the bottom crust and dot with the butter. Place top crust over the pie, seal and flute the edges. Cut several slashes in the top crust. Bake for 50 minutes.

Preparation time: 30 minutes
Baking time: 50 minutes

Natalie Payne

LEMON TART

This is a lovely and light English dessert.

1   8-inch pie crust
¼   cup butter
¼   cup sugar

2   eggs, separated
Grated rind and juice of 1 lemon

Preheat oven to 375 degrees.
Bake the crust for 10 minutes; remove from oven. Cream the butter and sugar. Add the egg yolks and beat well. Stir in the lemon rind and juice. Beat the egg whites until stiff but not dry then fold into the lemon mixture. Pour into the partially baked pie shell. Turn oven temperature down to 325 degrees and bake pie for 30 minutes.

Preparation time: 20 minutes
Baking time: 40 minutes

Gladys Schlesinger

CHOCOLATE SATIN PIE

The most chocolatey chocolate pie in town

1 12-ounce package semi-sweet chocolate morsels	4 eggs, separated
¼ cup milk	1 teaspoon vanilla
¼ cup sugar	1 9-inch baked pie shell
Pinch of salt	Whipped cream

Combine the chocolate, milk, sugar and salt in the top section of double boiler. Cook over hot water until mixture is blended and smooth; cool slightly. Add egg yolks, one at a time, beating well after each addition. Blend in the vanilla. Beat egg whites until stiff and fold into chocolate mixture, blending thoroughly. Pour into pie shell and let set for 2 to 3 hours. Serve with whipped cream.
Note: If pie has been refrigerated, let stand at room temperature for at least one hour before serving.

Preparation time: 30 minutes
Chill one hour   Carol Meyer

FUDGE NUT PIE

1 ounce unsweetened chocolate, melted	1 teaspoon vanilla
½ cup butter, melted	2 eggs
½ cup flour	¼ cup chopped walnuts or pecans
1 cup sugar	Vanilla ice cream

Preheat oven to 350 degrees.
Combine all ingredients except the nuts and ice cream; mix until smooth. Pour into a greased 9-inch pie pan. Sprinkle with the nuts then bake for 25 minutes or until sides begin to pull away from the pan and top springs back when lightly pressed.
Serve warm or cold with ice cream.

Preparation time: 10 minutes
Baking time: 25 minutes
Easy   Peggy Dasovic

OZARK PIE

1	egg	½	cup chopped apples
¾	cup sugar	½	cup chopped nuts
⅛	teaspoon salt	1	quart vanilla ice cream
1½	teaspoons baking powder	2	Heath bars, crumbled
¼	cup flour		

Preheat oven to 350 degrees.

Combine the egg, sugar, salt, baking powder and flour and beat well. Stir in the apples and nuts. Pour into a greased 10-inch pie pan and bake for 25 minutes. While pie is baking, remove ice cream from freezer to soften. When pie is done, spread with ice cream and top with crumbled Heath bars. Freeze.

Note: Type and size of candy bar can be varied.

Serves 8-10
Preparation time: 10 minutes
Baking time: 25 minutes
Easy

Bill Goodwin

BRANDY ALEXANDER PIE

1	envelope unflavored gelatin softened in ½ cup cold water	¼	cup creme de cocoa
⅔	cup sugar, divided	2	cups heavy cream, whipped
⅛	teaspoon salt	1	8 or 9-inch graham cracker crust
3	eggs, separated		Chocolate curls
¼	cup Cognac		

Place gelatin-water in a heavy saucepan. Add ⅓ cup sugar, salt and egg yolks; stir to blend. Cook over low heat, stirring constantly until gelatin dissolves and mixture thickens. Do not boil. Stir in Cognac and creme de cocoa; chill until mixture starts to mound slightly.

Beat the egg whites until foamy. Gradually beat in remaining sugar, continuing to beat until stiff peaks form. Fold into egg yolk mixture then fold in half the whipped cream.

Turn into the crust and chill for several hours or overnight. Decorate with remaining whipped cream and chocolate curls.

Preparation time: 30 minutes

Virginia Andreae

HEAVENLY PIE

Heavenly!

16 marshmallows
4 regular sized (1.45 ounce) Almond Hershey bars

¼ cup milk
1 cup heavy cream, whipped
1 baked graham cracker crust

Place the marshmallows, candy bars and milk in the top of a double boiler over simmering water. Cook, stirring constantly, until candy and marshmallows are completely melted. Let cool.

Gently fold the cooled chocolate mixture into whipped cream and pour into prepared crust. Refrigerate for 24 hours.

Preparation time: 20 minutes
Chill: 24 hours
Easy

Loretta Miles
handed down from
Bertha Miles

RUSSIAN CREME

1½ cups sugar
3 cups light cream
3 tablespoons unflavored gelatin
1½ cups cold water

3 cups sour cream
3 tablespoons vanilla
2 packages fresh raspberries, or frozen berries, thawed

In a medium saucepan combine the sugar and cream and heat until sugar is dissolved. Combine the gelatin and cold water and let soften for 5 minutes, then add to the warm cream mixture and stir until dissolved. Let cool.

Place the sour cream in a large bowl and gradually add sweet cream mixture by the spoonful, stirring well, until thoroughly incorporated, then add the vanilla. Pour into a lightly oiled 8-cup mold, or transfer to a glass serving bowl. Refrigerate for 6 hours or longer. When ready to serve, unmold, or spoon out directly from serving bowl and top with fresh fruit or fruit sauce.

Serves 12
Preparation time: 25 minutes
Chill

Joyce Byrwa

CHOCOLATE MOUSSE CREPES

It is well worth your effort for this make ahead dessert

CREPES

1	cup milk	2	tablespoons cocoa
½	cup flour	1	tablespoon butter, melted
¼	cup sugar	1	teaspoon vanilla
2	eggs		

Place all ingredients in a blender. Blend on low speed for about ½ minute, until smooth; do not over mix. Allow batter to rest, covered, in refrigerator for 1 hour.

To make the crepes: lightly grease an 8-inch crepe pan with butter then heat. Pour ¼ cup batter into the hot pan, lift pan off the heat and swirl until batter coats the bottom. Return pan to the heat and cook for about one minute. Turn out onto a piece of waxed paper. Watch closely as both the chocolate and high sugar content can cause crepes to burn. Let crepes cool.

MOUSSE

12	ounces chocolate chips	1½	cups heavy cream, heated
1	teaspoon vanilla		to boiling
¼	teaspoon salt	6	egg yolks

Combine the chocolate chips, vanilla and salt in a blender. Process until chocolate is well chopped. Add the hot cream and blend until the chocolate melts. Add the yolks and mix about 5 seconds longer. Allow the mixture to cool.

When both mousse and crepes are cool, put about 1½ tablespoons of mousse on uncooked side of each crepe. Roll and set seam side down on baking sheet. Place in the freezer. When frozen, store in an airtight plastic bag. Crepes can be kept frozen for about 1 month.

When ready to serve, remove from freezer and let sit at room temperature for about 1 hour. Place crepes on individuals plates and spoon warm custard sauce over the top.

CUSTARD SAUCE

4	egg yolks	1½	cups coffee cream
½	cup sugar	1	teaspoon vanilla

Combine the egg yolks and sugar; beat until fluffy. In a saucepan, heat coffee cream. Slowly add the yolks and sugar, beating constantly. cook, over low heat stirring constantly, for about 15 minutes or until custard coats the back of a spoon. Remove from heat and add the vanilla. Serve warm.

Maria Arnold

RHUBARB CRUMB

Serve with whipped cream or ice cream for a truly outstanding dessert

1   cup flour
¾   cup oatmeal
1   cup brown sugar
½   cup butter, softened
6   cups diced rhubarb (about 2 pounds)

1½   cups sugar
1   cup orange juice, apple juice or water
3   tablespoons cornstarch

Preheat oven to 350 degrees.
In a mixing bowl combine the flour, oatmeal, and brown sugar. Cut in the butter until mixture is crumbly. Press ¾ of the mixture into the bottom of a 9x13-inch baking pan. Place the diced rhubarb on top. Combine the sugar, juice and cornstarch. Bring to a boil and cook over medium heat, stirring constantly, until clear and thickened. Pour over rhubarb and sprinkle with the remaining crumb mixture. Bake for 1 hour.

Serves 8-12
Preparation time: 15 minutes
Baking time: 1 hour
Easy

"Fat Bob" Taylor
the Singing Plumber

PLUM PUDDING

Traditional at Christmas

1   cup raisins
1   cup dry Sherry
1   cup butter, softened
1   cup sugar
1   cup flour
1   teaspoon baking soda
½   teaspoon salt
4   eggs, lightly beaten
1   tablespoon grated orange peel
1   tablespoon grated lemon peel
2½   teaspoons cinnamon

½   teaspoon cloves
½   teaspoon nutmeg
¼   teaspoon mace
1½   cups grated carrots
2   cups chopped dates
1½   cups chopped nuts
1   cup dry bread crumbs
1   cup milk
1   cup currants
¼   cup molasses
½   cup Cognac
Lemon Brandy Hard Sauce

Soak the raisins in the Sherry for at least 4 hours.

Generously butter a 2-quart pudding mold with a tight-fitting lid. Cream the butter with the sugar. Blend in the flour, baking soda and salt. Stir in the raisins with the Sherry then add the remaining ingredients except the Cognac and the hard sauce; incorporate thoroughly. Transfer mixture to the prepared mold and cover tightly.

Place the mold on a rack in a deep kettle. Add enough water to come half way up the side of the mold. Bring the water to a boil, lower heat and simmer gently for 5 hours. Check occasionally to make sure that water remains at the same level. When done, remove mold from the kettle and remove lid. Let pudding cool for 30 minutes then loosen edges with a sharp knife and invert mold onto a platter leaving the mold over the pudding until it separates from the mold and is completely cool. Wrap pudding well in foil and refrigerate until ready to serve.

To serve: Steam pudding for 1 hour in a well-buttered mold. Invert onto a serving platter. Heat the Cognac, ignite, and pour over the pudding. Serve with Lemon Brandy Hard Sauce.

Serves 8-12
Freeze well   Brenda Pangborn

LEMON BRANDY HARD SAUCE

1½   cups powdered sugar   1   teaspoon vanilla
½   cup sweet butter, softened   1½   teaspoons grated lemon
¼   cup brandy   peel

Combine all ingredients in a bowl and beat until light and fluffy. Chill at least 6 hours before serving.

Makes 2 cups
Freezes well   Brenda Pangborn

379

HISTORIC HOLLY HOTEL
MARBLE CHEESECAKE

Cheesecake seems to be the all-American favorite. Here's an unusual and interesting version.

3	8-ounce packages cream cheese	1	tablespoon vanilla extract
1	cup sugar	1	teaspoon almond extract
Eggs to equal 1 cup		6	tablespoons hot Kahlua sauce

Beat the cream cheese until very smooth. Add sugar, scraping down the sides of the bowl. Add the eggs, two at a time, and beat until smooth. Add the extracts and blend well. Pour into a 9-inch spring-form or cake pan lined with parchment paper. Swirl in the hot Kahlua sauce.

Place the pan in a larger pan and fill halfway up the side with water — the water bath is imperative as this cheesecake does not have a crust. Bake for 1 hour. Let cool then chill for several hours before serving with additional Hot Chocolate Kahlua Sauce.

HOT CHOCOLATE KAHLUA SAUCE

8	ounces Baker's Sweet German chocolate	¼	cup Kahlua
		½	cup cream

Melt the chocolate with the Kahlua. Add the cream and stir well. Keep warm.

Preparation time: 15 minutes
Baking time: 1 hour
Easy

Rick Halberg, Executive chef
Historic Holly Hotel
Holly, Michigan

PRALINE PARFAIT SAUCE

Serve this in parfait glasses layered with vanilla ice cream. Top with whipped cream and pecan halves . . . scrumptious!

2	cups dark corn syrup	⅓	cup boiling water
⅓	cup sugar	1	cup chopped pecans

Combine all ingredients in a medium saucepan over medium heat. As soon as mixture reaches the boiling point, remove from heat. Cool and store in a covered jar.

Don Swanson

SNOW PUDDING

GELATIN

1 box strawberry gelatin	2 egg whites

Prepare gelatin according to package directions. Let sit until just ready to "jell", then whip until fluffy.

Beat the egg whites until stiff but not dry. Blend into the gelatin and refrigerate until cool. Serve with Vanilla Sauce.

VANILLA SAUCE

2 cups whole milk	2 egg yolks
2 tablespoons sugar	1 teaspoon vanilla
Pinch of salt	

Warm the milk in a small saucepan over low heat; blend in the sugar and salt. Beat the egg yolks and slowly add the milk, stirring constantly over heat until thickened, about 10-15 minutes. Remove from heat and add the vanilla. Do not overcook or sauce will curdle. Refrigerate until ready to serve over the gelatin mixture.

Note: Different flavors of gelatin can be used.

Serves 4

Richard Hayman
"Pops" Condustor and Arranger

CREME DE MENTHE FUDGE DESSERT

½ cup butter	20 chocolate sandwich cookies, crushed
3 ounces unsweetened chocolate	½ gallon vanilla ice cream, softened
3 eggs	
2 cups powdered sugar	½ cup creme de menthe liqueur

In a saucepan combine the butter, chocolate, eggs and sugar. Bring to a boil over medium heat; set aside. Spread the crushed cookies in a 9x13-inch pan. Pour the fudge sauce over the cookie crumbs; refrigerate. Mix the ice cream with the liqueur and spread over fudge. Freeze. To serve: Cut into squares.

Serves 15
Preparation time: 15 minutes
Refrigerate
Easy

Jean Smetana

NEW YEAR'S GATEAU

Irresistible!

MERINGUES
3   egg whites
Pinch cream of tartar
¾   cup sugar, divided

Preheat oven to 200 degrees.
Lightly grease and flour 2 *non-stick* baking sheets. Trace four 8-inch circles on the sheets.
In a mixing bowl, beat the egg whites with the cream of tartar at low speed. When whites begin to foam, increase the speed to high and beat until soft peaks form. Continue beating on high speed, adding half the sugar, 1 tablespoon at a time, beating well after each addition. At this time the whites will be glossy and dense, forming stiff peaks. Sprinkle the remaining sugar over the beaten whites. Using a spatula, gently fold the sugar into the whites until thoroughly incorporated. Spread the batter into the circles formed on the baking sheets to a thickness of ¼ inch. Place remaining batter in a pastry bag fitted with a small star tip and make 12 "kisses" in another area of the baking sheet. Bake for 1 hour, lowering temperature if the meringues begin to color. When thoroughly stiff and dry to the touch, remove from oven and let cool on racks.

FILLING

5	egg yolks	3	ounces unsweetened chocolate
1	cup sugar		
⅓	cup water	1¼	cups sweet butter, softened

In a medium mixing bowl, beat the egg yolks until pale in color. In a medium saucepan, combine the sugar with the water over high heat and bring to a boil. Cook, uncovered, until the syrup reaches the soft ball stage, 240 degrees on a candy thermometer.
Meanwhile, melt the chocolate in the top section of a double boiler over simmering water. Remove from the heat and let chocolate cool to lukewarm.
With mixer running, gradually pour the syrup into the egg yolks in a slow steady stream. Continue beating at high speed until cooled to lukewarm — about 5 minutes. Gradually beat the softened butter, 2 tablespoons at a time, into the cooled egg mixture. When the butter is thoroughly incorporated, beat in the chocolate.

ICING

2 cups heavy cream
2 tablespoons dark rum
¾ cup sugar

In a large chilled bowl, whip the cream at high speed. When it begins to thicken, add the rum and gradually beat in the sugar. Continue beating until quite stiff. If the cream spatters, you might want to do this in two batches.

ASSEMBLY

4 prepared meringues
Chocolate filling
4 medium bananas, sliced

1 Recipe Icing
½ pint perfect fresh raspberries or strawberries

Line a serving plate with four strips of waxed paper. Place one meringue on the serving plate with the waxed paper lying just under the edges of the circle. Spread ¼ of the chocolate filling to the edges. Place one sliced banana evenly over the chocolate filling and cover with a thin layer of icing. Repeat process until all meringues, filling and bananas are used. Frost with the remaining whipped cream and place the meringue "kisses" evenly around the edge of the gateau. Carefully fill the center with berries. Remove the waxed paper strips before serving.

Separate components can be made ahead with the final assembly done at the last moment.

Serves 8-12

John Merrill

LEMON ICE

Nice to clear the palate between courses or as a dessert served with fresh strawberries

2 cups strained fresh lemon juice

2 cups water
2 cups sugar

Combine the lemon juice and water in a saucepan. Stir in the sugar and bring to a boil over medium heat, stirring constantly. Remove from heat and let cool to room temperature. Pour mixture into a shallow 8-inch cake tin and place in freezer for 3-6 hours or until iced. Serve in hollowed-out lemon halves.

Marian Impastato

BRULEE

1   8-ounce package cream cheese
1   cup heavy cream, whipped
½   cup chopped nuts
1½   cups crushed pineapple, drained
1   teaspoon freshly grated nutmeg
1½   cups brown sugar

Preheat oven to broil.
In the bowl of a mixer beat the cream cheese. Add the whipped cream and mix well. Stir in the nuts, pineapple and nutmeg and thoroughly incorporate. Place in an 8x8-inch glass baking dish. Sift the brown sugar over the surface. Broil 5 inches from source of heat until the sugar melts and starts to bubble — watch carefully! Cool, then refrigerate 1-2 hours.
To serve: Break crust by tapping, then cut.

Serves 8-9
Preparation time: 15 minutes
Easy   Suzanne Boyce

FOUR LAYER TORTE

1   cup flour
½   cup butter, softened
½   cup walnuts, finely chopped
1   cup powdered sugar
1   8-ounce package cream cheese, softened
1   16-ounce container Cool Whip topping
2   3⅝ ounce packages *instant* lemon pudding
3   cups cold milk
Chopped nuts

First layer: Combine the flour, butter and ½ cup walnuts. Blend thoroughly and press into a 9x13-inch pan. Bake in a 350-degree oven for 20 minutes. Let cool.
Second layer: Mix together the powdered sugar, cream cheese and half the Cool Whip. Spread over the cake layer.
Third layer: Combine the lemon pudding with the milk. Mix well and let set for 15 minutes. Pour over the cheese layer.
Fourth layer: Top with remaining Cool Whip and sprinkle with nuts.

Serves 15   Susan Bratkowski

INDIAN PUDDING

A traditional New England favorite

⅓ cup yellow cornmeal	2 tablespoons butter
⅓ cup molasses	1 cup raisins
Pinch of salt	¼ teaspoon ginger
⅓ cup brown sugar	1 teaspoon nutmeg
3 cups hot milk	1 cup cold milk
2 eggs, beaten	Vanilla ice cream

Preheat oven to 275 degrees.
In a large bowl combine the cornmeal, molasses, salt and brown sugar. Add the hot milk and let stand for 5 minutes. Add the eggs, butter, raisins and spices. Transfer to a 6-cup buttered baking dish and bake for 20 minutes. Add the cold milk and stir gently. Return to the oven and bake for 2 hours longer. Serve with vanilla ice cream.

Serves 12
Preparation time: 15 minutes
Baking time: 2½ hours

Robert Pangborn
DSO

RICE PUDDING

1 quart milk, divided	4 eggs, beaten
⅓ cup butter	1 teaspoon vanilla
½ cup rice	½ teaspoon salt
½ cup raisins	Cinnamon
½ cup sugar	Nutmeg

Preheat oven to 325 degrees.
Cook 2 cups milk, butter and rice in top of double boiler until rice is very soft. Add remaining ingredients, except cinnamon and nutmeg, to the hot rice. Place in greased 1½-quart casserole. Sprinkle top with cinnamon and nutmeg to taste. Set in pan half full of warm water and bake for 45 minutes to 1 hour until set.

Preparation time: ½ hour
Baking time: 1 hour
Easy

Loretta Miles
handed down from
Bertha Miles

CHOCOLATE CHEESECAKE

This is the piece de resistance of chocolate desserts

¼	cup butter	1	cup sugar
1	cup crushed chocolate wafers, about 18	3	eggs
¼	teaspoon cinnamon	2	teaspoons unsweetened cocoa
8	ounces semi-sweet chocolate morsels	1	teaspoon vanilla
3	8-ounce packages cream cheese, softened	2	cups sour cream

Preheat oven to 350 degrees.

In a medium saucepan, melt the butter. Add the crumbs and cinnamon and mix well. Press crumb mixture on the bottom of an 8-inch spring-form pan. Chill.

In the top of a double boiler, melt the chocolate, stirring occasionally. In a large bowl, beat the softened cream cheese until fluffy and smooth. Beat in the sugar then add the eggs, one at a time, beating well after each addition. Stir in the melted chocolate, cocoa and vanilla. Add the sour cream and incorporate thoroughly. Pour the mixture into the prepared springform pan. Bake for 70 minutes.

Remove from oven . . . the mixture will still be runny, but will become firm as it cools. *Do not overcook!* Cool at room temperature, then chill in the refrigerator for at least 5 hours before serving. If any cracks develop in the top, decorate with chocolate shavings.

Pat Young

ANOTHER SINFUL CHOCOLATE CHEESECAKE

1⅓	cups chocolate wafer crumbs	3	8-ounce packages cream cheese, softened
¼	cup butter, melted	1	cup sour cream
2	tablespoons sugar	2	tablespoons cornstarch
1	cup heavy cream	1	teaspoon almond extract
8	ounces semi-sweet chocolate cut into bits		Pinch of cream of tartar
4	eggs, separated		Pinch of salt
¾	cup sugar, divided		Garnish: Whipped cream and chocolate curls

In a bowl combine the chocolate crumbs, butter and 2 tablespoons sugar. Mix well then press into the bottom and halfway up the sides of a well-buttered 9-inch springform pan. Chill shell while making filling. Preheat oven to 300 degrees.

In a saucepan, scald the cream. Remove pan from the heat and let cool for 5 minutes. Add the chocolate and stir until chocolate is melted. Transfer to a mixing bowl and beat until mixture is cooled and light in texture.

In a separate mixing bowl beat the egg yolks with ½ cup sugar until mixture is thick and lemon colored and forms a ribbon when the beaters are lifted. Add the chocolate mixture and beat until well blended. Combine the cream cheese, sour cream, cornstarch and almond extract and beat until mixture is smooth. Add to the chocolate mixture and mix well.

In another bowl, beat the egg whites with cream of tartar and salt until they hold soft peaks. Fold into the chocolate mixture and incorporated thoughly. Pour into the chilled shell.

Place the springform pan in another deep pan and fill with water to come halfway up the sides. Bake for 90 minutes. Turn off the heat and let sit in oven for 1 hour but *do not open oven door*. Remove pan to a rack and let cake cool completely. Chill, loosely covered, for at least 2 hours then remove the sides of the springform pan and transfer cake to a serving plate. When ready to serve, garnish with whipped cream and chocolate curls.

Preparation time: 45 minutes
Baking time 90 minutes   Carol Ann May

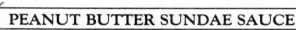

PEANUT BUTTER SUNDAE SAUCE

2	cups sugar	1 cup Half & Half
½	cup water	1 tablespoon vanilla
1	pound creamy peanut butter	Vanilla ice cream

Place the sugar and water in a saucepan. Bring to a boil and cook, stirring, until sugar dissolves and syrup is clear. Transfer syrup to the container of a food processor fitted with the steel blade or a blender. Add the peanut butter, Half & Half and vanilla and blend well. Serve at room temperature over vanilla ice cream.

Makes about 4 cups   Chef George Srabian
                                                 Savoyard Club
                                                 Buhl Building

BONNIE'S BRANDIED CUSTARD PEAR FLAN

DOUGH

1 cup flour	1 egg yolk
1 tablespoon sugar	1 tablespoon water
3 tablespoons butter, chilled	

Mix the flour and sugar together. Cut the cold butter into small pieces and cut it gently into the flour mixture until it resembles fine cornmeal. Mix the egg yolk and water together. Make a well in the center of the flour-mixture and pour in the egg yolk mixture. Combine mixtures until it forms a smooth paste. Refrigerate for 1 hour before rolling out.

Roll out into an 11-inch removable bottom fluted flan pan. Chill for at least 1 hour.

CUSTARD

4 eggs	1 capful of brandy
¼ cup sugar	½ teaspoon vanilla
1 cup Half & Half	Freshly grated nutmeg

In a small bowl mix the ingredients, in order listed, with a whisk.

ASSEMBLY

1 Recipe dough	3 ripe pears
1 Recipe custard	

Preheat oven to 375 degrees.

Line the chilled flan shell with foil and weigh it down with another pan. Bake for 10 minutes, remove foil, then bake for an additional 5 minutes. Reduce oven temperature to 350 degrees.

Peel and slice the pears lengthwise ⅛-inch thick. Arrange the slices in concentric circles in the flan shell. Cover with the custard and return to the oven for 20-30 minutes or until custard is set. Serve warm or at room temperature.

Serves 10-12
Preparation time: 30 minutes
Baking time: 30 minutes

Bonnie Fishman
Southfield, Michigan

SARAH'S CHEESECAKE

CRUST

1½ cups graham cracker
    crumbs
½ cup finely ground pecans

¾ teaspoon cinnamon
½ cup butter, melted

Thoroughly combine all ingredients and pat on bottom and sides of 9-inch springform pan

FILLING

3 8-ounce packages cream
    cheese, softened
4 egg whites

1 cup sugar
1 teaspoon vanilla

Preheat oven to 350 degrees.
Beat cream cheese until fluffy and set aside. Beat egg whites until stiff. Add sugar and vanilla and incorporate thoroughly. Fold egg white mixture into cream cheese. Pour into crust; bake for 40 minutes.

TOPPING

2 cups sour cream
2 tablespoons sugar

½ teaspoon vanilla
Slivered almonds

Increase oven temperature to 475 degrees. Mix sour cream, sugar and vanilla. Spread on top of cheesecake, then sprinkle with slivered almonds. Bake for 5 minutes. Chill well — at least 8 hours — before serving.

Serves 8

Lee Green
DSO

WHITE CHOCOLATE ZABAYONE

Beautiful . . . serve with a strawberry and sliced Kiwi fruit.

4 egg yolks
1 scant cup sugar
4 ounces white chocolate
¼ cup plus 2 tablespoons
    creme de banana

2 cups heavy cream
¼ teaspoon vanilla extract

Whip egg yolks with sugar over boiling water until very light and thickened. *Do not overcook.* Meanwhile, melt chocolate with liqueur. Combine with yolks and cool slightly. Whip the cream with vanilla. Fold all ingredients together and spoon into champagne glasses.
Variation: Use dark chocolate, Grand Marnier, Amaretto or Sherry.

Serves 8
Preparation time: 20 minutes

Rick Halberg, Executive Chef
Historic Holly Hotel
Holly, Michigan

QUICK BUTTER TARTS

This is an easy version of a delicious pastry.

1 cup currants	3 tablespoons butter, melted
1 egg, beaten	Crust for one 9-inch pie
1 cup brown sugar	

Preheat oven to 375 degrees.

Combine the currants, egg, brown sugar and melted butter in a bowl and mix thoroughly. Place dough on a lightly floured board. Roll out to ¼-inch thickness. Cut circles with a 2½-inch cookie cutter and press each circle into the bottom and ¾ way up the sides of muffin tins. Drop 1 heaping teaspoonful of the filling in each cup. Bake for 25 minutes or until pastry is golden brown.

Yield: 12 tarts
Preparation time: 15 minutes
Baking time: 15 minutes
Easy   Elizabeth McCartney

SUJI HALWA

A delicious East Indian dessert

2 pods cardamon or ½ teaspoon ground cardamon	2½ cups milk
	⅓ cup sugar
1 cup semolina	¼ cup raisins, softened in hot water
¼ cup ghee or clarified butter (Ghee is available in shops where Indian foods are sold)	¼ cup raw cashews

If using whole cardamon, remove seeds from the pods and crush with a mortar and pestle or rolling pin; set aside.

In a large skillet, dry roast the semolina over low heat, stirring constantly, until it darkens slightly in color and starts to smell good. Add the ghee or butter and stir to coat the semolina well. Increase heat to medium and roast for 2 minutes longer. Gradually add the milk, stirring vigorously, until mixture is the consistency of porridge. Add the sugar, raisins, cardamon and cashews and cook, stirring constantly, until mixture becomes thick and pudding-like in texture. Transfer to a serving dish and shape into a mound, or spread it in a flat pan and cut into diamond-shaped pieces, one inch wide; let cool. Serve at room temperature.

Barry Shapiro

FRESH FRUIT TORTE

½ cup butter, softened
1 cup sugar
2 eggs
1 cup flour
1 teaspoon baking powder
1 teaspoon vanilla

Fresh fruit: blueberries, peaches, plums, and apples, peeled cored and sliced
Cinnamon
Sugar

Preheat oven to 350 degrees.
Cream the butter and sugar. Add eggs and mix well. Beat in the flour and baking powder then add vanilla. Pour the batter into a greased 9-inch round cake pan. Arrange fresh fruit on top of the batter and sprinkle with cinnamon and sugar to taste. Bake for 1 hour. Cool and remove from pan. Allow to set overnight before serving.

Serves 6-8
Preparation time: 15 minutes
Baking time: 1 hour
Easy

Linnoah Grenzke

BANANA SPLIT DESSERT

This is a delicious, non-bake recipe.

2 eggs
1½ cups powdered sugar
1 cup butter, softened
2 graham cracker crusts, crumbled and pressed into a 9x13-inch pan
1 8-ounce can crushed pineapple, well drained

2 large bananas, sliced
1 package prepared whipped topping or 1 container frozen topping
Garnish: Finely chopped nuts, maraschino cherries

Beat the eggs for 10 minutes on high speed. Add the sugar and butter and beat until light and fluffy. Spread on top of the graham cracker crust. Add, in layers, the pineapple, bananas, and whipped topping. Sprinkle with nuts and cherries. Refrigerate for 2 hours before serving.
Note: 2 large packages of drained, frozen strawberries may be added with the pineapple.

Serves 12-18
Preparation time: 15 minutes
Easy

Peggy McCourt

CHOCOLATE BAG
1   6½-inch bag
5   pounds bittersweet
    chocolate, shaved

Cut 3½ inches off the top of the bag. Spray bag heavily with vegetable spray. Slowly melt the chocolate in the top section of a double boiler or in a microwave oven. Take care that *no* moisture or steam touches the chocolate! When the chocolate has melted and is smooth, begin painting the chocolate on the inside bottom and sides of the bag. Use a 1½-inch wide, very soft bristle pastry brush and paint chocolate liberally. Leave in a cool place, but do not refrigerate. When chocolate has set, brush on a second coat; let dry.

WHITE CHOCOLATE MOUSSE
2   tablespoons instant freeze-dried coffee
2   tablespoons hot coffee
3   tablespoons Tia Maria
5   egg whites
Pinch of cream of tartar
2   cups superfine sugar
5   ounces white chocolate, melted
Juice and zest of 1 lemon
2   cups heavy cream

Combine the instant coffee powder, hot coffee and Tia Maria; set aside. Beat the egg whites with the cream of tartar until frothy. *Slowly* add the sugar. Continue beating until meringue is tight and shiny. Fold the meringue into the melted chocolate. "Do not answer the telephone or doorbell, just get the meringue folded into the melted chocolate." Mixture should be marshmallow-like in consistency.
Add the lemon juice and zest; mixture will thin down slightly. When mixture is cool, whip the cream and fold in gently. Divide the mixture equally between two bowls. Carefully fold the coffee mixture into one of the portions of meringue.
Note: If desired, 1 ounce of melted chocolate may be mixed with the hot coffee for a mocha flavor.

CHOCOLATE MOUSSE
5   ounces bittersweet chocolate
5   ounces sweet butter
5   large eggs, separated
1   teaspoon vanilla
2   tablespoons Cognac

Melt the chocolate with the butter. Add egg yolks and mix well; stir in the Cognac. Beat the egg whites until stiff but not dry, then fold into the chocolate.

ASSEMBLY

Using a pastry bag fitted with a #5 tube tip, fill the chocolate bag, taking care that you do not hit the chocolate shell. Fill bag in any combination of mousse — white, chocolate and coffee. Refrigerate if mousse or bag seems to be softening too much. Leave one inch from the top of the chocolate bag; freeze. When frozen, carefully peel off the layer of paper bag and refrigerate for a few hours. Top with fresh raspberries or strawberries.

RASPBERRY SAUCE

Place a package of frozen raspberries in a saucepan and bring to a boil. Cook until thickened. Strain and cool. When ready to serve Sac de Bonbon, spoon some raspberry sauce on a plate and place the mousse-filled chocolate sac on top.

Makes 2 bags
Serves 12-14

Chef Duglass
Southfield, Michigan

DAIQUIRI CHEESECAKE

The combination of lemon, lime and rum makes a wonderfully interesting variation on the cheesecake theme.

1¼	cups graham cracker crumbs	2	teaspoons grated lime peel
¼	cup sugar	1	teaspoon grated lemon peel
6	tablespoons butter, melted	½	cup lime juice
1	envelope unflavored gelatin	4	eggs, separated
1	cup sugar, divided	2	8-ounce packages cream cheese
½	cup rum	1	cup heavy cream, whipped

Combine the crumbs, sugar and butter. Pat into bottom and sides of a springform pan, reserving 2 tablespoons of mixture for garnish; chill. In a medium saucepan, combine the gelatin and ½ cup sugar. stir in the rum, lime and lemon peel, lime juice and egg yolks. Cook, stirring constantly, over medium heat for 8-10 minutes or until thickened. Remove from heat and beat in the cream cheese or until smooth. In a separate bowl beat the egg whites until soft peaks form. Gradually add the remaining ½ cup sugar and beat until stiff but not dry. Fold beaten egg whites and whipped cream into the gelatin mixture. Spoon into the prepared pan and sprinkle around the edge with the reserved crumbs. Cover and chill at least 12 hours.

Preparation time: 40 minutes
Chill

Martha Bowman

ROLFE'S ENGLISH TRIFLE

1 12-ounce pound cake	1 tablespoon superfine sugar
½ cup raspberry jam	2 cups fresh raspberries, or
½ cup slivered almonds	two 10-ounce packages
¾ cup dry Sherry	frozen raspberries, defrosted
¼ cup brandy	and drained
1 recipe Custard Cream	¼ cup slivered almonds for
1 cup heavy cream	garnish

Cut the pound cake into 1-inch thick slices and spread with the raspberry jam. Line the sides and bottom of a glass bowl with the cake slices, jam side up. Cut any remaining cake into 1-inch squares and scatter on the bottom of the bowl. Add ½ cup slivered almonds. Pour the Sherry and brandy over the cake and let steep for 1-2 hours. Meanwhile, prepare the custard cream. (See recipe below.)

To assemble, whip the cream, gradually adding the sugar, until the cream forms stiff peaks. Scatter all but 15 of the raspberries over the cake. Spread the custard cream over the raspberries, then cover with the whipped cream. Garnish with the reserved raspberries and the remaining ¼ cup slivered almonds. Refrigerate until ready to serve, but no longer than 2 hours.

CUSTARD CREAM

2 cups milk, divided	⅓ cup sugar
¼ cup cornstarch	2 teaspoons vanilla
3 large eggs	½ cup heavy cream

Mix ¼ cup of the milk with the cornstarch to form a thin paste, then beat in the eggs, one at a time, beating after each addition. In a 2-quart saucepan, heat the remaining milk and the sugar until it is hot, but not boiling. Pour ¼ cup of the hot milk into the egg mixture, blend well, then, stirring constantly, slowly add the egg mixture to the hot milk in the saucepan. Lower the heat and continue to cook for 2-3 minutes until the custard thickens and any lumps have disappeared. Remove from the heat, stir in the vanilla, and set aside to cool to room temperature. When cooled, whip the cream and gently fold into the custard.

Makes 3 cups

Benedicta Gray-Sorton
DSO

SCOTCH AND RUM MOUSSE

2	envelopes plain gelatin	⅓	cup Scotch
1	cup water	4	egg whites
1	cup sugar	2	cups heavy cream, whipped
3	tablespoons rum		

Lightly oil a 1½-quart mold. Soften the gelatin in the water. Cook over low heat until gelatin is dissolved. Stir in the sugar, rum and Scotch. Chill until the mixture begins to thicken — watch carefully as this occurs quickly. Remove from refrigerator and beat until foamy. Beat the egg whites until smooth and glossy; gently fold into gelatin mixture. Fold in the whipped cream and chill until ready to serve.

Serves 6
Preparation time: 30 minutes
Chill

Pat Young

CHOCOLATE MOUSSE TORTE

7	ounces almond paste	1	teaspoon instant coffee powder
1	tablespoon unsweetened cocoa	1	tablespoon brandy
5	eggs, divided	2	tablespoons sugar
6	ounces semi-sweet chocolate	½	cup heavy cream

Preheat oven to 350 degrees.
Crumble almond paste into blender or food processor. Add the cocoa and 2 eggs; blend until smooth. Pour into a greased and floured 9-inch springform pan; bake for 15 minutes. Remove from oven and let cool. Melt the chocolate over hot water. Separate 2 eggs, set aside whites, and place yolks in a mixing bowl along with the remaining egg; beat well. Blend in the coffee powder, brandy and melted chocolate. In another bowls, whip egg whites, adding sugar gradually and beating until moist, stiff peaks form. Fold into chocolate mixture. Whip the cream and fold into mixture. Spread evenly over cooled cake and freeze.

To serve: Let sit at room temperature about 1 hour. Garnish with shaved chocolate and chopped almonds. Unmold and cut into thin wedges.

Serves 16-20
Freeze

Kitchen Stuff
Gourmet Cookware Shop
Birmingham, Michigan

CHOCOLATE MOUSSE

A classic dessert that's always a favorite.

6	ounces semi-sweet chocolate morsels	2	teaspoons vanilla extract
¼	teaspoon salt	¾	cup heavy cream
2	tablespoons water	1½	teaspoons superfine sugar
4	large eggs, separated		Chocolate shavings

Combine the chocolate, salt and water in the top section of a double boiler. Place over hot water and stir until chocolate is melted. Beat the egg yolks until light and lemon colored, then gradually beat in the melted chocolate. Stir in the vanilla extract.

Beat the egg whites until they form soft peaks, then fold them into the chocolate mixture. Whip ½ cup of the cream and fold into the chocolate mixture. Spoon the mousse into a decorative serving dish or into sherbet glasses and chill until ready to serve. Whip the remaining ¼ cup cream with the sugar and put on top of the mousse. Decorate with chocolate shavings and chill.

Serves 6
Preparation time: 25 minutes
Chill
Ken Harris

SWEDISH MAZARINE TORTE

PASTRY

½	cup butter	1	tablespoon plus 1 teaspoon sugar
1	cup plus 1 tablespoon flour	1	egg yolk

Cut the butter into the flour until the mixture resembles coarse corn-meal. Add the sugar and egg yolk and mix until the dough forms a ball. Chill for 1 hour.

Preheat oven to 400 degrees. Remove dough from refrigerator and roll out on a lightly floured surface. Line a false bottom 9-inch quiche pan with the dough and bake for 10-15 minutes or until pastry is lightly browned.

FILLING

⅓ cup butter	2 eggs
½ cup sugar	1 teaspoon flour
¾ cup ground almonds	Slivered almonds
1 teaspoon almond extract	Powdered sugar

Cream the butter and sugar. Add the ground almonds and extract and mix well. Add the eggs, one at a time, beating well after each addition. Add the flour and mix well. Pour into the prepared pastry. Lower oven heat to 325 degrees and bake the torte for 20 minutes. Place slivered almonds on top of the torte and bake for 10 minutes longer. Cool and sprinkle with powdered sugar.

Variation: Spread ½ cup raspberry jam on crust before adding the filling.

Preparation time: 30 minutes
Baking time: 30 minutes   MariAnn Eklund Halladay

BAVARIAN CHEESECAKE

½ cup butter, softened	¼ cup sugar
⅓ cup sugar	1 egg
¼ teaspoon vanilla	½ teaspoon vanilla
¾ cup flour	1 15-ounce can blueberries, drained
⅔ cup finely chopped pecans	
1 8-ounce package cream cheese	½ teaspoon cinnamon mixed with 1 teaspoon sugar

Preheat oven to 450 degrees.

In large bowl, beat the butter, ⅓ cup sugar and ¼ teaspoon vanilla until well mixed. Stir in the flour and pecans. With lightly floured hands, press mixture into bottom and 1-inch up the sides of ungreased 9-inch springform pan.

In small bowl, beat the cream cheese and ¼ cup sugar until smooth. Beat in egg and remaining vanilla; pour mixture into crust. Combine fruit with cinnamon-sugar mixture and toss well. Arrange on top of the cheese mixture. Bake 10 minutes. Reduce heat to 400 degrees and bake 25 minutes longer. Open oven door and let cheesecake cool in the oven. When cooled, refrigerate at least 6 hours before serving.

Note: Can use peaches, pears or other desired fruit.

Preparation Time: 30 minutes
Baking time: 35 minutes   Lynell Smith

PEACH BOMBE WITH RASPBERRY SAUCE

Light and delicious

1 quart rich French vanilla ice cream, softened
6 large peaches, peeled and pureed — about 1½ cups
4 ounces shaved bittersweet chocolate

2 cups toasted chopped almonds
⅔ cup Triple Sec or Grand Marnier
½ cup heavy cream
⅓ cup brandy

Lightly oil a 2-quart mold. In a large bowl, combine all ingredients and blend well. Pour mixture into the prepared mold and freeze until firm.

To serve: Run a sharp knife around inner edge of the mold. Quickly dip bottom of the mold into hot water and invert onto a serving platter. Serve with raspberry sauce.

Serves 12
Preparation time: 10 minutes
Chill
Easy

Carol Ann May

RASPBERRY SAUCE

3 cups fresh or unsweetened frozen raspberries, pureed and strained
½ cup Triple Sec or Grand Marnier

¼ cup brandy
½ cup sugar
½ cup heavy cream, lightly whipped

Combine all ingredients and mix well. Let stand at room temperature for at least 1 hour before serving.

Yield: 4½ cups
Preparation time: 10 minutes

Carol Ann May

To make super-fine sugar, process in a blender for 2-3 minutes or until very fine.

CHOCOLATE ICE BOX DESSERT

1 baked angel food cake	6 tablespoons water
6 eggs, separated	2 teaspoons vanilla
1 12-ounce package chocolate morsels	1 teaspoon salt
¼ cup sugar	2 cups heavy cream, whipped

Line a flat 9x9-inch cake pan with waxed paper. Slice the cake and place half the slices in the bottom of pan. (Angel food cake slices more easily when frozen.)

Beat the egg yolks. Melt the chocolate chips in top section of double boiler over hot water. Add the sugar and water, stirring until sugar dissolves. Remove from heat and gradually stir the hot chocolate mixture into the beaten egg yolks. Beat until smooth; set aside to cool. When slightly cooled, add vanilla and salt; mix well. Beat the egg whites until stiff. Fold the egg whites and whipped cream into the cooled chocolate mixture. Place half of the chocolate mixture on the sliced cake, then add another layer of cake slices and cover with the remaining chocolate. Place in refrigerator and chill overnight.

This may be frozen, but chill overnight before freezing.

Mrs. Gerald R. Ford

HOT FRUIT COMPOTE

4 cups drained canned fruit: peaches, pears, apricots, cherries pineapple	½ cup slivered almonds
	¼ cup brown sugar
	½ cup Sherry
12 dried macaroons, crumbled, divided	¼ cup butter

Preheat oven to 350 degrees.

Butter a 2½-quart casserole. Combine drained fruits. Sprinkle ¼ of the macaroon crumbs on the bottom of the casserole. Alternate layers of mixed fruit and macaroons, ending with macaroons. Sprinkle with almonds, sugar and Sherry. Bake for 30 minutes. Melt the butter and pour over compote. Serve hot.

Serves 8
Preparation time: 10 minutes
Baking time: 30 minutes
Easy

Dick Purtan
Radio and TV personality

HOT BENGAL TIGER SUNDAE

This receipe was created to pay tribute to Archibald, a captain in the Scottish Bengal Lancers, who served and fell in battle in India.

¼ cup butter
2 Delicious apples, peeled, cored and diced
3 bananas
½ cup Major Grey's chutney, chopped
½ cup Sultana raisins
1 tablespoon orange zest (remove all pith)
¼ cup brown sugar
1 heaping tablespoon curry powder

½ teaspoon salt
1 cup papaya juice or apple juice
Juice of one lemon
Juice of one orange
3 tablespoons cornstarch
Whipped cream
Macadamia nut or rum raisin ice cream
¾ cup chopped Macadamia nuts

In a large pan, melt the butter. Add the apples, 1 banana, diced, chutney, raisins, and orange zest. Sauté until fruit softens slightly. Add the brown sugar, curry powder and salt and mix well. Add papaya and lemon juices. Combine the orange juice with cornstarch and add to the pan. Cook over medium heat until juice forms a syrup, about 5 minutes.

Slice remaining bananas. Spoon sauce over ice cream and top with whipped cream. Garnish with sliced bananas. Sprinkle with chopped nuts.

Note: The sauce served chilled is an excellent condiment for hot curry dishes.

Serves 8
Preparation time: 20 minutes

Jim Lehane,
Chef
Archibald's
Birmingham, Michigan

SUMMER PUDDING

This English recipe was given to me by my grandmother.

1½ pounds fresh fruit — raspberries, strawberries or currants
¾ cup superfine sugar

8 slices stale white bread, crusts removed
Sweet cream

Pick over and wash the fruit. In a heavy saucepan simmer fruit with the sugar until juices begin to run out. Line a 3-cup pudding mold with the bread. It is important that the slices fit well, so you may need to trim them to shape. Add the stewed fruit and cover the top with more slices of bread. Compress the pudding by placing a plate inside the mold and weighing it down. Chill in the refrigerator overnight.

When ready to serve, remove the weight and plate. Pour off any excess juice and reserve. Place a serving plate on top and turn mold upside-down to unmold the pudding. Pour the reserved juice over to color any unstained portions. Serve with a jug of cream.

Serves 4
Preparation time: 25 minutes
Chill overnight

Gillian Von Drehle

CHOCOLATE TRIFLE

½ cup apricot preserves
3 tablespoons rum, divided
24 ladyfingers
2 3-ounce packages chocolate pudding, cooked according to package directions and cooled

1 cup heavy cream or 1 cup commercial whipped topping
½ cup slivered toasted almonds or chocolate curls

Combine the apricot preserves and 2 tablespoons of the rum. Coat the flat side of each ladyfinger with the mixture. Sandwich 8-10 ladyfingers together and arrange on the bottom of a 1½-quart casserole or glass serving bowl.

Press a layer of single ladyfingers vertically around the side of the bowl with the coated side facing inward. Spoon ½ of the chocolate pudding into the center. Arrange a layer of ladyfingers on top of the pudding and sprinkle with the remaining tablespoon of rum; top with the remaining pudding. Cover and refrigerate overnight.

Just before serving, whip the cream and spread a layer over the pudding. Garnish with the almonds or chocolate curls.

Serves 6-8
Preparation time: 25 minutes
Chill

Moira Prekel

POACHED STUFFED PEARS

PEARS

6	firm pears (not Bosc)	2	1.5 liter bottles white wine
½	cup chopped walnuts	3	cups sugar
½	cup chopped raisins		Garnish: Chopped pistachio
½	cup honey		nuts

Core the pears from the bottom, leaving stem on, then peel. Make a paste of the walnuts, raisins and honey. Stuff the pears and seal opening with a plug of foil.

Combine the wine and sugar and simmer just until sugar is dissolved. Poach pears in the liquid until tender. Remove pears and reduce the poaching liquid to the consistency of syrup; save for use with ice cream or pancakes. Cool pears and serve with the following sauce.

SAUCE

½	cup sugar	2	cups Half & Half
1	teaspoon cornstarch	1	tablespoon vanilla
6	egg yolks, well beaten		

Combine the sugar and cornstarch; add to the beaten yolks. Scald the Half & Half and add slowly to the egg mixture. Cook over very low heat, stirring constantly, until the mixture coats a spoon or until it reaches 160 degrees on a candy thermometer. Remove from heat and continue stirring for 2-3 minutes, then add the vanilla. Strain through a fine sieve; cool.

To serve, coat pears with the sauce and sprinkle with the chopped nuts.

Note: To keep the foil plugs from falling out during poaching, tie each pear in a cheesecloth bag. This also facilitates removal of pears from the hot liquid.

Serves 6   Bill Chapman

TONTILLE AUX FRAISES

¾	cup hazelnuts		Pinch of salt
1	cup butter, softened	2	cups heavy cream
½	cup sugar	2	cups strawberries
1¼	cups flour		Powdered sugar

Heat oven to 200 degrees. Toast nuts until lightly browned. Remove from oven and rub in a dry towel to remove skins. When cool, finely chop nuts.

Cream the butter and sugar until pale and fluffy. Sift flour with the salt and add to the butter mixture. Add prepared nuts and mix well. Chill for 30 minutes.

Preheat oven to 350 degrees. Divide pastry into three parts and press into three 9-inch cake pans. Bake for 10 minutes or until layers spring back when lightly touched. Place on racks to cool.

When cooled, whip the cream and spread on one layer. Cover with berries and place second layer on strawberries. Cover with whipped cream, layer with berries, and place third layer on top of this. Spread with whipped cream, layer with berries and sift powdered sugar generously over torte.

Serves 8   Helen Addison

APPLE WALNUT PAN CAKE

This is a terrific, no-mess cake.

CAKE

1	21-ounce can apple pie filling	1	teaspoon salt
1	teaspoon cinnamon	2	eggs
¼	teaspoon ground nutmeg	1	teaspoon vanilla
2	cups flour	⅔	cup vegetable oil
1	cup sugar	¾	cup chopped walnuts, divided
1½	teaspoons baking soda		

Preheat oven to 350 degrees.

Spread the pie filling in the bottom of a 9x13-inch pan; cut up the large pieces of apple. Stir in the cinnamon and nutmeg. Combine the flour, baking soda and salt and sprinkle over the pie filling.

In a small bowl, combine the eggs, vanilla, oil and ½ cup of the nuts. Mix well and pour over the mixture in the pan. Stir only until blended and smooth evenly in the pan. Bake 35-45 minutes, or until done. Remove from the oven and prick all over with a fork. Pour topping over cake and sprinkle with the remaining chopped nuts.

TOPPING

1	cup sugar	½	teaspoon baking soda
½	cup sour cream		

Combine ingredients in a medium saucepan. Cook, stirring, over medium heat until the mixture boils. Pour over the warm cake immediately.

Serves 12-16
Preparation time: 20 minutes
Baking time: 45 minutes
Easy   Ann Rumpsa

CHOCOLATE CREAM TORTE

1   cup flour
½   cup butter
1   cup sliced almonds
1   8-ounce package cream cheese, softened
1   cup powdered sugar
2   cups heavy cream, whipped

1   3-ounce package instant chocolate pudding
1   3-ounce package instant vanilla pudding
3   cups milk
Chocolate curls for garnish

Preheat oven to 350 degrees.
Combine the flour, butter and almonds. Mix well and pat into a 9x13-inch baking pan. Bake for 20 minutes, then cool.
Combine the cream cheese and powdered sugar and beat well. Fold in 1⅓ cups whipped cream and spread over the almond layer. Combine the puddings and mix with the milk until thick. Pour over the cream cheese mixture. Top with the remaining whipped cream; chill. When ready to serve, top with chocolate curls.

Serves 18-20
Preparation time: 30 minutes
Chill
Easy   Christine Kiehl

CREPES FITZGERALD

4   heaping teaspoons cream cheese, softened
¼   cup sour cream
4   prepared crepes
1   tablespoon butter
2   tablespoons sugar

½   teaspoon cinnamon
1   cup strawberries
2   tablespoons strawberry liqueur
2   tablespoons Kirschwasser

Combine the cream cheese with the sour cream and mix well. Fill the crepes and roll into an oblong shape; place 2 crepes on each plate. In a chafing dish melt the butter, sugar and cinnamon. Add the strawberries and cook for 2 minutes. In a separate saucepan combine the liqueurs and heat but do not boil. Ignite the liqueur and pour over the strawberries. Spoon the strawberries and sauce over the crepes.

Serves 2
Preparation time: 20 minutes   Don Swanson

SINFUL SOUFFLE

From an old Swedish recipe call Soufle Nobis

1   7-ounce stick marzipan
¾   cup creme de cacao
6   egg yolks
½   cup sugar

1   tablespoon coffee powder
2   pints heavy cream, whipped
Shaved chocolate

Grate marzipan and add to liqueur; set aside. Beat egg yolks with the sugar until pale and fluffy. Combine marzipan mixture with the egg yolks; add coffee powder and mix well. Whip the cream and carefully fold into marzipan-egg yolk mixture. Spoon into a souffle dish and place in freezer for at least 6 hours. Sprinkle shaved chocolate on top. Variation: Substitute coffee liqueur for creme de cocoa and cocoa powder for coffee.

Serves 8

Lee Green
DSO

PRALINE CHEESECAKE

1   cup graham cracker crumbs
3   tablespoons granulated
    sugar
3   tablespoons butter, melted
3   8-ounce packages cream
    cheese, softened
1¾ cups firmly-packed brown
    sugar

2   tablespoons flour
3   eggs
1½ teaspoons vanilla
½   cup finely chopped
    pecans
Maple syrup
Pecan halves

Preheat oven to 350 degrees.
Combine the crumbs, granulated sugar and butter. Mix well and press into the bottom of a 9-inch springform pan. Bake for 10 minutes. Beat the cream cheese until fluffy. Add the brown sugar and beat until well blended. Beat in the eggs and vanilla; stir in the chopped nuts. Pour into crust. Bake in a 450-degree oven for 10 minutes. Reduce oven temperature to 250 degrees and bake for 30 minutes longer. Loosen cake from rim of pan. Cool, then remove rim; chill well. Brush with maple syrup and garnish with pecan halves.

Preparation time: 20 minutes
Baking time: 40 minutes

Kathy Brassell

HOT FUDGE SAUCE

This mouthwatering hot fudge keeps well in the refrigerator for several weeks

1 cup butter
1 pound powdered
  sugar
¼ pound sweet chocolate
¼ pound unsweetened baking
  chocolate

1 13-ounce can evaporated
  milk
1 teaspoon vanilla
Dash salt

In the top section of a double boiler combine the butter, sugar, sweetened and unsweetened chocolates, and milk. Cook over simmering water for 20-30 minutes, stirring constantly, until thick. Remove from heat and beat in the vanilla and salt.

Makes 2½ cups

Millie Schembechler
"Mrs Bo"

FLIM FLAN

CARMELIZED MOLD
½ cup sugar

2 tablespoons water

Place the sugar and the water in a 6-cup metal mold and bring to a boil over moderate heat, swirling the mold constantly, until the syrup carmelizes. Immediately dip the mold in a pan of cold water for 2-3 seconds to cool it slightly, then, tilting the mold in every direction, coat the bottom and sides with the caramel. Set aside.

FLAN FILLING
2 3-ounce boxes Jello Golden
  egg custard mix
1 quart milk

2 egg yolks
3 ounces Grand Marnier
Freshly ground nutmeg to taste

In a large saucepan blend the custard mix with the milk. Add the egg yolks and the Grand Marnier and bring to a boil, stirring constantly. Add fresh nutmeg and pour mixture into the carmelized mold, the mixture will be thin. Chill until set.

To serve: Invert the mold onto a serving plate.

Serves 6

Susan P. Martin

DESSERT PIZZA

Great conversation piece. Kids of all ages love this.

PIZZA

1   10-inch baked flattened
    pie crust (Use either a pate
    brisee or frozen puff pastry)
½   cup strawberry or raspberry
    jam

3   ounces white chocolate
    melted with 1 teaspoon oil
Mock pepperoni (recipe below)
Mock sausage (recipe below)

Spread the jam to within 1 inch of the edge of the baked circle. Spoon the white chocolate over the jam and spread unevenly to resemble melted cheese. Top with the mock pepperoni and sausage.

MOCK PEPPERONI

1½ ounces sweet chocolate
1   teaspoon sweet butter
1   tablespoon sugar
2   tablespoons golden raisins,
    finely minced

2   teaspoons honey
¼   cup slivered almonds or
    pine nuts

Combine the chocolate, butter and sugar. Mix in the raisins, honey and nuts. Form into a 1½ inch log on waxed paper. Freeze until firm then slice thinly.

MOCK SAUSAGE

1   ounce chocolate, melted   ¼   cup granola

Mix ingredients well. Form into small crumbled pieces, resembling sausage, on a piece of waxed paper. Chill.

Serves 8   Bobbi Pincus

POTS DE CREME AU CHOCOLAT

5 ounces semi-sweet
chocolate (I recommend
Lindt "zart bitter")
2 tablespoons sweet butter,
softened
5 tablespoons sugar

5 eggs, separated
1 teaspoon flavoring —
vanilla, coffee, fruit liqueur,
or brandy
1 cup heavy cream, whipped
Filberts or pistachio nuts

Melt the chocolate in the top part of a double boiler over hot, but not boiling water. Add the butter and sugar, mixing with a wooden spoon. When creamy, remove from heat and beat in the egg yolks; add flavoring. Beat egg whites until they are stiff but not dry then gently fold into the chocolate mixture. Divide evenly between 6 "petite pots" and refrigerate.

To serve: Spoon a dab of whipped cream over the top and sprinkle with toasted, grated filberts or pistachio nuts.

Serves 6
Preparation time: 20 minutes
Chill   Charity de Vicq Suczek

BAKLAVA
(BOUTLAWA)

A traditional Lebanese dessert.

SYRUP

4 cups sugar
2 cups water
Juice of ½ lemon

1 teaspoon orange blossom
water

Combine ingredients in a saucepan and boil until clear. Set aside to cool.

BAKLAVA

2 pounds filo dough
2 pounds sweet butter

2 pounds ground walnuts
mixed with ¼ cup sugar

Preheat oven to 300 degrees.
Keep filo dough covered with a damp cloth to keep it from drying out. Divide the butter between 2 saucepans and melt. When the butter

separates, pour off the clear butter and discard the milky residue. Alternate the pans on the burner while making Baklava so that the butter will remain hot.

Using a pastry brush, butter the bottom of an 11x17-inch pan. Place one sheet of filo in the pan and brush generously with melted butter. Continue layering the dough and butter until 1 pound of filo is used up Sprinkle with the nut mixture. Continue layering dough and butter until the second pound of filo is used.

With a very sharp knife, cut 4/5 through the dough and nut mixture in a diamond pattern — corner to corner. Bake for 2 hours or until the pastry is lightly browned.

When done, pour all of the syrup evenly over the pastry. Cool for 15 minutes, then cut completely through the Baklava.

Note: One half of the recipe will fill a 9x13-inch pan. Be sure to tuck in any excess dough.

Freezes well   Vicki DeShaw

UPSIDE-DOWN APPLE TART

CRUST

1 cup flour	6 tablespoons butter, softened
¼ cup sugar	2-3 tablespoons ice water
½ teaspoon salt	

Combine the flour, sugar and salt. Cut in the butter with a pastry blender until mixture is the size of peas. Add the water and form into a ball — handling as little as possible. With a lightly floured rolling pin, roll into a 9-inch circle.

FILLING

6-8 medium cooking apples	1 teaspoon cinnamon
1 cup brown sugar	½ teaspoon nutmeg
¼ cup butter	

Preheat oven to 425 degrees.

Pare, core and slice the apples into a 9-inch pie plate. In a small saucepan over low heat, combine the brown sugar with the butter, cinnamon and nutmeg. Cook, stirring, until sauce becomes carmelized, then pour over the apples. Cover with the prepared pie crust and bake for 35-40 minutes or until the crust is golden brown and filling is hot and bubbly. Remove from oven and invert on a plate. Serve hot with vanilla ice cream or maple flavored whipped cream.

Serves 6   Reiko Kubo
                                                               Bob Shafer

HARVEST TORTE

4 cups tart apples, diced but unpared
1 cup sugar
½ cup sifted flour
2 teaspoons baking powder
1 egg, beaten
1 tablespoon melted butter
1 teaspoon vanilla
1 cup chopped walnuts
1 cup chopped dates

Preheat oven to 400 degrees.
Combine all ingredients and stir, **do not beat,** until thoroughly mixed. Turn into a greased 8x8-inch pan. Bake for 40 minutes or until apples are tender. Cut into squares and serve hot or cold with whipped cream or ice cream.

Serves 6-8
Preparation time: 10 minutes
Easy   Marian Walters

CREAM CHEESE CAKES

2 8-ounce packages cream cheese, softened
¾ cup sugar
1 tablespoon lemon juice
2 eggs
1 teaspoon vanilla
1 box vanilla wafers
Cherry, blueberry or strawberry pie filling or combination
Small-sized muffin pan
Paper liners

Preheat oven to 350 degrees.
Combine the cream cheese, sugar, lemon juice, eggs and vanilla. Beat at high speed for 5 minutes.
Place a paper liner in each muffin opening. Put one vanilla wafer in each liner and top with a teaspoon of the cheesecake mixture. Bake for 15 minutes or until top just cracks. Let cool then refrigerate.
When ready to serve, top with a dollop of pie filling.

Yield: 50-60 cakes
Preparation time: 10 minutes
Baking time: 15 minutes   Kay-Ellen Murphy
                                         DSO

BEDFORD SPECIAL

1	egg	½	cup chopped walnuts
½	cup sugar	½	cup chopped, peeled apples
3	tablespoons flour	1	quart vanilla ice cream
⅛	teaspoon salt		or iced milk, softened
1½	teaspoons baking powder	3	tablespoons coffee
1	teaspoon vanilla		

Preheat oven to 350 degrees. Line the bottom of an 8-inch spring-form pan with waxed paper.

Beat the egg until frothy. Gradually add the sugar while continuing to beat mixture; set aside. Sift the flour, salt and baking powder; blend into the egg mixture. Stir in the vanilla, nuts and apples and incorporate thoroughly. Pour into a buttered 9-inch pie plate. Bake for 30 minutes. Let cool.

In the bowl of a mixer, combine ice cream with the coffee. Spread ½ of the ice cream in the bottom of the springform pan. Remove the baked mixture from the pie plate and crumble ½ over the ice cream. Spread the remaining ice cream over the crumbled mixture and sprinkle with remaining crunch. Freeze until solid, about 6-8 hours. To serve: Cut with a hot, wet knife.

Serves 8   Mado Lie

CHOCOLATE CHESTNUT CREAM

1	9-ounce can *sweetened* chestnut puree (not the pure chestnut puree)	2	tablespoons sugar
		1	ounce sliced almonds
2	tablespoons brandy	2	ounces dark chocolate, melted
1¼	cups heavy cream		

Beat chestnut puree and brandy until smooth. Whip the cream and sugar until thick peaks form then fold into the chestnut mixture. Spoon into a large pastry bag fitted with a star tube. Pipe the mixture into small dessert dishes.

Toast the almonds in a 350-degree oven for 5 minutes or until golden brown; let cool. Sprinkle almonds over the chestnut cream, and drizzle with the melted chocolate. Refrigerate until ready to serve.

Juanita Hamel

PEACH KUCHEN

½ cup butter
2 cups sifted flour
¼ teaspoon baking powder
½ teaspoon salt
1 cup sugar, divided

1 teaspoon cinnamon
12 fresh or frozen peach halves (do not use canned peaches)
2 egg yolks
1 cup sour cream

Preheat oven to 350 degrees.
Work butter with flour, baking powder, salt, 2 tablespoons sugar and cinnamon until mixture resembles coarse corn meal. Pat into the bottom and sides of a 9-inch square pan. Arrange peaches over and sprinkle with the remaining sugar. Bake for 15 minutes.
Combine the egg yolks and sour cream and mix well. Pour over the peaches and bake 30 minutes longer. Serve hot or cold.

Preparation time: 15-25 minutes
Baking time: 45 minutes
Easy

Rho Blanchard

FROZEN CHOCOLATE TORTE

6 tablespoons unsalted butter
1¾ cups fine graham cracker crumbs
2 tablespoons powdered sugar
2 tablespoons sweetened dry cocoa mix
½ cup sugar
½ cup water
2 eggs

6 ounces semi-sweet chocolate, broken into small pieces
2 tablespoons Cognac or brandy
¼ cup chocolate flavored liqueur
1 cup heavy cream, whipped
1 cup chopped pecans or toasted almonds
Whipped cream for garnish

In a medium saucepan, melt the butter. Add the graham cracker crumbs, powdered sugar and cocoa mix. Stir until thoroughly mixed and press into the bottom and sides of an 8-inch springform pan. Freeze until solid, about one hour.

Meanwhile, in a small saucepan, combine the sugar and water. Heat until sugar is completely dissolved; keep warm. In a food processor or blender, combine eggs and chocolate pieces. Add hot sugar-water mixture and process until chocolate is melted and mixture is smooth. Stir in the Cognac or brandy and liqueur, and refrigerate until thickened, about two hours. Fold thickened chocolate mixture into whipped cream then add the nuts. Turn mixture into prepared crust and freeze until solid, about four hours, or up to one month, wrapped well in plastic wrap.

To serve: Remove from freezer. Run a sharp knife around edges of pan and remove sides of pan. Let stand 10 minutes before serving.

Serves 10-12   Moira Prekel

BAVARIAN APPLE TORTE

CRUST

| ½ | cup butter | ¼ | teaspoon vanilla |
| ⅓ | cup sugar | 1 | cup flour |

Preheat oven to 450 degrees.
Cream the butter and sugar; beat in the vanilla. Blend in the flour; the mixture will be crumbly. Pat into the bottom and 1½ inches up the sides of a 9-inch springform pan.

FILLING

| 8 | ounces cream cheese | 1 | egg |
| ¼ | cup sugar | ½ | teaspoon vanilla |

Beat together the cheese and sugar. Add egg and vanilla and mix well. Pour into the prepared crust.

TOPPING

⅓	cup sugar	2	teaspoons orange peel,
⅓	teaspoon cinnamon		optional
4	cups apples, peeled and	Sliced almonds	
	sliced		

Combine the sugar, cinnamon and apples. If desired, add orange peel. Spoon evenly on top of the cheese filling then sprinkle with sliced almonds. Bake for 10 minutes then reduce temperature to 400 degrees and bake for 25 minutes longer. Loosen torte from the rim of the pan. Cool before removing torte from the pan.

Serves 8-10   Eileen Hitz

PEACH RUM MOUSSE

4   large fresh peaches
½   cup honey
½   teaspoon almond extract
3   tablespoons dark rum
¼   cup fresh orange juice
2   tablespoons fresh lemon
    juice
1½ tablespoons unflavored
    gelatin

1   envelope whipped topping
    mix
½   teaspoon vanilla
½   cup lowfat milk
4   egg whites
Pinch of salt
Mint leaves for garnish

Place foil or waxed paper collar around a 1½-quart souffle dish. Dip peaches into boiling water and peel. Remove pits and cut into pieces, reserving ½ peach, sliced, for garnish. Puree pulp in blender with honey and almond extract.

Heat rum, orange juice and lemon juice in small saucepan. Remove from heat and stir in gelatin, stirring until gelatin is completely dissolved. Blend into peach puree. Prepare topping mix according to package directions using the vanilla and milk then fold into peach mixture. Chill until slightly thickened.

Sprinkle egg whites with pinch of salt and beat until stiff but not dry. Gently fold into peach mixture. Spoon into prepared souffle dish and chill 4 to 5 hours.

When ready to serve, remove collar and garnish with peach slices and mint leaves.

Serves 8-10
Prepare ahead
Chill 4-5 hours

Judy and Larry Liberson
DSO

FRENCH APPLE TARTE

1   package frozen puff pastry
10 firm Golden Delicious
    apples
1   cup sugar

½   cup butter
¼   teaspoon almond extract
Whipped cream

Defrost puff pastry and cut into a 12-inch circle. Peel and core apples and cut in half lengthwise. In a heavy 10-inch skillet with an oven proof handle, (or cover handle with heavy duty aluminum foil), combine the sugar, butter and almond extract over medium heat. Cook, stirring occasionally, until butter is melted — sugar will not be completely dissolved. Remove from heat and arrange the apple halves, cut side to the center (bottom side down), in the skillet, packing tightly to keep apples upright. Place skillet over medium heat, and bring to a boil. Cook for 20-40 minutes or until sugar mixture becomes carmelized, length of time will depend on the juiciness of the apples. Remove from heat.

Preheat oven to 450 degrees. Arrange the pastry circle on top of the apples and with a fork, gently tuck the edges of the pastry into the skillet. With the tip of a sharp knife, cut 3-4 slits in pastry top. Bake for 20-25 minutes or until pastry is puffed and golden. Remove from oven and let sit for 10 minutes. Invert onto a serving platter and serve with whipped cream.

Serves 12   Nancy Bluementhal

GRAHAM CRACKER TORTE

Children especially love this

TORTE

Whole graham crackers (about 1 pound) *Do not crush.*

2 packages instant French vanilla pudding

2 cups milk

1 8-ounce carton Cool Whip or Dream Whip

Butter a 9x13-inch pan and line with 1 layer of graham crackers. Mix the pudding with the milk. Fold in the whipped topping. Pour half the pudding mixture over the graham crackers. Cover with second layer of crackers. Pour on remaining pudding mixture. Cover with third layer of graham crackers.

ICING

2 ounces unsweetened chocolate, melted

3 tablespoons butter

3 tablespoons milk

2 tablespoons light corn syrup

1½ cups powdered sugar

Combine ingredients, mixing well. Spread over the torte. Refrigerate for 24 hours.

Serves 15
Preparation time: 30 minutes
Chill 24 hours
Easy   Jean Smetana

PAPAYAS TUCKER

"You've heard of Bananas Foster? Try this instead!"

1   *very ripe*, fresh papaya
Cold milk
1   teaspoon powdered sugar
¼   teaspoon almond flavoring
    or vanilla extract

Fresh berries for garnish
1   cup heavy cream

Trim the skin completely from the papayas. Clean out seeds and cut fruit into chunks. Place the chunks of papaya in a blender and add enough cold milk to just cover the fruit. Add the sugar and flavoring and process until papaya turns to a soft custard. Mixture should be very creamy in consistency. If mixture is not creamy, blend for a few seconds longer. Serve cold in crystal bowls and garnish with fresh berries and sweetened whipped cream.

Serves 2

Barbara Tucker

TRADITIONAL CHEESECAKE

CHEESECAKE
⅔   cup sugar
2   8-ounce packages cream
    cheese, softened

3   eggs
¼   teaspoon almond extract

Preheat oven to 325 degrees.
Combine the sugar, cream cheese, eggs and almond extract; beat until smooth. Pour into well-buttered 10-inch pie pan. Bake for 25 minutes. Cool for 20 minutes.

TOPPING
1   cup sour cream
1   teaspoon vanilla

2   tablespoon sugar

Combine ingredients; blend well. Cover cake with topping and bake 5 minutes longer.
Cool, then refrigerate.

Serves 6-8
Freezes well

Millie Schembechler

Index

Weights and Measures

U.S. LIQUID	VOLUME	METRIC
Dash	Less than ⅛ teaspoon	
1 teaspoon	60 drops	5 ml
1 tablespoon	3 teaspoons	15 ml
2 tablespoons	1 fluid ounce	30 ml
4 tablespoons	¼ cup	60 ml
5⅓ tablespoons	⅓ cup	80 ml
6 tablespoons		90 ml
8 tablespoons	½ cup	120 ml
	⅔ cup	160 ml
12 tablespoons	¾ cup	180 ml
16 tablespoons	1 cup	240 ml
1 cup	8 fluid ounces	240 ml
2 cups	1 pint	480 ml
1 pint		.551 liters
1 quart	2 pints	.95 liter
2.1 pints	1.05 quarts	1 liter
2 quarts	½ gallon	
4 quarts	1 gallon	3.8 liters
1 ounce	16 drams	28 grams
1 pound	16 ounces	454 grams
1 pound	2 cups liquid	
2.2 pounds		1 kilogram

8 quarts = 1 peck
4 pecks = 1 bushel

⅓ of ¼ teaspoon = pinch
3 teaspoons = 1 tablespoon
⅓ of 1 tablespoon = 1 teaspoon
⅓ of 5 tablespoons = 1 tablespoon plus 2 teaspoons
1 tablespoon = ½ ounce
½ tablespoon = ¼ ounce = 1½ teaspoons
2 tablespoons = ⅛ cup = 1 ounce
5 tablespoons plus 1 teaspoon = ⅓ cup
⅓ of ¼ cup = 1 tablespoon plus 1 teaspoon
⅓ of ⅓ cup = 1 tablespoon plus 2¼ teaspoons
⅓ of ½ cup = 2 tablespoons plus 2 teaspoons
⅓ of ⅔ cup = 3 tablespoons plus 1¾ teaspoons
½ of ¼ cup = 2 tablespoons
½ of ⅓ cup = 2 tablespoons plus 2 teaspoons
½ of ¾ cup = 6 tablespoons

419

420

R

430

431

O DELIGHT EVERY COOK AND
COOKBOOK COLLECTOR

From its dazzling full-color cover through its 432 pages of carefully chosen, edited and tested recipes — **Culinary Counterpoint** makes an exceptional addition to any kitchen bookshelf. Send orders to:

CULINARY COUNTERPOINT c/o Detroit Symphony League, 20 Auditorium Drive, Detroit, Michigan 48226.

Please send me ___ copies at $12.00 per copy (tax included) plus appropriate shipping charges*

Name _____

Address _____

City _____ State _____ Zip _____

Add $1.50 shipping and handling charge (additional copies add $1.00 per copy).
Enclose check or money order payable to The Detroit Symphony League.

O DELIGHT EVERY COOK AND
COOKBOOK COLLECTOR

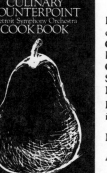

From its dazzling full-color cover through its 432 pages of carefully chosen, edited and tested recipes — **Culinary Counterpoint** makes an exceptional addition to any kitchen bookshelf. Send orders to:

CULINARY COUNTERPOINT c/o Detroit Symphony League, 20 Auditorium Drive, Detroit, Michigan 48226.

Please send me ___ copies at $12.00 per copy (tax included) plus appropriate shipping charges*

Name _____

Address _____

City _____ State _____ Zip _____

Add $1.50 shipping and handling charge (additional copies add $1.00 per copy).
Enclose check or money order payable to The Detroit Symphony League.

O DELIGHT EVERY COOK AND
COOKBOOK COLLECTOR

From its dazzling full-color cover through its 432 pages of carefully chosen, edited and tested recipes — **Culinary Counterpoint** makes an exceptional addition to any kitchen bookshelf. Send orders to:

CULINARY COUNTERPOINT c/o Detroit Symphony League, 20 Auditorium Drive, Detroit, Michigan 48226.

Please send me ___ copies at $12.00 per copy (tax included) plus appropriate shipping charges*

Name _____

Address _____

City _____ State _____ Zip _____

Add $1.50 shipping and handling charge (additional copies add $1.00 per copy).
Enclose check or money order payable to The Detroit Symphony League.